Nelson's Annual
Preacher's Sourcebook

Nelson's Annual
Preacher's Sourcebook
Volume 1

KENT SPANN AND DAVID WHEELER, EDITORS

THOMAS NELSON
Since 1798

NASHVILLE DALLAS MEXICO CITY RIO DE JANEIRO

Published in Nashville, Tennessee, by Thomas Nelson. Thomas Nelson is a trademark of Thomas Nelson, Inc.

Thomas Nelson, Inc., titles may be purchased in bulk for educational, business, fundraising, or sales promotional use. For information, please email *SpecialMarkets@ThomasNelson.com*.

Typesetting by Gregory C. Benoit Publishing, Old Mystic, CT.

Spann, Kent and David Wheeler (ed.)

Nelson's annual preacher's sourcebook, Volume 1.

ISBN 10: 1-4185-4896-0

ISBN 13: 978-1-4185-4896-4

Printed in the United States of America

1 2 3 4 5 6 7 8 RRD 12 11 10 09

CONTENTS

INTRODUCTION

Recently, I (Kent Spann) did a funeral service where I actually rode with the funeral director. It was a long drive, so there was plenty of time to talk and get acquainted. On the drive back, I decided to ask him how he got into the funeral business, and what he liked about it. His story was an interesting one. After he told his story, he turned to me and said he had a question that he had always wanted to ask a preacher. His question was simply this: "How do you come up with sermons every week?"

That was the question I had when I first started. As a young pastor, I had to produce three messages a week. Twenty-seven years later, I am closing in on my fifteen-hundredth sermon. I have certainly preached more times than that. That question still comes to mind.

One of the helps that I shared with the funeral director was sermon material like the book that you are holding in your hands. It is the reason that David Wheeler and I got involved in this project. It is why we spend the countless hours necessary to gather, edit, and compile the material you just purchased. We have a passion to help preachers like you. It is the reason that Thomas Nelson Publishers keeps putting out new editions each year.

After a long, dry sermon, a minister announced that he wished to meet with the church board following the close of the service. The first man to arrive and greet the minister was a total stranger. "You misunderstood my announcement. This is a meeting of the board members," explained the minister. "I know," said the man, "but if there is anyone here more bored than I am, then I'd like to meet him." We want to help God's preachers produce dynamic messages from the most exciting book in the entire world: the Bible.

New Format

One of the things you will notice about this year's volume is that it is not tied to the calendar. There are 52 weeks of sermons, three each week. The reason for the new format is to make the book useable for the long haul. When you put a date on it, it becomes dated once the year has passed. We will be creating new volumes each year with different emphases.

Each volume will still contain holiday sermons such as Christmas, New Year's, and Easter. Instead of going by the date, look under "Special Occasion Sermons" in the table of contents for the holiday sermon you need. Each volume will still contain worship services to help you put together a total service. Feel free to move the services to fit the sermon or week you need them. Finally, each volume will include funeral sermons to help you when you receive the call to preach a funeral sermon.

You will also notice also that we have added a longer second sermon. Now, in addition to the longer sermon, there is a medium sermon and a short sermon. We hope the addition of the longer second sermon will give you more material.

New Focus

This year's volume will focus on preaching on the family. There are three series: *Faith in the Family*, *The Missional Family*, and *Single and Satisfied*. In addition, there is a standalone short message in week 6. David Wheeler has prepared an article on the importance of preaching on family.

New Material

As always, there is new material by new preachers. I am delighted to welcome many new contributors whose material I think will really bless you. I am thrilled that Love Worth Finding ministries gave us permission to publish some of the late Dr. Adrian Rogers' sermons. His preaching was so powerful.

Make It Yours

Dr. Rogers said on one occasion, when talking about using his sermon material, that if you can fit it in your gun then shoot it. He wasn't saying take his message and preach it verbatim; he was saying take the material and make it your own. Put it in your words. Speak it in your congregation's language. Fill it with your illustrations. Make your own applications.

That is what you need to do with this book. It is not a substitute for getting into the Word and hearing God. It is not an escape from the hard work of sermon preparation. It is a primer. Some of the sermons include personal stories by the preachers. Replace their story with your story that is very much like theirs. You can also use their story by telling it from their viewpoint.

Feedback

David and I welcome your feedback. Some of it we can put into action. Some of it we cannot do because of size limitations. You can reach David Wheeler at *dwheeler2@liberty.edu* and Kent Spann at *spann@highlandgrovecity.org*.

You are the real heroes to David and me, and we so appreciate you. We are honored that you bought this book. May God use it to encourage and nourish you.

David Wheeler and Kent Spann

Editors

ABOUT THE 2012 WORSHIP SERVICES

This section of the 2012 Preacher's Sourcebook includes fifty-six separate orders of worship: one for each of the fifty-three calendar Sundays for 2012, two Christmas Eve services, and a service for baby dedication. Included are suggestions of choice songs for worship, an order of worship, time for greeting, time for prayer, and appropriate scriptures for almost every week of the year.

Format

The format varies for each service order. Each service can be used independently according to need or in its entirety as one service. Six elements are included with each worship service: (1) each worship service has an opening song, Scripture, or call to worship; (2) included with each service is a song or worship set to be used during a welcome or time of greeting; (3) each service includes a time for intercessional prayer, followed by a song or worship set; (4) an invitation or call for response is included with each service; (5) each service includes a song or worship set to be used during the time of offering or worship through giving; and (6) each order includes an optional concluding song to be sung after the benediction.

Song Selections

Song selections for the worship services do not follow any particular stylistic preference, be it either contemporary or traditional. Rather, worship services are designed according to the Scriptural idea, theme, or subject. Most songs selected for use are taken from a list of well known hymns and gospel songs, and these songs are songs of encouragement, theology, invitation, dedication, or faith. Stylistically, every effort is taken to make the services practical and broad enough for use by the entire evangelical community.

Scripture Readings

Scripture readings are written for use by small reader's theatre teams or the congregation with the worship pastor. A variety of Biblical translations and paraphrases are identified as follows: KJV (*King James Version*); NCV (*New Century Version*); NLT (*New Living Translation*); NASB (*New American Stan-*

dard Bible); *The Message*; NKJV (*New King James Version*); and HCSB (*Holman Christian Standard Bible*).

Worship Sets

Worship sets are grouped into one, two, three, or four songs. Most song selections are organized by key relationships, theme compatibility, and function.

Resources

Resources for song selection primarily include *The Baptist Hymnal* (2008), *The Celebration Hymnal* (1997), *Red Tie Music* (*redtiemusic.com*), *The Songs for Praise and Worship Series*, *LifeWayWorship.com*, *worshipideas.com*, and *Praisecharts.com*. Most songs used for these order of services are taken from the new Baptist hymnal (NBH), also known as *The Baptist Hymnal* (2008).

Several newer songs are used in the service orders. Take advantage of your church's resources, such as the praise team, small ensembles, or the choir, to teach new songs. It is good to take time to teach new songs ahead of time. And it is suggested that, when teaching these songs, the worship leader take an opportunity to have the congregation sit during the "learning process." Once the congregation is familiar with the new songs, invite them to stand, participate, and worship.

Finally, may God bless you as you use these worship services to facilitate worship in your fellowship. May you worship the Lord in all of His fullness.

Enthusiastically His,

Vernon M. Whaley, Ph.D.

2012 CONTRIBUTORS

Rev. Brian Bill

Senior Pastor of Pontiac Bible Church in Pontiac, Illinois, where I have served for eleven years. I have written several articles for various websites and newspapers, along with two evangelistic tracts. I am also a Featured Contributor at *SermonCentral.com*. Full-text sermon manuscripts are posted at *www.pontiacbible.org*.

Dr. Bill Bright (1921–2003)

Founded Campus Crusade for Christ, the world's largest Christian ministry. His booklet "The Four Spiritual Laws" has been printed in 200 languages and distributed to more than 2.5 billion people. He also produced the *Jesus* film, which has been viewed by more than 5.1 billion people.

Dr. Jimmy Draper

Dr. Jimmy Draper, Former President of Lifeway Christian Resources, Nashville, TN.

Dr. Bill Elliff

Directional Pastor of The Summit Church in North Little Rock, Arkansas. He is a frequent conference speaker, writer, and consultant to churches, drawing from his forty-plus years of pastoring and revival ministry.

Dr. Duane Floro

Currently serves as Ministry Evangelism Strategist for the State Convention of Baptists in Ohio. Previously, he pastored churches in Kentucky, West Virginia, Indiana, Arizona, and Oklahoma.

Rudy Hernandez

Founder of Rudy Hernandez Evangelism, Inc. He has represented World Ministries of the Southern Baptist Convention on special preaching-teaching missions around the world.

Junior Hill

Author and world-renowned evangelist. He has conducted over 1,700 revivals and numerous foreign crusades.

Rev. David Hirschman

Associate Dean, Liberty Baptist Theological Seminary, Online Programs.

Victor Lee

Victor Lee is a Christian journalist and Minister of Single Adults at First Baptist Concord in Knoxville, TN.

Dr. Richard Lee

Founding Pastor of First Redeemer Church in Atlanta Georgia, with over 5,000 members. He is also the speaker for "There's Hope America" radio and television ministry.

Dr. Larry Lewis

Pastor of First Southern Baptist Church, San Diego. He also serves on the staff of the Mission America Coalition as National Facilitator of Denominational Ministries.

Rev. Robert Matz

Teaching fellow and PhD student at Liberty Baptist Theological Seminary. He has pastored churches in Virginia and Texas, as well as serving on two church staffs in Tennessee.

Dr. James Merritt

Senior pastor of Cross Point Church near Atlanta, Georgia, and host of the television broadcast Touching Lives. He also was the President of the Southern Baptist Convention from 2000–2002.

Dr. Calvin Miller

Research Professor and Distinguished Writer in Residence, Beeson Divinity School. Artist and author of over forty books.

Dr. Karl Ray Minor

Senior Pastor of Beck's Baptist Church in Winston-Salem, NC since 2002, and the Research Assistant for Clayton Carnall World-Wide Ministries, Inc.

Dr. Doug Munton

Senior Pastor of First Baptist Church, O'Fallon, IL since 1995. Author of *Warriors in Hiding: The Surprising People God Chooses and Uses* and *Seven Steps to Becoming a Healthy Christian Leader*.

Dr. Phil Newton

Senior Pastor of South Woods Baptist Church in Memphis since 1987. He is the author of *Elders in Congregational Life* (Kregel, 2005), co-author of *Conduct Gospel-Centered Funerals* (with Brian Croft; Day One Publications, 2011), and co-author of *Venturing All upon God: The Piety of John Bunyan* (with Roger Duke; Reformation Heritage Books, forthcoming), as well as contributor to other books and journals.

Dr. Dean Register

Founder and Sr. Pastor of Crosspoint Community Church in Hattiesburg, MS. Author of *Romans: God's Amazing Grace* and contributor to *The New Quest Study Bible*.

Dr. Dwight "Ike" Reighard

Senior Pastor of Piedmont Church in Marietta, Georgia, and author of three books.

Dr. Mark Roberts

Senior Director and Scholar-in-Residence for Laity Lodge, a retreat center and multifaceted renewal ministry in the Texas Hill Country. Formerly, he was Senior Pastor of Irvine Presbyterian Church for sixteen years, as well as an adjunct professor for Fuller Theological Seminary. He is also author of several books.

Dr. Adrian Rogers (1931–2005)

The legendary pastor of Bellevue Baptist Church from 1979 to 2005. Under his leadership, Bellevue grew from 9,000 to more than 30,000. His messages are still heard on Love Worth Finding.

Ruth Schenk

A writer for the faith-based newspaper, "The Southeast Outlook," of the Southeast Christian Church in Louisville, Kentucky.

Dr. Bailey Smith

Founder and president of Bailey Smith Ministries. He is a former pastor and author of several books including the best seller *Real Evangelism*.

Dr. Bryan E. Smith

Senior pastor of the 3,500 member First Baptist Church in Roanoke, Virginia. In addition to his role as a pastor, Dr. Smith has served in numerous positions of responsibility at both the state and national levels of the Southern Baptist Convention.

Dr. Kent Spann

Pastor of the Highland Baptist Church in Grove City and co-editor of *Nelson's Annual Preacher's Sourcebook*.

Dr. Jerry Sutton

Dean and Vice President of Academics at Midwestern Baptist Theological Seminary. He has ministered as Senior Pastor for 31 years, and is the author of three books. His latest book is *A Primer on Biblical Preaching*.

Dr. David L. Thompson

Senior pastor of the North Pointe Community Church, which he started in 1999.

Rick Warren

Founding Pastor of 20,000 member Saddleback Church in Lake Forest, California. His wildly popular book, *The Purpose Driven Life*, has sold more than 30 million copies, making it the top selling hardcover book of all time.

Dr. Vernon Whaley

Director of the Liberty University Center for Worship, and Chairman of the Department of Worship and Music Studies in Lynchburg Virginia.

WORSHIP SERVICES

Dr. David Wheeler

Professor of Evangelism, Liberty University and Liberty Baptist Theological Seminary, Lynchburg, VA, and co-editor of the *Nelson's Annual Preacher's Sourcebook*.

PREACHING SERIES

Many of the messages are placed in series. Series offer many advantages. First, they assist the preacher in planning and preparation. Second, they build continuity for the audience. Third, they help the worship leader plan the upcoming worship services. Fourth, if you use powerpoints, visual aids, or notes, you can create a visual aid for the series instead of one for each individual message.

The user is free to preach individual sermons out of the series, change the order of the sermons, select another time of the year, and change the title of the series.

The Missional Family (Week 1–5)

The Missional Family Series is designed to lead families into self-examination and exploration of five aspects of Christian living that can guide them into missional living. A missional family will be thankful, and the result of living thankfully with right priorities and right purpose that are rooted in the Word will be holy living. If God aligns your family with the truths contained here, you will be "On Mission!"

Family Matters (Week 1–9)

Family matters to God, so matters of the family are important to God. This series looks at some of the things that matter, such as fidelity, growing in marriage, parenting, and being the mother and father God intended.

Obey Anyway (Week 7–10)

There are times that we are pumped and ready to go, while there are other times when we really don't want to take the next step. In this series, Dr. Dean Register reminds us that, even when we don't feel like obeying, we need to obey anyway.

Single and Satisfied (Week 16–19)

This series speaks to an often overlooked group of people in the church: singles. Their needs are special, especially widows. Dr. Karl Minor shines the light of God's Word on this very important group of people.

The Gospel Truth (Week 10–28)

The gospel was under assault in Galatia. Paul masterfully defends the doctrine of justification by faith and his apostleship in this book that is sometimes called Paul's mini-Romans. This nineteen-week series will take your congregation on an exciting journey through Galatians.

Enough (Week 31–34)

Believers live in two worlds: the kingdom of this world, and the kingdom of our God. Paul teaches us in Colossians 3 how to live with this dual citizenship in such a way that the heavenly kingdom is brought to earth through us. In this series, Dr. Bill Elliff shows us how God's kingdom can come and His will be done on earth as it is in heaven in our personal lives, our churches, and our homes.

The Forgotten Kingdom (Week 35–37)

Christ's first public message announced the entrance of a new kingdom. To experience its fullness, we must learn how to enter the kingdom, live passionately for the kingdom, and share the kingdom with others. Join Dr. Bill Elliff, as he shows you how to enter, live, and share the kingdom.

He is Jehovah (Week 38–43)

There is no greater subject to occupy the mind than to consider the person of God. One of the special names for God is Jehovah. The name Jehovah is often attached with a powerful descriptor revealing His character. In this six part series, you will look at some of those important names.

Reluctant Prophet, Sovereign Lord: Jonah (Week 33–42)

If ever there was a reluctant prophet, it was Jonah. God had a plan to use this reluctant prophet. Join Dr. Phil Newton as he mines the riches of Jonah. You will see the greatness of our God.

A Theology of Christmas (Weeks 49–52)

Theology is the study of God, His attributes, and His activities. In this Christmas series by Dr. Jerry Sutton, you will find a unique opportunity to explain how, why, and in what ways God relates to humanity.

WEEK 1

SERIES: MARRIED WITH CHILDREN

The Biblical Model for the Family

Proverbs 22:6
By Dr. David Wheeler

Introduction

Think about it: if you wanted to destroy a building, would you not aim your most destructive blows at the foundation? In a very direct manner, that is exactly what Satan has been doing to the family for many years.

Faith Runs in the Family

Pastors and church leaders are often guilty of overlooking the fact that God created the family before He created the church. In fact, I believe it was God's intent all along that one's faith should be passed along generational lines. Consider what the Bible says in Deuteronomy 6:

> And these words which I command you today shall be in your heart. You shall teach them diligently to your children, and shall talk of them when you sit in your house, when you walk by the way, when you lie down, and when you rise up.
>
> —Deuteronomy 6:6, 7

From this passage, it is obvious that God places a high value on the family. Imagine for a moment what it would have been like to live in a home that hosted several generations of the same family. This concept of passing biblical faith to the third and the fourth generations becomes much more understandable when you consider that parents and grandparents shared meals and performed daily tasks together.

From birth, children in households like this learned the stories and doctrines of faith while sitting around the dinner table each evening and by working in the fields daily with older family members. In doing so, children learned to both love God and to love others with all of their hearts!

This cycle of biblical mentoring was repeated as new generations came along. As a result, we still talk about movements of God from thousands of years ago. Even with the advent of the Church in the New Testament, as it was in the days of Moses in Deuteronomy, I believe that family remains the foundation from which to build.

Restoration of the Godly Family

"Raise up a child in the way he should go, and when he is old, he will not depart from it" (Proverbs 22:6). In a day where the family has deteriorated and the church is losing its influence on society, this simple passage holds several profound keys to restore the family back to the purpose for which God originally intended. The question is whether or not we are willing to do what it takes. There are four main points:

1. **The Imperative of the home and family.** The phrase, to "raise up" is not written as a suggestion. Rather, it is a command that has three very descriptive meanings.

    A. **It means to "put something sweet in the mouth of babes."** One of the responsibilities of the home is to create a positive impression related to faith. However, we are not talking about compromising biblical faith in order to make it easy for a child to believe. On the contrary, like a child who is unwilling to give up a candy bar because it is so fulfilling, this phrase instructs parents to teach their children that God and faith are never to be abandoned.

    B. **It means to "build an altar."** At this point, it is worth noting that it is significant for the writer of Proverbs to use a phrase in reference to the family that reflects back to the Jewish temple. After all, the temple was considered to be the highest and holiest place in Jewish society. Could it be that God is placing the family at the same level? That everything one brings into the home is to be placed on an altar as if it were an offering to God? I believe so!

C. Finally, the phrase also means "to dedicate." This is another meaning that comes from the temple. The process of dedication was evoked every time the priests would prepare the holiest of holies for a time of sacrifice. They would purify the temple and everything in the temple as a symbolic practice of honoring God's holiness. After all, when they laid down the offering, God was expected to show up.

Let's compare this to the home. If the home is to be a place of daily worship as well, should it not also be representative of God's holiness? Thus, everything one watches on TV, along with every word and attitude, is to be scrutinized under the same expectation of purity. In other words, if our homes are to be places of worship, should we not treat it that way? The home and family need to be rededicated to God!

2. **The initiation of the home and family.** This comes from the reference to "Raise up a Child."

A. **All too often, parents miss out on many of the most influential years of a child's life** because they are pursuing worldly things, such as acquiring a larger home, fancier car, or a more secure bank account. The truth is, there is nothing inherently wrong with nice things—but at what sacrifice? It seems that parents are spending way too much time away from home; paying other people to pour their values into their children. In turn, the parents buy their kids more stuff to fill the void.

The bottom line is, children don't need more stuff. What they desperately need is their parent's willingness to be a spiritual mentor! If not, how will the next generation learn to follow Christ? True parenting begins when a child is a child—regardless of the cost.

3. **The instruction of the home and family.** This comes from the reference to "raise up a child in the way he should go." The key here is that parents have to instruct and discipline their children. Too many parents have bought into the approach that their child should be their friend.

There is also the unbiblical concept that a parent should allow children to do as they desire so that they can learn from their mistakes. Please note that the instruction from Proverbs says to lead a child in the way that he "should go" not "would go." Parents have a responsibility to discipline their children!

4. The impressions of the home and family. Finally, keep in mind that when everything is said and done, all that is left are the impressions of the home and family. This comes from the reference, "and when he is old, he will not depart from it."

Conclusion

The bottom line is that, after children leave the home, the "impressions," both positive and negative, live on in the lives of future generations. In other words, if a child is expected to "not depart from" (Proverbs 22:6) biblical teachings, then they must be modeled in the lives of the parents!

As the old saying goes, true lessons in life are usually "caught" more than "taught." If all a child knows about following God is to go to church on Sundays, don't be surprised when the child "departs" from the faith when he leaves the home. Real faith is a daily process of dying to self and fully surrendering to Christ!

ADDITIONAL SERMONS AND LESSON IDEAS

The Missional Family Is Permeated by the Teachings of the Word

Deuteronomy 6:1–9
By Rev. Victor Lee

Introduction

The family that lives on mission will start and end with the truth of the Word of God. It will permeate the family. God's Word will be the family's guiding light, its counsel, its statement of record, and its reference point.

Knowing the truth, and living by the truth, will cause your family to be a missional family. Restated, a family living by the Word of God will be on mission.

The Call to Live According to the Word of God Is a Generational Call (Deut 6:2)

The phrase "you and your son and your grandson" commands us to look beyond ourselves to future generations, even to parallel generations of siblings and cousins. From your position within your immediate family, you can influence other lines of the family and future generations.

The Call to Live According to the Word of God is a Call with a Reward (6:2, 3)

The passage reads, "that your days may be prolonged" and "that it may be well with you, and that you may multiply greatly as the Lord God of your fathers has promised you—a land flowing with milk and honey."

Our Father desires to give good gifts to His children (Matt. 7:11; Luke 11:13). He wants to bless you as you pass on the blessings of His wisdom and truth and as the Holy Spirit moves through you and others to reach the next generation.

The Call to Live According to the Word of God Requires Steadfast, Intentional Thought and Effort (6:7)

"You shall teach them diligently" calls us to teach without fail. The Hebrew word translated *diligently* means "sharp pointed," as in "you shall zero in on the truth of the Word of God and focus the application where needed in your home!" This understanding of diligence fits perfectly with the declaration in Hebrews 4:12 that the Word of God is "sharper than any two-edged sword."

The Call to Live According to the Word of God is a Comprehensive Call (6:7, 8)

"And shall talk of them when you sit in your house, when you walk by the way, when you lie down, and when you rise up." This passage tells us that we are to teach the Word of God in all situations.

The Word of God is always:

- Relevant
- Applicable
- Useful
- Encouraging

The Call to Live According to the Word of God is a Specific Call to your Household (6:8)

"You shall bind them as a sign on your hand, and they shall be as frontlets between your eyes." God is saying in this verse that the Word of God is the lens through which you should see life! The home must establish the Word as the lens for each family member.

The Call to Live According to the Word of God is an Evangelistic Call (6:9)

"You shall write them on the doorposts of your house and on your gates." What is written on the gates announces the standard of the home to passers-by. As they get closer, it is announced again, even on the door posts.

Conclusion

The best thing we can do for our families is to teach and then live the Word of God!

A God Blessed Nation

2 Chronicles 7:12–16
Dr. Robert Matz

Introduction

In 2 Chronicles 7:12–16, it quickly becomes apparent that our nation needs the blessings of God. America needs God's blessing in order to:

1. Live (v. 13*a*)
2. Be financially stable (v. 13*b*).
3. Have physical and moral well-being in our nation (v. 13*c*).

How Can It Happen?

1. God's blessing of America depends on God's People (v. 14*a*). God will not change America until He changes us.
2. God's blessing of America demands our humility (v. 14*b*).
3. God will bless America as His People are developed through prayer (v. 14*c*).
4. God will bless America when His People desire His presence (v. 14*d*). God's people must seek favor (*bakash*, Hebrew meaning "to seek favor") by doing what God says in His Word.
5. God will bless America when His People are disgusted by their own sin (v. 14*e*). A God-blessed America is one where Christians return God.

What happens when we return to Him?

1. God hears us.
2. God forgives us.
3. God heals us personally and nationally.
   God is waiting on us to get right with Him so He can heal our land.

Conclusion

God wants to bless America. The only thing stopping God from blessing America is us getting right with Him.

WEEK 2

SERIES: FAITH IN THE FAMILY

What Every Marriage Needs

Gen. 2:18–3:13
By Dr. Doug Munton

Introduction

Stu Weber tells a story about two men, Bill and Jim, serving together in the terrible trench warfare of World War I. They labored and fought together and became true friends amidst the fighting and death.

One day, after a fruitless charge on enemy trenches, all of the men scrambled back to the safety of their own trench—all of the men, that is, except for Jim. He fell severely wounded between the lines—alone.

Bill wanted to go to Jim to provide whatever assistance he could. The officer in charge, however, would not allow it because of the imminent danger. But when the officer turned his back, Bill rushed into the fray, ignoring the bullets and shells, and made it to Jim.

He managed to get Jim back to the trenches, but it was too late. Jim was gone. His officer asked cynically if it had been worth the risk. Bill responded without hesitation.

"Yes sir, it was," he said. "My friend's last words made it more than worth it. He looked up at me and said, 'I knew you'd come.'"[1]

Marriage is much like life in the trenches. Marriage is about two people living, serving, and growing together. Every marriage needs a partner who will say, "I am here for you. I'll be here when you need me. You can count on me."

The Bible gives us clear instructions for what every marriage needs. The early chapters of Genesis show us God's blueprint for marriage, and how our marriages can be what God intends them to be.

Three Principles that Every Marriage Needs (2:18–3:13)

1. **Every marriage needs to live its purpose (2:18–25).** God gave marriage a purpose. He is the One who formed the institution. He is the One who gave the first bride to the first groom. He formed the union of Adam and Eve and He gave that union purpose—a reason for being. Two very important purposes for marriage are evident.

   A. Family. Marriage is at the core of family relationships. Children are described in the Bible as a blessing from God, and a strong, healthy marriage is a blessing to children. Marriage is the foundation of family life, and a healthy marriage—with a healthy man and woman—is the ideal environment for the growth of children.

   B. Fellowship. God gives the gift of physical intimacy to a husband and wife (v. 23). It is a part of the emotional and spiritual intimacy of marriage. He also gives the fellowship of unity (v. 24) to marriage. Close, intimate fellowship between a husband and wife is one of the reasons God created marriage. We need to take steps to guard and strengthen that fellowship. Married couples should:

   ⁓ Talk daily. Keep connected through regular conversation.

   ⁓ Date weekly (not "weakly"). Go out together and have fun together.

   ⁓ Depart annually. Get away from all the distractions and pressures and reconnect with each other.

2. **Every marriage needs to know its dangers (3:1–9).** The world's first marriage—and every marriage since—faced grave dangers which need to be identified and guarded against.

   A. Temptation. "Did God really say?" the enemy asked (v. 1). "Isn't sin really pleasurable and God is just trying to keep you from this pleasure?" he intimates (v. 4–6). Those in strong marriages know that God calls us to obedience and that this obedience is ultimately for our own benefit.

   B. Disobedience. Men can be passive in the face of danger, as Adam was in Eve's conversation with the serpent (v. 6). Temptation can turn into disobedience in a moment. Our disobedience affects our relationship with the Lord and with others.

C. Hiding. Our response to our own sin is often to try to hide from God rather than to repent (v. 8). Running from God and from others is a common, but ineffective, response to sin.

3. **Every marriage needs to own its responsibilities (3:9–13).** Blaming our wrong choices on others is a practice as old as Adam and Eve. Adam blamed Eve for his sin, and he blamed God for making Eve. Eve blamed the serpent and his deception. Often we place the blame for our own poor choices or lack of commitment to our marriages on everyone and everything but ourselves.

A. I'm not responsible for their choices. We can only do our part. You can't make your spouse do right. You can, however, pray and encourage, support and love.

B. I'm responsible for my choices, mistakes, and sins. Every marriage partner brings baggage into that marriage—our past, our hurts, and our own sinful tendencies. While we are not responsible for the choices of others, we are responsible for our own choices. Genuine repentance always involves us being honest with God and with ourselves.

C. I can lay down that baggage. I don't have to cling to my past problems, sins, or failures. I don't have to remain in bondage to my past. My marriage can have the benefit of God's forgiveness and His mercy and grace.

Conclusion

Your marriage—like every marriage since Adam and Eve—has needs and difficulties and dangers. You are two fallen people who are sinners like all of us. But God can put two people together as husband and wife and make your marriage something that honors Him and brings joy to your life. You can experience the joy of family and fellowship through this wonderful gift of marriage. Ask God to make your marriage what it needs to be.

Endnotes

[1] Stu Weber, *Locking Arms* (Sisters, OR: Multnomah Press, 1995), 87–88.

ADDITIONAL SERMONS AND LESSON IDEAS

The Missional Family Wins the Good vs. Best War

Luke 10:38–42
By Rev. Victor Lee

Introduction

Americans are dominated by selfish desires. Christians are no exception. Once a person is a Christ-follower, his or her salvation cannot be reversed. So Satan, the enemy, goes to Plan B, which is to minimize the believer's effectiveness so that he or she is not effective in influencing others to follow Christ!

In short, the enemy wants to keep you and your family from living on mission. He is doing a great job in most of American Christian culture. It is the war of good versus best. The enemy wants to distract you and your family!

Many of us Christ followers are doing things that honor and serve God, but we face a daily dilemma; a challenge many of us are likely not meeting well. Here are some questions for you to deeply consider:

- Are there some "treasures on earth" that look good and that really aren't bad?
- What is the difference between earthly and heavenly treasures?
- What eternal purpose is served by anything you amass on earth?
- How far do you go in eschewing earthly treasure for eternal treasure?

Our challenge is to live out God's mission for our lives and our families' lives, rather than to be another average church family that says, "We go to church and do good things, but we live with no power or deep purpose!"

Good vs. Best (Luke 10:38–42)

This is the best passage to illustrate good versus bad:

> Now it happened as they went that He entered a certain village; and a certain woman named Martha welcomed Him into her house. And she had a sister called Mary, who also sat at Jesus' feet and heard His word. But Martha was distracted with much serving, and she approached Him and said, "Lord, do You not care that my sister has left me to serve alone? Therefore tell her to help me." And Jesus answered and said to her, "Martha, Martha, you are worried and troubled about many things. But one thing is needed, and Mary has chosen that good part, which will not be taken away from her."

Another way of saying it is, "Martha, thanks for the hard work. The kitchen looks real nice. But Mary is at my feet learning eternal truths, and that is what matters. She won't be coming to help you."

Look at your life. Are you missing Him? Is activity consuming you? Are your time, money, and relational energy being spent on what is temporary? Are you a Martha?

Contextualizing Good vs. Best

Here are ways to contextualize good versus best:

- God vs. World; self vs. others; earthly treasure vs. eternal treasure.
- Earning more money vs. being with your family.
- Kids very active in extracurricular activities versus intimacy with family and God.

Conclusion

There is likely no American Evangelical Christian who cannot see meaningful changes that need to be made to his or her priorities, which will then move them more assertively toward living on mission. Lay up treasures in heaven, where neither moth nor rust destroys, and where thieves do not break in and steal!

Three things last forever: God, His Word, and People. What will you invest in?

The Bible: the Word of God or just Another Book?

2 Timothy 3:15–17
By Dr. Robert Matz

It is easy to be deceived, but we needn't be because there is one source of certain truth: God's Word.

Background to Passage

1. Paul writing to Timothy at the end of His life
2. Timothy is facing trials (2 Tim. 3:2–4, 3:13)
3. Paul gives Timothy Advice

The Bible Is the Source of All Truth

If you are going to be certain in one thing, be certain in the Bible. It is God's very Word.

1. You can trust the Bible because of its message: Salvation (v. 15). Every part of the Bible tells of Jesus and His saving work.
2. You can trust the Bible because of its source: Divine Illumination (v. 16*a*).
   A. All Scripture is inspired by God.
   B. Explanation: God-breathed (Greek, *theoktonos*); this is the only time the word occurs in the Greek New Testament. It is the image of the Power of God.
3. You can trust the Bible because of its goal: your Sanctification (v. 16*b*).
   A. Teaching: What we are to believe.
   B. Reproof: What we are not to believe.
   C. Correcting: What we are not to do.
   D. Training in All Righteousness: What we are to do.
4. You can trust the Bible's because of its result: Completion (v. 17).

Conclusion

If you want to be used of God, you must submit yourself to the Bible.

WEEK 3

SERIES: FAITH IN THE FAMILY

How Not to Start a Marriage

Judges 14: 1–20
By Dr. Doug Munton

Introduction

Samson has to be one of the most intriguing men in the Bible. He is stronger than an ox. His abilities in battle are spectacular. He makes Olympic weightlifters look as wimpy as me. He is unbelievable! And yet, it sometimes seems that his head is filled with muscles instead of brains.

If ever there is a time for a man or woman to use his brains, it is as they plan for marriage. A good start to a marriage pays long term dividends. That is why premarital counseling should be required. We need to do everything we can to help marriages get off to a good start.

I once spoke to a man who asked me about performing his wedding ceremony with his wife-to-be. I told him that one of the requirements I had for performing a wedding was to do pre-marital counseling. "Oh," he said, "I won't need that. I've already been married several times." Hmmm. . . I wonder if there might be some misunderstanding here?

Strong marriages are built on strong foundations. Weak marriages are built on flimsy foundations. Samson is kind enough to show us in Judges 14 how not to start a marriage.

1. **Shallow People Build Shallow Relationships.** (vv. 1–2, 7). The basis of Samson's relationship with his intended wife is external rather than internal. We get the impression that he has seen the woman (v. 2) but hasn't really spoken to her (v. 7). Samson is immature. He is demanding of his parents, impetuous in his decisions, and weak in his faith. Not surprisingly, he finds himself wanting to marry a woman who is willing to whine, deceive, and undermine. One immature person is drawn to another.

A. **Healthy relationships aren't built on external factors like beauty and wealth (v. 2).** Verse two is fascinating. Samson says to his parents, "I have seen a Philistine woman in Timnah; now get her for me as my wife." Apparently, Samson bases his need to marry the woman on the fact that he has seen her and he likes what he sees. What a shallow basis for a marriage. External factors are the most unstable sort of foundation for a lasting relationship.

B. **Healthy relationships are built on internal commitments like honesty and trustworthiness (v. 7, 16–17).** First Samuel 16:7 tells us, "Man looks at the outward appearance, but the Lord looks at the heart." Beauty and wealth will fade. Relationships are to be based on who we are on the inside. The lack of internal commitment becomes quickly evident in the relationship between Samson and his unnamed girlfriend.

Vickie and I have been married for close to thirty years now. I am balder, more wrinkled, heavier, and less muscled than I was when we married. I am so glad she married me for who I am on the inside and not what I look like on the outside!

2. **Strong Relationships Build on a Foundation of Faith (v. 3).** Samson's parents were deeply concerned that he would marry someone who did not worship the Lord God. Can I tell you one of the most unpopular verses in the bible? Second Corinthians 6:14, "Do not be mismatched with unbelievers." Yet this verse gets to the heart of the importance of faith in building a strong marriage.

A. **A common faith leads to:**

i. **Common values.** Faith is the basis of our common values in marriage or any family relationship. Our love for our family is a commitment we make based in our faith in God's love. Our common faith leads us to common values like love, commitment and integrity.

ii. **Common commitments.** Faith leads a husband and wife to a common commitment to marriage. We sometimes say, "Divorce is not an option—murder maybe—but not divorce!"

iii. **Common goals.** With a common faith, we work towards the same goal of honoring the Lord with our marriage and our family. Our goal in life should be to honor the Lord. We are to love Him supremely and love others as we love ourselves. (See the great commandment.) This becomes the goal of our lives as Christians and of our marriages as we serve the Lord together.

B. **A compromise of faith leads to:**

i. **Compromise of moral standards.** Samson's compromise of faith led to deception and exasperation. (vv. 15–17). Both Samson and his hoped-for bride are willing to compromise God's standards of holiness and honesty.

ii. **Compromise of spiritual responsibilities.** Samson was called to be a judge—a leader—in Israel. Yet his compromises of faith kept him from fulfilling his leadership responsibilities. Perhaps the reason divorce is so common in our country is that we are unwilling to face our marriage responsibilities. Compromising those responsibilities seems to be the easy way out.

iii. **Compromise of personal potential.** Samson was filled with potential. He could have been a great leader. But his compromise of faith kept him from being the man God called him to be.

Conclusion

You are preparing for your future every day. For those of you who will contemplate marriage one day, God wants to begin to prepare you right now for the kind of husband or wife you need to be. Deepen your own faith right now. Grow in your commitment to the Lord and His purposes and plans for you and for your future. Become the kind of person your future marriage partner will need you to be. Make some wedding plans right now and let those plans be to become all that God wants you to become.

ADDITIONAL SERMONS AND LESSON IDEAS

The Missional Family Lives out the Purpose of Jesus

Luke 19:10
By Rev. Victor Lee

Introduction

Everyone should have a purpose. A study of the Word will reveal thirty five to forty statements that can be construed as "mission statements" or "purpose statements" of Christ. The crux of all of those statements can fit under one overarching statement: "For the Son of Man came to seek and to save that which was lost" (Luke 19:10).

Combine that with the Great Commission statements, and it's clear that Jesus' purpose is to be our purpose. He does the saving, but we are to do the seeking. In order to carry out Jesus' mission, we must do four things.

ENGAGE the Lost

1. This means to seek out the lost; Jesus came to seek out the lost.
2. The Bible tells us the shepherd leaves the ninety-nine and risks his life to find the one lost sheep.

   That is the way we're to live; being willing to leave the safety of the Christian fold and go after—that is, pursue in love—the lost.

ENDEAR the Lost

1. This means to serve people. When you serve people, they will pay attention to you. Jesus had a servant's heart and actions to match. He got people's attention through serving them.
2. Jesus was greater than the disciples, but He washed their feet.

3. Endearing yourself to people simply means giving them a reason to pay attention to you, a reason to come to you, etc. The best way to attract someone is to serve them.

EDUCATE the Lost

That simply means we must tell them *how* they can know Jesus personally.

1. 1 Peter 3:15. "Always be prepared to give an answer to everyone who asks you to give the reason for the hope that you have. But do this with gentleness and respect."
2. Thomas asked, "Lord, how can we know the way?" People today are asking the same thing. It's not enough to go to them, to love and serve them; we must tell them why it's important to know Jesus. Jesus answered Thomas, "I am the way, the truth, and the life. No one comes to the Father except through me" (John 14:6).

EXHORT the Lost to Make a Decision About Jesus

This means to lead challenge them to give their life to Jesus Christ.

1. Jesus said to Peter, "Who do you say I am?"
2. Jesus said to the woman at the well, "whoever drinks of the water that I give will never thirst."

   So many Christians go to people, love people, even share their testimony, but pull up short of graciously challenging them to make a decision

Conclusion

In order to carry out the mission of Christ, you must do as He did. Jesus engaged, endeared, educated, and exhorted the lost.

When Money Costs Too Much

Matthew 6:19–24
Dr. Robert Matz

> The care of $200,000,000 is enough to kill anyone. There is no plea-sure in it.
>
> —W. H. Vanderbilt

Introduction

Money, things, and treasure are not evil. They are tools to help us accom-plish God's goals for our lives. Yet when we long for money, a nice house, a new car, and the finer things in life, we end up spiritually broken.

Things to Consider

1. The cost of money
   A. It leaves you bankrupt (v. 19). If your treasure is here on earth, it is at best insecure. When your desire is for stuff, Jesus says you will ultimately end up bankrupt.
   B. It leaves you blind (v. 22). If you love money, you will miss everything that matters.
   C. It leaves you in bondage (v. 24). When your treasure is anything other than Jesus Christ, you will find yourself in bondage to it.
2. The value of God
   A. There is security in the pursuit of God (v. 20–21).
      i. Heavenly treasure lasts.
      ii. It is the believer's reward.
   B. There is sight in the pursuit of God (v. 23). We see what matters and can thrive in life.
   C. When we make God our treasure, He sets us free to serve Him (v. 24). We are either free to serve God or enslaved to temporary possessions.

Conclusion

Preacher Graham Scoggie said, "There are two ways in which a Christian may view his money, 'How much of my money shall I use for God?' or 'How much of God's money shall I use for myself?'"

WEEK 4

SERIES: FAITH IN THE FAMILY

Drink Water from Your Own Cistern

Prov. 5:15–23
By Dr. Doug Munton

Introduction

I'm going to give you a tip for understanding this passage of Scripture. This passage isn't talking about water or cisterns. If you are looking for some help in building or strengthening the water cistern in your home, this is not the sermon for you. Maybe they can help you at the local hardware store.

This passage is talking about something far more important. It is speaking of sex, and the intimate relationship between a husband and wife. The cistern is really an illustration for us—a method of teaching us—about the important topic of intimacy and faithfulness in marriage.

God is not shy in talking to us about sex. He is, after all, the Creator of the topic. God is the author of this subject and He speaks to it often. He tells us of the purpose and the parameters of sex. He reminds us of the special role of sex in the life of a husband and wife. But He also points out to us the dangers of sex outside of the confines of marriage.

Proverbs 5:15–23 is both a reminder of the purpose of sex in marriage and the danger of sex beyond marriage. We see clearly that God gives the gift of sex to a husband and wife in marriage. But we are also warned that those parameters are given for a reason and are not to be taken lightly. Learning and living are important principles concerning our marriages and are critically important to building the kind of marriage relationship the Lord wants for us.

Four Principles of Marriage

1. **Be faithful to your marriage (v. 15–17).** God is very clear about our responsibility to faithfulness in marriage. We are not to allow our "springs [to] flow

in the streets." The Bible tells us over and over to avoid adultery and immorality. The first fourteen verses of this chapter of Proverbs are clear warnings against adultery.

Sin is packed well. Movies and television shows make adultery look harmless and fun. Popular music often makes sex outside of marriage seem natural and wonderful. Media makes sin look attractive, but we must remember that it leads to destruction. Therefore, God warns us of the danger of adultery and reminds us of the importance of faithfulness in our marriages.

2. **Enjoy your spouse in marriage (v. 18–19).** The Bible tells you to "take pleasure in the wife of your youth." Sex is a gift that God gives to a husband and wife. It certainly has the purpose of conceiving children, but sex is also a pleasurable gift that God made for a husband and wife to share together. A husband can be "lost in her love forever." What a picture of romance! This is a picture of genuine intimacy between man and wife.

There is an interesting event that happens in Finland each year. It is a "wife carrying contest." Husbands line up for a race of 253 meters (832 feet), which includes a water obstacle. The catch, of course, is that the husbands must carry their wives on their backs the entire distance. I don't know how much fun it is, but you must admit that it is an interesting concept!

Husbands and wives, we are joined together in this race of life. We are to take delight in our spouse. This passage tells us that we are to be satisfied with our spouse's love and guard it. Intimacy is a gift that God gives to a marriage that is to be carefully guarded and fully enjoyed.

3. **Follow the Author of your marriage (v. 20–21).** Perhaps you think of adultery as relatively harmless. "No one else has to know," you reason. But the Bible reminds us that our sin is always known by the Lord. Verse 21 points out that "a man's ways are before the Lord's eyes." The Lord calls us to holiness in our marriage relationship because He is holy. God has set the parameters of marriage because those parameters are right and holy. Ultimately, we discover that it is in our own best interest to respect those parameters.

Marriage is God's idea and, therefore, is to be taken seriously by us. God wants our marriages to be honoring to Him and pleasing for us. His plan for your marriage is always the right plan.

4. **Avoid damage to your marriage (v. 22–23).** Adultery, like all sin, "entraps" us as verse 22 states. Verse 23 reminds us that sin is like a rope that entangles the sinner. Adultery is even called "great stupidity" in verse 23.

I like fishing on occasion, but there is one part of fishing that I hate. It seems I get a tangled line almost every time I fish, and I just hate it. I'll get a backlash and notice my line is a tangled mess and find myself spending all my time just trying to undo the damage.

Adultery, and all sin for that matter, is like that terrible knot. It takes the joy out of marriage and damages this precious gift that God gives to a married couple. How foolish we are to become tangled in such a terrible and avoidable act.

Conclusion

God gave the gift of marriage to husbands and wives. It is a wonderful blessing that includes the gift of sexual intimacy. Guard that closeness and that intimacy and enjoy the wonderful gift of marriage God gives. And, whatever you do, be sure to drink water from your own cistern!

ADDITIONAL SERMONS AND LESSON IDEAS

The Missional Family is a Thankful Family

Luke 17:11–19
By Rev. Victor Lee

Introduction

The family living on mission is a thankful family. They are thankful for what they have, not sorrowful about what they have given up. Have you ever noticed that some of the most thankful people you've ever met are some of the greatest servants you've ever met? Why? It's because they have their accounts straight with God. They know who owes whom; they know why they were created.

Pastor James MacDonald says, "Thankfulness is the attitude that perfectly displaces my sinful tendency to complain and thereby releases joy and blessing into my life."[1] The key word in James McDonald's definition is *releases*. God releases His joy, purpose, and blessings through us to serve others.

Thankfulness Is Engendered by Genuine Obedience

As Luke 17:11–19 shows, obedience isn't always genuine. Jesus tells the men to go show themselves to the priests (they had to do this to have permission to go back to their families), so they headed off in that direction. "As they went" they were cleansed. Game over for nine of them!

Nine lepers displayed temporary, pragmatic obedience. This is often what our children do, and frankly, often what we as parents do. They obey up to the point that they get what they want and then they are done—done with Jesus, done with the leader, the authority, the parent, etc.

We must teach and demand obedience from our children, not just because we are the authority—though that is true—but because it engenders the qualities that lead to real thankfulness and service.

Humility is a Prerequisite for Obedience ("And one of them, when he saw")

Humility and obedience go hand in hand. The one man saw that he was a leper but now was healed. He realized that he could go to his family; if he had a wife and kids, he could now touch them. He didn't have to live the humiliation of yelling "unclean" everywhere he went. When you and I and our family members realize what we've been given, we'll want others to have it! And we'll take it to them in the power of the Holy Spirit.

The other nine lepers were self-focused. Their obedience was not genuine; well, it may have been genuine, but it was genuinely self-serving! The disingenuous person is rarely thankful. Sincerity isn't evident in his life, because his life is about himself. And people who live for themselves don't live on mission.

Humility and Obedience Lead to Thankfulness, Which Leads to Worship

Thankfulness to God leads to worship, and worship is a form of proclamation. Missional people proclaim the truth of God in word and action, which gives credibility to their words—"when he saw that he was healed, he returned, and with a loud voice glorified God, and fell down on his face at His feet, giving Him thanks."

Conclusion

Only one leper was completely healed. Jesus said to the one who returned to give thanks in verse 19, "your faith has made you well." The other nine were healed on the outside but they were still lepers on the inside. How so? They were still self-serving.

Thankfulness leads to wholeness. As a missional family, let us be thankful!

Endnotes

[1] James McDonald, *Lord, Change My Attitude: Before It's Too Late* (Chicago: Moody Publishers, 2001, 2008), 53.

Pay Attention

Hebrews 2:1–4
By Dr. Robert Matz

Introduction

In the Christian life, there are numerous distractions and sources of discouragement designed to make us quit on Christ and His Church. In Hebrews 2:1, we see that is easy to get distracted and discouraged and to give up.

Pay Attention to Jesus

If we are to survive, we must pay attention to Jesus. Why? The writer of Hebrews gives us two reasons:

1. The condemnation that comes through the Law (v. 2*a*; see Deut. 33:2, Gal. 3:19)
   A. It is reliable (v. 2*b*).
   B. It condemns (v. 2*c*).
   C. Yet, there is good news, the law is inferior to Jesus (v. 3*a*).
2. The Salvation that comes through Jesus (v. 3*a*).
   A. Jesus announced it (v. 3*b*). Salvation is not through keeping the law but instead through God Himself.
   B. The Apostles confirmed it (v. 3*d*).
   C. The Church heard it (v. 3*c*). Christianity is not the product of some rogue preacher, but instead is directly descended from the men who were taught by Jesus Himself.
   D. God testified to it (v. 4*a*). God has supernaturally intervened in humanity.

Conclusion

The entire Bible is telling us that we must pay attention to the message of Jesus if we are to be saved and then thrive as Christians.

WEEK 5

SERIES: FAITH IN THE FAMILY

How to Parent While Keeping Your Sanity

Ephesians 6:4, Hebrews 12:5–11
By Dr. Doug Munton

Introduction

There are no perfect parents. There, I said it out loud. I'm not a perfect parent and you won't be either. What's more, your children will not be perfect. If you are not yet a parent, or if your children are babies, you may find that hard to believe. If you have children who are two years of age or older, I don't have to tell you that your children are imperfect, do I? You already have all the evidence you need!

While parenting is one of the most rewarding things we can do, it is also one of the most challenging. It can be exciting and exhausting, thrilling and frightening.

When your children are small, you worry about all that might happen. You rush them to doctor's offices with fevers. You fret over them on stormy nights. When they get older, a whole new set of problems and worries present themselves.

Mark Twain gave some advice to parents of teenagers. He suggested that, when children reach the age of about twelve or thirteen, you should put them in a barrel, nail the lid shut, and feed them through a knothole. He then said, when they turn about sixteen years of age, you should plug the knothole!

I don't advocate parenting barrels with or without knotholes. It might sound tempting on occasion, but it is not a good idea! Actually, the Bible tells us that children are a gift from God and that parenting is a wonderful opportunity as well as a great responsibility. You can parent well if you understand and follow God's direction and purpose.

Ephesians 6:4 and Hebrews 12:5–11 give us some key responsibilities for every parent. These verses help us to see what we are to do, and to appreciate the importance of following some basic guidelines God gives to us as parents.

Three Responsibilities of Every Parent

1. **To Practice Love (Heb. 12:5-6).** One of the most basic responsibilities we have as parents is to love our children. We are to love them with the same love God shows to us. Love is the first and most foundational element of our parenting responsibilities.

   A. **We provide an atmosphere of unconditional love.** We must show the same sort of unconditional love to our children that our Heavenly Father shows to us. The love the Lord showed to us on the cross of Calvary is the kind of love we are to show to our family.

   B. **We demonstrate an attitude of encouragement.** Our goal is not to exasperate our children (Eph.6:4) but to encourage them. When I played basketball, our cheerleaders had a special cheer when we shot free throws. They called out your name. They said, "Sink it, Doug, sink it." I loved that cheer! Pretty girls called out your name for all to hear! I am to be my children's greatest cheerleader. I am the one who encourages them to do their best. I want them to know I am on their side and cheering for them to become everything God wants them to become.

2. **To Provide Discipline (Heb. 12:7–11).** Discipline is not a dirty word. It is, instead, an important part of our parenting responsibilities. Far too many parents in this generation have lost sight of the importance of godly, loving discipline.

   A. **The relationship of discipline and love**

      i. **Neglectful parents.** Low love, low discipline. Paul Harvey told of a motorcyclist who had the following words printed on the back of his shirt. "If you can read this, my girlfriend fell off."

      ii. **Harsh parents.** Low love, high discipline. These parents show discipline, but not as a result of their love.

      iii. **Permissive parents.** High love, low discipline. They love their children, but they hamper them by not providing the discipline and parameters children need.

      iv. **Balanced parents.** High love, high discipline. Balanced parents know that discipline is not the opposite of love; it is the result of love. Because they love their children, they set boundaries and teach consequences.

    B. Two kinds of discipline.

        i. Punishment and rewards (Heb. 12:10–11). Our children need to learn the important principle that there are consequences for our choices. Learning the lesson of consequences is one of the most important lessons we can teach our children.

        ii. Training in responsibilities. Learning the discipline that comes with doing chores, helping in the family, and being responsible is an exceptionally valuable life lesson.

3. To Promote Teaching (Eph. 6:4).

    A. Teach truth. We are to bring up our children in the training and instruction of the Lord. That is, we teach them what God says and what God wants from us. One of the great ways we can do that is to bring our children with us to church. But it also involves parents teaching godly principles to their children in their home.

    B. Model Morality. Children tend to follow our example and not just our words. After a snowstorm, my little children would sometimes try to walk in my footprints in the snow. Dads and moms, your children will tend to follow your footprints in life. Be sure you are going where God wants you to go.

    C. Demonstrate Discipleship. Reportedly, President George H. W. Bush was asked what his greatest accomplishment in life was. He said, "My children still come home." Of all the things you might think are important in life, nothing will be able to replace your family.

ADDITIONAL SERMONS AND LESSON IDEAS

The Missional Family Lives a Holy Life

1 Peter 1:13–26
By Rev. Victor Lee

Introduction

Holiness is a scary subject, because it strikes us as so utterly unattainable. Indeed, there is only one we know who has lived a perfectly holy life—Jesus Christ. Yet we are commanded in Scripture to live holy lives. It is to be our persistent pursuit. Sanctification is the pursuit of holy living.

> Holiness is the habit of being of one mind with God, according as we find His mind described in Scripture. It is the habit of agreeing in God's judgment, hating what He hates, loving what He loves, and measuring everything in this world by the standard of His Word. He who most entirely agrees with God, he is the most holy man.[1]

So, you see, holiness is not perfection—though we strive for that—as much as it is agreement with God, and actions that are consistent with that agreement. The missional family lives a holy life. They agree with God about the Great Commission, about the sacrifice of self, about seeking and leading to salvation that which is lost.

There are five aspects of holy living found in our text.

The Motivation for Holy Living (1:13)

Verse 13 reads in part, "set your hope completely on the grace to be brought to you at the revelation of Jesus Christ." Our motivation to serve will be unhindered when we can focus, focus, focus on the truth about who He is, who we are, what He's done for us, and what is to come. When we stop resting our hope on anything except the hope of Christ and the glory to come, we will find "holy living" to be right where we are!

The "Left Behind" of Holy Living (1:18–19)

There are a lot of things we have to leave behind in order to live a holy life. Peter calls them the "empty way of life inherited from the fathers." The question for you and your family is what are the "empty" ways of life, habits, actions, past-priorities, etc. that you must "leave behind?" How do you leave them behind?

The "Moving Ahead" of Holy Living (1:13)

Verse 13 reads in part, "Therefore get your minds ready for action, being self-disciplined. . . ." You and I will be self-disciplined when our hearts and minds catch up with the truth of what Christ has done for us! We will be "'ready for action!" Go home, and after you contemplate what is to be left behind, contemplate what has to come in so that you can move ahead in holy living.

The "How To" of Holy Living (1:22)

So how do we live this holy life? We live by "obedience to truth." In other words, you leave out of your life the things that aren't true, and you put in the truth by steady meditation on the Word of God. This results in "purifying yourselves" and leads to sincere love from a pure heart.

The "Why" of Holy Living (1:23–25)

At this stage of life, I hope you don't need much more motivation to live by the Word of God, but in case you do, let's finish with an excerpt from 1 Peter 1:

> All flesh is as grass, and all the glory of man as the flower of the grass. The grass withers, and its flower falls away, but the Word of the lord endures forever.

Conclusion

The Missional family lives a holy life because they are a part of God's family. God calls His family to live a holy life.

Endnotes

[1] J. C. Ryle, *Holiness*, (Chicago: Moody Publishers, 2010), 81.

God Forsaken?

Matthew 27:45–50
By Dr. Robert Matz

Introduction

This passage has long confused the faithful and the heretical. Luther was puzzled by it. Muslims argue that it means that Jesus wasn't God and one with God the Father. What is the message of this passage?

- God Provides for His Son (27:45).
- God the Father was still in control. He made the whole world dark to call attention to His Son's plight.

Jesus' Faith in the Father is Unaffected (27:46a)

"My God" is the God whom Jesus knows personally, and since He is still God, Jesus believes He is in control and able to change events. Therefore, Jesus cries out to Him.

Jesus Atones for Our Sins (27:46)

The cry is in Aramaic to call attention to its Old Testament parallel in Psalm 22. There, to be "forsaken by God" means that one is in:

1. **Uttermost Sin (Ps. 22:6–8).** Jesus, bearing our sins, is "forsaken" by God as our sins require (1 Peter 2:24).
2. **Uttermost Sorrow (Ps. 22:2–5, 11–18).** Jesus knew sorrow as fellowship within the Trinity was temporarily altered. The Father turned away from the sin that was on the Son.

Jesus' Sacrifice Was the Only Way for Us to Be Saved

The cross alone, through Christ alone, was the only acceptable way of paying for mankind's sin, hence the Father's silence.

Conclusion

Even in the darkest hour the world has known, God was there providing for His Son, and His Son was there providing for you. Will you trust Him as your Savior?

WEEK 6

SERIES: FAITH IN THE FAMILY

What Every Child Needs

Proverbs 4:1–15, 23
By Dr. Doug Munton

Introduction

Bo Jackson was one of the most famous athletes in America during the '80s and '90s. He starred in both professional football and baseball. His commercials catapulted him to even greater fame. But there was something missing in Bo's life: a father.

Jackson spoke candidly to *Sports Illustrated* magazine about missing that relationship with a father who was not involved in his life. He said:

> My father has never seen me play professional baseball or football. I tried to have [a] relationship with him, gave him my number, said, "Dad, call me, I'll fly you in." Can you imagine? I'm Bo Jackson, one of the so-called premier athletes in the country and I'm sitting in the locker room and envying every one of my teammates whose dad would come in and talk. . . . I've never experienced that.[1]

All children need parents who love them and are involved in their lives. Parents have a crucial role in their children's lives. This passage in the book of Proverbs tells us some specifics of what every child needs his or her parents to be: a teacher, a cheerleader, and a coach.

1. **Every child needs a teacher: parents who teach the truth** (v. 1–4). Parents are teachers who instruct their children in right living based on a commitment to following the truth. Parents are to teach the lessons of life, holiness, and truth to their children.

A. **Instruction: showing the proper way.** Parents serve as teachers who give the daily instructions of life. The writer of Proverbs notes for his child how his own father had instructed him in life. Parents become the "instruction manuals" for their children's successful lives. Instruction manuals can be complicated, but failure to follow them can lead to unnecessary problems.

B. **Sound learning: teaching based on truth.** Verse 1 commands the son to "listen" and to "pay attention". These lessons of life are grounded in the truth of God's word, and because of that they are extraordinarily valuable to our lives.

2. **Every child needs a cheerleader: parents who encourage wisdom (v. 5–9).** Parents need to be cheerleaders for their children. We urge them on to become the best they can be. Our encouragement and support plays a critical role in our children becoming all God wants them to be.

A. **All children need encouragement.** We are to encourage our children to become their best and to follow God's purposes and plans.

B. **All children need wisdom.** We urge them to follow wisdom because "wisdom is supreme" (v. 7).

I loved having cheerleaders at my basketball games as a youth. Pretty girls cheering for me; that was awesome! My favorite part was free throws. In our high school, the cheerleaders had a special cheer before you shot your free throws. They said, "Sink it, Doug, sink it." Pretty girls cheering my name; that was doubly awesome! I prayed that someone would foul me just so I had a chance to hear that cheer!

Parents, we are the cheerleaders that our children need. We cheer for their success and urge them to do their best. We cheer for them to "get wisdom, and whatever else you get, get understanding" (v. 7–8). We are the ones most excited when they succeed and most concerned when they face the critical free throws of life. No one cheers them on more loudly than a godly parent.

3. **Every child needs a coach: parents who train in right living (vv. 10, 11, 14, 15, 23).** Parents serve as coaches to their children. A great coach can help us become the best athlete we can be—often better than we thought we could be. Similarly, parents coach their children to be more than they could otherwise be.

A. Parents who teach and model right living (v. 10–11). Like a coach, we show our children what we want from them. Our best coaching comes through serving as a model for our children by presenting our own behavior and attitude.

When walking outside in the snow, I noticed that my young children would often try to put their feet where mine had been. It reminds us to walk very straight when our small children are already following in our path. Your example is more powerful to your children than your words.

B. Parents who set clear boundaries (v. 14–15). Every child needs boundaries. We should set clear parameters out of love for our children. "Don't set foot on the path of the wicked," verse 14 says. Out of our love, we keep our children from playing on a busy street. Out of our love, we set clear rules for our children to keep them from danger and harm. Out of our love, we use words like "no" and "you are not allowed." Our children need coaches who clearly keep them within the rules of the game given to us by the Lord.

C. Parents who encourage a godly spirit (v. 23). One of my church members told me the story of a conversation he had with his young daughter. "Beth," he said, "what will you remember about me when you've grown up?" She answered with three things.

"First", she said, "I'll remember that you loved me." Dad responded by giving Beth a kiss on the cheek. "Next", she continued, "I'll remember that you made my lunches." Dad responded with laughter. "Finally", she said, "I'll remember that you will be with me in heaven someday." Dad responded in the only way he could: with tears.

Parents, your children need you. No one else can fully take your place. They need you to be their teacher, their cheerleader, and their coach. I pray that you will fulfill your great and wonderful responsibility to the fullest.

Endnotes

[1] Richard Hoffer, "What Bo Knows," *Sports Illustrated*, October 30, 1995, 110.

ADDITIONAL SERMONS AND LESSON IDEAS

Finish Well

2 Timothy 4:6-8
By Dr. Kent Spann

Introduction

A journalist in charge of the obituaries page found himself without any deaths to record one day, so he put a sheet of blank paper into his typewriter, typed his own name at the top, and wrote the following:

> "I have been a good husband and a fine father. I have contributed to a number of worthy causes. I have left a reputation of absolute integrity. My friends are many."

The journalist had written his own obituary. That is, in essence, what the Apostle Paul did in 2 Timothy 4:6–8. If I could sum up what Paul says in the passage in a simple sentence, it would be: "I finished well for God."

The sad truth is that many professing Christians do not finish well. A study of Bible characters in the Old and New Testament will show that most ended poorly. A study of a church's turnover rate will show that most Christians do not end well. Why is that so? The answer is very simple: becoming a Christian is easy, but living the Christian life is not.

How can we finish well? Paul shares five keys to finishing well in these verses.

Serve the Lord Sacrificially (4:6).

The Christian life involves sacrifice. Sacrificial service means:

1. **We lay our life on the altar (Rom. 12:1).**
2. **We adopt His agenda instead of ours.**
3. **We pay whatever price is required for obedient service.**

Fight the Fight Successfully (4:7).

The word *fight* refers to an intense struggle. It pictures a contest where a person is expending a great deal of energy and effort. All true believers walking with Christ are engaged in a fight. Who or what are we fighting against? We are fighting against Satan (Eph. 6:11, 12), the flesh (Rom. 7:14–25), and the world (1 John 2:15).

If we are going to win this fight, it is going to require some things.

1. Exertion (Col. 1:29).
2. Discipline (1 Cor. 9:24–27).
3. Vigilance (Col. 4:2).
4. God's Power (Col. 1:11).

Run the Race Enduringly (4:7).

1. We get into the race.
2. We stay in shape spiritually.
3. We don't quit, no matter how painful it gets.
4. We get back up if we fall down.

Keep God's Word Faithfully (4:7).

The word *faith* refers to the revealed Word of God: the Scripture. He means the faith as revealed to us in the Word of God. How do we keep the Word of God faithfully?

1. We know the Word of God.
2. We defend the Word of God (1 Tim. 2:15).
3. We live the Word of God.
4. We share the Word of God.

Focus on the Finish Line Eagerly (4:8).

John "The Penguin" Bingham is an American marathon runner. What is his secret? This quotation by him reveals it. "As I stand at the starting line, I know that somewhere out there is a finish line." Paul knew the finish line (4:8), and so must we.

Conclusion

Let's run the race and finish well like the Apostle Paul!

Turning Houses into Homes

Psalm 127
By Dr. Kent Spann

The housing market is in trouble in America. Even more troubling is the fact that the "home market" is in crisis. How do we turn our houses into homes?

1. **We need the Lord's Presence in order to turn houses into homes (127:1–2).** It is vain to try to build a home without God.
   A. **We need God's plan (1a).** Just as building a house requires an architectural blueprint, building a home requires God's blueprint.
   B. **We need God's power (1a).**
   C. **We need God's protection (1b).**
   D. **We need God's provision (2).** It takes more than brick and mortar to build a home; it needs His provision of love, forgiveness, kindness, patience, self-control, etc. (Gal. 5:22–23).

2. **We need the Lord's Blessing in order to turn houses into homes (127:3–5).** The focus of this blessing is on children, but the Bible speaks of many other blessings that God gives to the home. How do we receive God's blessings?
   A. **We accept them.**
   B. **We appropriate them.**
   C. **We acknowledge them.**

Conclusion

James Dobson summed it up best: "The concepts of marriage and parenthood were not human inventions. Seek divine assistance." Let's seek divine assistance in building our homes.

WEEK 7

SERIES: FAITH IN THE FAMILY

Dysfunctional Families Can Change

Genesis 37
By: Dr. Doug Munton

Introduction

I've watched the development of television families in my lifetime. When I was very young, I watched *Leave it to Beaver*, which featured a loving mother, a wise and caring father, and two sons who were respectful of their parents. Later came *The Brady Bunch*. Two widowed parents married and blended their sons and daughters into a loving, somewhat hectic, family. The parents loved one another and provided thoughtful and firm direction to their children.

Somewhere along the way, families on television began to change. Divorce or living together outside of marriage became the norm. Television children today regularly smart off to their dimwit parents as a part of the laugh line. Dysfunction in family life is often seen as the norm.

Some of you grew up in solid, godly homes for which you are, no doubt, exceedingly grateful. But many of you grew up in homes with deep problems and even spiritual chaos. I am glad that the Lord can heal our homes and our lives, just as He can heal our hearts.

One of the greatest men in the Bible is a man named Joseph. He lived with great integrity and became a wonderful leader for us to emulate. But his early home was marred by dysfunction, jealousy, and dangerous anger.

The Choices We Make Will Affect Our Families (vv. 2–8).

Family life is a fabulous gift from God. , but we need to be reminded that the choices we make have an effect on our family members. My grandfather was not a believer in his early years. He drank heavily when he had the money to do so and caused great problems for his family. His subsequent conversion to Christ—and the positive changes which came out of that, including his sobriety—became a great blessing to his wife and children.

1. **The parents**
   A. **Marital difficulties (v. 2).** Jacob had two wives who were rivals for his affection and attention. They magnified the problem by giving their servant girls to him for him to impregnate. This is a *Jerry Springer Show* episode waiting to happen!
   B. **Favoritism (v. 3).** Jacob clearly showed favoritism to Joseph in the presence of his brothers, symbolized by an ornate robe. This brought the family dysfunction to another level.
2. **The brothers**
   A. **Unresolved anger (v. 4).** Joseph's brothers struggled to deal with a father who failed to show them the love they so deeply desired. The favoritism shown to Joseph led to anger which festered. Perhaps you have allowed anger to go unresolved in your life and family. Unresolved anger builds, and it clouds our thinking.
   B. **Jealousy (v. 5–8).** Seeing God's work in the life of Joseph only intensified the feelings of jealousy. Verse seven even gets to that awful and powerful word *hate*. Unresolved jealousy can quickly turn to hatred.

Unresolved conflict will damage our relationships (vv. 17b–20, 25–28)

The story takes a most unpleasant turn. The brewing conflict remains unresolved and the animosity builds. Finally, the brothers plot to kill Joseph. They change the plan to selling their brother into slavery, but what could they have done?

1. **They could have chosen to love.** One of the most important choices a family member makes is to love. The Bible tells husbands to "love your wives, just as also Christ loved the church and gave Himself for her." (Ephesians 5:25).

Love is a choice, the Bible teaches, and not just an emotion that can't be changed. We choose to love, or we choose not to love. You can love others regardless of whether they love you in return.

2. They could have chosen to forgive. Just as love is a choice, forgiveness is also a choice. You can hold on to the wrongs done to you, let them build and fester, or you can choose to forgive.

When you choose to forgive, you free yourself from the bondage of bitterness and hatred. Forgiveness is not saying that you like the fact that you were wronged. It says that you choose not to live under the bondage of unforgiveness, but instead choose the freedom that comes with forgiving those who have wronged you.

God Can Bring Good Out of Our Bad Situations (v. 36)

Joseph experienced dysfunctional parenting and sibling betrayal. It is a terrible story of family life gone wrong. Yet God used it for good. Eventually, God would use Joseph's situation in Egypt to provide deliverance for his entire family.

Conclusion

Many of you have been on the receiving end of hurt, betrayal, and unresolved conflict from your own family background. You cannot change your past. You can't undo the wrongs—but you can allow God to bring good out of the bad.

God can use you to help others who are going through the same sorts of situations you have gone through. If you are divorced or are in the process of getting one, seek out a divorce care program filled with wounded hearts. The greatest sources of healing help for those who are divorced often comes from others who have been wounded themselves. Members will find the comfort that comes from the Lord and from His forgiveness, and now they can pass that healing love on to others.

Some of you are here who need to choose to love. Your marriage is damaged and your love has grown cold. Will you commit yourself today to love as Christ loves you? You can't force your spouse to love, but you can commit to love him or her as Christ loves you.

Some of you need to choose to forgive. Forgiveness can only come by the grace and power of the Lord. But knowing that Christ forgives you, you can choose to live with an attitude of forgiveness. And with that choice will come renewed freedom from the dysfunction of your past, and an opportunity to grow to become the person God wants you to be.

ADDITIONAL SERMONS AND LESSON IDEAS

SERIES: OBEY ANYWAY!

When You Would Rather Be Excused

Exodus 3:11–4:16

By Dr. Dean Register

Introduction

The Bible clearly teaches us the value of obedience to God's Word. The problem, however, is that we prefer obedience on our terms rather than on His. Consequently, we grow proficient at making excuses, and we become deficient at obeying His instructions. When we do obey God, here is what we discover.

God's Presence Answers Our Insecurity (3:11–12)

In response to God's command, Moses voiced the unworthiness deep within his soul. "Who am I?" is a question that thousands of us have raised, and an excuse that thousands of us have hidden behind. Admittedly, we are all unworthy of God's grace and unsuitable for His grandeur. God chooses to use us in spite of our insecurity, however. As He affirmed to Moses, so He also affirms His presence to us by the statement: "I'll be with you." It represents God's unfailing character and the resources of Heaven! In God's presence, there is no circumstance that can destroy our security. Without God's presence, there is no security that circumstance cannot destroy.

God's Authority Dispels Our Confusion (3:13–14)

We live in a culture of confusion. It's hard to know truth from error without a reliable authority. Moses wanted to know what authority would support his obedience. God responded by saying, "I am who I am." God essentially said, "I am who I have always been, and I am who I will always be. I am the unchanging, infallible, all-powerful, awesome, and only authority for now and eternity." Unless an individual surrenders to God's authority and determines to obey God, he will stumble in confusion and fall back upon a litany of excuses.

God's Power Calms Our Anxiety (4:1–7)

Moses was not completely convinced that he should take God's assignment. He contracted the "what if?" virus: "What if they won't believe me?" The "what if?" virus infects entire congregations of believers. It renders them lethargic and anemic. It raises their anxiety to a feverish level and confines them to the infirmary of fear. God, however, boldly demonstrated His power by turning Moses' staff into a serpent. If God can change worms into butterflies, tadpoles into frogs, and snakes into sticks, He has the power to handle whatever we may face. Why should we worry about what we can accomplish in our strength when we have the power of God available to us?

1. God's Provision Covers Our Inadequacy (4:10-16).

At the core of his heart, Moses would rather be excused. Furthermore, he would rather inform God about the type of leader God needed for the assignment. God had answered Moses' every objection. God had explained the mission, but Moses felt inadequate as a spokesman. He thought eloquence was the quality God looked for, but he learned that obedience was the virtue God expected. God provided Aaron to help Moses, but He didn't allow Moses' excuses to deter the call to obedience.

Conclusion

Sometimes God puts us in places where we would rather not be in order to grow us to a place where we should be.

A Plea for Revival

Psalm 85
By Dr. Kent Spann

Have we gone too far? Have we reached the point of no return? The Psalmist must have felt that way as he surveyed his native land and saw the people of God living in sin. It led him in verse 6 to cry out for revival. Will God send revival? Can we boldly ask for revival?

1. **We can boldly ask for revival because God has revived His people in the past (85:1–3).**
   A. **God showed His favor towards His people in the past (85:1).**
   B. **God restored His people in the past (85:2).**
   C. **God turned His judgment from His people in the past (85:3).**
2. **We can boldly ask for revival because we need God to revive His people in the present (85:4–7). We are prone to wander. We are prone to go back to the old ways.**
   A. **We need to cry out to God in repentance (84:4).** Restoration is the idea of repentance.
   B. **We need to cry out to God for mercy (85:5).**
   C. **We need to cry out to God for revival (85:6).**
   D. **We need to cry out to God in faith (85:8, 9).** The psalmist was confident that God would answer his plea, which is why he was waiting and listening. He believed salvation was near.

Conclusion
What happens when God sends revival?

∽ We see God's attributes gloriously blended together (85:10).
∽ We experience God's blessing, and we prosper (85:12).
∽ We walk in righteousness and truthfulness (85:11, 13).

WEEK 8

A Godly Mother Models Godly Living

Genesis 2:18; Ephesians 5:22
By Rev. Victor Lee

Introduction

Mothers, you have a difficult job in today's culture. The typical "soccer mom" is everything to everybody—bus driver, cook, schedule-keeper, boo-boo fixer, counselor, tutor... you probably got tired just listening to the description, and it is incomplete.

How do you do it all? Imperfectly, no doubt, as being a mom is a hard, hard task. But you can do it, if you stay focused on your number one job. And what is job number one? We must look at two verses that will help you focus in a way that brings success.

The Role of a Wife

In Genesis we read, "Then the Lord God said, 'It is not good that man should be alone; I will make him a helper fit for him'" (2:18). And then in the New Testament, Paul writes, "Wives, submit to your own husbands, as to the Lord" (Eph. 5:22).

Ladies, don't get too anxious about these words. They neither belittle you nor put you down. Indeed, they set a direction, a course, and a baseline that is the foundation for success. Note that in Genesis 2:18, God said that you are a "helper fit for [man]." You are a good "fit." You are a perfectly coupled companion. The godly man and the godly wife fit together in every way by God's perfect design, and so that extends to the parenting roles, to the effective mothering of your children.

The Hebrew word translated "helper" is *ezer*. It means "one who supplies strength in an area." The term does not imply that the helper is either stronger or weaker than the one helped. Wives, mothers—you are doing what a husband cannot and was not created to do.

Ephesians 5:22 instructs a woman to "submit" to her husband. The key here is the following phrase: "as to the Lord." I am sure you quickly found out that your husband is imperfect. You do not submit to him because he is perfect; you submit to him as to the Perfect One, the Lord. When you submit to him as to the Lord, you set the right course for your family. First, you have Christ in view; and then second, you have your husband in view.

What are the benefits of Christ-focused parenting? If you start a journey of several hundred miles just a few degrees off course, you will not realize that you are en route to the wrong place for quite some time. In the end, you will miss the mark. A Christ-centered execution of your role as wife or mother is vital to the success of your family. A successful mother raises children who are Christ-honoring, Christ-serving people. When you have Christ in proper focus, you arrive at the right destination.

Many a woman has lived the first few years of marriage or motherhood without particular concern for her proper role according to the Word, and those years were not necessarily bad. But perhaps when challenges came, when conflict arose, they could not re-center, and trouble erupted.

Defining Actions of a Christ-Centered Mother

1. **A Christ-centered mother shows her children where to focus.** A Christ-centered mother shows her children the way. She exemplifies the love of Christ.

    Mothering is about so much more than specific instructions on how to do this or that. As important as those things may be, the first thing a mother should teach her children is where to look for guidance and comfort. Mothers are often nurturers—though they should not be exclusively that. When a child leaves his mother, he must know where to turn for nurturing—to the Lord! A mother who teaches her child to love the Lord equips him to live in the wholeness that God intends for him.

2. **A Christ-centered mother shows her children how to submit to authority.** Dad isn't perfect, but when children see mom love dad anyway, care for him anyway, be kind and gracious when he is gruff—and on and on the

examples could go between any two humans—then a child sees Christ in action! Christ loved us despite our rejection of Him.

You are first and foremost not submitting to your husband because he is right—he is sometimes, he is not sometimes. You are submitting because it is your God-given role and responsibility. Your children will not submit to teachers, coaches, bosses, etc., because they think that they are always right—in reality, they are right sometimes, but not all the time. Children submit because it is their role.

3. **A Christ-centered mother shows her children where she goes for comfort and counsel.** Mothers encounter many problems and challenges. Matters related to your marriage, to your children's schooling, to their conduct, their extracurricular activities, their health, and family finances are just a few. Where do you get the wisdom to face these challenges? When it is all overwhelming, where do you find comfort?

Surely you don't fancy your husband to be your all-sufficient comfort? A few years of marriage, maybe just a few weeks, will make it clear that the comfort of your husband is not sufficient by itself. You surely can't rely on your children to be your all-sufficient comfort—though, sadly, many misguided mothers do. Where does that all-sufficient comfort come from? Christ!

The Christ-centered mother models problem-solving and comfort-receiving by pointing the way to a relationship with Christ through the Holy Spirit.

The Word of God says, "And I will ask the Father, and He will give you another Helper, to be with you forever, even the Spirit of Truth, whom the world cannot receive, because it neither sees Him nor knows Him. You know Him, for He dwells with you and will be in you" (John 14:16–17).

This Helper, the Holy Spirit, is your Comforter and Counselor. Your children should see you running to the Word of God for counsel. When they are 18 at college, 26 struggling in a new marriage, 42 wrestling with a wayward child, 57 battling severe illness, they should remember that their mother ran to the Word for counsel and got it! They should remember that she was comforted in hard times by the Spirit living in her.

Conclusion

Mothers, what difference does it make if your child grows up knowing how to clean his room, fold his clothes, obey his teachers, and groom himself well, but doesn't learn to focus on Christ? If he has not learned submission to Christ? If he does not know the only true source of counsel and comfort?

If you are a single mom, your job is harder, no doubt, but your ability to focus on Christ might even be increased. Whether there is a "Daddy" in your home or not, the point is the same: you should model for your children how to focus and rely on Christ.

ADDITIONAL SERMONS AND LESSON IDEAS

SERIES: OBEY ANYWAY!

When Catastrophe Strikes!

Job 1:1–42:17

By Dr. Dean Register

One day your life is carefree and happy. The next finds you engulfed in catastrophic events. Questions swirl like powerful whirlpools threatening to suck you under. Why is this happening? What have I done to deserve this?

Meet Job. He was a godly man from the land of Uz. He honored God and took seriously his call to a holy lifestyle, but unexpected chaos turned his life upside down. When catastrophe strikes, we face three big questions, just as Job did.

1. **Will you obey during the time of your deepest grief?** One day a messenger arrived at Job's home to tell him that the Sabeans had attacked. They took his donkeys and oxen and murdered all but one of his employees. Soon two other devastating reports followed. A bolt of lightning wiped out Job's sheep and all of his shepherds except for one. Furthermore, Chaldean marauders attacked more of Job's employees and took away all of his camels. The worst report came last, however. A freak storm struck and killed ten of Job's sons and daughters.

   Imagine his grief. Job's entire world crumbled. Behind the scenes, Satan counted on Job's faith to falter so that he would dishonor God. Job, however, chose to obey God during a moment of supreme heartbreak. He fell to the ground and blessed the name of the Lord. Job wept openly, but he also worshiped deeply.

2. **Will you remain devoted when others criticize and condemn you?** Unfair and disparaging comments can throw us into a ditch of depression—especially when the comments come from those we considered as friends. One friend told Job that the catastrophe was due to Job's personal sin. Another friend told him that God withdrew His blessings because Job lacked integ-

rity. A third called him a babbling idiot who would "gain understanding as soon as a wild donkey was born a man" (11:12 HCSB).

To Job's credit, he withstood the bad theology and reviling opinions of his friends. He said, "God knows the way I have taken and when He has tested me I will emerge as pure gold" (23:10 HCSB). Job didn't allow the voice of his critics to mute the voice of God. He pressed on. He remained devoted. We would do well to remember that lightning often strikes the tallest tree. The taller we stand for the Lord, the more likely we are to draw fire from critics.

3. **Will you continue to follow when God seems silent?** If you're like me, you find God's silence to your prayers harder to bear than His denial of your petitions. During Job's experience, God remained silent for 38 chapters. When God finally spoke, He revealed that the answer Job needed was found in "who," not "why". If we know who discerns infinity, determines the universe, and displays eternal glory, we can rest in the assurance that a "why" is wrapped into His perfect character. God gave Job a glimpse of His revelation that needed no explanation. To follow the Lord when heaven seems silent may be the noblest expression of love.

Discerning the Times

1 Chronicles 12:32
By Dr. Kent Spann

Introduction

We live in perilous times. The church needs people who can understand and interpret the times. David had such men who served with him—the men of Issachar. We can learn from these men of discernment.

1. **We need to discern the times.** The men of Issachar were men of discernment who analyzed their times and accurately interpreted them.

   A. **We must understand our times.**

   i. **We must understand what is happening around us, which means we study our culture, our communities, and our churches.** We must be interpreters of our times. In order to understand what is going on in our times, we need to discern what events mean for Christianity, Christians, and the church.

   B. **We must understand God's times.**

   i. **We need to discern what God is doing in the world.**

   ii. **We need to discern what God is doing in our church.**

   iii. **We need to discern what God is doing in our lives.** It has been said that ignorance is bliss; the truth is that ignorance is fatal.

2. **We need to discern the course of action.** The men of Issachar knew what to do. If all we do is discern our times but never take action, then we are just more informed knowledgeable people. We must take the next step and determine what to do in light of the times. This requires seeking God, getting good counsel, and making good decisions.

WEEK 9

A Godly Father Will Lay His Children on the Altar

Genesis 22
By Rev. Victor Lee

Introduction

Dads, this is probably not the warm and fuzzy type of message you might expect on Father's Day, but stay with me. In the end, we will see the power and deliverance of God through the family to accomplish His purposes. In Genesis 22, we see a father and son who glorified God. Through it all, we see His power.

The title of this message is frightening, taken at face value: "A Godly Father Will Lay His Children on the Altar." But we must consider the fact that we will lay them either at the altar of God, or at the altar of the world. We will give them over to something, and giving them over to nothing is giving them over to the world.

Keys to Laying Your Child(ren) on the Altar

1. **Simply obey God.** That's what Abraham did. In verse 3 of chapter 22, he immediately does exactly what he was told to do in verse 2.

   This requires recognition that your children are a gift from God, they are not merely your creation. Abraham understood this, perhaps better than anybody, because approximately 100-year old people don't make babies— but Abraham and Sarah did because God said they would!

   This depth of obedience requires seeing the big picture and keeping it in mind. He is God and you are not. A godly father sees life through the lens of God's purposes and plans, realizing that God's thoughts are not his thoughts, nor his ways God's ways (Isa. 55:8).

Do you, as a father, have to understand what God's will is? Does it have to come easily? Abraham obeyed under great duress. He was not merely giving up a child, but the prized child, the one born so late in life, who brought joy to the parents and laughter to Sarah. And he was doing it in a place, the "land of Moriah," where pagans in Canaan regularly sacrificed their children. Abraham was being tested as to whether he was as committed to the Lord as the pagans were to their gods.

2. **Understand that giving your children to the Lord is an act of worship.** Abraham was not kidding when he said to his servants on the day of the sacrifice, "we will go over there to worship." You've heard the expression, "the sacrifice of praise." To *worship* is literally to bow down before God. If we bow down, we are subservient. If the One to whom we bow down wants something, we give it, or we are not truly worshipping. Abraham gave his best in worship.

3. **Maintain confidence in God.** Abraham's comment, "We'll come back," is often overlooked, or perhaps sometimes dismissed as a throw-away line to keep from arousing concern. In fact, he was expressing confidence in God. Abraham's confidence was not based on the belief that God would not actually ask him to sacrifice his son. On the contrary, Abraham's confidence was in the fact that God would raise Isaac from the dead if he obeyed God!

It is important for fathers to stay attentive to the journey. God may interrupt. God may shock you. His favor may come when you least expect it. What seems so hard may not be as hard as we think, and if it is hard, it may come with a profound reward that exceeds the hardship.

Abraham followed through on God's instruction. It is worth noting that he followed through with meticulous detail. He had the wood and the fire. He was up early and about the Lord's business.

God was very pleased with Abraham's confidence and perfect obedience. When asked by his son Isaac about the lack of a lamb for the sacrifice, Abraham said, "God Himself will provide the lamb for the burnt offering, my son."

4. **Remember what happens when we obey.** God shows favor, and pours Himself out through us even more! As Abraham was about to obediently

sacrifice Isaac, God interrupted and said, "Do not lay a hand on the boy or do anything to him, for now I know that you fear God since you have not withheld your only son from Me."

God the Father gave His only Son for us! Should we be willing to do any less? In whatever form He asks? Maybe it doesn't cost your child's life, but perhaps God calls your child to do something that is not quite what you had in mind. Maybe instead of choosing a career path that you envisioned for your child, such as being a banker, attorney, doctor, or professional athlete, Christ calls him to do something else. He might call your child to serve in a distant land that doesn't impress the world.

After Abraham's obedience and God's intervention, God says, "By Myself I have sworn, because you have done this thing and not withheld your only son, I will indeed bless you and make your offspring as numerous as the stars of the sky and the sand in the seashore. Your offspring will possess the gates of their enemies. And all the nations of the earth will be blessed by your offspring because you have obeyed my command" (22:15–18).

The Father who loves you and desires to give you good things will respond with joy and blessing at your obedience. What a profound blessing He bestowed on Abraham!

Conclusion

As a father, you cannot figure out what is best for your child. You cannot plot his course, nor guide him on it. You need the perfect Father, God Himself, to do that for you. How do you allow God to do that? You lay your children on the altar and say, "Here is my son, here is my daughter! I know that you know best!" When you do that, God will accomplish His will through your child.

ADDITIONAL SERMONS AND LESSON IDEAS

SERIES: OBEY ANYWAY!

When You Feel Like Giving Up

Luke 18:1–8

By Dr. Dean Register

If we conducted a survey and asked, "Have you ever felt like giving up?" it would be fair to assume that 99 percent of people polled would respond "yes"—and the other one percent would be lying. At some point along the journey of life, everybody has felt the urge to throw in the towel. In C. S. Lewis' classic book *The Screwtape Letters*, the senior demon reminds the junior demon that their cause is never more in danger than when a Christian feels abandoned and has no desire to follow the Lord, but still obeys anyway.[1] So how do you "obey anyway" when you feel like giving up?

1. **Practice persistence.** First-century widows often faced mistreatment. Medicaid, life insurance, and social security did not exist. Powerful landowners often confiscated property that had been owned by a widow's husband. Unless a judge intervened, the situation would be hopeless. In Luke 18, the widow in Jesus' parable faced a ruthless judge. Her persistence, however, became her most valuable asset. Day by day, she peppered the judge until her persistence proved more powerful than his resistance.

2. **Pursue righteousness.** Experiencing injustice can drive a person to the brink of despair. The judge didn't care about justice. "Fair" and "balanced" were not words in his vocabulary. Furthermore, he held no love or respect for God. The widow, however, refused to surrender her pursuit of righteousness simply because the judge was corrupt. She did not sacrifice holiness in order to court his favor. Justice may be abandoned by the laws of man, but it is front and center in the character of God. The contrast between the hell-bent judge and Holy God reinforces our need to follow in the path of integrity without quitting.

3. **Pray passionately.** Jesus used the parable to drive home the necessity of prayer. By contrasting the judge with God, Jesus encouraged the disciples to pray passionately to the One who is perfectly just and infallibly fair. God hears and answers those who "cry out to Him day and night" (18:7). When we are tempted to succumb to discouragement, we can call upon God to invade our situation. When we feel like giving up, we can surrender our feelings to God in prayer. When we are urged to join the "quitting business," it is our serious business to pray for strength not to quit.

Vance Havner was fond of saying, "If you can't pray like you want to, pray as you can. God knows what you mean. And you have good help—the Advocate who is God's Son and the Paraclete who is God's Spirit. They will take your feeblest prayer and make it perfect".[2]

Endnotes

[1] C. S. Lewis, *The Screwtape Letters* (New York: Macmillan, 1961), 47.

[2] Dennis Hester. *The Vance Havner Quote Book* (Grand Rapids: Baker, 1986), 166.

"Don't Look Back!"

Genesis 19:25–26
By Dr. David L. Thompson

In Luke 17:32, Jesus' warning was simple: "remember Lot's wife." What are we to remember? She looked back and turned into a pillar of salt. That is not what Christ had in mind when He said that we are to be the salt of the earth. Trust me!

Lot's wife could not let go of the world. It had its hold on her. The admonition is simple: "Don't Look Back!" Don't let the world get hold of you. Our Lord accentuates it by adding that no one is worthy to follow when looking back. So don't even think you can get away with it.

1. **Don't look back on what God has already judged.** The Scripture states that God overthrew the land and all living things including the vegetation. What sounded like the radiation fallout from a nuclear plant melt down was the judgment of God on a culture of rebellion and sexual immorality (Gen. 18:16–19:5).

    The jury is not still out on the issues of the day. God has spoken out against all forms of immorality and rebellion against God's laws. God forbids it. Don't think God has changed. We shouldn't look back and long for what God has already judged.

2. **Don't look back, because God is not in the rear view mirror.** Lot's wife looked back, but that was not where God was. She should have been looking ahead. We need to keep our eyes looking ahead to Jesus (Heb. 12:2).

WEEK 10

SERIES: THE GOSPEL TRUTH

Accept No Imitations

Galatians 1:1–10

Part 1
By Dr. Kent Spann

Accept No Imitations

"Buyer beware, don't be fooled by cheap imitations!" It seems for everything genuine there is a cheap imitation. You can get imitation diamonds, Rolex watches, pearls, iPhones, etc. An imitation is anything pretending to be something it is not. If you want a true Rolex watch, then accept no imitations. If you want a real diamond, then accept no imitations.

The same is true when it comes to the gospel. There are all sorts of imitation gospels out there for people to pick and chose. If you want the true gospel, you must not accept any imitations.

That is Paul's message to the Galatian believers. You would think that, if anyone would not be fooled by cheap imitations of the gospel, it would be the early believers who had Paul as their preacher—but even they were being fooled by cheap imitations.

Paul and the Galations (1:1–2)

1. The Importance of Galatians.

Merrill C. Tenney wrote:

Christianity might have been just one more Jewish sect, and the thought of the Western world might have been entirely pagan had it never been written. Galatians embodies the germinal teaching on Christian freedom which separated Christianity from Judaism, and which launched it upon a career of missionary conquest. It was the cornerstone of the Protestant Reformation, because its teaching of salvation by grace alone became the dominant theme of the preaching of the Reformers.[1]

2. **Context.** Galatians either refers to Northern or Southern Galatia, but most conservative scholars believe Paul is referring to Southern Galatia, because four of the churches mentioned in Acts are in Southern Galatia. The book was written between AD 50 and 52.

3. **Reason for Writing.**

A. **The Credibility of the Gospel.** The gospel of Christ was in danger of being lost at Galatia. A group called the Judaizers had infiltrated the ranks of the church. Judaizers were Jews who had made a "supposed profession of Christ" but turned back to Judaism and tried to make Christianity an extension of the traditional system of works righteousness or keeping the law.

B. **Credibility of His Apostleship.** In order for these Judaizers to make headway in the church, they had to discredit Paul, since Paul taught the opposite of what they taught. They attacked Paul personally by discrediting his apostleship, thereby undercutting his authority and doctrine.

Paul answers both attacks in the very beginning. In verses 1–2, he declares that he is an apostle and, in verses 3–5, he declares the true gospel in a nutshell.

The True Gospel (1:3–5)

What is the true gospel? The Gospel is the heart and soul of Christianity. Get it wrong, and you get Christianity wrong. If your compass gets true north wrong, then you will never get to your destination. The compass will lead you astray.

The true gospel is the message of grace and peace. Divine grace is the basis of the gospel, and peace between God and man is the result of this divine grace.

1. **The gospel is theocentric (1:5).** God is the focal point of the gospel. The heresy of imitation gospels is that they are anthropocentric, which means that man is the focal point. They make man the focus of attention.

During construction of Emerson Hall at Harvard University, president Charles Eliot invited psychologist and philosopher William James to suggest a suitable inscription for the stone lintel over the doors of the new home of the philosophy department. After some reflection, James sent Eliot a line from Greek philosopher Protagoras: "Man is the measure of all things."

James never heard back from Eliot, so his curiosity was piqued when he spotted artisans working on a scaffold hidden by a canvas. One morning, the scaffold and canvas were gone. The inscription? "What is man that thou art mindful of him?" Eliot had replaced James's suggestion with words from the Psalmist. Between these two lines lies the great distance between the God-centered and the human-centered points of view.[2]

The gospel is God glorified in salvation (Eph. 1:3–14). Salvation is not about us first and foremost; it is about God. It is about who He is and what He does. It is about His great love coupled with his uncompromising holiness.

2. **The gospel is the bad news that we are sinners under the control of this present evil age (1:4*b*).** We live in a sinful world. I guess that is stating the obvious, isn't it? You could be blind, deaf, and dumb and still know that we live in an evil world. Even children at a very early age understand that we live in an evil world. That is why they love stories with good and bad characters.

The bad news is that we cannot escape the claws of sin (Rom. 3:23).

3. **The gospel is the good news that Jesus Christ freely gave Himself for our sins and rescued us from this present evil age (1:4*a*).**

A. **Jesus freely died for us to pay in full the penalty for our sin (*for sins*).** Jesus, who never knew sin, became sin for us (2 Cor. 5:21).

B. **Jesus freely died for us to set us free from the power of sin (*rescue us*).** Grace does not free us to sin; rather, it frees us to live righteously (Rom. 6:1–4).

4. **The gospel is God's free gift to all who believe and receive it (1:3).** Paul says the gospel is from God. It was God who willed it. It was God who initiated it. That is grace (Rom. 3:24; 5:15; 11:6; Eph. 2:8–9; 1 Tim. 1:12–14). This was God's plan from the beginning (1 Peter 1:18–20; 2 Tim. 1:8–10)

John Calvin said, "So glorious is his redemption that it should ravish us with wonder."

Accept No Gospel Imitations

The market is flooded with all sorts of cheap gospel imitations. New ones pop up while old ones are still being pawned. God's people must accept no cheap imitations. There is only one true gospel. It is the gospel that Paul preaches in Galatians.

Endnotes

[1] Merrill C. Tenney, *Galatians: The Charter of Christian Liberty*, (Grand Rapids: Eerdmans, 1957), 15.

[2] Warren Bird, "Christianity and Humanism," *www.preachingtoday.com/illustrations/2000/january/5563.html*.

ADDITIONAL SERMONS AND LESSON IDEAS

SERIES: OBEY ANYWAY!

When You Need a Cause to Live By

Acts 20:22–24

By Dr. Dean Register

Saul radically opposed the spread of the Gospel. He persecuted Christians whenever and however he could, until he encountered Jesus Christ. Then everything changed. Saul was converted. He took a new name—Paul, and he took the message of Jesus across the Roman Empire. Paul's entire life was consumed with a cause to live by! There are scores of worthy causes that solicit our attention. Many of them appeal to our benevolent nature. There is only one cause, however, that is truly worth living for: the cause of Jesus Christ. The cause of Christ gave Paul a compelling ministry and a driving purpose to obey the Lord, regardless of what he faced. Three axioms of obedience unfold in Paul's testimony to the Ephesian leaders.

1. **Obedience helps you live on the edge of whatever happens.** Paul explained his strong sense of obedience with the phrase "bound in my spirit" (v. 22 HCSB). The Greek word (*dedemenos*) rendered "bound" conveys a powerful fastening by heavy chains or strong ropes. Paul didn't know what would happen to him at Jerusalem. He only knew that He was bound to Christ and obedient to His cause.

   Everybody likes the idea of a cause to live by, but few live by their cause when conditions turn perilous. The Holy Spirit gave Paul a glimpse of hardships ahead, but Paul didn't back up or let up.

2. **Obedience teaches you an eternal prospective.** Paul didn't measure his life by temporal fame or fleeting adulation. Years of obeying Christ taught him to ignore the seduction of the world, the flesh, and the devil. He learned to see through the lens of eternity so that present trials could be sifted through the sieve of God's sovereignty. When he said, "I count my life of no value to

myself" (v. 24 HCSB), he was asserting that his life belonged to the Lord, and that he would give it away to glorify the cause of Christ.

Look at Paul, the veteran apostle. Feel the pathos in his words. Listen to his perspective. It's been said that the two greatest moments in our lives are (1) the moment we are born and (2) the moment when we realize why we were born. Paul knew why he was born. He wanted to obey Christ and finish the course Christ had given him. Paul's all consuming drive was to obey anyway!

3. **Obedience satisfies our deepest longing.** There is a place inside of us that cannot be satisfied by the awe of achievement or the wow of wealth. It can only be filled by God's grace in Christ. Paul never claimed that he earned his cause. He never boasted that he was worthy of his cause. Paul consistently said he "*received* it from the Lord Jesus" (v. 24 HCSB). Having received redeeming grace from Jesus, Paul pursued a redeeming cause to spread the Gospel. He could go to Jerusalem with the deep satisfaction that he obeyed Christ.

Praise the Lord

Psalm 150
By Dr. David L. Thompson

Can you ever praise God enough? This final "Hallelujah" psalm challenges believers to find out. The psalmist praises God in every verse and with everything.

1. There are preferred places for praise (150:1).
   A. Praise Him in the assembly ("in the sanctuary").
   B. Praise Him in creation ("in the firmament"). God should be praised for His creation. It's His and no one else's. "The earth is the Lord's and the fullness thereof" (Psalm 24:1)
2. There are practical purposes for praise (150:2).

   A. Praise His mighty acts. John closes his Gospel stating that the world is not enough to contain the acts of Jesus (John 21:25). God is working all things together for good for those that love Him and are called. God never ceases working mightily on our behalf.
   B. Praise His surpassing greatness.
3. There are plentiful practices for praise (150:3–5).
   A. Everything provides a way to praise God.
   B. Everything is to be used to praise God.

Conclusion

"Let everything that has breath praise the Lord." That means you. There are no exceptions. There is never an excuse not to praise the Living Lord! If you only have one breath left, use it "praising God!"

WEEK 11

SERIES: THE GOSPEL TRUTH

Accept No Imitations

Galatians 1:1–10

Part 2
By Dr. Kent Spann

Introduction: Unbelievable!

What comes to your mind when you hear the word *unbelievable*? Is it the U.S. Congress passing the healthcare bill? Maybe it is a seemingly impossible catch made by a football player, or a successful businessman throwing away his career for a one-night stand with a woman. For Paul, it was the Galatian believers deserting the gospel of Christ.

Review the True Gospel from Part 1.

What in the World Were You Thinking? (1:6–7a)

Paul's response is strong. Paul says that he is astonished, dumbstruck, blown away, bewildered, flabbergasted, floored—yes, even amazed—that the Galatians had deserted the gospel. The Greek word translated "deserting" or "turning away" (*metatithēmi*) was used of military desertion, which was punishable by death during a time of war. Even today we don't look favorably on deserters. The Galatians had gone AWOL.

The Galatians had *quickly* deserted the gospel. The Greek word conveys the idea of time and ease. Paul is astonished that they so swiftly deserted the gospel. He is also astonished that they so easily deserted the gospel.

◦ They deserted *Christ* who saved them by grace.
◦ They deserted the gospel for a *different gospel* that was worthless.

The Galatians had traded the true gospel for a worthless imitation, and Paul was incredulous.

Clear Instruction

Paul gives sound but stern instructions to the Galatians and to us today.

1. **Don't accept cheap perversions of the Gospel (1:6–7).**

   A. **If the message doesn't say grace by faith, it is just a worthless imitation (1:6-7a).** Paul is dealing with the Judaizers. The Judaizers believed many correct things. They believed that Jesus was the Messiah and that He died and was raised from the dead. They believed in the oneness of God. They believed in the sinfulness of man. So what was the problem with their belief system? Judaizers believed that more was needed than just belief in Christ. The work of Christ was not completely sufficient. They weren't completely overthrowing the gospel, just adding to it (Acts 15:1; Gal. 4:10). They were teaching a "Christ-plus salvation."

   B. **If the message doesn't say grace by faith, it is just an attempt to confuse you (1:7a).** The scene after the 2010 earthquake in Haiti was total chaos and confusion. People didn't know what to do. Others in the confusion began to loot.

   Paul says that the Judaizers are confusing and disturbing the believers. They are unsettling the church at Galatia. False teachers and their doctrine always confuse people. Confusion causes chaos, which causes some to stray from otherwise favorable behavior.

   Many people in the church today are confused. They say that they believe in Christ, but will then go on to say that they must live a good life in order to be saved. In essence, they are saying that the work of Christ is insufficient because there is more they must do.

   C. **If the message doesn't say grace by faith, it is just a perversion of the gospel (7b).** As subtle as it seemed, the false teachers were turning the true gospel on its head by making it into something it was not.

   D. **If the message doesn't say grace by faith, it is a desertion of the gospel of grace (1:6).** When a person adds to or accepts another gospel, he deserts the true gospel. He becomes a traitor of the true gospel.

   E. **Modern Day Imitations of the True Gospel**

i. **Mormonism teaches that Christ died on the cross for sins but that His death only provides immortality, not salvation.** It is only by obeying the teachings of Mormonism that one can be saved.

ii. **Jehovah's Witnesses believe that Christ died on the cross but that His death was not sufficient for salvation.** In addition to having faith, a person must be baptized by immersion, be actively associated with a Kingdom Hall, perform works as defined by Jehovah's Witnesses, and be absolutely loyal to Jehovah—as they define Jehovah.

iii. **The Church of Christ teaches that you have to be baptized to be saved.** On top of that, if you aren't baptized in a Church of Christ church, then you aren't saved.

In each case, these groups are teaching that salvation is Christ plus something else, which is false. According to the true gospel, salvation is by faith in Christ alone!

2. **Don't be fooled; stay true to the Gospel (1:8–10).** Paul makes his strongest statement yet about listening to a false gospel

A. **It doesn't matter who the person is, if he doesn't preach the true gospel, you must reject it (1:8a, 9a).** The Judaizers had some impressive credentials. They came from Jerusalem, which was the home of the mother church. These guys knew their Old Testament backwards and forwards. They had degrees from the finest Jewish schools. They were masters of persuasion. Who could dispute them?

Paul doesn't care if it is himself or even an angel who preaches a different gospel. Reject it. It doesn't matter how many degrees they have at the end of their name or how big their church is, if they don't preach the true gospel, reject it.

i. **Reject it because it is false.**

ii. **Reject it because those who preach a different gospel are eternally condemned.** Paul uses the word *anathema*. It is the strongest condemnation that Paul could possibly use. It translates to "let them be under God's curse."

Some may wonder whether Paul could be a little more tolerant. Post-modernism says that all beliefs are equal and, therefore, you have no right to judge another person's belief. There is a word for that: "Hogwash!"

Paul wouldn't compromise one inch of ground when it came to the gospel. Paul didn't care what anyone thought about him when it came to the gospel (1:10). We can't give an inch either.

B. It doesn't matter who the person is, if he doesn't preach the true gospel, you stay true to the Gospel (1:10).

Conclusion: Does it really Matter?

Paul sounds the warning against any gospel that is not the true gospel of salvation by faith in Christ alone. In Phuket, Thailand, Tilly Smith, a determined ten year-old girl, saved her parents and dozens of fellow vacationers from the deadly tsunami because she had studied a school geography lesson, and then she courageously spoke what she knew to be true.

Tilly's family was enjoying a day at Maikhao Beach when the sea began to bubble and rush away from the shore. "Mummy, we must get off the beach now!" Tilly said. "I think there's going to be a tsunami." The adults didn't understand her warning until she called it a tidal wave.

They heeded her warning and evacuated the beach. That was the only section of beach along the shores of Phuket where no one was killed or even seriously hurt. It was all because they heeded a girl's warning.[1]

Paul warned the Galatians and all believers. Will you heed the warning to accept no imitations of the true Gospel?

Endnotes

[1] *www.thaivisa.com/forum/topic/23997-10-year-old-girl-saves-dozens-from-tsunami/* (accessed March 22, 2011).

ADDITIONAL SERMONS AND LESSON IDEAS

A Time to Testify

1 Peter 3:13–15
By Dr. Dean Register

If you were asked to tell a friend about one of the most significant events in your life, you would talk about it with conviction and passion. That's because the events and experiences that shape you most convincingly are also the ones you share most readily.

Ask a hunter about the ten-point trophy deer he shot, and he will talk about it with gusto. Could you imagine him saying, "I don't want to talk about it because I don't understand everything about gun powder"? Would he likely decline to tell his story because he feared that others would have a different opinion about hunting?

Obviously, most of us will never bag a trophy buck. If we are Christ-followers, however, we are trophies of God's grace. Simon Peter compelled first generation Christians to witness, and he emphasized four factors involved in a testimony (v. 15).

1. The Courage Factor

Fear is one of the main reasons that believers don't share their faith in Christ. We fear rejection. We fear conflict. We fear embarrassment. We fear suffering. Peter stressed the necessity of courage when he admonished believers not to be afraid or disturbed by those who oppose the gospel.

Courage is not the absence of fear, but the overcoming of it. Courage to bear witness for Christ necessitates a resolve to honor Him in spite of all anxiety, intimidation, and threats.

2. The Preparation Factor

The directive to "always be prepared" is a challenge to remain alert and ready to testify. Opportunities seldom announce their significance, but exalting "Christ as Lord" enables us to seize moments for evangelism.

Billy Graham wondered if he missed a golden opportunity to witness to President John F. Kennedy. Following the 1963 National Prayer Breakfast, Kennedy eagerly wanted to talk to Graham and invited him to the White House. Graham was fighting a fever and not feeling well. He asked if they could talk some other time. President Kennedy understood, but Graham sadly acknowledged that it was the last time he was with the President. He realized that the opportunity was "an irrecoverable moment."[1]

3. The Reason Factor

Christianity is a reasonable faith because it provides God's answer to sin, suffering, and death. Unfortunately, many believers want to suspend testifying until all possible objections can be resolved. Peter's instruction to give a "reason for the hope that is in you" is a challenge to declare the trustworthiness of the gospel regardless of objections (v. 15). In the New Testament, the word *hope* is not a vague and fragile wish, but a robust and confident trust. True faith is never unreasonable, but altogether sensible, because the object of such faith is the reliability of Jesus Christ.

4. The Respect Factor

Testifying about Christ in an arrogant manner is not endorsed in the New Testament. Consequently, Peter wrote that we are to evangelize with "gentleness and respect." Notice how Jesus witnessed. He never compromised truth, but He always drenched it in an appealing style. To the woman at the well He spoke authoritatively but tenderly. To the rich ruler He answered with dignity and countered the man's hesitation with an invitation to salvation.

Endnotes

[1] Billy Graham, *Just As I Am*, (New York: HarperCollins, 1997), 399.

"Transformed"

Matthew 17:1–8
By Dr. David L. Thompson

Is transformation possible for every believer? Is it a requirement for entrance to Heaven? The transformation that Jesus experienced on the mount proves that He is God and proves the possibility of transformation for all Christ's followers. Three truths are revealed in this passage.

1. The deity of Jesus overrules Jesus' humanity.
   A. Only those closest to Him were allowed to see His glory.
   B. Jesus reveals Himself today to those seeking intimacy with a personal and powerful Savior.
   C. The word *transfigured* (17:2) literally means an inward change that radiates from the inside out.
   D. It changed His countenance and His clothes.
   E. Similarly, Moses face reflected the glory of God (Ex. 34).
   F. In the same way, we are to reflect God's glory as we are transformed into the image and likeness of Christ (Romans 8:29, 30).
2. The death of Jesus is the reason for His humanity.
   A. Moses and Elijah appear representing the Law, the Prophets, and the saints of the ages for the purpose of urging Christ on to the cross.
   B. Luke's gospel reminds us that they spoke of Christ's departure and work in Jerusalem.
3. The divinity of Jesus is exposed for our humanity.
   A. God explodes from the cloud, "listen to Him!"
   B. God reveals Himself, not for our entertainment, but for our exposure to His Word. "Listen to Him" is the command of God.
   C. "To Him," not to Moses and Elijah; the law and Prophets are gone. In the end, Jesus alone stands as the preeminent one.
   D. The greatest need in the world and the Church is to "listen to Jesus!"

Conclusion

Jesus was transformed on the mount because of who He was. Because of who He is, we as believers are transformed.

WEEK 12

SERIES: THE GOSPEL TRUTH

It's the Gospel Truth

Galatians 1:11–2:10
By Dr. Kent Spann

Introduction: To Tell the Truth

In the early days of television, there was a game show called "To Tell the Truth." In the game, three challengers were introduced, all claiming to be the same person. Only one of them was the real person, and the job of the panelists was to ask questions that would help them to identify which it was.

People face the same challenge with competing claims of religious truth. Best estimates place the number of world religions at approximately 4,200.[1] All of them claim to be the way to God and to provide real life. People have to determine which religion is true and which is false.

For the sake of simplicity, there are only two ways of salvation offered in the world: good works and grace.

The Gospel of Good Works

If you study all the major religions of the world, you soon find a common thread: good works. The good works may differ, but the system is basically the same. Do this and you will gain eternal life.

The Gospel of Grace

- God is absolutely holy and must punish sin.
- Man is a sinner and cannot save himself.
- Jesus Christ is God's solution to man's problem.
- God offers forgiveness as a free gift to all who will receive it.
- When a person believes in Christ as his Savior, he is instantly made right with God.

⸺A person is justified by faith in the finished work of Christ and nothing in and of himself.

The Gospel of Grace is the Gospel Truth

So which is true, the gospel of good works or the gospel of grace? In Galatians 1:11–2:10, Paul proves that the gospel of grace is the gospel truth. In these verses, Paul also defends the credibility of his apostleship.

1. **The gospel of grace is the true gospel because it is God's message (1:11–12).** Paul begins with a strong statement: "I want you to know." The Greek word for "know" (*gnōrizō*) means to know with certainty and confidence.

   A. **The gospel was not manmade (1:11).** If Paul had made up the gospel, it would look like all the other religions of the world. It would have been a works-oriented system.

   B. **The gospel was not taught to him by anyone (1:12*a*).** One of the big issues in our day is plagiarism, the act of taking someone else's work and claiming it to be your own. Paul was not guilty of plagiarism when it came to the gospel of grace.

   C. **The gospel was revealed to him by Christ (1:12*b*).** Paul declares that the gospel of grace was not manmade or man taught but was received by revelation. The word *revelation* means an unveiling of something previously a secret. What Paul received was something that he had never heard or understood before. Paul would never have understood it unless Christ had revealed it to him. He never could have dreamed up anything like the gospel of grace.

2. **The gospel of grace is the true gospel because it is the life-changing message (1:13–24).** Paul substantiates his claim that this gospel of grace was given to him by divine revelation by sharing about his life.

   A. **His life before Christ proved that it is the true gospel (1:13, 14).** Before his conversion, Paul hated Christianity and tried to eradicate it. He was not a likely candidate for conversion.

B. His conversion proved that it is the true gospel (1:15, 16). When Paul was converted (Acts 9:1–19; 22:1–21), he was on his way to Damascus to arrest and kill Christians. He wasn't looking for this God of grace, but the God of grace was looking for him. Paul's salvation was the work of God.

C. The radical change in his life proved that it was the true gospel (1:16b–24). Salvation is more than God saving you from Hell; it is a personal relationship in which He reveals Himself to you. That is the message of grace.

3. **The gospel of grace is the true gospel because it is the unchanging message (2:1–10).** Paul claimed that God revealed the gospel of grace to Him (1:16, 17). All religious leaders and cult leaders make the same claim as Paul. They claim to have received a vision from God or that God spoke directly to them.

In 1820, Joseph Smith, the founder of Mormonism, claimed to have received a vision in which both God the Father and God the Son appeared to him. He was told in the vision that all churches were abominations to God and that he was being charged as a prophet to restore the true gospel to the world. In 1823, the angel Moroni appeared to him and told him about a number of golden plates which he later uncovered and translated. He claimed several other revelations.

How do we know that the revelation which Paul received was any more valid than Joseph Smith or Muhammad the Islamic prophet, who both claimed to receive a revelation from God? I could stand up on a street corner and claim that I received a new revelation from God. The key word is *new*. When someone starts a religion or claims a revelation, watch for the word *new*. The gospel of grace was not a new message, as Paul shows in 1:18–2:10.

A. It was the same message held by the Apostles (1:18–2:10).

B. It was the same message held by Peter and James (1:18–20).

C. It was the same message held by the church (1:21–24).

D. It was the same message held by all the apostles (2:1–5).

E. It was the same message held by the church leaders (2:6–10).

The gospel of grace is the timeless, eternal, unchanging message of God.

4. **The gospel of grace is the true gospel because it is based on the person and work of Christ (1:3–5, 12b).**

We don't believe that Christianity is true because it works (pragmatism), or because it feels right (subjectivism), or because it's true for us (relativism); rather, we believe that Christianity is true because it's based on the person and work of Christ (John 14:6).

Conclusion

I have nothing new to offer you today. It is the same old story that man is not saved by good works but by grace through faith in the finished work of Christ. That is the gospel of grace.

The gospel of grace is the true gospel, and that is gospel truth.

Endnotes

[1] Michael Vlach, "Classical World Religions List," *http://www.theologicalstudies.org/classical-religionlist.html* (accessed December 28, 2010).

ADDITIONAL SERMONS AND LESSON IDEAS

Wanted: Dangerous Disciples

Romans 12:1–2
By Dr. Dean Register

The men and women who carve the deepest imprint and exert the best influence upon their generation live as dangerous disciples. They are a danger to Satan's schemes. They pose a threat to the kingdom of evil. Throwing caution to the wind, they risk their lives to advance the sacred honor of Christ. Many are reserved and humble, like William Tyndale. Some are staunch and unflinching, like Athanasius. Others are passionate and focused, like Jim Elliot. Elliot's prayer captures the conviction of every dangerous disciple: "Father, make of me a crisis man. Bring those I contact to decision. Let me not be a milepost on a single road. Make me a fork, that men must turn one way or another on facing Christ in me."[1]

Although every dangerous disciple is unique, there are three qualities that they share:

1. **A life surrendered on the altar of God's purpose.** The image of sacrifice is indelibly stamped upon the heart of a dangerous disciple. We are called to a radical surrender of our agenda to God's purpose. Consequently, the "mercy of God" (v. 1) motivates us to attempt outrageous things for Him. Since we have been drenched in soul-saving mercy, we can present ourselves as a "living sacrifice". The verb "present' is rich with imagery from Old Testament sacrificial practice. As worshipers would offer a prized lamb to the priest for sacrifice, so also dangerous disciples offer themselves to the perfect High Priest, Jesus Christ. His purpose takes precedent over our ambitions.

2. **A mind renewed by a holy transformation.** Dangerous disciples think outside the box of secular reason. They practice nonconformity toward worldly wisdom. The command to resist conformity to the prevailing culture is a daily order for dangerous disciples. The Greek word rendered "conformity" (*syschēmatizesthe*) refers to blending into something else. However, we are called to "stand out" and make known the Savior rather than camouflage our

devotion. Furthermore, dangerous disciples testify to a life-changing transformation. The Greek word for "transform" (*metamorphousthe*) denotes a metamorphosis from one stage of life to another. The transformation of our minds from selfish and foolish thinking toward holy wisdom does not happen by human effort, however. Dangerous disciples understand that Christ alone creates the renewal. He is the divine Agent that accomplishes eternal change and makes ordinary individuals extraordinarily dangerous.

3. **A will devoted to God's glory.** Dangerous disciples harbor a passion for pleasing God. They are committed to God's glory and relentlessly pursue God's will at the expense of their own will. They discern and desire God's will by obeying God's pleasure. They cause demons to flee by their boldness and make Hell's army shiver. Dangerous disciples know that the mark of a good soldier is that he worries the enemy. They worry the devil by faithfully yielding the will of their flesh to the will of their Savior.

Endnotes

¹ Elisabeth Elliot, *Shadow of the Almighty: The Life and Testament of Jim Elliot*, (New York: Harper and Brothers, 1958), 59.

Literal or Liberal

John 17:17
By Dr. David L. Thompson

The communicator of God's word must hold to a literal interpretation. Anything else is a liberal interpretation, which ultimately deifies humanity.

1. **The *Word* is God's Word.** God spoke through men to pen the Scripture. God used their personalities to season the holy text, yet it is not of men. The text is all of God.

    The Bible is God-breathed. The Bible doesn't contain the Word of God; it is the Word of God. God anoints the preacher that stands solely on the truth of His Word. Some tell it like it is; some yell it like it is. Either works when the teacher has a literal interpretation and not a watered down man-centered approach.

2. **The *Word* is Truth.** There is no error in the whole of Scripture. Words like *inspired, infallible,* and *inerrant* are used to describe Scripture. *Truth* is Jesus' favorite description. We should not fear that word.

Conclusion

Truth is the only source of freedom. Germany led the way in the Reformation, yet pseudo-intellectuals introduced a liberal interpretation of Scripture. The next generation allowed Hitler to take control of the church and then the country. Dietrich Bonhoeffer was one who stood for truth of God's Word in the face of Nazism, and it cost him his life. Like Bonhoeffer, we must take our stand that Scripture is God's Word, and thus it is true. We must take that stand no matter what it costs us.

WEEK 13

SERIES: THE GOSPEL TRUTH

The Mask

Galatians 2:11–16
By Dr. Kent Spann

Introduction

Stanley Ipkiss was a mild-mannered goofball bank clerk on a dead end street to nowhere until he found the mask. When he put on the mask, he was no longer the clumsy bank clerk; no, my friend, when he put on the mask—he was *smokin'*! He went from zero to hero!

Masks can be great. They let you be someone you are not. You can put on a mask and pretend to be someone else entirely. But according to Paul, not all masks are good (2:11–16). In Galatians, Paul had to confront Peter because Peter had put on a mask, as we shall soon see.

Background on Antioch (2:11)

This is the city of Antioch in Syria, not the Antioch in Pisidia. It was the capital city of the Roman province of Syria. Except for Jerusalem, no city of the Roman Empire played as important a role in the early church. It was first evangelized by some of the Christians who were scattered abroad after Stephen's death (Acts 11:19). It was in Antioch that the disciples were first called Christians (Acts 11:26)

The Incident at Antioch (2:12–13)

Saul and Barnabas returned to Antioch at the end of their first missionary journey to report what God had done (Acts 14:26–28). It was at this time that Peter came to Antioch (2:11). Evidently Peter joined in fellowshipping with his newfound Gentile brothers and sisters in Christ (2:12). Then a group of men came down to check things out as well. They were Judaizers who claimed to be from James but were not. They may be the ones referred to in the Jerusalem Council (Acts 15:24).

When the men arrived, something happened that takes place at school cafeterias all across America. Joe sits down at a table where one of the guys is an outcast, not part of the "in crowd." Soon Joe gets the glaring glances from his football buddies at another table. He knows what they are saying: "If you stay at the table with that guy, you are not one of us." Joe knows what he has to do, so he gets up and joins his football buddies at the other table.

That is exactly what Peter did when he saw the glaring glances from those men. Peter put on his mask, picked up his tray, and went to their table (2:12). Soon others followed his lead (2:13).

Paul Confronts Peter (2:11, 14)

It was showdown time. In front of everybody, Paul "opposed" Peter. The word *opposed* is a strong word meaning, in some cases, hostile resistance. This was no lightweight confrontation. Paul was confronting Peter the great apostle!

Peter had put on the mask! Actors in that day were called "hypocrites." Actors couldn't alter their face digitally or with makeup, so to play the part of an animal or person, actors wore masks. They wore mask to pretend to be someone they really weren't. Peter was a hypocrite because he acted like someone he was not. He had put on the mask!

Paul confronted Peter's hypocrisy. Peter was "not acting in line with the truth of the gospel" (2:14). The Greek word translated "straightforward" (NJKV) is *orthopodeo.* We get our word "orthopedic" from it. The literal translation is that Peter and the others were not walking orthopedically—that is, with straight feet or a straight course. They were walking a crooked path. That is a good definition of hypocrisy.

Peter's Hypocrisy (2:14–16)

1. **He was a hypocrite because he told others what to do and then didn't do it himself (2:14).** Peter had set aside the traditions and laws of Judaism to eat with Gentiles. How could he now demand by implication that these Gentiles keep the same laws and traditions he had laid aside?

2. **He was a hypocrite because he contradicted what he professed and preached (2:15–16).** Paul and the others who joined him said by their actions that the Judaizers were right; you *do* have to keep the law in addition to Christ. That was a contradiction of the gospel of grace.

Hypocrites in the Church

How many times have I heard that the church is filled with hypocrites? It is funny that the pagans see what people in the church don't often see themselves: our hypocrisy!

﹏When we don't practice what we preach, we are hypocrites!
﹏When we contradict the message of grace, we are hypocrites!

When an African American isn't welcome at a predominately white church, that is not the gospel of grace. When a church or group makes it a rule (spoken or unspoken) that you have to wear certain clothes to come to church, that is not the gospel of grace. When a church demands that people clean up their act before they come to church or to Christ, that is not the gospel of grace. When the church creates "hoops" for people to jump through, that is not the gospel of grace.

The Impact of Hypocrisy

1. **It convolutes the gospel of grace.** Churches today are full of people who are totally confused about the gospel. They think they are saved by their good works. These are people sitting in the pews of Presbyterian, Lutheran, Methodist, and Baptist Churches, as well as Catholics. The gospel has been so muddy that people don't know the truth.
2. **It negatively affects others, especially non-Christians.**
3. **It destroys the credibility of our witness.** A police officer pulled a driver over and asked for his license and registration. "What's wrong, officer?" the driver asked. "I didn't go through any red lights, and I certainly wasn't speeding."

"No, you weren't," said the officer, "but I saw you waving your fist as you swerved around the lady driving in the left lane, and I further observed your flushed and angry face as you shouted at the driver who cut you off, and how you pounded your steering wheel when the traffic came to a stop near the bridge."

"Is that a crime, officer?"

"No, but when I saw the 'Jesus loves you and so do I' bumper sticker on the car, I figured this car had to be stolen."

Conclusion

Believers, we must guard against any action that contradicts the gospel of grace and sends the wrong message. If we are not preaching and practicing the gospel of grace, we are hypocrites! We have put on the mask!

ADDITIONAL SERMONS AND LESSON IDEAS

Get Out Of Your Rut

John 5:1–9
By Dr. Dean Register

Life is full of ruts. It's easy to fall into a rut and difficult to get out. You can fall into a rut at work, at home, or at church. Ruts are created in the boggy confines of hopeless routines. One day, Jesus met a man stuck in a rut. For thirty-eight years, the man had suffered from paralysis, and his dreams had slowly evaporated. Perhaps he still imagined what it would feel like to walk into Jerusalem, to run through fields of barley, to throw his leg over the branch of a tree, or to dance at a wedding festival. The years had taken a toll. The man's future dangled by a thread until Jesus challenged him to get out of a rut in three ways

1. **Take an honest look at where you are.** Jesus asked a question that seemed insensitive: "Do you want to get well?" Why did Jesus ask such a harsh question to a helpless man? Could the answer lie with the man's honesty? Jesus forced him to face his true condition and to answer a gut-deep dilemma. Wellness and healing meant change, and a man unwilling to be changed is unlikely to be honest with Jesus. Individuals miss out on adventures with the Lord by pretending where they're not instead of confessing where they are. Brutal honesty is a first step out of a rut.

2. **Stop waiting for ideal circumstances.** The man's reply indicated that his attention was not fixed on Jesus but on circumstances around the pool. He was convinced that the only way to get out of the rut of paralysis was to claw and crawl into the water faster than everyone else. Competition was fierce and someone always arrived at the pool before he did. What the man didn't realize, but needed to know, was that circumstances can't transform withered legs. Sadly, many people remain in a rut spiritually and emotionally because they put their faith in situations instead of in the Savior. If you wait for ideal circumstances before taking a step out of a rut, you'll remain frustrated by every turn of events.

3. **Trust Jesus immediately.** Jesus gave the man a brief and powerful command to stand. When you are in a rut, you must actively be faithful at the instant Jesus speaks. You don't have time to weigh the merits and demerits of risk taking. A rut feeds upon doubt and uncertainty. It dines at the table of hesitation. When Jesus says "Get up!" you can count on His power to enable you to pick up your mat and walk.

Your defining moment occurs when you make a decisive commitment to Him. Your choice affects your present condition and your future state. You must choose to trust Christ with the direction of your life, or instead you allow the rut to make the choice for you. One act of true faith is more valuable than thirty-eight years of wishful thinking.

"Knock Knock!" "Who's There?"

Revelation 3:20–22
By Dr. David L. Thompson

We have all used that child's riddle "knock knock." But Jesus was not using a child's riddle. Our text illuminates the church's condition and that of many would-be Christians. The good news is that Jesus is near. The bad news is He is just outside the door.

There are five key questions that must be answered from this text.

1. **Who's there?** It is Jesus and only Jesus! Buddha, the Allah of Islam, and all others will never stand at the door.
2. **What's He doing?** Knocking! Your attention is required. You must "hear" before you can open. It takes two things to be wise. The first is silence. The second is listening.
3. **What does He want?** He wants to come in. The Laodiceans thought they were good with Jesus. Wrong! They thought Jesus was on the inside, when in reality He was on the outside. What a tragedy when a church or a believer shuts Jesus out of their life.
4. **What will happen?** If we answer the door and let Him come in, we will have sweet fellowship with Him (1 Cor. 1:9).
5. **How do I open the door?** I open the door of my heart by admitting my true condition and my need for Christ.

Conclusion

If you hear a knock at the door of your heart and it is Jesus, let Him come in so that you can experience sweet forgiveness and fellowship.

WEEK 14

SERIES: THE GOSPEL TRUTH

The Most Important Question

Galatians 2:15–16
By Dr. Kent Spann

Introduction

What is the most important question in life? Is it, "What will I be when I grow up?" "How do I succeed in life?" "Will you marry me?" "Will the kids ever move out of the house?" "Is the threat of global warming real?"

In fact, the most important question is this: "How can a person be right with God?" That is the question that Paul answers in Galatians 2:15–21.

Two Essential Questions

Before we answer the most important question, there are two essential questions that we must answer.

1. **Is there something wrong in our world?** Everyone would answer "yes" to that question. So what is the problem? People will admit there is a problem while denying the real problem. They will say that global warming, politicians in Washington, big business, education, poverty, etc. is the problem. All of those are problems, but they are not *the* problem.

The problem is that man is a sinner!

In Galatians 2:15, Paul makes a universal statement that Jews and Gentiles alike realize that things are not right between God and them. Paul is not saying that the Jews are better than the Gentiles. He is saying that the Jews, who have the Law from God, know better than anyone else that man is not right with God. That was the design of the Law (Gal. 3:22).

People live in denial that sin is the main problem that plagues our world. What makes sin so serious?

A. **Our sin is a debt.** God has told us what to do, but we have fallen short of the obligation (Rom 3:23) so that now we owe God a debt which must be paid (Ezek. 18:4).

B. **Our sin is enmity (Eph. 2:1–3).**

C. **Our sin is a crime (James 2:10).** A crime is an infraction of the law. Sin is an infraction of the divine law.

2. **Why do we need to be right with God? We need to be right with God because we are under the wrath of God (Rom. 1:18; 2 Thess. 1:6–9).**

> Whoever believes in the Son has eternal life, but whoever rejects the Son will not see life, for God's wrath remains on him.
>
> —John 3:36 (NIV)

The bottom line is that we have a big problem: we are not right with God!

The Most Important Question

That leads us to the most important question, "How can we be right with God?" Paul gives the answer in Galatians 2:16: justification by Faith! We cannot get right with God by good works, religion, spirituality, etc.

Justification by Faith (2:16)

Justification by faith is the instantaneous act of God whereby He declares the sinner, who solely believes in Christ, to be forgiven and righteous in His sight.

1. **Justification by faith is a onetime instantaneous act of God.** It is not something that happens over a period of time. Once it is done, it is done!

2. **Justification is the imputation of our sins to Christ and His righteousness to us.** The key word is *imputation*. God imputes our sin to Christ and His righteousness to us. The word "imputation" means to reckon or charge to someone's account.

God made him who had no sin to be sin for us, so that in him we might become the righteousness of God.

—2 Corinthians 5:21 (NIV)

This transfer is a double transfer. Our sins are imputed or transferred to Christ, so God declares us forgiven in His sight. Christ's righteousness is imputed to us, so God declares us righteous in His sight.

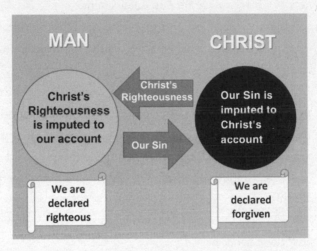

The Double Imputation of God's Justification

We are not righteous in the sense that we are morally perfect; rather, we are declared righteous in God's eyes by God.

3. **Justification is a legal declaration by God that we are right with him.** God declares sinners as righteous. He doesn't make the ungodly righteous in the sense of changing them internally and making them morally perfect. This is where the Catholic Church gets it wrong. The Catholic Church says that a person is justified by infused righteousness. In other words, God puts righteousness into the sinner and actually changes his moral character.

The Bible teaches that God declares the sinner as righteous. He is the Judge and Sentencer; therefore, He has the authority to make such a declaration because it is He who must be satisfied.

Let's say you are a dirt poor country boy from West Virginia. You can't pay your bills, the creditors are after you, and the sheriff is on his way to arrest you. Out of nowhere, a billionaire transfers five billion dollars to your account. Are you dirt poor now? No, you are a billionaire. Are you a billionaire because you earned it or because it was credited to your account? No—you are billionaire because it was credited to your account.

God declares us to be righteous, not because we earned it, but because the righteousness of Christ was credited to our account.

4. **Justification is granted by God in response to our faith.** We are not justified on the basis of the merits of our faith. Faith is simply the instrument through which justification is given to us.

Why faith? Because faith is the opposite of works. In works we, the individual, try to accomplish something. Faith is the exact opposite. Faith is relying or depending on someone other than ourselves. Faith is trusting God to provide what we cannot provide, giving us what we could never get on our own and accomplishing what we could never accomplish. Horatius Bonar said it this way:

> Not what these hands have done
> Can save this guilty soul;
> Not what this toiling flesh has borne
> Can make my spirit whole.
> Not what I feel or do
> Can give me peace with God,
> Not all my prayers and sighs and tears
> Can bear my awful load.
> Thy work alone O Christ,
> Can ease this weight of sin;
> Thy blood alone, O Lamb of God,
> Can give me peace within.
> Thy grace alone, O God,
> To me can pardon speak,
> Thy power alone, O son of God,

Can this sore bondage break.
I bless the Christ of God;
I rest on love divine;
And, with unfalt'ring lip and heart,
I call this Savior mine.[1]

Conclusion

The most important question in our lives is this: "How can we be right with God?" The answer to that question is justification by faith in Christ alone.

Endnotes

[1] *http://www.lutheran-hymnal.com/lyrics/tlh389.htm* (accessed March 22, 2011).

ADDITIONAL SERMONS AND LESSON IDEAS

Secrets Of A Strong Prayer Life

Selected Scripture

By Dr. Dean Register

Many of us have an average prayer life. We casually tell Jesus that we love Him. We express token gratitude for our food and shelter, and we plead with Him when trouble strikes. Our mediocrity mocks us and stands in sharp contrast to the passion and power of prayer warriors in the Bible. A closer look, however, reveals that these prayer warriors were ordinary individuals who developed an extraordinary capacity to communicate with God. If we could interview them today, they would disclose several secrets of a strong prayer life.

1. **A constant confession of neediness.** The depth of our prayer life never exceeds the depth of our confession. Whenever we deny our neediness, we defile our prayer life. David expressed his soul-wrenching need when he cried out, "I acknowledged my sin to you and did not cover up my iniquity" (Ps. 32:5 NIV). The main reason we don't voice our daily need for God's intervention lies in our own self-sufficiency. Pride injects the heart with the subtle toxin of arrogance. Consequently, Simon Peter explained, "God opposes the proud, but gives grace to the humble. Humble yourselves therefore under God's mighty hand that He may lift you up in due time" (1 Peter 5:5, 6).

2. **A consuming confidence in God's ability.** Whereas pride overestimates the power of self, unbelief underestimates the ability of God. If we don't believe that God is able to handle our requests, we are not likely to engage in habitual prayer. When we are consumed with God's sufficiency, we grow indifferent to the obstacles facing us. Consequently, Moses prayed and the waters parted (Ex.14:15, 16). Elijah prayed and the fire fell (I Kings. 18:38). Daniel prayed and the lions slept (Dan. 6:21). Nehemiah prayed and the wall was erected (Neh.14; 4:9; 6:16). The disciples prayed and the gospel spread (Acts 2:42).

When a Sidonian woman asked Jesus to help her daughter, He tested her confidence with a curt reply. At stake was not His reluctance but her resolve. She believed that the crumbs of His grace could restore her child. What an example of confidence in God's ability (Matt. 15:21–28).

3. **A continual quest for holy intimacy.** A strong prayer life is essentially a deep love life with Jesus. Calvin Miller described spiritual intimacy as a union of two in the closet of prayer.

> The closet of prayer is the only place you may be able to tell God everything you are feeling. There, no betrayal is possible. In the closet there is absolutely no possibility that some other human auditor will misunderstand your heart.[1]

> The basis of effective prayer is not rhetoric to dress it in eloquence, nor logic to keep it orderly, but intimacy to feed its passion. Jesus said that, when we abide and thrive in Him, we bear much fruit, but separated from Him we are absolutely impotent. Intimacy requires time and consistency, but the reward is a rich, deep, and powerful relationship that moves mountains.

Endnotes

[1] Calvin Miller, *Conversations with Jesus* (Eugene OR: Harvest House, 2006), 151.

What a Book!

Proverbs 30:5, 6
By Dr. Kent Spann

Agur makes some rather bold claims about God's Word.

1. **God's Word is pure (30:5).** The Hebrew word translated "flawless" (NIV) means to refine, try, smelt, or test. The image is gold that has been refined in the fire.

John Phillips writes about the refining process.

> Years ago my friend Stan Ford visited a gold mine in South Africa. Watching the refiners at work, he saw them heat the ore in a furnace, skim off the dross, and repeat the process again and again until only pure gold was left. The pure gold was then taken to the assayer, who put it in the fire. Stan asked the tour guide if this step was another part of the refining process. The guide said, "Oh, no! The gold has already been refined. The work of the assayer is not to refine the gold any further, but to prove that it is already fully refined."[1]

God's Word doesn't need any refining.

2. **God's Word is perfect (30:6).** This is a warning not to add anything to the Word of God. There is no need for any additional books like "The Book of Mormon" or "Pearl of Great Price." It is perfect; therefore, there is no need for further revelation.

Conclusion

The point is that the Bible is the final authority for the believer because it is pure and perfect.

Endnotes

[1] John Phillips, *Exploring Proverbs Volume 2: An Expository Commentary*, (Grand Rapids: Kregel, 1996), 547.

WEEK 15

SERIES: THE GOSPEL TRUTH

The Two Don't Mix

Galatians 2:17–21
By Dr. Kent Spann

Introduction

There are some things that don't mix.

- Oil and water
- Drinking and driving
- Taxes and our wallets
- Frugality and government
- Honesty and politicians
- Gas and fire
- Republicans and Democrats
- Peace and war

In Christianity, there are two other things that don't mix: justification by works and justification by faith.

Catching Up (2:11–16)

For context, let's look at the incident when Paul confronted Peter in Galatians (2:11–14). The incident highlights two very different claims: justification by works (keeping the Law), and justification by faith in Christ alone (2:15–16).

Justification by Faith is the instantaneous act of God whereby He legally declares the sinner, who solely believes in Christ, as forgiven and righteous in His sight. The Judaizers said that it is a combination of faith and works. Paul makes it clear that it is an "either/or" situation.

Why Don't the Two Mix?

The Judaizers tried to blend the two together. That is what people do today. It is called *syncretism*. Syncretism is the reconciliation or fusion of differing belief systems. So you pick a little of this and a little of that and fuse them together and you have a new religion.

People still try to mix law and grace together. People in evangelical churches will profess their faith in Christ while still believing that there is something they have to do in addition to having faith in order to go to heaven. Paul's answer to Religious Syncretism is that the Law and grace don't mix. He further explains why the two don't mix in verses 17–21.

1. **You can't mix the Law and grace because it is hypocritical and revolting** (2:17). It is hypocritical because you are saying one thing and doing another. Peter professed justification by faith in Christ, but by his actions said that we are justified by faith plus our works.

    A. **Combining the two is revolting because, by combining them, you are saying that Christ is a sin-promoter.** Who was the One that told Peter to go and eat with Cornelius the Gentile? Jesus (Acts 10:9–23). Now follow this. If the Judaizers are right in that you have to keep the Law to be right with God (and thus, in this case, not eat with Gentiles), then Jesus told Peter to do something that was sinful, and thus Jesus is a sin-promoter.

    Jesus taught that we are justified by faith so, if we are really justified by the Law, then Christ promoted sin by teaching the wrong way.

    B. **You can't mix the two because, in doing so, you become a lawbreaker** (2:18). Paul had spent his Christian life tearing down the system of justification by works. The Greek word translated "destroy" (*kataluō*) is a strong word meaning to demolish or totally raze to the ground.

    Notice that Paul changes from the plural *we* (v. 17) to the singular *I* (v. 18). If he builds up what he tore down, it means that he, the apostle Paul, is a lawbreaker. The Greek word translated "lawbreaker" or "transgressor" (*parabatēs*) means to transgress or violate the law. If a police chief takes down the crime mob in town but then personally rebuilds it, he is nothing more than a lawbreaker like the people he took down. The same thing happens when a person professes justification by faith in Christ alone, but then rebuilds the false notion of justification by the Law through his actions.

2. **You can't mix the two because the Christian is dead to the law and alive to God (2:19).**

   A. **Christ liberated us from the condemnation of the law (2:19a).** The Law does not save us, but it does condemn. It does declare that we are guilty, but it does not absolve the guilt. It does show us God's standard, but it can't empower us to live it perfectly. It tells us sin's penalty, but it can't do anything about that penalty.

   The Law has no authority over the Christian because Christ fulfilled completely the demands of the Law through His death on the cross. The Law can't condemn us or judge us. Dr. Grant C. Richison illustrates it this way:

   The law has no remedy for sin. It has a double power: 1) it declares us sinners and 2) states our penalty for being sinners. Suppose a person committed the terrible crime of murder. He deserves the death penalty or life in prison. The authorities arrest him, bring him before a judge, and arraign him for murder. They call the witnesses one by one. They all testify with one accord to the man's guilt. There seems to be no defense for him at all. The jury finds him guilty. He is guilty according to the law and the law requires he be put to death.[1]

   Before the judge pronounces the sentence, something suddenly happens to the accused. While he is on the stand, the man suddenly slumps down and dies. A physician pronounces him dead. What does the judge do now? Does he continue with the penalty? He cannot carry out any penalty. The law cannot try, convict, or carry out a penalty on a dead man. He is beyond the reach of the law. All that the judge can do is rap his gavel and solemnly dismiss the case and adjourn the court. The man is dead in the eyes of the law.

In the case of this illustration, the man cheated the law. The law had the right to put him to death but could not do so because he was already dead. In our case, Christ fulfilled all the requirements of the law (Romans 8:2–4).

Christ died for us. Through His death, we die to the Law's condemnation.

B. Christ made us alive to God (2:19*b*). See Ephesians 2:4, 5.

2. **You can't mix the two because you make the Law, not Christ, the basis of your relationship with God (2:20).**

3. **You can't mix the two because you render the death of Christ useless or pointless (2:21).** If a person can get right with God by keeping the Law, then Christ's death was pointless. If Christ's death wasn't sufficient, it was useless. Any human merit invalidates the cross of Christ and its purpose (Heb. 10:29–31).

Conclusion

You cannot mix legalism and grace or faith and works because they are mutually exclusive!

Endnotes

[1] Verse by Verse Commentary, Grant C Richison, *http://versebyversecommentary.com/2000/01/16/galatians-219b/* (accessed December 30, 2010).

ADDITIONAL SERMONS AND LESSON IDEAS

The Perils of Procrastination

Acts 24:24–27
By Dr. Dean Register

Procrastination is a thief. It steals virtue, pilfers courage, and robs integrity. A tragic example of procrastination unfolded in the September heat of 1862. Two Union soldiers found a copy of Gen. Robert E. Lee's battle plan and forwarded it to Union Gen. George B. McClellan. Union forces outnumbered confederate forces three to one near Sharpsburg, Maryland. Lee's army was divided and vulnerable, and McClellan had a decisive advantage. President Lincoln urged McClellan to attack, but he hesitated. Sadly, his procrastination proved perilous. Lee was able to maneuver his forces and, by the end of the Battle of Antietam, there were nearly 23,000 Union and Confederate casualties.[1]

Procrastination is seductive. When the trumpet of duty sounds, procrastination whispers, "Relax. Take it easy. You have plenty of time." When Christ stirs the heart, procrastination mutters, "Wait for a better occasion."

The danger of procrastination lurked near Felix as he listened to Paul. The Governor was acquainted with "the way" (24:22), but acquaintance and acceptance are different matters. Felix's response indicates three perils of procrastination.

1. **It neglects God's righteousness.** Felix enjoyed hearing about religious issues, but refused to embrace God's righteousness. Deep inside the soul of every person is a need to be right with God. Paul declared that God's righteousness comes to those who believe through faith in Christ (Rom. 3:22). Felix heard the truth, but neglected to act on it. Procrastination worked its poison into his heart. Jesus promises grace to cover our sins, but He does not promise to cover our procrastination tomorrow. Like Felix, many individuals today enjoy hearing theological teaching and doctrinal sermons. They listen but draw no conclusions. They see no pressing need to change. They never reach a verdict about God's righteousness.

2. **It shirks the necessity of personal morality.** The reason the subject of "self-control" troubled Felix is that he was a man of unbridled self-indulgence. He had a flawed moral compass that pointed toward decadence and hedonism. Tacitus, the Roman historian, wrote that Felix was "a man full of lusts." A life out of control desperately needs self-control. Paul, no doubt, argued that self-control was the mental discipline of conforming our actions to the Holy Spirit. Procrastination, however, shows indifference to moral convictions and virtuous actions. It prefers personal pleasure at the expense of godliness, and casually dismisses God's ideal.

3. **It postpones a faith decision.** The Bible declares that there is a moment to decide and a moment when it's too late. Paul pitched the truth of "judgment" into the bull's eye of Felix's conscience. The spear of truth tipped with the razor sharp reality of accountability before God terrified Felix. His eternal destiny hung in the balance, but he shouted, "Enough! Leave! When it's convenient I'll hear you again." Felix waffled. He delayed the greatest opportunity of his life. He postponed a faith decision, and there is no record that he ever trusted Christ. Ironically, every time a person hears the Gospel and refuses to embrace it, he makes himself less capable of receiving it at another time. Procrastination is perilous.

Endnotes

¹ National Park Service, "Antietam: Casualties of War," *http://www.nps.gov/anti/historyculture/casualties.htm*.

Affluenza

1 Timothy 6:6–10
By Dr. Kent Spann

In 1997, PBS debut a one-hour television special entitled "Affluenza." It looked at the high social and environmental costs of materialism and overconsumption, and offered solutions. God's Word long ago warned against these things, stated their detrimental impact, and gave its solution.

The Detriment of Affluenza

1. Powerful Temptations (6:9)
2. Deadly Traps (6:9)
3. Foolish or Harmful Desires (6:9)
4. Personal Ruin (6:9)
5. Spiritual Disaster (6:10)

The Cure for Affluenza

The cure is godliness with contentment (6:6). We need to cultivate contentment.

1. Practice gratitude for what you have (6:7; *For we brought nothing into the world*).
2. Hold onto stuff loosely (6:7; *and we can take nothing out of it*).
3. Simplify your life (6:8; *But if we have food and clothing, we will be content with that*).
4. Stay close to God (6:10).

The way to keep from wandering is to cultivate your faith and walk with God.

A. Love God supremely (Matt. 22:37–40).
B. Obey God with your possessions.
C. Maintain a Kingdom Focus (Matt 6:33, 34).

Conclusion

God has a word to our materialistic culture: Be content in God!

WEEK 16

SERIES: THE GOSPEL TRUTH

Living by Grace

Galatians 2:19–20
By Dr. Kent Spann

Introduction: Justification by Faith

The most important question is: "How can we be right with God?" That question implies that there are problems. What are the problems?

1. We are sinners (2:15a).

— Our sin is a debt we owe God.
— Our Sin is enmity toward God.
— Our Sin is a crime against God.

2. Our sin requires that a penalty be paid (Heb. 9:27).

— We will physically die (Rom. 5:12)
— We are separated from God (Isa. 59:2).
— We will spend eternity in Hell (Rev. 20:11-15).

Knowing these problems, how can we get right with God? We learned in the previous sermon that justification through faith, not by good works, is what gets us right with God. Justification by faith is the instantaneous act of God whereby He legally declares the sinner, who solely believes in Christ, as forgiven and righteous in His sight.

Objection!

You can imagine that those who follow the Law might object, "The doctrine of justification by faith or grace removes the Law, which undermines the basis for right living. You eliminate man's moral responsibility. Paul, according to your doctrine, a person can be saved and then go out and sin like crazy—it doesn't matter, since they are going to heaven. Paul, you are promoting lawlessness."

Objection Overruled!

Justification by faith or grace doesn't promote sin or lawlessness; the very opposite is true! Justification by faith produces a level of righteous living that cannot be obtained by the doctrine of works. Grace is superior to Law in producing right living.

1. **We have a new relationship with God (2:19).** You have all heard the saying, "you have got to have the right tool for the job." That axiom means that you have to know the purpose of the tool and match it with the kind of job it was made for.
   A. **The Law was not given to give life.**
      i. **The Law reveals sin (Rom. 7:7).**
      ii. **The Law reveals the penalty for sin.**
      iii. **The Law was not given to give life.**
   B. **God is the one who gives life (Rom 8:1–4).** When we are justified by faith, God infuses new life in us.
2. **We have been crucified with Christ (2:20a).** Certainly Paul didn't mean that he had been physically crucified with Christ. So what does he mean? At this point, we are on very sacred ground. It must be understood that the death of Christ was unique and unrepeatable. It was not the act of crucifixion that made Christ's death unique, because on either side of Him were thieves being crucified. The uniqueness of His death was the substitutionary suffering and a vicarious death for others. He was carrying the sins of others.

   What then does Paul mean when he says that we are "crucified with Christ"? He is saying that the believer is identified with Christ in His death and resurrection. It was a co-crucifixion. What happened to Christ physically happened to Paul legally. He was identified with Christ and thus died. As Calvin put it, "As long as Christ remains outside of us, and we are separated from him, all that he has suffered and done for the salvation of the human race remains useless and of no value for us."[1]

A. **The believer's crucifixion through Christ is a once and for all death.** When you trusted Christ for your salvation, in that moment, you died.

B. **The believer's crucifixion was something that God did to him.** When Paul says, "I have been crucified with Christ," it is in the passive voice in the Greek (*sustauroō*), which means that the subject is being acted on. Paul cannot brag and say, "I crucified myself;" rather, he was crucified.

What does this mean from a practical standpoint? First, we are dead to the law and its condemnation. Second, and most importantly as it relates to sanctification, we die to sin and the self-life.

What shall we say, then? Shall we go on sinning so that grace may increase? By no means! We died to sin; how can we live in it any longer?

—Romans 6:1, 2 (NIV)

3. **We have the indwelling life of Christ (2:20b).** At salvation, we die but we also come to life. This is a new life in Christ (John 12:24, 25; Col. 1:27).

A. **Christ dwells in us.**

B. **We dwell in Christ.** How can we say this? If I go to the Pacific coast and fill a bottle with water from the Pacific Ocean, I can say that the Pacific Ocean is now in the bottle. If I then take the bottle a hundred miles out to sea and drop it in the Pacific Ocean, I can now say that the ocean dwells in the bottle and the bottle in the ocean. This is the principle of John 15:4. Jesus says that we abide in Him and He in us.

3. **We have a new *modus operandi* (2:20c).** Here is where the Judaizers got it all wrong and where many still get it wrong today. They say that we are saved by faith but sanctified by works.

Paul says that it is by faith from salvation to sanctification (Col 2:6, 7). We trusted Christ to provide what we couldn't provide: salvation. In the same way, we trust Christ to do what we can't do in our own power: live the Christian life. The Christian life is not about trying harder and harder to get right with God; it is trusting Christ more and more to live His life through us. Living by faith is our new *modus operandi*.

4. **We have a higher motive for living a righteous life (2:20d).** Paul says that he lives this new life for the One "who loved me and gave Himself for me." This new life in Christ gives a new reason for living. We live for the One who loved us and made the ultimate sacrifice for us.

Conclusion: Living by Grace

The doctrine of grace, as Paul teaches, does not produce lawlessness; rather, it produces true righteousness. It is not a license to sin; it is a license to live. It is not a relationship of law and obligation; rather, it is one of love and devotion. It is not about trying harder and failing more. It is about trusting more and letting Christ live in us. It is not about what we as Christians have to do; it is about what we should want to do.

ADDITIONAL SERMONS AND LESSON IDEAS

SERIES: SINGLE AND SATISFIED

Don't Waste Your Singleness

1 Corinthians 7
By Dr. Karl Ray Minor

Introduction

Pastor and author John Piper has encouraged his readers to take full advantage of the opportunities that God has given them in his book *Don't Waste your Life*. Piper has followed his own advice in his essay about dealing with his own prostate cancer, "Don't waste your Cancer," reminding his readers that even cancer is an opportunity to know Christ and glorify God.

In First Corinthians 7, Paul describes being single as a good gift from God. The apostle spells out in detail that singleness is a gift given for a season of life for the ultimate good of knowing Christ and serving His Church.

But Paul also gives warning to singles in 1 Corinthians 7. He says to the single people in Corinth, "Don't waste your singleness." The gift given for their good and God's glory can be spoiled in four different ways.

Choosing Immorality (vv. 1, 2)

The Apostle Paul does not discount the natural sex drive. He admits that it can become a "burning passion" (v. 9). At the same time, Scripture is clear that singleness for Christians means celibacy. An immoral relationship brings shame and guilt, and robs the person of his Christian witness. One cannot fulfill God's purpose while at the same time living outside the will of God.

Getting Married Just to get Married (v. 8)

Abraham and Sarah grew impatient waiting on God's timing for a son, and instead produced their own son through Hagar. In a similar way, singles face the temptation to run ahead of God and find a spouse—any spouse—to fulfill their desire to be married. This produces a permanent problem from a short-term solution. An ill-matched marriage will bring all the troubles of marriage without adding the benefits and will waste your gift of singleness.

Patience is the faith that God's timing is perfect. Don't lower your standards; allow God to bring someone into your life who is worthy of you.

Living a Divided Life (vv. 33, 34)

Paul reminds his single readers that this season of their life is a gift because it allows them the time to live a life focused upon building their relationship with Jesus Christ. But singles are subject to the common temptations of us all. It becomes very easy for singles to throw themselves into a hobby, a job, or any other activity that consumes their time. What happens when single people don't take advantage of this opportunity? They waste their singleness.

Becoming Self-Absorbed (v. 32)

Singles also have the opportunity to be about "the things of God" by investing their lives in the lives of others. But it is possible for singles to become so distracted by their own situation that they close their lives to others, thereby wasting their singleness. Open yourself once again to the people whom God has placed into your life.

Conclusion

Singleness is a good gift. Don't waste it.

Praying for your Pastor

1 Thessalonians 5:25
By Dr. Kent Spann

Paul was a man in need of prayer. In fact, all ministers of the gospel are people in need of prayer.

1. Pray for his spiritual life, and that he will:
   A. Love God with all of his being (Deut. 6:5; Matt. 22:37–40).
   B. Be filled with the Spirit (Eph. 5:18; Gal. 5:22–25).
   C. Grow spiritually (2 Peter 3:18).
   D. Develop in character (2 Peter 1:5–9).
   E. Be devoted to prayer (Col. 4.2; Acts 6:4).
   F. Be protected from the evil one (2 Thess. 3:1–3; Eph. 6:12, 13).

2. Pray for his personal life, for him to:
   A. Be pure (Matt 26:41; 1 Tim. 4:11).
   B. Be a witness (Col. 4:5, 6; Acts 1:8).
   C. Manage his time well (Eph. 5:15, 16).
   D. Have a proper view of himself (Rom. 12:3).
   E. Experience God's healing (Isa. 61:3).
   F. Be well-rounded (Luke 2:52).
   G. Have a strong family life (Eph. 5:22–6:4).

3. Pray for his ministerial life, and that he will:
   A. Not allow the pressure of the ministry to get him down; and if it does, that he find rest in Jesus (2 Cor. 11:28; Matt. 11:28–30).
   B. Experience joy in his ministry (Heb. 13:17).
   C. Preach the Word (1 Tim. 4:13; 2 Tim. 4:2).
   D. Remain doctrinally sound (1 Tim. 4:15, 16; Titus 1:9).
   E. Be a man of vision (Prov. 29:18).
   F. Be a good shepherd of his flock (1 Peter 5:1–4).

WEEK 17

SERIES: THE GOSPEL TRUTH

The Case for Faith

Galatians 3:1–14
By Dr. Kent Spann

Introduction

Is faith in Jesus Christ really the only way to get right with God? Isn't there something we must do? Isn't keeping the Law and doing good works part of the salvation equation? Paul teaches in Galatians that we are justified by faith in Christ, not by works. Faith in Christ alone is the only way to get right with God!

By Faith Alone

In Galatians 3:1–4, Paul makes the case for faith alone.

1. **We know it is by faith because that is the way we were saved (3:1–5).** In the '60s and '70s, there was a popular television show called *Bewitched* starring Elizabeth Montgomery. Her character Samantha used her magical powers to cast spells over her husband's boss and their neighbor Harriet. In other words, she bewitched them.

   Similar to the characters in the TV show, the Galatians had been "bewitched." They were held spellbound by an irresistible power. How were they being bewitched? Paul preached justification by faith in Christ alone to the Galatians. They believed and were converted. After Paul left, Judaizers came to the Galations. The Judaizers believed that it was not enough to believe in Christ; they believed that the Galations should also keep the Law to be saved or justified. They taught a "Christ-Plus" doctrine. Sadly, the Galatians, like many today, were bewitched by this message of Christ-Plus, and the Galatians bought into it.

   Paul reminds the Galatians of their salvation experience and ours as well.

A. **By faith we believed Christ died for our sins (3:1).** Paul says, "I placarded Christ as crucified before you. I put up an official notice that it was the death of Christ that secures a person's salvation. I described for you the crucifixion of Christ and what it meant."

The cross of Christ was the central message of Paul's preaching (Gal 6:14) and must be of ours. It is through the cross that we are saved.

B. **By faith we received the Holy Spirit (3:2–5).** The Jews believed that the evidence of the Lord's coming would be the pouring out of the Spirit. Paul reminded them that they received the Holy Spirit when they trusted Christ (Rom 8:15, 16). He reminded them of how they received the Holy Spirit by asking a series of rhetorical questions in verses 2–5.

2. **We know that justification is by faith because that is the way Abraham, the patriarch of the Jewish people, was saved (3:6–9).** The Judaizers appealed to Moses the lawgiver as the basis for keeping the Law for salvation; Paul goes back further to the father of the nation, Abraham, as the basis for salvation by faith.

A. **Abraham was declared righteous in response to his faith in God (3:6).** This is based on the account of Abraham in Genesis 15:1–6. He was declared righteous by faith before the law was given.

B. **The true children of Abraham are the children of faith (3:7, 9).** Paul says that those who believe in Christ are of Abraham, not those who keep the Law. He is not talking about being descended literally from Abraham; he is talking about being spiritually descended from Abraham (Galatians 3:29).

C. **Salvation by faith was God's plan from the very beginning (3:8).** The gospel of faith was announced in Abraham's experience which predated the giving of the law. Paul solidifies the case for justification by faith through Abraham, the Father of the Jews.

3. **We know that justification is by faith because that is the only way to be saved (3:10–14).** Paul makes his strongest argument for justification by faith by showing from the Old Testament the impossibility of salvation by keeping the Law.

A. **The Curse of the Law (3:10–12)**

i. **You can't keep the Law; therefore, you are cursed (3:10).** In other words, Paul says, "Ok, you want to insist on keeping the Law as the way to get right with God, well understand that right off the bat you are cursed!" To be under the curse is to be under the sentence of divine judgment and the ruin or punishment that follows it. He is actually quoting Deuteronomy 27:26. See James 2:10.

ii. **God never intended for you to get right with Him by keeping the law (3:11).** See Habakkuk 2:4.

iii. **Faith and Law cannot be combined (3:12).** See Leviticus 18:5.

B. **The Cure for the curse (3:13, 14).** Christ doesn't put us under the curse of the Law as the Judaizers would do; He redeems us from the curse. The word *redeem* means to buy back. How did He buy us back? By becoming a curse for us. He quotes Deuteronomy 21:22, 23. He was cursed for us so "that the blessing given to Abraham might come to the Gentiles through Christ Jesus" (NIV). It was all according to God's plan from the very beginning (1 Peter 1:18–20).

And how is this wonderful redemption secured by the individual? Look at the end of verse 14: "so that by faith we might receive the promise of the Spirit." There you have it. Case closed.

Conclusion

Actress Sophia Loren said in *USA Today* (2-4-99):

I'm not a practicant, but I pray. I read the Bible. It's the most beautiful book ever written. I should go to heaven; otherwise it's not nice. I haven't done anything wrong. My conscience is very clean. My soul is as white as those orchids over there, and I should go straight, straight to heaven.

Boy has she got it wrong, thinking that her good works will get her into heaven! Dr. Robert Webber tells of a conversation he had on a plane:

I was traveling on a plane from San Francisco to Los Angeles a few years ago. I was sitting next to the window, reading a Christian book. The man next to me, obviously from the Eastern hemisphere, asked, "Are you a religious man?" "Well, yes," I said. "I am too," he responded. We began talking about religion. In the middle of the conversation I asked, "Can you give me a one-liner that captures the essence of your faith?" "Well, yes," he said. "We are all part of the problem, and we are all part of the solution."

We talked about his one-liner, a statement I felt was very helpful. After a while I said, "Would you like a one-liner that captures the Christian faith?"

"Sure," he responded.

"We are all part of the problem, but there is only one Man who is the solution. His name is Jesus."[1]

Endnotes

[1] Robert Webber, *Who Gets to Narrate the World?* (Downer's Grove: InterVarsity Press, 2008), 26.

ADDITIONAL SERMONS AND LESSON IDEAS

The Good Gift of Singleness

1 Corinthians 7
By Dr. Karl Ray Minor

Introduction

We all have occasions in our lives that are marked by gifts. We receive graduation gifts, birthday gifts, and Christmas gifts, to name a few. Each gift is for our benefit and happiness. Each gift marks a moment or season in our lives.

In 1 Corinthians 7, Paul is answering various questions from the church in Corinth, and he speaks about one of God's good gifts: the gift of singleness. And like all other gifts, this gift is for our benefit, and marks a season of our lives. Notice what Paul says about singleness.

It is a Good Gift (vv. 7, 8)

"For I wish that all men were even as I myself. But each one has his own gift from God. . . . But I say to the unmarried and to the widows: It is good for them if they remain even as I am" (1 Corinthians 7:7, 8).

God is a good God and every gift He gives to His children is good (James 1:17). God works all things to the good of those who love Him (Rom. 8:28).

It is For a Season (v. 26)

"I think then that this is good in view of the present distress, that it is good for a man to remain as he is" (1 Cor. 7:26).

Scholars differ on what Paul means by the phrase "the present distress." Regardless of the exact interpretation, the point is the same: the moment is temporary. So it is with you. Whether you have not yet married, or you find yourself single after divorce or death, this season of your life is only temporary.

It is for a Purpose (v. 35)

"This I say for your own benefit. . . to secure undistracted devotion to the Lord" (1 Cor. 7:35).

Paul reminds us that marriage is not God's ultimate will for our lives. Becoming conformed to the image of His Son is God's highest purpose for us. Paul states that God works all things for our good because the greatest good is to become like Christ (Rom. 8:28, 29).

Those who are married are rightly divided between the cares of the family and the Lord (1 Cor. 7:33) so that they may try to please both. The season of singleness in our lives is a good gift that allows us to focus single-mindedly upon Christ.

It is for Others (v. 32)

"But I want you to be free from concern. One who is unmarried is concerned about the things of the Lord, how he may please the Lord. . ." (1 Cor. 7:32).

Paul speaks nowhere of the single life being a lonely life. In fact, the gift of singleness allows you to invest yourself in "the things of the Lord." The good gift of singleness allows you to give yourself away to others.

Conclusion

Thank God for giving you the good gift of singleness.

Temptation Island

James 1:13–18
By Dr. Kent Spann

The Source of Temptation (1:13)

We cannot excuse our sinning by saying that God tempted us. The source of temptation is within us.

The Steps of Temptation (1:14, 15)

1. **Desire (1:14a).** The only reason that Satan is effective in tempting us is because of a problem within us. We have a connection to Satan. It is called evil desire. There is no use going around and blaming circumstances, environment, other people, etc., because the problem is ours.
2. **Deception (1:14b).**
   A. "Dragged away" means to draw out as a hunter does to his prey.
   B. "Enticed" means to deceive like the hunter, who puts out bait to lure his prey into the open.
3. **Disobedience (1:15b).** James uses the analogy of childbirth. The desire has now conceived, but the goal is not getting pregnant; the goal is to give birth to disobedience.
4. **Death (1:15b).**

The Victory Over Temptation (1:16–18)

1. **Stay on guard (1:16).**
2. **Remember God's Goodness (1:17).** At the heart of sin's temptation is the question of God's goodness (Gen. 3:1–5).
3. **Put on the new self (1:18).** The clear teaching is that we have experienced a new birth so that we now have a new nature.

WEEK 18

Law and Promise

Galatians 3:15–24
By Dr. Kent Spann

Introduction

One of the most popular crime shows on TV is "Law & Order," launched in 1990. There have been many spin-offs since the show first aired. There is another version of "Law & Order" that long preceded the one launched in 1990. It is called "Law & Order: Israel." The Law was central to Israel. It was the key to ordering their life. The Judaizers still insisted that a person had to keep the Law in order to be saved.

Paul clearly teaches that a person is saved or justified, not by keeping the Law, but by faith (Gal. 3:1–5). That has been God's plan beginning with Abraham (Gal. 3:6–14). The Promise (salvation by faith) is superior to the Law. The Judaizers would agree; Abraham was saved by faith but, when the Law was given, everything changed. The basis of salvation was now the Law. The Judaizers said that keeping the Law is superior to the Promise.

The Promise is Superior to the Law

Paul changes the "show" from "Law & Order" to "Law & Promise." He proves that the Promise is superior to the Law.

1. The promise is superior to the Law (3:15–18).
   A. The Promise is superior to the Law because it is irrevocable and unchangeable (3:15). Paul uses the analogy of a human covenant or contract to make his point. A contract binds two parties. The covenant Paul speaks of here is the one given by God in Genesis 15.
   i. God declares the Promise to Abraham (15:1–5).

ii. Abraham believes God and it is credited as righteousness to him (15:6).

iii. Abraham asks how he will know that all this will happen (15:8).

iv. God makes a covenant with Abraham (15:9–21). The ratification of a covenant took place when both parties walked between the two halves. In this case, only God walked between the two halves (15:12–21). This was not a covenant between Abraham and God. It was a covenant by God. It was unilateral. It was God's covenant. Paul's point is that it cannot be revoked (Heb 6:16–20).

B. The Promise is superior to the Law because it is centered in Christ (3:16). The heir of the Promise given to Abraham was not *seeds*, referring to the nation of Israel, but instead *seed*, which refers to Christ. See 2 Corinthians 1:20.

C. The Promise is superior to the Law because it preceded the Law (3:17). Four hundred-thirty years refers to the time that elapsed between God's last statement of the Abrahamic covenant to Jacob in Genesis 28:15 and the giving of the Law to Moses at Sinai.

The Abrahamic covenant did not establish the principle of salvation by faith; it only verified and typified it. From the time of Adam's fall, faith had been the only means of man getting right with God. The Law didn't void it. Salvation by faith has always been God's plan.

D. The Promise is superior to the Law because it is a gift (3:18).

E. The Promise is superior to the Law because it was delivered by God Himself (3:19*b*, 20). Paul contrasts the delivery of the Law with the Promise. The Law was decreed by God but delivered by angels to Moses on Mount Sinai (Acts 7:53; Heb. 2:2). The Promise, however, was delivered directly by God (1 Tim. 2:5).

2. The Law pointed to the Promise (3:19–25). The Jews and the Judaizers tried to make the Law do something it was never intended to do.

A. The purpose of the Law (3:19–20)

i. The purpose of the Law was to expose and restrain sin (3:19*a*).

ii. **The purpose of the Law was to reveal our need for a Savior, a Mediator (3:19*b*-20).**

B. **The place of the Law (3:21–25).** Is the Law opposed or contradictory to the Promise in God's scheme? Absolutely not, Paul answers. The Greek here (*ginomai mē*) is stronger than the translation "absolutely not." "May it never be" is a stronger translation. The Law has its place as Paul shows us.

i. **The Law reveals the hopeless condition of mankind (2:22).** Paul says that the Scripture imprisoned us under sin. The word *imprisoned* means to securely lock down. The Law locks us down in a prison of sin that we cannot escape. In other words, the Law shows us our utter hopelessness and destitution. The Law has to be preached because it is only when a person crashes into the demands of the Law that he sees the utter hopelessness of his state.

ii. **The Law restrains the sinfulness of people (3:23).**

iii. **The Law harshly disciplines people (3:24).** The Greek word for "put in charge" is *paidagōgos*. In Roman and Greek culture, a slave would often be employed to supervise (*paidagōgos*) young boys on behalf of the parents. They took them to school, made sure they did their assignments, kept them out of trouble, and made them obey. The dominant image of the *paidagōgos* was a harsh disciplinarian. The Law disciplined until the coming of Christ. It was demanding.

C. **The Law leads us to salvation in Christ (3:25).** We couldn't keep the demands of the Law, but Christ did. He fulfilled the demands of the Law so that we no longer have to be under the governance of the Law in our relationship with God. The Law was never given to save but to point us to Christ.

Conclusion

Paul F. M. Zahl provides a powerful picture of the Law and the believer in *Who Will Deliver Us?*

A duck hunter was with a friend in the wide-open land of southeastern Georgia. Far away on the horizon he noticed a cloud of smoke. Soon he could hear crackling as the wind shifted. He realized the terrible truth: a brushfire was advancing, so fast they couldn't outrun it.

Rifling through his pockets, he soon found what he was looking for—a book of matches. He lit a small fire around the two of them. Soon they were standing in a circle of blackened earth, waiting for the fire to come.

They didn't have to wait long. They covered their mouths with handkerchiefs and braced themselves. The fire came near—and swept over them. But they were completely unhurt, untouched. Fire would not pass where fire had already passed.

The law is like a brushfire. I cannot escape it. But if I stand in the burned-over place, not a hair of my head will be singed. Christ's death is the burned-over place. There I huddle, hardly believing yet relieved. The law is powerful, yet powerless: Christ's death has disarmed it.[1]

Endnotes

[1] Craig Brian Larson, *Illustrations for Preaching & Teaching from Leadership Journal*, (Christianity Today, Inc. and Baker, 1993), 127.

ADDITIONAL SERMONS AND LESSON IDEAS

SERIES: SINGLE AND SATISFIED

The God who sees Me

Genesis 16:1–13
By Dr. Karl Ray Minor

Introduction

I once saw a Christian short film about a man who received a special pair of sunglasses from a mysterious stranger. The sunglasses allowed the wearer to see a caption about every person at whom he was looking. The man wearing the glasses was then able to see beyond a person's smiling façade and see the issues and problems beneath.

If we had such a pair of sunglasses, when we looked at the young woman in Genesis 16, the captions would be overwhelming. "Single and pregnant." "Unemployed." "Runaway." "Abused." "Utterly alone." "No place to go and no place to return to." "A woman without hope or future."

Few people have found themselves in such a dire situation as we find Hagar in Genesis 16. Yet, in the midst of this dark night of the soul, Hagar discovers something about God that changes her situation and gives her hope and a more promising future: She discovers that God is a God who sees her.

"You are a God who sees me" (Gen. 16:13)

Perhaps you find yourself in a situation similar to Hagar's. You think you are completely alone. You wonder where God is in the midst of your hurt.

God is a God who Sees

The Bible is clear that God is a God who sees everyone and everything.

> "For He looks to the ends of the earth and sees everything under the heavens" (Job 28:24).

~ "For His eyes are upon the ways of a man, and He sees all his steps" (Job 34:21).

~ "The LORD looks from heaven; He sees all the sons of men. From the place of His dwelling He looks on all the inhabitants of the earth" (Ps. 33:13, 14).

But Hagar's discovery was not simply that God was a God who sees, but that God is a God who sees individuals.

God is a God who sees Me

Before murderer Joseph Jernigan was executed by lethal injection on August 5th, 1993, he bequeathed his still young and healthy body to science. What science did with the mortal remains of Joseph Jernigan is amazing. First anatomists froze him solid at minus 100 degrees Fahrenheit. Then they sliced him, like a loaf of bread, into one-millimeter thick sections—1,871 of them. After each slice, they made a fine-grained photo of his cross-section. Every millimeter of Joseph Jernigan can be seen at the Visible Human Project.[1]

As thoroughly as we can see Joseph Jernigan, God sees us far more intimately. He knows every problem and every failure. He knows our thoughts and hearts. He knows our yesterdays. He knows our tomorrows. There is not a part of our life that God does not see.

Because God sees, and because God is in control, whatever God has allowed to enter our life is a part of His purpose to bring about good in our lives (Rom. 8:28, 29).

Conclusion

There has never been a moment of your life when God has not seen you. Trust the One who knows you best.

Endnotes

[1] D. T. Wheeler, "Creating a Body of Knowledge," *The Chronicle of Higher Education*, February 2, 1996, A6–A7, A14.

Accomplishing God's Plan, Pt. 1

Nehemiah 2:11
By Dave Hirschman

Introduction

The Scriptures reveal the overall plan of God: to redeem fallen mankind through his son, Jesus Christ. But the Scriptures also provide evidence of God's other plans: to accomplish specific measures in the lives of individuals, groups, and nations. Within the context of God's plan for Nehemiah, a noticeable sequence may be seen. Using this sequence as a guide, we can begin to recognize God's ways and join Him in accomplishing His plan.

God's plan begins with a burden (Neh.1:1-4a).

The Lord brought information to Nehemiah to create a burden, so that God's plan could unfold to assist the people in Jerusalem, to rebuild the walls of Jerusalem, to reestablish his people in the land of Israel. The Lord brings information to his children and churches to create a burden for His plan to become reality: the plan to exhibit the love, mercy, and grace of God in our lives, to extend that love, mercy, and grace to others, to encourage others to experience the love, mercy, and grace of God personally!

God's plan takes shape with prayer (Neh. 1:4, 6, 11)

Things can be accomplished without prayer. Plans can be made, implemented, and completed without anyone ever consulting with God. God's plans, however, cannot be accomplished without prayer. Nehemiah had the burden of knowing that Jerusalem was in distress, but without prayer he did not have the bearing or directions for how to carry out God's plan. Prayer prepares, informs, and arranges the circumstances of God's plan.

Conclusion

People of God, let the burden of God's plan for you begin and the prayer take shape!

WEEK 19

Series: The Gospel Truth

Sons of God

Galatians 3:26–4:7
By Dr. Kent Spann

Introduction

Has someone ever dropped a bombshell on you? I am talking about news or an announcement that was unexpected or startling. In our passage, Paul drops a bombshell on the Judaizers. He had been building a case against the Judaizers who said that it is not enough to believe in Christ; you must also keep the Law.

In Galatians 3:26, Paul reaches the most important point in his presentation of salvation by faith or the gospel of grace. He says that we "are all sons of God through faith in Christ Jesus." Paul's statement was shocking because, in Jewish literature, the title "sons of God" was a title of highest honor. Paul was saying that, not only could a Jew be a son of God, but also Gentiles could be called "sons of God." That is what he meant by *all*.

What does it mean for us to be sons of God? It means that we are no longer children of wrath or children of the devil. It means that we have a right relationship with God.

How do we become sons of God?

1. **We are sons of God through faith in Christ (3:26–29).** We don't become sons of God by right, birth, or good works; we become sons of God by faith in Christ (John 1:12). When we believe, we are placed "in Christ." We are sons of God because of our union with Christ.

   What does it mean to say that we are sons of God?

   A. **We are members of God's family (3:27).** Paul uses two very powerful images to make it clear that we are members of God's family. We have been baptized into Christ, and we have been clothed with Christ. What does that mean for us?

    i. **We carry on the family "tradition," meaning that we should continue to do the things that Jesus did here on earth.**

    ii. **We are responsible for the reputation of the family name.**

    iii. **We can never escape the love of God.**

B. We are one with all sons of God (3:28). There is no distinction on the basis of race or nationality, economics or social standing, or gender. Christianity lived out is the only equalizer we need. Jesus is the one that unites and tears down the divisions among us. It is the cure for discrimination.

    i. **It means that we must learn to live with one another.**

    ii. **It means that we must learn to love one another.**

    iii. **It means that we must rid ourselves of our pride.**

    iv. **It means that we must work together.**

C. We are heirs with Christ (3:29). In Galatians 3:16, Paul said that the promise was to Abraham and his seed. He went on to identify who the seed was: Jesus Christ. Now he takes it to its logical conclusion. If Christ is the seed and we are a part of Christ, then we are also Abraham's seed and thus heirs with Christ.

2. **We are sons of God with all of the rights and privileges (4:1–7).**

A. We have been freed from slavery (4:1–5). Paul uses the analogy of the child and heir (4:1, 2). The promise of the inheritance lies in the future, but the child does not possess it yet. He goes on to say that a child is nothing more than a slave under the authority of trustees. What were we slaves to? As the NIV translates it, we were slaves to "the basic principles of the world." There is much debate about what Paul meant by this. I think it is simply the power of sin and Satan (John 8:34, 44).

God sent His Son in the fullness of time to redeem us from slavery and to make us sons (4:4, 5*a*). The Son of God became the Son of Man, so the sons of men can become the sons of God.

B. We received the Holy Spirit (4:6*a*).

C. We call God our Father (4:6*b*). The title "Abba, Father" is a title of endearment. It is the title of filial relationship. The privilege of calling him

Father means that we enjoy the blessings of calling him Father, which are many.

D. We are heirs (4:7). We are joint heirs with Jesus (Romans 8:17).

Conclusion

The great preacher Donald Grey Barnhouse tells a powerful story about a friend who was preaching in Latin America. At the close of the sermon in which he had set forth the necessity of the new birth as the only way in which a member of the human race could become a child of God, two men came to him to challenge his statement.

One of them said to the preacher, "You admit do you not, that we are all descended from Adam?" "Certainly," replied the preacher. "And you admit that Adam was created by God?" they continued. Again the preacher agreed. "Well, then," said the questioner with an air of triumph, "does that not prove that we are all the children of God?" The preacher pointed to one of the benches in the little chapel and said, "Who made that bench?" They looked at it and replied, "The carpenter." "Well, do you call that bench the son of the carpenter, or the child of the carpenter?" "Certainly not," they replied. "Why not?" insisted the preacher. "Because it does not have the life of the carpenter in it," one of them replied. Then with great directness, the preacher asked, "Do you have the life of God in you? I am not talking about physical life, mere animal existence. I am talking about the spiritual life of God."

The debaters had no answer.[1]

The question for you today is: "Are you a son of God?" Do you have the life of Christ in you?

Endnotes

[1] Donald Grey Barnhouse, *Romans: God's Heirs Romans 8:1-39*, (Grand Rapids: Eerdmans, reprinted 1999), 63.

ADDITIONAL SERMONS AND LESSON IDEAS

SERIES: SINGLE AND SATISFIED

Pure Faith: The Biblical Mandate to Care for Widows

Various Scriptures
By Dr. Karl Ray Minor

Introduction

Our culture is obsessed with youth. The oldest among us are pushed into the shadows and are rarely recognized as important or vital.

The Church should not make the same mistake. The Scripture tells us that God has a unique concern for those who are helpless and alone: the widow. If our Heavenly Father has a unique concern for the widow, so should we.

The Bible tells us:

God has a Unique Concern for the Widow.

1. **God promises to respond if a widow cries out to Him (Ex. 22:22–24);**
2. **He will punish those who harm her (Ps. 68:5).** Because she has no one to stand for her, God Himself stands as the Judge and the Defender of the widow.

God's People are Called to Have a Unique Concern for the Widow

1. In the Old Testament:
   A. The widows were given special protection in lending (Deut. 24:17)
   B. God gave specific provision for meeting the needs of the widow through food stored in each community as Israel's third-year tithes. (Deut. 24:19-21; 26:12, 13).
3. In the New Testament:

A. The first major Church conflict arose of the care of the widows (Acts 6:1).

B. Jesus condemns the Pharisees as hypocrites because they "devour the widow's houses" (Luke 20:47).

C. Timothy is told to honor the widow (1 Tim. 5:3).

D. James calls his readers to visit the widow in their distress (James 1:27).

Practical Ways that We can Demonstrate a Unique Concern for the Widow

1. **Educate our congregation on the eventuality of death.** Ministry to widows begins before they become widows by helping couples to prepare together for the decisions that must be faced in the eventuality of death.

2. **Lead congregational prayer.** Prayer brings the power and presence of God into one's life. It is a way to keep the names and needs of the widows before the congregation.

3. **Involve widows in ministry to other widows.** The best person to minister to a widow is another widow. A widow can identify and comfort another widow in a way that no other can. This fulfills God's admonition in 2 Corinthians 1:3–4, "Blessed be the God and Father of our Lord Jesus Christ, the Father of mercies and God of all comfort, who comforts us in all our affliction so that we will be able to comfort those who are in any affliction with the comfort with which we ourselves are comforted by God."

4. **Develop a widow's ministry designed to meet the physical and emotional needs of the widow.** James 1:27 tells us "to visit the widows in their distress." James speaks here of meeting needs in much the same way that a shepherd would provide for his flock. A simple social call does not fulfill James' admonition.

Conclusion

The Church has a biblical mandate to minister to the widow. The Church can become the presence and peace of God to a group for which God has a unique concern.

Accomplishing God's Plan, Pt. 2

Nehemiah 2:11
By Dave Hirschman

Introduction

We see three things in the first two chapters of Nehemiah:

1. God's plan begins with a burden (Neh. 1:1–4*a*).
2. God's plan takes shape with prayer (Neh. 1:4, 6, 11)
3. God's plan generates action (Neh. 2).

Things begin to happen when God's people have prayed (Neh. 2:5, 7, 8; Acts 4:31). Nehemiah was granted a promotion, leave of absence, and pay for the way. Impossible things are accomplished when we pray.

God's Plan Produces Strength (Neh. 6:3, 9)

Not everyone gets overjoyed at seeing plans go forward and being accomplished. There will always be opposition. God's plan, prepared with prayer, produces strength sufficient to meet and overcome opposition.

God's Plan results in Accomplishment (Neh. 6:15, 16)

When we allow ourselves to be burdened, we must pray for direction. We must act in faith when we pray for direction and details. When we act in faith, we will see the plan accomplished, right here!

Conclusion

God is looking for people through whom He can work to accomplish His plans, ultimately leading to salvation and redemption. When we are familiar with His ways, we can begin to discern His movements, and recognize what He is calling us to do. As we see His ways unfold, we can be confident that we are joining Him to accomplish his plan.

WEEK 20

A Personal Plea

Galatians 4:8–20
By Dr. Kent Spann

Introduction

Paul, in the book of Galatians, makes an appeal in three different ways to the Galatians not to be led astray by the Judaizers.

- Doctrinal Appeal (1:6–4:7)
- Allegorical Appeal (4:21–31)
- Personal Appeal (4:8–20)

In 4:8–20, Paul changes the whole tenor of his approach and makes a personal appeal. Luther said of these verses, "These words breathe Paul's own tears."

A Journey Down Memory Lane (4:8–11)

Paul's appeal begins with a journey down memory lane, reminding the Galatians of their conversion experience. He reminds them that, in their life before Christ (4:8), they did not know God. They were slaves to gods that were not gods. All of that changed when Paul came to Galatia during his first missionary journey and preached the gospel of salvation by grace through faith (4:9). Paul reminds the Galatians that this is when they came to know God and God came to know them. The kind of knowing that Paul speaks of here is not an intellectual knowing; it is a personal intimate knowing. They personally knew God, and God personally knew them.

That leads to Paul's inquiry of why the Galatians were backsliding doctrinally (4:9*b*–10). They had turned away from God and His truth and back to their old ways. Like the old hymn "Come Thou Fount of Every Blessing," we are

Prone to wander—Lord, I feel it—

Prone to leave the God I love.

Paul laments and is dismayed (4:11). Paul wondered if all that he went through—the stonings, the beatings, the hardships, the long hours of teaching, etc.—had been a waste of his effort. Why would Paul say that, since they made a "supposed confession of faith in Christ?" Paul's goal was not merely to get the Galatians into the kingdom; his goal was for the King to be formed in them (4:19).

Paul's Personal Appeal (4:12–20)

Paul's personal appeal is based on his ministry among the Galatians. We can learn a lot about ministry from Paul's personal appeal.

1. **The manner of his ministry (4:12–16)**

   A. **We proclaim the gospel loudest by living a life that others want to emulate (v. 12a).** Paul modeled the gospel for them and invited them to model him (v. 12a). What do people see when they look at us? What are we inviting them to become? Do they see bitterness, anger, and unforgiveness, or forgiveness, love, and kindness? Paul was not saying that he was a perfect role model, because none of us are. He was, however, a model of grace.

   B. **We proclaim the gospel loudest by identifying with those we are trying to reach with the gospel (v. 12b "became like you").** Paul didn't speak down to or at the Galatians. He spoke as one of them. Paul practiced an incarnational gospel (1 Cor. 9:19–23). In other words, he changed his methods based on who he was trying to reach. We must do the same in ministry.

   C. **We proclaim the gospel loudest by seizing divine opportunities (4:13).** We can't pinpoint with accuracy the nature of the illness. It may have been malaria, epilepsy, or ophthalmia. Whatever it was, it led Paul to stop in the region of Galatia. While there, he preached the gospel.

   The opportunity to preach the gospel to the Galatians wasn't planned. It occurred because Paul was sick and had to stay in Galatia. Paul saw it as divine appointment or opportunity to preach the gospel.

D. We proclaim the gospel loudest by relying on God's power and the power of the gospel (4:14–15). Paul didn't have it all together when he preached to the Galatians. He was a very sick man. Dr. Timothy George sums it well:

What prompted the Galatians to respond so well to this fat little bald man with a crooked nose, this tent-making preacher at whom most people would be tempted to spit? Nothing in the character of the Galatians makes us think they were naturally disposed to receive with gracious hospitality the sort of figure Paul portrayed himself to have been. No, it was the simple preaching of the cross in the power of the Holy Spirit that softened the hearts of the Galatians and brought them to a saving knowledge of the Christ Paul proclaimed.[1]

God does his greatest work through weak and inadequate vessels (1 Cor. 2:26–31). People are not impressed by our power, but they are impressed by God's power. David Ring is an evangelist; he also has cerebral palsy. He would challenge people to quit making excuses for not sharing Christ. He would say, "I have Cerebral Palsy, what's your problem!"

D. We proclaim the gospel loudest by speaking the truth with unwavering conviction (4:16). Paul loved them enough to speak the truth even if it hurt or offended them. He didn't water down the truth to be popular; he didn't preach messages that tickled everyone's ears. He spoke the truth with conviction.

2. **The motivation of his ministry (4:17–20).** Paul contrasts the motives of the Judaizers with his own, and then challenges the Galatians to choose the loftier motivation.

A. The motives of the Judaizers (4:17–18). He acknowledges that the Judaizers were zealous. It is great to be zealous, but it is dangerous to be zealous for the wrong thing. The Judaizers were trying to draw the Galatians away from Paul and the gospel of grace. There are still all sorts of groups and people whose motive is to draw you away from God's people and the gospel. It can be a cult, a boyfriend or girlfriend, or even a lifestyle that attempts to draw you from grace.

B. The motive of Paul (4:19–20). Paul's motive was simple: that Christ be formed in the Galatians' lives. The word *form* means to take shape. He longed for them to take the shape of Christ. Paul was passionate about this. Over and over again he shares this passion (Rom. 8:29; 1 Cor. 15:49; 2 Cor. 3:18; Phil 1:9–11; Col. 1:9–13; 1 Thess. 5:23; 2 Peter 1:4; 1 John 3:2).

Conclusion

Paul makes a powerful personal appeal to the Galatians and to us not to abandon the Gospel of Grace for the bondage of legalism.

Endnotes

[1] Timothy George, *Galatians, The New American Commentary, vol. 30* (Nashville: Broadman & Holman Publishers, 1994), 324–25.

ADDITIONAL SERMONS AND LESSON IDEAS

Rise Up, O Lord!

Psalm 17:1–15
Dr. Mark D. Roberts

Introduction

I have a hard time asking people for things. I have been "request-challenged" all of my life. However, I do know people who aren't like me. A college friend, for example, could ask anyone for anything. Once he asked a movie theatre manager if he could have one of the promotional posters for a popular film. I thought my friend was crazy until he got the poster! If he is as bold when talking with God as he is when talking with people, then he'd sound like David in Psalm 17.

David's Bold Prayer in Psalm 17

1. **David makes seventeen requests in only fifteen verses.**
2. **David is bold in his requests, especially in verse 13:** "Rise up, O Lord, confront them, overthrow them!" David speaks as if he is God's alarm clock. Seen also in Psalm 35:23: "Wake up! Bestir yourself for my defense." Do you ever pray with this kind of audacity?
3. **Psalm 17 exemplifies the most basic kind of prayer, the prayer of asking.** Some people say we ought not to pray this way. But it is taught here and throughout Scripture. In the prayer of asking, we come as needy children before our Heavenly Father.

Reasons for David's Boldness in Prayer

1. **David is desperate.** He is surrounded by enemies who are attacking him with their words (Ps. 17:9–12). Nothing encourages bold prayer like desperation.

2. **David has confidence in the Lord, knowing that he can speak freely, with the expectation of God's help.** David identifies God as the "savior of those who seek refuge" (Ps. 17:7). Therefore, David has confidence to pray, "Guard me as the apple of the eye; hide me in the shadow of your wings" (17:7–8). Here, David applies to himself God's devotion to Israel. In Deuteronomy 32:10–11, Moses celebrates the fact that God "guarded [Jacob] as the apple of his eye" and cared for Israel as an eagle "hovers over its young." David prays with bold assurance because he knows he is special to God, just as Israel is.

The Deeper Purpose of Bold Prayers of Asking

1. **Why do we ask in prayer?** This might seem like a silly question. We ask God boldly because we want God's help. We see this in Psalm 17.
2. **But this psalm points to a deeper reason for prayers of supplication.** Notice that David begins by crying out to God for help. Yet, by the end of Psalm 17, he says, "As for me, I shall behold your face in righteousness; when I awake I shall be satisfied, beholding your likeness" (Ps. 17:15). As David prays, he discovers that his deepest desire is not what God can do for him, but for God himself. He yearns for God's presence, that which alone will satisfy his soul.

Conclusion

Psalm 17 invites us to lay our requests before God with bold freedom. The God who saves and loves us will answer when we pray. But this psalm also points to the deeper purpose of open-hearted supplication. When we lay ourselves before the Lord, we come to know him more deeply and intimately.

(Scripture quotations from nrsv.)

Why Am I Here: To Know God

Luke 10:21–24; John 14:19–23
By Dr. Dave Hirschman

Introduction

We live in a world of conflicting values that produce widespread confusion as to what the real purpose of life is. At various points in life, people face significant events that cause them to question their purpose and reason for living, asking themselves, "Why am I here?" Ask yourself that very question. Expand on it, and ask yourself, "Is there some purpose in my being alive? What about in being a Christian?" Luke 10:22 reveals one overriding answer.

We are Here to Know God (Luke 10:22).

Say to yourself:

1. **I can know God, because He can be known (John 14:23)!** To "know God" in this context means not hypothetically but personally; not generally but specifically; beyond general terms, but in personal specifics ("I remember when God _____); not mystically but in reality— at the living level of life—through daily living, decisions, and difficulties.
2. **I should know God, because He can transform my life (John 14:21)!**
3. **I must know God, because only He can guarantee the future (John 14:19)!**
   There are no guarantees about the future, except with God!

Conclusion

There is more to life than meets the eye. God desires to bring meaning and purpose to your life. Finding and having a meaning and purpose begins with knowing God!

WEEK 21

SERIES: THE GOSPEL TRUTH

Roots

Galatians 4:21–5:1
By Dr. Kent Spann

Introduction

In 1976, Alex Haley's book *Roots: The Saga of an American Family* came out. He earned a Pulitzer Prize for the work, which is an account of his family history. He wanted to know where he came from.

Our roots are important. They tell a lot about us. They also give insight into who we should be. Paul was writing to a congregation in Galatia that had lost touch with their roots; the roots of grace. The Galatians had moved from a people of grace to a people of the Law.

Paul was making three appeals to the Galatians:

- doctrinal (1:6–4:7)
- personal (4:8–20)
- metaphorical (4:21–5:1)

Paul makes it clear in verse 24 that he is using a metaphorical interpretation. The NIV translates it, "These things may be taken figuratively." The ESV translates it more literally: "Now this may be interpreted allegorically." An metaphor is a tool whereby a writer conveys hidden, mysterious truths by the use of words which also have a literal meaning.

Paul is using a metaphor to teach a spiritual truth from a historical event. He sets it up with a question in 4:21. Paul points out the hypocrisy of the Judaizers, who claimed to be under the Law and yet didn't even listen to it or understand it.

He uses the term *Law* twice in the passage. In the first use, he refers to the Law given at Mount Sinai. In the second use of the word, he is referring to the Old Testament Scriptures.

The Historical Event (4:22–23)

Paul is going to use the story of Abraham's two sons to show the difference between law and grace. The account of Sarah and Hagar, as well as that of Isaac and Ishmael, is found in Genesis 15–21.

Historical Account Genesis 15; 16; 21	
Hagar	Sarah
Slave	Free
Concubine	Legitimate wife
Slave Son, Ishmael	Free Son, Isaac
Result of Sarah's word (Gen. 16:2)	Result of God's word (Gen. 15:4)
Arabs	Israelites

The Figurative Meaning (4:24–27)

Paul takes the story of a dysfunctional but historical family and shows how it applies to the conflict between works and grace.

Metaphorical Account Galatians 4:24–27	
Hagar Ishmael	Sarah Isaac
Covenant of Law given at Mount Sinai (4:24, 25)	Covenant of Promise given to Abraham (4:26–27)
Slavery	Freedom/Grace
Result of self-effort, flesh (4:23)	Result of promise (4:23, 28)
Mount Sinai (4:24, 25)	Mount Zion (4:26)
Earthly Jerusalem (4:25) Citizens of earth	Heavenly Jerusalem (4:26) Citizens of heaven
Persecutes/Condemns (4:29)	Deliverance/Joy (4:27)

Paul makes a powerful argument for grace through this story.

1. **Grace came before the Law.** Sarah was Abraham's wife before he had relations with Hagar. In the same way, grace came before Law. Grace has always been God's way of dealing with us (2 Tim. 1:9–10).

2. **Grace gives life, but the Law brings death.** Hagar was not meant to bear a son to Abraham. She bore a son because Abraham and Sarah were impatient with God. In the same way, the Law was never given with the intention to save. The Law cannot save, because the Law cannot give life (3:21). In fact, the Law kills. Only grace gives life (2 Cor. 3:6–7).

3. **The Law was given to serve grace.** Hagar was never to be a wife to Abraham; she was to be a servant to Sarah. The Law was given to serve grace. It makes us aware of our sinfulness and hopelessness as we try to keep it but can't. It condemns us. It brings us to the point where we realize that, apart from God's grace, we have no hope.

4. **Grace results in freedom; the Law results in slavery.** Hagar was a slave, so her son was a slave. Sarah, on the other hand, was a free woman, and so her child was a free son. The children of grace are truly free.

5. **The covenant of works has ceased to be a covenant, while the covenant of grace is still in effect.** Hagar with her son Ishmael was cast out with God's approval (Gen. 21:12), never to return. Only Sarah remained. The covenant of Law or works was done away with after Christ. The Galatians were foolish to think that they were saved by faith plus works. They were inviting Hagar to come back and reside once again.

6. **Salvation by grace is the work of the Spirit; salvation by Law is the work of the flesh.** The birth of Ishmael and Isaac were entirely different, according to verse 23. Ishmael was conceived as a result of works; Isaac was the result of promise. Salvation by the Law is a work of the flesh. Salvation by grace, on the other hand, is God working in our lives and producing a new birth, a supernatural birth (John 3:3).

The Application of Grace (4:28–31)

1. **We who have trusted Christ are the children of promise (4:28).** We were supernaturally conceived and miraculously born. We are the offspring of God's promise to Abraham, fulfilled in Christ. We don't have to work or perform to be a child of God; we are sons of God.

   Imagine your son coming to you and saying, "I want to be your son; therefore, I am going to work hard to become your son. I am going to perform my best so that you will love me." How would you respond? At first, you would be broken-hearted that your son felt that way, but you would also be insulted as he continued to strive to become your son, even after you confirmed that he is your son. Quit striving to be a son and enjoy being a son!

2. **We will be persecuted and condemned by legalists (4:29).**

3. **We are the true heirs (4:30).**

4. **We should live in our freedom (4:31–5:1).**

5. **We are free from the bondage of the Law (4:30).** Sadly, many still live as though they are under the Law. They are like the man who moved to the United States from another country whose laws prohibited a person to walk on the sidewalks after 6 p.m. After arriving in the United States, he decided to see the sights and so went for a long walk. Suddenly, he realized that it was getting close to 6 p.m. and he was far from where he was staying. In desperation, he stopped a stranger who was getting into an automobile and in halting English said, "Please, sir, help me! It is almost six and I am too far from my hotel to walk back before I will be arrested. Can you give me a ride?"

   The stranger at first was confused but then realized that the man was new to the United States and so said to him, "Sir, let me assure you that, in the United States, we do not arrest people for being out after six."[1]

   The man was living under the law of his former life. As children of grace, we no longer have to live under the Law.

6. **We are free to live God's way (5:1).** Paul is going to show us how to live the life of a free person in chapters 5 and 6. Grace doesn't free us to sin; grace frees us to live the life that God intends.

An Indian pastor in Oklahoma was going to a pastors' conference. He went to the train station and caught a train to a mansion where the conference was being held. The theme of the conference was "Law and Grace." The Indian pastor listened intently to the lengthy theological discussions and arguments presented by each seminar leader. Finally, in a group-discussion period, he said, "It seems to me that the train station we all came in at demonstrates Law, and this house we are meeting in, grace. At the station was a sign 'Do not spit,' yet the men there did. Here there is no sign, yet no one spits."[2]

Grace frees us to live God's way.

Conclusion

We do not need to work to become sons of God; we become sons of God the moment we accept God's free gift of salvation through Jesus Christ. There is no work on our part—indeed, there is nothing we can do to earn or deserve our adoption as sons. So quit working to be God's child, and begin living like one!

Endnotes

[1] M. P. Green, *Illustrations for Biblical Preaching: Over 1500 Sermon Illustrations Arranged by Topic and Indexed Exhaustively* (Grand Rapids: Baker, 1989), Logos Electronic Bible Software.

[2] M. P. Green, *Illustrations for Biblical Preaching: Over 1500 Sermon Illustrations Arranged by Topic and Indexed Exhaustively* (Grand Rapids: Baker, 1989), Logos Electronic Bible Software.

ADDITIONAL SERMONS AND LESSON IDEAS

The Curious Faith of Peter

Matthew 14:22–33
Dr. Mark D. Roberts

Introduction

These are hard times. People are struggling financially. Families feel stressed by too much to do. Marriages are vulnerable to division and divorce. Government services are being cut, leaving many people feeling desperate. Churches are downsizing. What should we do when we seem to be sinking into a ravenous sea?

Peter: The Paragon of Great Faith

1. **Set up:** After a miraculous feeding of 5,000, Jesus sent his disciples ahead in a boat while He remained behind to pray. A storm began to batter the boat. In early morning, Jesus approached the boat, walking on the sea. The disciples feared that He was a ghost. Jesus reassured them, saying, "Take heart, it is I; do not be afraid" (Matt. 14:27).
2. **Peter's Response:** "Lord, if it is you, command me to come to you on the water" (Matt 14:28). Jesus obliged, and Peter started walking on the water.
3. **Peter exemplifies bold, active, risky faith.** True faith in Jesus calls us out of our "boats," our comfort zones, where we have no choice but to trust Jesus.
4. **We are drawn to, yet fearful of the adventure of bold faith.**

Peter: The Paragon of Little Faith

As Peter was walking on the stormy sea, his common sense got the better of him. As his faith weakened, he sank into the water. In desperate fear he cried, "Lord, save me!" (Matt. 14:30).

I can relate to such debilitating fear. When I was learning how to kayak in the ocean, I accidentally tipped over my kayak and was trapped underwater.

Fear of drowning obliterated my good sense for several moments before I thought clearly enough to set myself free.

Peter, the paragon of great faith, becomes the paragon of little faith. Can you relate? Have there been times in your life when you have trusted God in a big way, only to panic when little things didn't work out quite as you had expected?

What Should We Do When We Are Sinking?

1. **Our first impulse is to rescue ourselves, which usually makes matters worse.**
2. **Peter shows us where to begin.** We cry out, "Lord, save me!" We realize how much we need God's help and turn to Him in prayer.

Jesus Saves

1. **Jesus reached out to Peter, saying, "You of little faith, why did you doubt?"** (Matt. 14:31).
2. **Notice that Jesus did not require Peter to have great faith in order to save him.** Little faith was plenty. What an encouragement this is for us when we struggle with doubt and fear!

Conclusion

How might Peter have avoided sinking into the water in the first place? Matthew says he was doing fine until "he noticed the strong wind" and "became frightened" (Matt. 14:30). Peter took his eyes off of Jesus and focused on the challenges and dangers.

How can we keep our eyes on Jesus? Through prayer. Through claiming the promises of Scripture. Through focusing on His mission. Through resting on His love and grace, knowing that nothing in all creation can separate us from His love (see Rom. 8:38–39).

An Appointment with Purpose

John 1:14; Luke 22:47–54; John 18:33–37
By Dave Hirschman

Introduction

At this point in Scripture, the most significant time in human history is ending with Christ's imminent death. Thirty-three years have passed since an innkeeper told a young couple that there was no room for them. Roughly three years have passed since a man named John said, "Behold the Lamb of God." Now it is going to end. But, why?

Finding Purpose?

1. **God clothed Himself in flesh to live among us** (John 1:14). He lived among us, not to discover anything or investigate, but to reveal Himself to us (Luke 10:22, John 14:9). He revealed Himself:
   A. **Through His knowledge** (Nathanael: John 1:48; The Samaritan Woman: John 4:17).
   B. **Through His power: miracles, healings.**
   C. **Through His wisdom: parables, teachings, wisdom**
   D. **Through His love**
2. **God surrendered Himself in rejection to pursue us** (Luke 22:47–54a).
3. **God sacrificed Himself in death to redeem us** (John 18:33–37, "for this cause I am come"). He came to redeem us from sin, separation, and death; to redeem us to Himself as His own children; and to redeem us to Himself for eternity.

Conclusion

Jesus' earthly ministry was an appointment with purpose. He came to accomplish what no one else could, and what He accomplished changed history and many lives. Will you let him change your life, too?

WEEK 22

SERIES: THE GOSPEL TRUTH

Free at Last

Galatians 5:1–12
By Dr. Kent Spann

Introduction

Begin the sermon with a video or simply read the final section of Dr. Martin Luther King Jr.'s speech "I Have a Dream," delivered on the steps of the Lincoln Memorial August 28, 1963.

And if America is to be a great nation this must become true. So let freedom ring from the prodigious hilltops of New Hampshire. Let freedom ring from the mighty mountains of New York. Let freedom ring from the heightening Alleghenies of Pennsylvania!

Let freedom ring from the snowcapped Rockies of Colorado!

Let freedom ring from the curvaceous slopes of California!

But not only that; let freedom ring from Stone Mountain of Georgia!

Let freedom ring from Lookout Mountain of Tennessee!

Let freedom ring from every hill and molehill of Mississippi. From every mountainside, let freedom ring.

And when this happens, when we allow freedom to ring, when we let it ring from every village and every hamlet, from every state and every city, we will be able to speed up that day when all of God's children, black men and white men, Jews and Gentiles, Protestants and Catholics, will be able to join hands and sing in the words of the old Negro spiritual, "Free at last! free at last! thank God Almighty, we are free at last!"

Free At Last (5:1)

But when will we really be "free at last?" Paul tell us in 5:1 that we are "free at last" in Christ, but this is not the social and political freedom which Dr. King spoke of. It is the freedom of the soul liberated from spiritual bondage to sin (John 8:34), tyranny (John 8:44), and the Law (Gal. 3:10).

So how can we be freed from this bondage? Christ alone sets us free from sin, Satan, and the condemnation of the Law.

Stand Firm (5:2–12)

Once we have entered into this freedom, Paul says that we must stand firm in our freedom (5:2).

1. **We must stand firm against false teaching, which steals our freedom (5:2–6).** What happens when we put ourselves back under the Law or the system of works?

   A. **Christ is of no advantage to us (5:2).** On New Year's Day 1863, the Emancipation Proclamation was read declaring that all slaves were freed. The headlines of the newspapers read, "Slavery Legally Abolished." Many of the recently freed slaves in the south continued to serve their former owners.

   What value is Christ to you if you are still going to live a life of bondage to sin and the Law? Why have Christ at all if He is not your all?

   B. **We are obligated to keep the whole Law (5:3).** If we fail to keep one thing in the law, we are guilty of it all (James 2:10).

   C. **We fall from grace (5:4).** Is Paul saying that we can lose our salvation? Absolutely not. That would be a clear contradiction the rest of Scripture, which teaches the security of the believer (John 10:28–30; Rom. 8:1–17, 28–39; Eph. 1:13, 14; Phil. 1:6). So what is Paul saying here? It depends on which group you are in.

   i. **Unbelievers: The Judaizers heard the gospel of grace but rejected it.** They chose to believe that it is faith-plus, which is not the gospel. They never really came to a saving faith. They were exposed to the message of grace but fell away from it.

ii. **Believers:** What about the Galatians, whom Paul makes clear are believers? He is saying that, if they put themselves under the Law, they fall out of the sphere of grace. They don't lose their salvation, but they lose the blessing of it. They no longer operate in the realm of grace.

D. **We forfeit the victorious Christian life (5:5).** Living the victorious life is living by faith through the Spirit in hope (confident assurance) of righteousness (sanctification and glorification).

E. **We accomplish nothing (5:6a).** All those works we do to be right with God are for nothing! All that giving to the church is for naught. All those Sundays spent sitting and listening to a preacher and Sunday School teacher is for naught. All of those kind and charitable acts are for naught. All of those long hours at the church working on the building are for naught. All of those Sundays in the nursery are for naught. It doesn't gain you one ounce of ground with God. Only what Christ has done matters.

F. **We spoil the fruit of grace, which is love (5:6b).** Legalism leads to condemnation, negativity, criticism, judgementalism, etc. Grace leads to love. Show me a church where the people are negative, critical, and judgmental of one another or of the pastor, and I will show you a church living under legalism.

2. **We must stand firm against false teachers who steal our freedom (5:7–12).** Paul exposes the character of false teachers.

A. **They make believers stumble (5:7a, "you were running a good race").**

B. **They hinder the truth by distorting it and causing people to disobey (5:7b).**

C. **They are not from God (5:8).**

D. **They infect others (5:9).**

E. **They face God's judgment (5:10).**

F. **They persecute true teachers and believers (5:11).**

G. **They are hypocrites (5:12).**

One of the thriving mystery religions of Asia Minor was the worship of Cybele. Each year at the spring festival, the worshipers of Cybele would fast, pray, and mourn the death of Attis. Then the priests would castrate themselves, drink their own blood, and carry an image of the young god Attis to his grave in solemn procession. Paul's point is that, if they think circumcision is going to save them, then go all the way and castrate themselves. That would be even more powerful.

Paul's description of false teachers is just as accurate today as it was when he penned these words to the Galatians.

Conclusion

Shortly after the Emancipation Proclamation was passed by Congress early in 1863, Abraham Lincoln warned in a speech:

> We are like the whalers who have been on a long chase. We have at last got the harpoon into the monster, but we must now look how we steer, or with one flop of his tail he will send us all into eternity.[1]

You are free at last; don't be enslaved again by false teaching and teachers!

Endnotes

[1] *http://opinionator.blogs.nytimes.com/2010/12/06/misgivings/* (Accessed March 22, 2011)

ADDITIONAL SERMONS AND LESSON IDEAS

The Great Pastor

Hebrews 13:20–21
Dr. Mark D. Roberts

Introduction

When I was growing up, I had a great pastor. He was a not only a great pastor, but he was also a renowned preacher, a man of deep compassion, and someone who was committed to the biblical vision of the pastor as an equipper of God's people for ministry (Eph 4:11–13). Even though my pastor was great, he was not *the* Great Pastor. That title belongs to another.

Jesus is *the* Great Pastor

Hebrews 13:20 refers to Jesus as "the great shepherd of the sheep." The Greek word translated as "shepherd" is *poimen*. This same word is translated in Ephesians 4:11 in reference to "pastors and teachers" who equip God's people for ministry.

As our Great Pastor, Jesus guides, nourishes, cares for, equips, and protects us. He exercises His pastoral activity in our lives in a variety of ways, including through human beings who serve in the role of pastor. Yet, we must be careful not to expect our human pastors to do the job of the one and only Great Pastor.

God is at Work in Us, Equipping Us to Do His Will

The main clause of Hebrews 13:20–21 reads this way: "Now may the God of peace. . . make you complete in everything good so that you may do his will." The verb translated as "make you complete" is *katartizo*. This same verb appears in Ephesians 4:11–12, where church leaders, including pastor-teachers, are "to equip [*katartizo*] the saints for the work of ministry."

God is at work in us, equipping us with all we need to do His will. God does this through the Spirit and through human agents, including human pastors who teach, train, equip, and encourage all of God's people to be ministers of Jesus Christ in the church and in the world.

It's easy for Christians to forget that they are ministers and that God himself is equipping them for their ministry. They can expect their pastors to do the ministry for them, but the true pastor cooperates with God in the work of equipping people for service.

To God be the Glory!

Hebrews 13:20–21 concludes with a doxology (from the Greek *doxa*, meaning "glory") of God: "through Jesus Christ, to whom be the glory forever and ever. Amen."

What is the point of life? To what end is Jesus Christ our great pastor? Why is God equipping us as His ministers? The point of life is to seek God's glory. In seeking God's glory, we will certainly accomplish many good things, but our chief purpose in life is "to glorify God and to enjoy him forever" (*Westminster Shorter Catechism*, Question 1).

Conclusion

The more we turn away from our own profit and seek God's glory, the more we will live life to the fullest. The more we strive for our churches to glorify God, the more those churches will find new vitality, guided by the Great Pastor. God's people will be equipped by God in every way to do His will, "working among us that which is pleasing in his sight, through Jesus Christ, to whom be the glory forever and ever. Amen" (Heb 13:21).

Leaving a Lasting Impression, Pt. 1

Luke 15:11–20
By Dave Hirschman

Introduction

Have you ever noticed that the Bible is a book about the wonderful love of a father? It is the compiled account of God's actions toward the world, all rooted in His love. The ultimate expression of His love is seen in the giving of His son as the sacrifice to redeem your soul. I hope that you know God as your heavenly Father, and that you have experienced His wonderful love through Jesus Christ!

Luke 15 is the account of another father's love. You know this story by a different name: "The Prodigal Son." We usually focus on the son, and how he wasted his inheritance and ruined his life. But now we're going to view it from a different direction. It is important to see what the son knew about his father, and the lasting impression that shaped his decision to return home. The father had left a lasting impression upon his son; so much so, that the son knew exactly what to do.

A Principled Father

1. **The prodigal son knew he had a father who lived by principles (15:15–17).**
   A. **Principles are what you value.** Values are what you live by. They shape your actions. This account shows us the father's values. He treated his employees well—with respect, value, and decency. He cared for them even though they were employees.
   B. **Principles are what define you.** They become what you are known for. The son had watched his father's dealings. The prodigal son knew that his father was a man with principles!
2. **The prodigal son knew he had a father who could be trusted (15:18a).** The son was in trouble—trouble of his own making. He needed help, but he knew he didn't deserve it. However, he had confidence and knew who to go to: his father.

A. He knew his father's nature. His nature was fashioned by the principles by which he lived.

B. He knew his father's response. He knew he would be received and not rejected.

C. He knew his father's judgment.

Conclusion

He knew his father was fair and decent. The prodigal son knew he could trust his father.

WEEK 23

SERIES: THE GOSPEL TRUTH

Now What Do We Do?

Galatians 5:13–15
By Dr. Kent Spann

Introduction

The Road Runner and Wile E. Coyote have a long history together. The popular cartoon was an endless chase of the Road Runner by Wile E. Coyote. Finally, after countless episodes, Wile E. Coyote finally caught the Road Runner. When he did, he had the strangest look on his face, and then he held up a sign: "Okay, wise guys—you always wanted me to catch him, now what do I do?" He'd spent his life trying to catch the Road Runner and now he had him but didn't know what to do with him.

Have you ever felt like Wile E. Coyote? You spend your whole life pursuing something. Finally, the day comes and you accomplish it. There is this feeling of, "Now what?"

That is what the Galatians and most believers feel right after their conversion. Paul tells us in Galatians 5:1 that we are free. We are free from the performance treadmill of the Law, the fear of rejection by God, the prospect of Hell, bondage to sin and Satan, etc. We are free at last! Now what?

Living the Free Life

Freedom is a funny thing. Everyone wants it, but once they get it they don't know what to do with it. Sadly, many end up abusing it. Freedom for many people means the freedom to do whatever one desires. A visitor to America in the nineteenth century gave a speech to the American public and said, "America, I am impressed with all of your wealth and all of your ingenuity, but I have a question. What are you going to do with all these things?"

What does it mean to live free in Christ? Paul answers that question for us in verses 13–15.

1. **We are free to say "no" to the flesh (5:13a).** Paul begins with a negative. Paul introduces us to a very important phrase in verse 13: "the flesh." The word *flesh* translates the Greek word *sarx*. The NIV translates it as "sinful nature," but the literal translation is "flesh." *Sarx* is used primarily in three ways in the New Testament.

— It is used to refer to the physical flesh or the body (Gal. 2:20; Phil. 1:22).

— It is used to describe human effort (Gal. 3:3).

— It is used to describe the sinful inclination of fallen mankind, the old self, whose supreme desire is to do its own will and to satisfy its sinful appetites. It is the faculties of the body dominated and perverted by sin.

Paul says do not indulge or give opportunity to the flesh. In war, the Greek word translated *indulge* was used to denote the base of operation for a military campaign. In any military campaign, an army has a base of operations where supplies are kept and strategy is developed. Paul's point is that we are not to allow our freedom in Christ to become a base of operations for the flesh. Freedom is not a license to sin or indulge the flesh.

Grace is not the believer being free to sin, although you are free to sin. Grace is the believer being free to sin but choosing to obey God and turn away from sin through the power of the Holy Spirit. If the grace you claim does not give you the desire and will to obey, then, my friend, you know nothing of God's grace (Rom 6:1–4;15–18)! "For you are free, yet you are God's slaves, so don't use your freedom as an excuse to do evil" (1 Peter 2:16 NLT).

How do we apply what Paul tells us?

A. **We recognize that the flesh is at war with God (5:17).**

B. **We understand the nature of the flesh.** In other words, we know where the flesh is prone to attacks us.

C. **We call on God for His strength and power to resist the flesh.**

D. **We say "no" to fleshly desires.**

2. **We are free to love others (5:13b–15).** Now that we are free from the power of the flesh, we are free to really love others. The flesh is self-centered self-

will. When a person is living in the flesh, then he or she is self-centered because that is the nature of the flesh. The opposite of self-centeredness is love.
What does it mean to be free to love?

B. **We love by serving others (5:13*b*).** Did you pick up on the paradox in this
verse? Paul declares that we are free in Christ (v. 13) but then, in the last
part of the verse, he tells us that we are servants. Luther summed up this
paradox rather well: "A Christian is free and independent in every respect,
a bond servant to none. A Christian is a dutiful servant in every respect,
owning a duty to everyone."

Freedom is the ability to be what God wants you to be. Jesus made it very
clear what He wanted us to be in Luke 22:24–27: servants!

C. **We love by fulfilling God's Law (5:14).** "Wait a minute, Pastor," someone says, "I thought that, when we were saved, we were freed from the
Law?" That is correct. We don't keep the Law in order to be saved; we
keep it because now God's Spirit lives in us and enables us to truly keep it.

But don't miss Paul's point. He wasn't talking about the rules and regula-
tions; rather, he was talking about keeping the spirit of the Law. What is the
spirit of the Law? "Love your neighbor as yourself." That is what Jesus taught
in Matthew 22:38–40.

When a person is really living by grace, he will truly fulfill the law.

D. **We love by building one another up (5:15).**

Conclusion

We are set free in Christ. Now what do we do? We say "no" to the flesh and
"yes" to truly loving others.

ADDITIONAL SERMONS AND LESSON IDEAS

Avoiding Oldwineskinitis

Luke 5:33–39
Dr. Mark D. Roberts

Introduction

What if you went to your doctor for your annual checkup and learned that you had a potentially terminal disease? You'd do anything to get over it. Many of us are suffering with a spiritually terminal disease and we don't even know it.

The same is true for our churches. All around us, once vibrant churches are ailing. Some have closed their doors; others have cut their ministry and mission. Churches are plagued with the same disease that threatens our own spiritual health.

This disease is Oldwineskinitis, and it's ravaging God's people today. Luckily, we can diagnose it and be cured from it, if we are willing.

New Wine and Old Wineskins, According to Jesus

In Luke 5:37–39, Jesus used an image that would be familiar to his listeners. They stored wine in wineskins. These specially prepared animal skins, supple because they were previously unused, could expand to accommodate fermenting wine. Once a skin had been used and emptied, however, it was worthless. Reused wineskins would burst because of the expansion of new wine. Thus, Jesus said that "new wine must be put into fresh wineskins" (Luke 5:38).

Defining Oldwineskinitis

Oldwineskinitis can be defined as trying to put the new wine of Christ into old skins. It can also mean rejecting the new wine altogether in favor of the old skins. When we suffer from Oldwineskinits, we value our traditions and comforts more than the new work God seeks to do in and through us. If we cling to what's familiar and safe, we are unable to contain the new wine of the Gospel.

Oldwineskinitis in the Church

A church with Oldwineskinitis is stuck in "we never did it that way before." It invests more of its time, energy, and money in self-preservation than in mission. It pays more attention to the complainers than to the people with vision. It coddles the members rather than welcoming guests.

Virtually every church has at least a minor case of Oldwineskinitis. Thus, we are responsible to prayerfully consider what the new wine of the gospel is and what the wineskins are. For example, the good news of God's salvation through Jesus Christ is the new wine. But the ways of communicating this good news are wineskins. The church is challenged to impart the classic truth of God in forms, modes, and words that resonate with the people of today, especially the unchurched who are increasingly ignorant of anything having to do with authentic Christian faith.

Oldwineskinitis in our Personal Lives

God wants to do a new work in us. He calls us to a fresh, daring commitment to His kingdom. This inevitably leads to change. The new wine of God's work in us means that we must be open to new wineskins: new habits, new relationships, new values, perhaps even new locations. If we are stricken with Oldwineskinitis, we'll reject the stirring of God's Spirit out of fear or a desire to maintain the status quo.

When we put our trust in God and open our lives to the new work of the Spirit, we are healed of our Oldwineskinitis. We are set free to discover the new work God wants to do in and through us, for His kingdom and glory.

Leaving a Lasting Impression, Pt. 2

Luke 15:11–20
By Dave Hirschman

Introduction

We saw before that the prodigal son knew he had a father who lived by principles (15:15–17), and that the son knew he had a father who could be trusted (15:18*a*). But the son knew even more about his father.

The Knowing and Loving Father

1. **The prodigal son knew he had a father that he had to be honest with (15:18–19).** His father would know just by looking at his ragged, smelly, and humbled appearance. He would have to explain his state (penniless, having wasted everything his father had given him). His appearance would have consequences. The prodigal son knew he could be honest with his father.
2. **The prodigal son knew he had a father who still loved him (15:20).** His father had been watching and waiting for him. His father didn't wait, but ran to his son. The father had never stopped loving his son. The prodigal son never had a chance to finish what he planned to say! He was welcomed, received, and loved!

Conclusion

The prodigal son's father left a lasting impression on his life, so much so that, even in trouble of his own making, the son knew what to expect from his father. Are we leaving a lasting impression of godliness upon others? That's the kind of father our heavenly Father is to us. Let us run to Him!

WEEK 24

SERIES: THE GOSPEL TRUTH

The Great Conflict

Galatians 5:16–18
By Dr. Kent Spann

Introduction

If you were asked to name some of the great conflicts in human history, which ones would you name: the Revolutionary War, the Civil War, World War 1 or 2, the Arab-Israeli conflict? None of those are the great conflict. The greatest conflict is the conflict between the Spirit and the flesh (5:16–18).

The Heart of Conflict

What is at the heart of every conflict whether ethical, national, or spiritual? It is desire. As James puts it:

> What causes quarrels and what causes fights among you? Is it not this, that your passions are at war within you? You desire and do not have, so you murder. You covet and cannot obtain, so you fight and quarrel. You do not have, because you do not ask. You ask and do not receive, because you ask wrongly, to spend it on your passions.
>
> —James 4:1–3 ESV

The word *desire* in James 4:2 is the same Greek word translated *desires* in Galatians 5:16, 17. The word can be translated as "lust after" or "covet." This is not simply standing outside the window of a pastry shop and thinking, "I wish I had one of those pastries," and then walking on to work. It is passionately wanting it.

A pastor decided to go on a diet, which meant eliminating sweets. He announced his diet to the staff. A week or two later, he showed up in staff meeting with a huge pastry in his hand. He immediately noted the glaring stares of the staff and declared, "this pastry is God's will for my life!" "How so?" the staff asked. "I was driving to church, which requires me to pass by the pastry shop. As I made my way toward the office, I prayed, 'Lord if it is your will for me to get a pastry today, please open up a parking spot right in front of the pastry shop.'" The pastor went on to say, "After circling the pastry shop over and over again, the Lord opened up a parking space, so this pastry is God's will for my life today." That pastor passionately wanted that pastry.

The Location of This Conflict

The location of this great conflict is not on some far away battlefield out of mind and out of sight. It is not "over there;" it is in us.

"But," someone says, "I thought it was a cosmic struggle between God and Satan." You are exactly right. Satan desires to rule creation, but that is not going to happen. He has already been defeated and cast out of heaven. The next best thing for Satan would be to rule God's crowning creation (Gen. 1:26, 27). That battle takes place in Genesis 3. Man came under the dominion of Satan. Christ redeems us from the dominion of darkness by His death, burial, and resurrection (Col. 1:13, 14). But Satan doesn't throw in the towel. He has lost us to the Kingdom of God, but he still has an inlet to our lives—the flesh. So the war continues to wage in us (Rom. 7:14–23).

The Opponents in This Conflict

1. The flesh
   A. The description of the flesh
      i. It is the sinful inclination of fallen mankind, the old self, whose supreme desire is to do its own will and to satisfy its sinful appetites.
      ii. It is the sinful self-will.
   B. The desire of the flesh
      i. The flesh desires to do evil.
      ii. The flesh desires to glorify self.
2. The Holy Spirit

A. The description of the Holy Spirit

   i. The Holy Spirit is a Person, not a force like in Star Wars.

   ii. The Holy Spirit is God (Acts 5:3, 4).

   iii. The Holy Spirit indwells every believer (Gal. 4:6; Acts 1:8; Rom. 8:9–11).

B. The desire of the Holy Spirit

   i. The Holy Spirit desires holiness.

   ii. The Holy Spirit desires to glorify God.

Who Rules?

The word translated *walk* in the KJV and *live* in the NIV is very colorful. The students of Aristotle were known as the *Peripatetics* because of their habit of following the philosopher around from place to place as he dispensed his teachings. So *walking* in our text means to go where our Master goes, listen to His voice, discern His will, and follow His guidance. It is to live under the influence of another.

If we are walking in the flesh, it means that we are listening to the flesh, discerning what it wants and following its guidance. If we are walking in the Spirit, it means that we are listening to the Spirit, discerning what He wants, and following His guidance.

I want to give some practical insights into how we as believers can walk in the Holy Spirit.

— Desire to be filled with the Holy Spirit.

— Die daily to self (Luke 9:23, 24).

— Decide to yield to the Holy Spirit.

— Depend upon the Holy Spirit.

— Devote yourself to the Lord.

— Discipline your life through the spiritual disciplines (prayer, Bible study, fasting, witnessing, etc.).

Which Are You Feeding?

The cuckoo is a common bird in England. It is a strange bird because it never builds its own nest. When it feels an egg coming, it finds another nest, such as a mother thrush's. It seizes the moment by hurriedly laying its egg in the thrush's nest and taking off.

The thrush doesn't realize that there is an additional, much larger egg now in her nest. When they hatch, she has several little thrushes and one cuckoo, which is two or three times the size of the thrush babies. When momma thrush returns with the breakfast entrée—worms—there are several little mouths and a huge cuckoo mouth. The cuckoo gets the breakfast entrée. The result is that the cuckoo grows larger and the thrushes smaller and smaller. Eventually, the thrushes die, and the cuckoo throws them out of the nest.

The point is that what we feed grows, and what we starve dies. We are to feed the Spirit and starve the flesh.

ADDITIONAL SERMONS AND LESSON IDEAS

The Grace of Giving

2 Corinthians 8:1–9
By Dr. Bryan E. Smith

Introduction

Some Christians think about their giving as a burden or a difficulty, much like paying taxes or bills. But giving to God is intended to be an act of personal and corporate worship. It has been said that we're never more like Jesus than when we give. The Lord gave Himself for us and extends His grace to us, and we are to give back to Him as a demonstration of His grace in us. Four times in these eight verses, the Bible mentions God's grace in connection with giving. When we live like Jesus, then we will give like Jesus, because true giving comes from the work of God's grace in our hearts and lives.

Giving by Grace Surpasses Afflictions (2 Cor. 8:1–4)

1. The source of God's grace (John 1:14–16)
   A. The reason for Grace: Christ's Atonement (Eph. 1:7–8)
   B. The reach of Grace: to every church (2 Cor. 8:1).
2. The strength of God's grace (2 Cor. 8:1–4).
   A. It isn't hindered by our affliction.
   B. It isn't weakened by our poverty.
   C. It isn't limited by our inabilities.
3. The service of God's grace (2 Cor. 8:5).
   A. They gave of their own accord.
   B. They gave with a heartfelt desire.
   C. They gave in service to others.

Giving by Grace Puts Christ First (2 Cor. 8:5–8)

1. Giving by grace will surprise others (2 Cor. 8:5*a*).
2. Giving by grace starts with surrender to Christ (2 Cor. 8:5*b*).
3. Giving by grace inspire others (2 Cor. 8:6).
4. Giving by grace reflects living by grace (2 Cor. 8:7).
   A. They excelled in their faith.
   B. They excelled in their speech.
   C. They excelled in their knowledge.
   D. They excelled in their diligence.
   E. They excelled in their love.
   F. They were to excel in their giving (2 Cor. 8:8).

Giving by Grace has Christ as our Example (2 Cor. 8:9)

1. Jesus was very rich (2 Cor. 8:9*a*).
2. Jesus became very poor (2 Cor. 8:9*b*; Phil. 2:7).
3. Jesus makes us very rich (2 Cor. 8:9*c*; Phil. 2:8).

Conclusion

Giving by grace is God's work in our hearts. Giving should not be legalistic but an act of grace.

What the Resurrection Really Means

1 Corinthians 15:13–18
By Dave Hirschman

Introduction

There are certain days on the calendar that we attach special meaning to. We emphasize the historical and theological meaning of those days, and many times we celebrate the symbolic meaning—but we frequently miss the practical meaning. On a practical level, what does the resurrection of Christ mean for me?

I do not need to be afraid of death because Jesus replaced hopelessness with certainty (15:25–26).

People fear many things, one of them being death. Jesus' resurrection means that I do not need to fear death because Jesus went there and came back!

I can trust everything that God says because Jesus replaced doubt with confidence (15:51–57).

He really was raised from the dead and I will really be raised from the dead.

I can live life with confidence and expectation because Jesus is alive (15:58).

Because He is alive, I can stand firm and serve diligently.

Conclusion

Jesus' resurrection holds so much for his followers—truth that can change your life, now and forever!

WEEK 25

SERIES: THE GOSPEL TRUTH

The Litmus Test

Galatians 5:19–25
By Dr. Kent Spann

What is the litmus test of Christianity? What is the crucial indicator of what kind of Christian we are? This morning, Paul gives us the litmus test.

The Great Conflict

Last week, we learned that there is a great conflict going on inside us. Let's briefly review that conflict (the preacher can summarize the previous message).

The Spiritual Litmus Test

How do you know whether you are walking in the flesh or the Spirit? Paul gives us the litmus test: it is what we are producing. It is not what we say, profess, believe, etc.; it is what is produced in our lives.

1. **When you live by the flesh, you will produce the deeds, works, and acts of the flesh (5:19–21).** Paul says the works of the flesh are obvious. The problem is that they are not always obvious to believers; therefore, Paul has to list them. People who call themselves believers will attribute what they do to everything but the flesh. They will say, "It is the product of my environment," or "It is just my nature or personality." They will even claim that they are victims of other's behavior. The greatest travesty in America is the dumbing-down of Christianity by those who call themselves Christians! We have normalized the flesh. The church has become so accustomed to living in the flesh that it no longer realizes it is in the flesh. The funny thing is that pagans know the truth, which is why they reject the church and "western Christianity."

Paul doesn't dumb it down. He shoots it straight in verses 19–21. The list can be broken down into five categories of sin.

A. Sexual Sins (5:19 sexual immorality, impurity and debauchery). Paul begins with the sexual sins. This is characteristic of Paul's list. Why does he prioritize the sexual sins? Is it because they are the ultimate sin? Is it because they are more heinous? I think he starts with the sexual sins because they graphically display man's self centeredness and rebellion against God's norm which is the mark of the flesh.

B. Religious Sins (5:20 idolatry and witchcraft). Now Paul moves to the sins of religion. Interestingly, the flesh is very religious. Hey, the devil is very religious. Every person is very religious. Religion is not the organization of systems of belief and thought; religion is about who or what a person worships. The Christian worships God as revealed in Christ; the Muslims worship Allah; the Hindus worship any of thousands of gods; atheists worship man. So the flesh is very religious, but it is a sinful religion.

Idolatry is whatever replaces the worship of the true and living God (Rom. 1:24–25). Witchcraft is more than casting spells or dealing in black magic. The word translated *witchcraft* by the NIV is *pharmakeia*. We get our word *pharmacy* from this. It was used originally of medicines in general, but came to be used primarily of mood- and mind-altering drugs similar to those that create havoc in our day. The people took the drugs to have experiences or have their mood altered. In that altered state, they were indoctrinated in false religion; thus, they became associated with the occult. That is exactly what is happening in the modern day drug epidemic. People are taking drugs and, in so doing, opening themselves up to demons and the occult.

C. Social Sins (5:20, 21 hatred, discord, jealousy, fits of rage, selfish ambition, dissensions, factions, and envy). The third category deals with sins in relationships. While I see the first two categories often in the church, it is this category that is most evident.

D. Alcoholic Sins (5:21 drunkenness, orgies).

E. Et Cetera Sins (5:21 and the like).

His list is not meant to be exhaustive. It is an ugly list, isn't it? How ugly? It is so ugly that Paul ends this section with a warning in verse 21.

2. **When you live by the Spirit, you will produce the fruit of the Spirit (5:22, 23).** Paul contrasts the products of the Spirit and the flesh using two different words. When describing the product of the flesh, he calls them *acts*. When he describes the product of the Spirit, he speaks of *fruit*. I want to point a few things about this word *fruit*. First, it is singular, unlike the acts of the flesh. He didn't say "fruits of the Spirit." Second, it is the result of the overflow of the life of the Spirit in the believer. The acts of the flesh are what we produce; the fruit of the Spirit is different. Fruit is a result of the life of the tree, not the fruit itself. The fruit is merely the outward expression of the life of the tree. Finally, it is a process. Fruit ripens with time.

3. **What is this fruit of the Spirit?**

   A. **Love is sacrificial serving and caring for others (1 Cor. 13).**

   B. **Joy is not necessarily happiness, which is based on circumstances.** It is the sense of well-being that comes from knowing that things are right between you and God.

   C. **Peace with God and others (Eph. 2:11–22).**

   D. **Patience is longsuffering when hurt by others.** It is longsuffering in the face of irritating or painful situations. It is not being easily offended.

   E. **Kindness is a tender concern for others.**

   F. **Goodness is benevolence toward others.** It is actively doing good to others.

   G. **Faithfulness is loyalty and trustworthiness.**

   H. **Gentleness is a submissive and teachable spirit toward God that manifests itself in genuine humility and consideration toward others.**

   I. **Self-control is the restraint of passions and appetites.** It is mastery of self, not by self discipline but by the discipline and power of the Holy Spirit.

Walking In The Spirit

How do we walk in the Spirit instead of the flesh? Paul tells us in the final verses of this section.

1. We continually die to our flesh (5:24).
2. We continually walk in the Spirit (5:25)
   A. We desire to be filled with the Spirit.
   B. We ask the Holy Spirit to fill us (Eph. 5:18).
   C. We live in dependence upon the Holy Spirit.
3. We walk humbly with one another (5:26).

ADDITIONAL SERMONS AND LESSON IDEAS

Tithing Yesterday and Today

Deuteronomy 14:22–23
By Dr. Bryan E Smith

Introduction

Tithing was commanded by God and was meant to be practiced by His chosen people, the Israelites, as their acknowledgement of His goodness and a demonstration of their faith and obedience to Him. Tithing is a biblical principal for Christians today.

Tithing was Intended for Every Israelite (Deut. 14:22; Gen. 14:20)

1. In the Bible, a tithe is a tenth.
2. The tithe applied to "all the increase" (Deut. 14:22–23).
3. God was the source of their increase.
   A. They were dependent on God's provision (Lev. 27:30).
   B. They were dependent on God's protection (Gen. 14:18–20).

Tithing was Important for Every Israelite

1. Tithing reminded them of God's presence.
2. Tithing reminded them of God's promise (Mal. 3:10).
3. Tithing reminded them of God's preeminence (Deut. 14:23).
   A. To "fear" God is to reverence God above all others.
   B. God's child fears Him because he belongs to God.
   C. The "fear of the Lord" is a lifelong pursuit and practice.

Tithing is Intended for Every Christian

1. Tithing wasn't dropped by the Lord Jesus (Matt. 23:23; Luke 11:42).
2. Tithing was endorsed by the Lord Jesus (Matt. 23:23; Luke 11:42).
3. Tithing is giving to God through His Church (Mal. 3:10–11; 1 Cor. 16:2).

Tithing Should be Important for Every Christian

1. Tithing teaches the Christian to appreciate God's goodness (Ps. 103:2).
2. Tithing teaches the Christian to trust God for his needs (2 Cor. 9:6).
3. Tithing teaches the Christian to demonstrate his faith (Luke 16:10).
4. Tithing teaches the Christian to worship God in obedience (1 Cor. 16:2).

Conclusion

According to Empty Tomb, Inc., in 2008, the average church member gave 2.43 percent of his or her income. "If Americans who identify with the historically Christian church had chosen to give 10% to their congregations in 2008, rather than the 2.43% given that year, there would have been an additional $172 billion available for work through the church." They point out that $70 to $80 billion a year could address the basic needs of the poorest people around the world.[1]

Tithing is not out of date. It is a beginning point. It is God's plan for the church today.

Endnotes

[1] Empty Tomb, Inc. *http://www.emptytomb.com/potential.html* (accessed April 1, 2011).

Does It Really Matter What You Believe?

Acts 21:8–14; 23:11: 28:30–31

By Dave Hirschman

Introduction

How important to your life is what you believe? What people do or do not believe has a direct impact on how they live. Paul was a man who was affected by what he believed. He believed that Christ was Lord and Savior.

What Paul believed defined who he was and how he lived his life (Acts 21:8–14).

Paul lived by what he believed and could not be dissuaded (Acts 21:14).

What Paul believed determined how far he would go (Acts 23:11).

Paul was determined to follow wherever and however the Lord led him (Acts 23:11, 27:24). He was determined because what he believed mattered to him (Phil. 3:13–14; 2 Tim. 4:8).

What Paul believed demonstrated the true meaning of his life (Acts 28:30–31).

1. He had a singular focus (28:31*a*, "preaching the kingdom of God").
2. He had a singular love (28:31*b*, "Jesus Christ").
3. He had a singular commitment (28:31*c*, "confidence").

Conclusion

What we believe influences every aspect of our lives. Our beliefs define, determine, and demonstrate what we value. Paul's life was shaped and driven by what he believed about Christ. Does what you believe about Christ really make a difference in your life?

WEEK 26

SERIES: THE GOSPEL TRUTH

Good Saint Care

Galatians 6:1–5

By Dr. Kent Spann

Introduction

The medical care industry is obviously in the forefront of everyone's mind these days. Hardly a week goes by that something related to the medical field fails to make it into the news. Everybody wants good medical care. Good medical care is critical in the medical field; good saint care is critical in the church.

The Perfect vs. the Healthy Church

There is a huge misconception about the church. It is usually stated this way: "The Church is full of hypocrites." The misconception is that the church should be full of perfect people. Church is nothing more than the sum total of its people. And what do its people bring to the table? Paul tells us in Galatians. They bring battles with sin and the flesh (6:1) as well as burdens and baggage from life (6:2). You have probably heard the statement, "If you find a perfect church, please don't join it because you will ruin it!"

The Healthy Church vs. the Dysfunctional Church

The problem is not that the church is imperfect; the church is often dysfunctional. The church is dysfunctional because she doesn't know how to deal with people who sin and carry heavy burdens. Here are common ways that a dysfunctional church deals with sin and burdens of others and itself:

- Blame game
- Critical spirit
- Avoid the person who sins or is hurting
- Deny that there is a problem especially with sin.

—Gossip and slander
—Silence
—Cold shoulder
—Triangulate, or use go-betweens to communicate messages instead of directly communicating with the person.
—Sweep it under the rug or hide the issue.

We don't deal with our dysfunctions very well in the church. We need better saint care.

Good Saint Care

Good saint care involves correct diagnosis of the problem, qualified caregivers, proper treatment, compassionate care, and proper precautions. We can use those guidelines as we learn about good saint care from Paul.

1. **We seek to restore those who sin (6:1).**
   A. **Proper Diagnosis: Sin.** *Sin* is a nasty word that we don't like to hear. We don't want to talk about sin. Some preachers avoid it because they don't want to offend people. We find other ways to describe it, to excuse it, to justify it, etc.

   What does Paul mean by a brother "caught in sin?" It can refer to two situations. First, a fellow Christian catches another believer in the commission of a sin. Second, "caught in sin" can describe a situation where a fellow believer is overtaken by a sin before he is aware that he has done wrong.

   B. **Proper Treatment: Restore.** Paul tells how a healthy church handles sin in the life of the believer. The word Greek word for *restore* (*katartizete*) was a surgical term used of setting a bone or joint. It also means to mend or repair. At the end of the day, fisherman would check their nets and make sure that there were no holes where fish could escape. The fisherman would then mend or repair the net (Matt. 4:21).

   When a brother or sister falls, stumbles, or is caught in sin, proper saint care demands that we attempt to restore the person. That means that we seek to get them back on the right road. It means helping them face up to their sin, confess it, and put it away. It is helping believers be restored in their fellowship with God and walk with the Spirit.

C. **Qualified Caregivers: Spiritual believers.** Notice that Paul doesn't say that just anyone should be involved in this process. He says, "you who are spiritual." A spiritual person is one who is walking in the Spirit or living his life in dependence upon God's Spirit. Paul is not talking about position in the church or how long someone has been a Christian. He is talking about being Spirit-filled. You can be a new believer and be Spirit-fil,led and you can be a long-time believer and be Spirit-filled. Every believer ought to be Spirit-filled.

Who should not try to restore a sinning brother? A carnal or fleshly Christian should not attempt to restore another Christian. Why? Because the carnal Christian needs to first be restored.

D. **Compassionate Care: Gentleness.** We are not to be critical and judgmental in our attempt to help a fallen brother. That does not reflect grace. The work of restoration should be done with sensitivity and consideration and with no hint of self-righteous superiority.

E. **Proper Precautions: Watch yourself.** In a hospital, the caregivers have to take proper precautions lest they come down with the same disease as the one they are treating. Paul warns the caregiver to be careful lest he or she fall into the same sin.

2. **We bear the heavy burdens of others (6:2–5).**

A. **Proper Diagnosis: Heavy burden.** Life is full of burdens such as suffering or persecution, trials and tests, physical or emotional problems, issues with children, job loss, financial disaster, and the list goes on. Some burdens can be our own making but many are not. People with heavy burdens fill churches like ours.

B. **Proper Treatment: Carry.** Those carrying a heavy burden don't need the condemnation of believers. They don't need friends like those who "comforted" Job telling them everything they are doing wrong. They don't necessarily need fixers telling them how to fix everything. They need believers to help them carry their burden.

What does it means to carry another's burden? It doesn't mean that we take the burden off of their shoulder and carry it for them. When we do that, we take away the opportunity for God to develop character in their lives. It does mean that we join our brother or sister in helping them carry that burden. To bear another's burden means that we come alongside them and help them. It may mean sitting with them as they weep, praying for them, attentively listening, or helping them get back on their feet.

C. **Qualified Caregivers: Humble believers (6:3–5).** Humble believers have a proper view of themselves (6:3), are right with God (6:4), and fulfill their God-given responsibilities (6:5).

D. **Compassionate Care: Love (6:2).** What is the law of Christ? Christ told us in John 15:12.

E. **Proper Precautions: Test (6:4–5).** Make sure that we have the right attitude.

Conclusion

So there you have Paul's prescription for good saint care, which leads to a healthy church.

ADDITIONAL SERMONS AND LESSON IDEAS

Stewardship is Personal

Ezra 2:68–69
By Dr. Bryan E. Smith

Introduction

It should encourage us to know that God is serious about our stewardship and that He actually does care about what we do with our money. When we stop to consider the fact that God truly does own "the cattle on a thousand hills" (Ps. 50:10), yet He also cares for us and longs to help us manage His blessings, this should give us confidence. Our stewardship is personal with God, and it should be personal to us.

The Pace of Their Giving (Ezra 2:68)

1. The heads of the father's houses came.
   A. Only some Israelite's were represented (Ezra 2:68).
   B. Only some Christians are represented today (Heb. 10:25).
   C. The work needed everyone's support (Ezra 1:3–6).
   D. Many Christians today are missing out on giving to God.
2. They came to the "house of the Lord" (Ezra 2:68).
   A. The location of "God's House:" in Jerusalem (Ezra 2:68).
   B. The location of "God's House:" in your Church (Mal.3:10; 1 Cor. 16:2).
   C. The location of "God's House:" in your heart (2 Cor. 9:7).

The Practice of Their Giving

1. They gave freely (Ezra 2:68).
   A. God has freely given to us (Rom. 3:24, 6:23).
   B. We should freely give for Him (Matt. 10:8; 2 Cor. 9:7).
2. They gave purposefully (Ezra 2:68).

A. God's people wanted to build up the house of God (Ezra 2:68).

B. God's people today want to build up the kingdom of God (Luke 12:33–34).

3. They gave faithfully (Ezra 2:68).

A. God's work needed faithful givers in Ezra's day (Ezra 2:69).

B. God's work needs faithful givers in our day (2 Cor. 8:2).

4. They gave accordingly (Ezra 2:69).

A. They gave out of their own personal possessions (Ezra 1:4–6; 2:69).

B. Stewardship is managing what God has given to us (Ezra 2:69; 2 Cor. 8:12).

The Purpose of Their Giving

1. To obey God's command (Ezra 1:2, 3).
2. To support God's work (Ezra 3:7).
3. To rebuild God's temple (Ezra 1:2–4, 68, 69).
4. To fulfill God's purpose (Ezra 1:1).
5. To glorify God's name (Ezra 6:14–22; 7:27).

Conclusion

Stewardship is first and foremost a personal matter for every believer. It is a personal matter between God and the believer. Ezra provides a great model for our stewardship.

It's A Wonderful Thing!

Hebrews 10:24–25
By Dr. Kent Spann

Introduction

Paul makes it clear that gathering with other believers is important. Why do we need church?

We Need Others to Grow in Our Christian Faith.

1. We need to study the Bible together with other believers (Acts 2:42).
2. We need to worship together with other believers (Ps. 122:1).
3. We need the encouragement of other believers (Heb. 10:24; 1 Thess. 5:11; Prov. 27:17).
4. We need the love of the Body (John 13:34, 35; Rom. 12:10; Heb. 13:1; 1 Peter 1:22).
5. We need the service of the Body (Gal. 5:13).
6. We need the help of the Body (Gal. 6:2; 1 Thess. 5:14, 15).
7. We need the healing power of the Body (James 5:16).
8. We need others to fulfill the Great Commission (Phil. 1:3–6).
9. We need the positive influence of godly people in our lives (Phil. 3:17–21).
10. We need a place to bring our tithes and offerings (1 Cor. 16:1–3).

Others Need Us to Grow in Their Faith.

Every believer has a key role in the life of the church. Your presence is missed when you're not there.

1. Others need our gifts (1 Cor. 12:12–26).
2. Others need our service (Eph. 4:11–16).
3. Others need our gift of giving (Phil. 4:10–19).
4. Others need our partnership in the gospel (Phil. 1:4, 5).

Conclusion

You probably know Viggo Mortensen as Aragorn in "The Lord of the Rings." Commenting on the lessons learned from "The Lord of the Rings," Viggo said:

> The lesson, I guess, is that the union with others is more significant than your individual existence. It doesn't deny the importance of your individuality. It just means you're a better person the more you connect with others. You're going to know more. You're going to be stronger and you're going to have a better life if you get over yourself. That's part of growing up.[1]

Endnotes

[1] Bob Smithouser, "Life Lessons from Middle-Earth." Found at *http://www.focusonlinecommunities.com/blogs/pluggedin/tags/unity* (accessed April 4, 2011).

WEEK 27

SERIES: THE GOSPEL TRUTH

God's Inviolable Law

Galatians 6:6–10
By Dr. Kent Spann

Introduction

Ask a member of the congregation to stand next to you on the platform. Ask him or her to respond to the following series of true false statements:

- If you eat a diet of foods high in fat, cholesterol, and calories, you will lose weight—especially if you overeat every time.
- If you drink two bottles of vodka in a couple of hours, you will not get drunk.
- If you never sleep, you will never be tired.
- If you put your hand in a raging fire, it won't get burned.
- If you jump off the roof of the church, you will go up, not down.

Ask the congregation why the answer to all those statements is "false." Explain that this is because they are all based on an inviolable law. An inviolable law is a law that is incapable of being violated.

In Galatians 6:7, Paul introduces us to God's Inviolable Law. God's inviolable law says, "whatever a man sows, that he will also reap." In other words, choices and actions have consequences.

The Enforcer of the Inviolable Law (Gal. 6:7)

Buddhists and Hindus believe in a concept called Karma, which is akin to Paul's teaching that a man reaps what he sows. Paul is not teaching the law of Karma here. He is not talking about an impersonal system; rather, he tells us that God is at the heart of the inviolable law of sowing and reaping. God is the One who established the law, and He is the One who enforces the law of sowing and reaping.

The biggest mistake that we can make is to believe that we could somehow be exempt from the inviolable law of reaping what we sow. In Galatians 6:7, Paul says, "Do not be deceived, God is not mocked!" In other words, don't be fooled into thinking that you can be the exception to the rule. How many times have we thought that we could get away with doing something wrong, thinking that we will somehow be the exception? A person who has premarital sex thinks that he will be the exception to the rule and not get pregnant or contract a sexually transmitted disease. A person who drinks is sure that he will never become an alcoholic.

By the same principle, we must understand that, by doing good, we will reap positive benefits. God rewards those who _____ [fill in the blank].

This law of the harvest is inescapable, because God is the One who enforces it.

The Application of the Inviolable Law (Gal. 6:8)

1. **We can sow to the flesh and reap destruction.** It is our desire, contrary to God's will and standards, to sow to the flesh. Giving in to these desires means that we are doing what we want, not what God wants. Sowing to the flesh means operating in our own power to do what we want for our own glory and self-pleasure.

   Of course, we can sow to the flesh, but we must understand that, if we do, we reap destruction. You see, we don't get to determine the consequences of our sowing. The Greek word translated *destruction* (*phthora*) does not mean annihilation; rather, it means something going from bad to worse. The best illustration that I can give you is a steak. Steak is a delicious and decadent food, but if you lay it out on the table and leave it there for two or three weeks it decays, or corrupts. This truth applies to believers as well as unbelievers. Believers are guilty of sowing to the flesh. Comedian Fred Allen (1894–1956) illustrated this when he said, "Most of us spend the first six days of each week sowing wild oats, then we go to church on Sunday and pray for a crop failure." In other words, we don't live according to God's will, yet we expect to reap rewards.

2. **We can sow to the Spirit and reap eternal life.** What does it mean to sow to the Spirit? It means to walk in the Spirit (Gal. 5:18) and be filled with the Spirit (Eph. 5:18). Simply put, it means participating in selfless activities which will eventually foster spiritual growth. Paul gives it a specific application in our text.

    A. **We sow to the Spirit when we give to the Lord's work (6:6).** Paul uses the concept of sowing to the Spirit twice in the New Testament (2 Cor. 9:6; Gal. 6:7). In both of these passages, Paul refers to financial giving in support of those who teach the Word of God.

        According to Paul's example, by giving to the church and supporting the teachers, we sow to the Spirit. We prove by opening our pocketbooks the importance of the preaching of the Word.

        The way that we use our money is a reflection of what we value. If I looked at how you have used your money over the past 5 years or just this last year, what would it say about what you value? Most Christians give only a small percentage to the Lord's work. According to the Barna Research group, only five percent of Americans tithe.[1] Evangelicals were a little better than the average American, with twenty-four percent tithing. That means that, in the average evangelical church, seventy-six percent of the members don't tithe. That seventy-six percent does not value the work of the church. "But things are tight, pastor!" Are things tight on one hundred percent, or on the ninety percent that you live on after you have given to God? The question is not whether it is tight or whether you can afford to tithe; the question is whether you will sow to the Spirit, which in turn determines what you will reap.

    B. **We sow to the Spirit when we do good to others in His name (6:9–10).** We are to do good to others, whether in serving or giving. Jesus taught us to let our light shine by doing good deeds for the Father's glory (Matt. 5:16).

The Motivation for the Inviolable Law (6:9–10)

We will reap either now or later. I am not saying that, if you start giving, suddenly everything is going to turn around financially for you. It may; it may not. But don't lose heart: God will come through with the reward, either here or there.

The Unbeliever and the Inviolable Law

Is there an application for unbelievers? The answer is yes. The choices that you make now have eternal consequences.

Conclusion

Remember that what you do with Christ has eternal consequences!

Endnotes

[1] The Barna Group, "New Study Shows Trends in Tithing and Donating," April 14, 2008. *http://www.barna.org/barna-update/article/18-congregations/41-new-study-shows-trends-in-tithing-and-donating?q=giving* (accessed January 28, 2011).

ADDITIONAL SERMONS AND LESSON IDEAS

Money Matters of the Heart

2 Corinthians 9:6–8
By Dr. Bryan E. Smith

Introduction

Where does giving truly start? What motivates you to give? Why don't more Christians practice generous giving to God through their local churches? Could it be that they are looking at giving as a burden rather than a blessing? The Lord Jesus said, "It is more blessed to give than to receive" (Acts 20:35). When it comes to how we think about money, what matters most is the attitude of our hearts.

The Principle of Sowing Bountifully (2 Cor. 9:6)

1. What we receive corresponds to what we give.
   A. The law of sowing and reaping (Prov. 11:24).
   B. The limit of sowing and reaping (2 Cor. 9:6).
   C. The life of sowing and reaping (Luke 6:38).
2. Reasons why some Christians give "sparingly."
   A. They have misplaced priorities (Matt. 6:33).
   B. They have mismatched pleasures (1 Tim. 6:10).
   C. They have misguided pursuits (Matt. 16:26).
3. Reasons why some Christians give "generously."
   A. They are spiritually mature.
   B. They have the gift of giving (Rom. 12:8).
   C. They were taught to give as children.
   D. They are self-disciplined (Gal. 5:23).

The Practice of Giving Cheerfully (2 Cor. 9:7)

1. Giving should begin in the heart (Luke 16:15).
2. Giving shouldn't be seen as a burden (Matt. 11:30).
3. Giving should be done cheerfully.
   A. The joy of our salvation (Acts 8:8).
   B. The joy of our Savior (Neh. 8:10; Hab. 3:18).
   C. The joy of our service (Ps. 112:9).

The Promise for Giving Confidently (2 Cor. 9:8)

1. God will supply graciously (2 Cor. 9:10).
2. God will supply sufficiently (Phil. 4:19).
3. God will supply abundantly (Rom. 8:32).

Conclusion

A wealthy elderly man married a beautiful young woman. Not long afterward, he began to wonder if she married him for his money or love for him. He decided to consult a counselor.

"Doc, my problem is driving me crazy. I need to know if my wife really loves me or if she just married me for my money."

"The answer is simple," the counselor explained. "Give away all your money except just enough to live on. If your wife stays, she loves you. If she leaves, she loves your money."[1]

The counselor understood that money is a matter of the heart. Where is your heart today?

Endnotes

[1] Kent Crockett, *I Once Was Blind But Now I Squint* (Chattanooga, Tenn.: AMG, 2004), 62.

3-D Christianity

Luke 9:23–27
By Dr. Kent Spann

Today, advances in technology have made three-dimensional (3-D) movies and television commonplace. Jesus introduced an early version of 3-D over two thousand years ago. It came in the form of three important words.

Denial

Jesus makes it very clear right off the bat that, if you want to be a true disciple of His, you must deny yourself. Now what does that mean?

1. In the case of the lost sinner, it means:
   A. You renounce faith in anything other than Christ (religion, church, your own goodness, your best efforts, etc.) to save you (John 14:6).
   B. You trust in Christ alone to save you (Acts 4:12).
2. In the case of the true believer, it means:
   A. We put Christ first in our lives (Matt. 6:33).
   B. We seek His will, not our will
   C. We deny the desires of the flesh so that we can walk in the Holy Spirit (Gal. 5:16–18)
   D. We do what He wants instead of what we want.

Death

The cross is an instrument of death.

1. It means that we willingly accept the path that Christ chooses for us.
2. It means that we willingly accept the cost of being His disciple, whether it means ridicule or persecution.

Devotion

1. We obey Him (John 14:21; 15:14).
2. We trust Him (Matt. 19:16-21; Luke 18:18–22).
3. We follow Him (1 Peter 2:21).
4. We serve Him (John 12:26).

Conclusion

Jesus calls us to a 3-D commitment. It is a radical commitment, but it is what He calls for (Matt. 10:37–38).

WEEK 28

SERIES: THE GOSPEL TRUTH

The Centrality of the Cross

Galatians 6:11–18
By Dr. Kent Spann

Introduction

In Galatians 6:11–18, we see the end of Paul's letter to the Galatians. The primary reason for the letter was to respond to the Judaizers who were undermining the Gospel as well as Paul's authority as an apostle.

The Judaizers believed that Christians should follow the laws of the Old Testament, so that Christianity was an extension of the traditional system of Judaism that involved keeping the Law. Instead of using a secretary (*amanuensis*), Paul wrote the letter to the Galatians himself, which he emphasizes in verse 11. This illustrates the critical nature of his final words. In the final verses of Galatians 6, Paul defends his apostleship and the Gospel of Grace by contrasting what the Judaizers boasted in to what Paul boasted in.

These verses remind us that you can tell a lot about a person and what he values by paying attention to what he boasts about.

The Judaizers' Boasting (6:12, 13)

Paul writes that the Judaizers boasted in the flesh. Here, Paul is using "the flesh" to describe human self-effort independent from the power of God. The focus of Paul's comments is on the act of circumcision. A major plank of the Judaizers' teaching was circumcision. They insisted that Gentiles be circumcised in addition to believing in Christ for salvation because they thought that all Christians must also be Jews. In other words, to the Judaizers, faith in Christ was not enough to be a Christian. They believed that there is something beyond faith that a person must do in order to be saved, to be right with God. This, among other acts of self-effort, was commonly boasted about by Judaizers.

All religions besides Christianity are religions of self-effort. Only a faith in Christ brings freedom from self-effort. Paul exposes the self-effort movement.

1. **Self-effort is all about impressing others (6:12a).** The Judaizers wanted to make a good impression on those in their religious sphere. It was more important for them to make a good impression on their peers than it was to preach the truth about the Gospel.

   Think about what happens in the church. People do things to impress others in the church. They want people to think how spiritual they are, how godly they are, or how good a Christian they are. They are motivated by what others think, not by faith alone.

2. **Self-effort is driven by fear (6:12b).** The Judaizers didn't want to pay the price for following Christ and preaching the cross for a couple of reasons. First, they feared that they would be expelled from the community of the synagogue (John 12:42–43). Second, they would be persecuted (Gal. 6:12).

   When man, as opposed to Christ, is the center of religion, fear of what others think or do will drive the adherent.

3. **Self-effort is characterized by hypocrisy (6:13a).** The Judaizers were running around telling everyone what they need to do, when they weren't even doing it themselves. In other words, they weren't practicing what they preached. Self-effort is plagued with hypocrisy, because no one can measure up to the standards of God's Word (Matt. 5:48; Rom. 3:23).

4. **Self-effort is motivated by pride (6:13b).** The Judaizers wanted to boast about all of their converts. They wanted to go back to their community and give the numbers of people following them. At the heart of all human achievement and self-effort is pride.

Paul's Boasting (6:14–18)

Paul didn't boast in self-effort; he boasted in the cross of his Lord Jesus Christ. "May I never" is a very strong negative in the original language of this passage, indicating a virtual impossibility.

Wearing a cross today is fashionable. Seeing crosses on the top of church buildings or on lawns is commonplace. Modern culture has sanitized the cross.

Not so in Paul's day. The cross was repulsive to the people of Paul's day (1 Cor. 1:22–25), but most importantly it was repulsive to God (Deut 21:23). It was even repulsive to Christ (Luke 22:39–44).

If the cross is repulsive, why should we boast in it?

1. **We boast in the cross because we are liberated by the cross (6:14b).** In this verse, Paul uses "the world" to describe the evil world system ruled by Satan and his agents. The life of the person apart from Jesus Christ is that of a slave of the world system. It is a life of meaninglessness, depravity, hopelessness, and guilt. The cross of Christ liberated us from bondage to this dying, corrupt, sinful world.

2. **We boast in the cross because we are transformed by the cross (6:15).** Have you ever bought a car that turned out to be a lemon? Did you want the dealer to make some cosmetic repairs to the lemon, or did you want a brand new, mint-condition model?

   Christianity is not God taking a broken down lemon of a model (us) and making some cosmetic repairs. Essentially, Judaizers were offering cosmetic repairs with their self-effort salvation. The cross of Christ is not a self improvement program; rather, it makes us new creations (2 Cor. 5:17).

3. **We boast in the cross because we are saved by the cross (6:16).** A rookie at an NFL camp was worried about whether or not he would make the team. Lovie Smith, coach of the Chicago Bears, told the rookies in a talk to the 2010 class, "Make us put you on the team."

   Many people think that God makes the same sort of speech about getting to heaven. "Do you want to 'make the team' and have eternal life? Make me let you into heaven by being a good person." It is quite the opposite. God wants you to admit that you are a wretched, hopeless, helpless, lost sinner who cannot save yourself. It is casting your lot in the cross of Christ. The way of the cross is peace and grace.

4. **We boast in the cross because we are marked by the cross (6:17).** The Judaizers were marked by circumcision; Paul was marked by the cross of Christ.

Paul suffered for Christ. To bear the cross is to suffer for Christ. If we are devoted followers of Christ, we will face persecution and suffering!

Conclusion

Some years ago, a fourteen-foot bronze crucifix was stolen from Calvary Cemetery in Little Rock, Arkansas. It had stood at the entrance to that cemetery for more than fifty years. The cross was put there in 1930 by a Catholic bishop, and had been valued at the time at $10,000. The thieves apparently cut it off at its base and hauled it off in a pick-up truck. Police speculate that they cut it into small pieces and sold the 900-pound cross for scrap, which would have netted them about $450. They obviously didn't realize the value of that cross.[1]

They didn't understand the value of that bronze cross; do we understand the value of the real cross of Christ? The evidence that we value it is that we boast in it. If we boast in self-effort, we do not value the cross of Christ.

Endnotes

[1] Lee Eclov "The Agony of Victory," as found in *www.preachingoday.com* (Accessed January 28, 1957).

ADDITIONAL SERMONS AND LESSON IDEAS

The Widow's Mighty Mites

Mark 12:41–44
By Dr. Bryan E. Smith

Introduction

Is financially giving to God a joy or a burden? Do you give because of what is expected of you, or because you are grateful to God for how He has blessed you? If we're not careful, our giving to God can become more about how it pleases us than how it pleases Him. In our text, Jesus was more impressed by the attitude and actions of the widow's small gift than He was by the much larger amounts that were placed in the temple treasury that day. We need to remember that the Lord still sees today what His people give to Him and, more importantly, He sees their hearts, too!

God Sees our Offerings in Worship

1. Jesus saw who gave the offerings (Mark 12:41).

    A. Do you ever think about how Jesus sees you in worship? (Matt. 6:4)

    B. Would it make a difference if you could see Him in worship?

2. Jesus saw how the offerings were given.

    A. He knows our thoughts (Mark. 2:8).

    B. He knows our hearts (Acts 1:24).

    C. He knows our deeds (Matt. 6:18).

3. Jesus saw the amount of the offerings.

    A. How much do you give? A tithe? (Mal. 3:10; Matt. 23:23)

    B. How often do you give? Regularly? (1 Cor. 16:2)

God Knows our Circumstances in Worship

1. God is aware of our burdens (1 Pet. 5:7).
2. God is concerned about our difficulties (Matt. 11:30).
3. God is pleased with our faithfulness (Matt. 25:21).
   A. Sacrificial giving depends on God's supply (Phil. 4:19).
   B. Sacrificial giving demonstrates God's love (Rom. 5:8).
   C. Sacrificial giving declares God's glory (1 Cor. 10:31).

God Honors our Generosity in Worship (Matt. 6:4)

1. The widow didn't give out of pride but humility.
   A. The widow didn't let her poverty keep her from giving.
   B. The widow didn't know God's pleasure with her sacrifice.

Conclusion

Doris Hier in the *Christian Reader* tells a humbling story about her daughter. Her daughter worked in Chicago before she was married. One day on her way to work, a pan-handler stopped her to ask for a quarter. Hier wrote:

> Never one to cast judgment or ignore a need, she faced a dilemma. Looking straight into the man's eyes, she said, "I'm sorry but I don't have a quarter. I don't have any money to take the bus to work today." She was quite touched when the man, without saying a word, reached into his pocket and gave her a quarter.[1]

The one that had the least was willing to give sacrificially.

This is also the story of the widow in our passage. She gave to God from what little she had. Even though the amount she gave was small, her sacrifice touched the heart of God, just as the offering of a quarter by the beggar touched Doris Hier's daughter.

Have you learned the joy of giving sacrificially? Does your giving bring joy to the heart of God?

Endnotes

[1] Doris Hier, "The Generosity of a Begger," *Christian Reader*, Vol. 33, no. 5, as found in *www.preachingtoday.com* (accessed April 2, 2011).

Loose Tongue Disease

Proverbs 10:19
By Dr. Kent Spann

There is a disease that is an epidemic in our society, and the Center for Disease Control hasn't acknowledged it.

The Epidemic: Loose Tongue

Solomon says "when words are many, sin is not absent." There are many strains of loose tongue disease.

1. **Rumors and gossip** (Prov. 11:13)
2. **Idle talk** (Prov. 14:23)
3. **Lying** (Ps. 101:7; Prov. 21:6)
4. **Sharp tongues** (Ps. 140:1–3)
5. **Boasting** (Ps. 12:3, 4)

The sin of the Loose Tongue is Serious

The loose tongue inflicts deep wounds and pain in the lives of others, destroys relationships (Prov. 17:9), and ruins reputations. The sin does irreparable damage and brings judgment (Prov. 12:13; Matt. 12:36).

A little girl asked her mom, "Which is worse: to tell a lie, or to steal?' The mother replied that both were bad. The child replied, "I've been thinking about it lately, and I think it's worse to lie." "Why?" asked the mother. The child responded, "Well, if you steal, you can take it back or pay for it, but a lie is forever."

The Immunization: A Restrained Tongue

1. **We recognize the power of our tongue** (Prov. 18:21; James 3:1–12).
2. **We guard our tongue** (Prov. 13:3; Prov. 21:23; Ps. 39:1; Eph. 4:29; James 4:11; 1 Peter 3:10).

3. We find something positive to do or say (2 Thess. 3:11; 1 Tim. 5:13).

4. We weigh our words (Prov. 15:28).

5. We confess the sins of our loose lips (Lev. 19:16; Is. 6:5).

WEEK 29

How to be a Worshiper!

Psalm 51:14–17
By Dr. Vernon M. Whaley

Introduction

Psalm 51 is a fascinating account of how King David of Israel sinned against God. First, he committed adultery with another man's wife. Second, in an effort to cover up his sins, he had the woman's husband murdered. After the Prophet Nathan confronted the King about his sin, David sought God's forgiveness. Third, in so doing, He came to God as a broken person, asking God to restore the relationship they enjoyed together. He sought to once again be an active worshiper. How did David renew his worship with God? How did he become a worshiper?

According to Psalm 51:12–17, in order to be a Worshiper, one must be broken. What does it mean to be broken as a worshiper?

It Means Being Broken in Spirit.

1. **We must be broken of our attitude: what we think, the way we feel..**
2. **We must be broken of our arrogance: when we think we are better than the person next to us.**
3. **We must be broken of our small ambitions.** This involves what we think we want to be. Sometimes all we want is to be famous or wealthy. What God wants is for us to give ourselves to him in such a way that He controls who we are and what we become.

A good example of brokenness is when a horseback rider "breaks a horse." The rider places a bit in the horses mouth, uses reigns to determine the direction of the horse, sits on top of the horse (usually in a saddle), and controls where the horse is going and what they are going to do together. The horse's spirit is broken and, as a result, he submits to the rider's desire. So it is with

God. He wants our spirit broken. He wants us to submit to His control in our lives. When our spirit is broken, He will then show us His plans for our lives.

It Means Being Broken of Self

1. **We need to be broken over our sin.** This means that we rid ourselves of anything that separates us from fellowship with God. We repent of our sins. We turn away from that which we know is wrong.
2. **We need to be broken of our selfishness.** It is selfishness that compels us to only want what we want; only do what we want to do; and only include in our lives those things that will benefit us whenever we make decisions. It is when we live to please ourselves that we are serving our own ego and not the God that made us and loves us. God wants us to be broken of self.
3. **We need to be broken of our own desire to be self-sufficient.** This is when we think we don't need anyone else's help; we can do all that needs to be done in life by our own strength. In reality, God wants to be our sufficiency.

It Means Being Broken and Surrendered

I've met many a broken person who understands that their spirit is crushed. They also understand that they are broken of self. Many times, they come to me when they have spent their last dollar, and pushed away their families or sometimes their very best friend. But, even in their hurt, they cannot bring themselves to meet the final criteria for worship: surrender. We must be broken and surrendered. We need to be surrendered to the will of God for our lives, the working of God in our lives (Phil. 3:10), the wonder of God with our lives, and the worship of God for our lives.

Finally, God is in the business of using broken people. Jesus said that He "came to mend the broken heart" (Luke 4:17–21; Isa 61:1–3). The Psalmist says that God does "not want a sacrifice. . . or burnt offerings. The sacrifice pleasing to God is a broken spirit. God [does not] despise a broken and humble heart" (Ps. 51:16–18). He receives all that come to him in brokenness.

Conclusion

So, in order to be a true worshiper, we must be broken. When we experience brokenness, we will see that God is all we have. God is all that we need. God is all that we ever want!

ADDITIONAL SERMONS AND LESSON IDEAS

Redeeming Love

Ruth 4
By Dr. Adrian Rogers

Introduction

1. The book of Ruth began with weeping, but in this fourth and final chapter, joy has come (Ps. 30:5).
2. Remember that Ruth is a picture of the church, the bride of Christ. Boaz is a picture of the Lord Jesus Christ, our kinsman-redeemer.
3. The key word in Ruth 4 is "redemption" (Ruth 4:4).
4. In Ruth 4, we find three pictures of our Lord's gift of salvation.

Redeeming Love of Christ

1. A picture of our redeeming Lord (Ruth 4:1–6)
   A. Jesus is legally worthy.
      i. There are two laws from ancient Israel that come into play in Ruth 4:
         a. The law of the kinsman-redeemer (Lev. 25) said that, if a landowner went into bankruptcy and had to sell his land, a near relative (a kinsman-redeemer) could redeem that land and buy it back.
         b. The law of the Levirate marriage (Deut. 25) said that, if a married couple had no children and the husband died, then the man's brother was to take the man's wife, who was now a widow, marry her, and endeavor to have children with her in order to keep the man's name alive.

      ii. **Three things were necessary** in order for a man to be able to buy back the lost estate and to marry the widow who came with the estate where applicable:

      a. He had to have the legal qualifications.

      b. He had to have the money to buy it back.

      c. He had to be willing to buy it back.

      iii. Boaz, who represents our Lord, was legally worthy (Ruth 4:6).

         a. **The nearer kinsman who could not redeem represents Adam.** In Adam, we all die. The ten witnesses in Ruth 4:2 represent the Ten Commandments, which testify that our Adamic nature cannot save us.

         b. **Jesus is worthy and willing to redeem us** (Heb. 2:14; Rev. 5:1–9).

    B. **Jesus is lavishly wealthy (Ruth 2:1).** Jesus paid a greater price than Boaz paid: Jesus bought us back with His blood. (See 1 Peter 1:18, 19; 1 Peter 3:18; Ephesians 1:7; Revelation 5:9.)

    C. **Jesus is lovingly willing.**

      i. Boaz did not have to buy Ruth, nor did the Lord Jesus have to buy us.

      ii. We love Him because He first loved us (1 John 4:19).

2. **A picture of our renewed life (Ruth 4:7, 8)**

    A. **Ruth had three major problems, and without Christ, we share those same problems, as outlined in Ephesians 2:12, 13:**

      i. **Her past was cursed.** She was an alien from the commonwealth of Israel. Spiritually, she was born on the wrong side of the tracks (Deut. 23:3).

      ii. **Her present was crushed.** Ruth was a stranger to the things of God; she was without Christ.

      iii. **Her future was condemned.** Her future, without God, was hopeless.

    B. **The word *redeem* can mean "to purchase," "to buy back."** It can also mean "to buy out," "to take off the market place." It also means "to set free."

i. **When our Lord redeemed us, not only did He buy us, but He took us out of the market place; we are no longer for sale.** This speaks to our eternal security.

ii. **We are set free in Christ.**

C. **As was the custom, the nearer kinsman, who could not redeem, took off his shoe and handed it to Boaz (Ruth 4:8).**

i. **When Jesus paid for our sins, He took our place: He stands in our shoes.** As Boaz stood in the shoes of the nearer kinsman, Jesus stood in our shoes and paid the penalty for our sins.

ii. **Jesus became sin for us (2 Cor. 5:21).**

3. **A picture of our restored legacy (Ruth 4:10–17)**

A. **Ruth received a family (Ruth 4:10).** When we are saved, we become a part of the family of God.

B. **Ruth received a fortune (Ruth 4:10).** No longer is Ruth gleaning the fields; she *owns* the field. She shares in the wealth of Boaz. As Christians, we are joint heirs with Jesus.

C. **Ruth received fame (Ruth 4:11).** Even today, the name of Ruth is spoken with reverence. If we know Jesus, we will reign with Him forever.

D. **Ruth received fruitfulness (Ruth 4:11).** See John 15:16.

E. **Ruth received the future (Ruth 4:16, 17).** Ruth's son, Obed, was the grandfather of David, in the ancestry of our Lord Jesus Christ.

Conclusion

1. **Jesus bought us with a great price.**
2. **Just as Ruth was not ashamed of Boaz, neither should we be ashamed to proclaim that we belong to Jesus Christ.**

This sermon was aired on *Love Worth Finding* on March 21, 2010 and March 28, 2010.

Being Missional: Effectively Taking the Good News to All People

Acts 11:19–30
By Duane Floro

Introduction

To be missional is my calling. My relationship with Jesus Christ is personal and practical. I view the world around me differently than most because of the good news that is living within me.

Leading a Missional Life

Here are four steps to being missional:

1. **Advance the Kingdom.** Persecution or difficulty did not slow down the advancement; it accelerated the spreading of the Word (vv. 19–21).
2. **Provide encouragement.** What happened there encouraged other believers. When they witnessed it for themselves, they returned the favor by sharing what they knew with these new believers (vv. 22–24).
3. **Remain teachable.** The disciples taught in Antioch for a whole year. The evidence the people heard and understood is found in the latter part of verse 26: "The disciples were called Christians first at Antioch" (vv. 25–26).
4. **Be ready for life's transitions.** Even with the announcement of a coming famine, the believers did what believers do best: the church lived out the good news and met the needs (vv. 27–30)!

Conclusion

"Being missional" means more than hearing and receiving this message. It hinges upon how we live out" this message.

WEEK 30

The Day the Preachers Stopped Preaching

2 Chronicles 5:7–11; 6:2–11,40–41; 7:1–4
Dr. Vernon M. Whaley

Introduction

Students of the Great Awakening often tell us that, during the days leading up to an unusual time of revival or spiritual renewal, it is not unusual for God to move upon the hearts of His people. Sometimes, especially after weeks of home prayer meetings, 24-hour prayer vigils, and times of confession, revival would break out in the morning or evening services—even before the preacher would get up to preach. Often, when a song leader or soloists were in the middle of a song service, or at the end of an extended time of genuine singing of worship songs, right before beginning of the preaching, people would begin to walk to the front of the church and confess wrong doings, seek forgiveness of sin, and repent from various shortcomings. Many times, when these movements took place, the preacher would go ahead and extend the invitation to the entire congregation. The preacher did not get to preach. Such is the case with this most impressive account in 2 Chronicles 5.

The setting of 2 Chronicles is the dedication of the Temple. King David requested of the Lord the opportunity to build a house of worship for the people of Israel. God declined David's request. Instead, He told David that his son, Solomon, would build the temple. So, now the Temple was finished and everyone had met to dedicate it to the Lord.

Established was a place of worship. It was the new temple of God, a meeting place especially designated as the place of worship of Yahweh. The people meeting for worship included the priest, the preachers, musicians, the king, and the great assembly. The Bible tells us that all of the men, women, and children from each family in Israel met to worship. The preparation for worship involved sanctifying themselves for service to the Lord. The process of worship included singing, playing of instruments, shouting to the Lord, and praying.

So, what is it about their worship that makes this event so unique? How do you suppose we can see God work in our services in much the same way as He did in 2 Chronicles 5? God is still in the miracle-working business. He is still making his presence known to men and women—especially when they worship him in sincerity.

They Cultivated Unified Praise (5:13*a*)

They expressed their praise with one heart. The preachers, instrumentalists, families, and all that were in attendance, including the king, joined together in praise and worship. They worshiped with skill. They came with one voice. This is most unusual; the singers and the instrumentalists were "as one," and they sang with one voice—in unison, in one accord. Their ego was left outside the building, and God saw their sincere hearts.

They Crafted an Unselfish Praise (5:13*b*)

They exalted God with raised voices, bowed heads, and holy hearts. They sang to the Lord with hearts of thanksgiving. They praised and thanked the Lord by singing, "Blessed be the name of the Lord, may His mercy endure forever." They consciously gave God first place in their motives, manner, message, and methods. God was blessed, and He responded accordingly.

They Captured an Unexpected Presence (5:13, 14)

Third, because they cultivated unified praise and sought to craft unselfish praise, they were able to capture an unexpected presence of God. They actually experienced God's glory through their worship. In reality, the glory of the Lord was revealed because of their praise, and His glory overtook their ministry. The Bible says that the priest had to discontinue ministering to the Lord because the glory of the Lord filled the temple.

Solomon responded to God's presence by offering his own, very public time of prayer. Standing on a large platform constructed for this very purpose, Solomon praised God and gave the Lord first place in His worship (6:1–4).

Then, the King pledged to the Lord that *all the people, including himself as King, would be faithful to worship Yahweh all the days of their lives.* In His prayer, Solomon remembered God's goodness, recognized God's plan for the temple, and recognized God's place in the building (6:5–15). He reminded God of His purpose for the Temple (6:16–39) to be a place of healing, salvation, and worship. Finally, He asked God to help them as they practiced worship. Solomon simply invited God to take his "due resting place" (6:40–42). God responded by sending his power.

They Celebrated Undeniable Power (7:1–3)

Fourth, they celebrated the undeniable power of God. Everyone experienced the blessings of God because of their honest thanksgiving. The fire of God came down and consumed the altar. This was a rare endorsement by God of their worship. God was blessed by their honest, holy, and humble praise. This was the same fire that consumed the altar and sacrifice at the completion of the tabernacle. It was the same fire that came down when Elijah encountered and defeated the prophets of Baal. And, it was the very same kind of fire that came upon the disciples on the Day of Pentecost. God blessed the people with His power.

Conclusion

We have learned five things:

1. **Our success in public worship** is a direct reflection of our commitment to worshipping—in one accord, together—getting along with each other!
2. **Our success for genuine worship** replicates our heart motive for worship!
3. **Our success for acceptable worship** is not dependent upon ability or skill. No one is indispensable; God can do quite well without us!
4. **Our success for holy worship** exposes our own personal desire to see the glory of God revealed.
5. **Our success *in leading worship*** is in direct proportion to the presence of God upon our lives.

ADDITIONAL SERMONS AND LESSON IDEAS

The Unpardonable Sin

Matthew 12:22–32
By Dr. Adrian Rogers

Introduction

1. **What is the unpardonable sin?**
   A. The unpardonable sin is not some moral sin.
   B. The unpardonable sin is not intellectual sin.
   C. The unpardonable sin is not a verbal sin. God forgives blasphemy against God the Father and God the Son. The unpardonable sin can be committed without saying a word. The word *blaspheme* means "to speak hurtfully against;" but we can speak to God in prayer without saying words, and we can blaspheme God without saying words (Luke 6:45).
   D. The unpardonable sin is the blasphemy of the Holy Spirit.
2. **The blasphemy of the Holy Spirit**
   A. The unpardonable sin, the blasphemy of the Holy Spirit, is attributing to the devil the work of the Spirit of God. In this passage in Matthew 12, the Pharisees committed a three-fold sin.
   i. They sinned against redemption.
   ii. They sinned against reason (Matt. 12:24–26; Isa. 1:18).
   iii. They sinned against revelation (Matt. 12:28).
   B. The unpardonable sin, the blasphemy of the Holy Spirit, is a sin against light (Matt. 11:23–24; John 3:19).
3. **The consequences of the unpardonable sin**
   A. The deceiving power of this sin. A person who commits this sin opens himself up to deception. See 2 Thessalonians 2:11, 12; Romans 11:8.
   B. The deadening power of this sin. When a person commits this sin, something within him dies. See Hebrews 3:7, 8.

C. The damning power of this sin. When this sin is committed, it places a person beyond the pale of redemption. See Hebrews 6:4–6; Genesis 6:3.

Conclusion

If you desire to be saved, then you have not committed the unpardonable sin. See Revelation 22:17.

This sermon was aired on Love Worth Finding *on October 31, 2010.*

So, What do you See?

Genesis 13:14–18
By Duane Floro

Introduction

"Watch out for yourself, no one else will" has become the order of the day. What should one do to rise above the chaos? Abraham teaches a great lesson about "seeing." Despite strife within his family, he would not lose sight of God's purpose. He told his nephew Lot that there was no need for quarreling. The solution was not so much what was around them as what was within them.

Choices

1. Your choices are set in your heart before you see with your eyes (v. 14).
   A. Abraham chooses an altar (v. 18).
   B. Lot chooses an ambition.
2. Your choices reveal the world from God's perspective (v. 15).
   A. By giving up the least, Abraham found the most.
   B. By taking what seemed the most, Lot found the least.
3. Your choices affect those who come after you (vv. 16–17).
   A. Numerous lives are touched as one walks by faith with Him.
   B. Maximum impact occurs as one walks by faith with Him.

Conclusion

Paul the Apostle says, "For now we see only a reflection as in a mirror; then we shall see face to face. Now I know in part; then I shall know fully, even as I am fully known" (1 Cor. 13:12).

WEEK 31

SERIES: ENOUGH

Enough to Transfer Us to the Heavenlies

Colossians 3:1–4
By Dr. Bill Elliff

Introduction

I have had the amazing privilege of raising eight children. There's been a lot of love, and a lot of discipline! One day, I had to spank my firstborn son. After I had taken care of business, he looked up at me with soulful eyes and said, "Dad, could I rewind that and do it gooder?"

I think that most people come to church because they want to rewind it and do it "gooder," to really find significant change in their lives. Are you like that? Would you like genuine, substantive change in your life?

Paul knew how to see the miracle of change happen. Under God's inspiration, he unveiled some amazing truth that shows us exactly how we can change.

In the first part of the Colossian letter, Paul has been telling us about the sufficiency of Christ. Now, he's going to show us how substantive change can happen in our daily lives because of who Christ is and what He has done for us.

Change begins by realizing something amazing about yourself.

Read Colossians 3:1–4.

1. **If you are in Christ, you are a powerful person.** Paul explains what has happened to us as believers in four amazing statements.

   A. **You have died (Col. 3:3).** Who you used to be without Christ no longer exists. You will never again be a person without Christ.

   B. **You have been resurrected with Christ (Col. 3:1).** You have been moved to a new location and have a new power, which is the life of Christ in you.

C. **Your life is hidden with Christ in God (Col. 3:1).** You're forever pardoned

   i. **You're forever protected.**

   ii. **You're forever a part of Christ.** Christ is your life. Colossians 3:4 says, "Christ, who is your life." I have Christ, He has me. All He is, I have.

     If you are pardoned and have all power because you have all of Christ, any change is possible in your life!

     You may not realize this or be experiencing it, but just because you're living below what God has planned for you, don't blame or doubt God. If Christ is your life, anything's possible! But there's more.

2. **You are a powerful person, who has been transferred to a perfect place.** Again, Paul helps us see this through four more powerful ideas.

  A. **Christ is seated in another world.**

  B. **You are in Christ.** This means that, where He is, you are too!

  C. **You temporarily live in two worlds.** You now have dual citizenship. This is not just a theoretical truth, but a practical one. You have access to both of these worlds and live in both at the same time.

   i. **Earthly kingdom: broken, sinful, unsatisfying.**

   ii. **Heavenly kingdom: perfect, sinless, sufficient.**

  D. **One day, this will all be revealed, and everyone will see that you are with Christ in glory.** The 1999 movie *The Matrix* was a fascinating picture of a man living in two worlds. The main character, Neo, discovered that the world he lived in was a simulated reality. Behind that world was another world of reality.

     Similarly, we now live in two worlds. Both of these worlds, however, are very real. The kingdom of heaven is not a dream. Just because it is not physical does not mean it is not real. And it is a world in which the believer can now live and operate. This is why God calls His followers "aliens" (1 Peter 1:1).

3. **If you are in Christ, you are a powerful person who has been transferred to a perfect place, so don't go slumming!**

Slumming is a great theological phrase! The literal definition of *slumming* is "to visit slums, especially from curiosity; to frequent a place. . . considered to be low in social status."[1] It means to go to places that are beneath your social standards.

Paul tells us to do two things to prevent slumming. He says that we must keep setting our minds on things above, and keep seeking things above (Col. 3:1, 2).

The classic book *Oliver Twist* by Charles Dickens tells the story of a boy separated from his mother at birth. He grew up in the slavery of a work-house and then lived in the slums. Finally, through a strange turn of events, Oliver is taken in by a man who he tried to rob. He is a man who has everything this boy would ever need. At the end of the story, it is revealed that this is actually Oliver's true home, and his biological grandfather.

Why would Oliver ever go back to live in the slums once he discovered the truth about his family? Why would he eat porridge if he could have a feast, eating scraps when he could savor the riches of his true home? He would not set his mind in the slums or seek those things in that other world. In fact, he would do everything in his power to help others to come out of that world into the next.

We have a new home.

Again read Colossians 3:1–4.

This is where we live, and the realization of what we now have is the basis for lasting life-change. C. S. Lewis was right when he said:

> We are half-hearted creatures, fooling about with drink and sex and ambition when infinite joy is offered us, like an ignorant child who wants to go on making mud pies in a slum because he cannot imagine what is meant by the offer of a holiday at the sea. We are far too easily pleased.[2]

Conclusion

This amazing truth all begins with one important word in verse 1: *if*. That word transports us to another world. Gives us power to change. Causes us to live in another dimension. Opens the doors to our true home and the riches of our Father.

"If you are in Christ." Are you?

Endnotes

[1] "Slumming." *Dictionary.com Unabridged*. *http://dictionary.reference.com/browse/slumming* (accessed January 13, 2011).

[2] C. S. Lewis, *The Weight of Glory* (New York: MacMillan, 1949), 2.

ADDITIONAL SERMONS AND LESSON IDEAS

A Prayer for America

Daniel 9:1–8
By Dr. Adrian Rogers

Introduction

1. Prayer is our greatest resource.
2. God is our sure defense and our hope.
3. God does bring judgment upon sin.
4. Only believing and repenting prayer can hold back the floodtides of judgment and sin, and release the cleansing power of the Lord Jesus upon our personal lives and our nation.

How to Pray for America

1. We are to pray with serious concentration (Dan. 9:3)
   A. Prayer and fasting is the order of the day (Dan. 9:3; Matt. 6:5; 6:16)
   B. What is fasting?
       i. Fasting is going without food or water and other pleasures for a spiritual purpose.
       ii. Avoid the following when fasting:
         a. Exhibitionism.
         b. Legalism. Don't get the idea that you can buy a blessing from God.
         c. Ritualism.
         d. Asceticism.
         e. Egotism.
         f. Extremism.
         g. Bragging about fasting.

     iii. If you have health concerns, talk with your doctor before fasting. See Zechariah 7:5.

  C. Six things that fasting will do:

     i. Fasting strengthens your prayer life (Joel 2:12; Jer. 29:13).

     ii. Fasting subdues self (Ezek. 16:49).

     iii. Fasting stays the judgment of God (Jonah 3:5, 10; Jer. 18:7–8).

     iv. Fasting stops the enemies of God (2 Chron. 20:3, 4, 29).

     v. Fasting seeks guidance (Acts 13:2).

     vi. Fasting shatters strongholds (Isa. 58:6).

2. We are to pray with steadfast confidence (Dan. 9:4).

  A. Glance at your problem.

  B. Gaze at your God. See Daniel 9:7, 9, 14, 20, 21.

3. We are to pray with sincere confession (Dan. 9:4–14).

  A. Daniel confessed personal sins.

  B. Daniel confessed national sins. See Romans 3:23; 1 Peter 4:17; 1 John 1:9.

4. We are to pray with spiritual concern (Dan. 9:17–19).

  A. When Daniel prayed, he was not merely trying to get out of difficulty.

  B. When we pray, we need to pray for the glory of God. See Matthew 6:9–13.

This sermon was aired on Love Worth Finding *September 19 and 26, 2010.*

What Gets you up in the Morning?

1 Peter 1:18–19
By Duane Floro

Introduction

Remember what made it difficult to get up in the morning when you were young? For me, it was the knowledge that I had to go to school. I knew that it was important, but I would stay under the covers until the very last minute. But on the special days when my dad would take me with him to his office, I would rise at his first call. I guess it didn't hurt that I knew we would stop for breakfast on the way. It was this little boy's dream to spend that time with his father. My day was energized by the opportunity to be with my dad . Observe what energized Peter to get up and go.

Alert Mind (v. 13–16)

1. **Clear thinking**
2. **Transformation living**

Amazing Company (vv. 17–19)

1. **Enjoy being around Him.**
2. **Enjoy being with others who love Him, too.**

Abundant Gift (vv. 20–21)

1. **Jesus paid the price.**
2. **The gift is eternal.**
3. **All hope is found in Him.**

Conclusion

Job records how this truth is nothing new. It enabled Job to get up from his pain, suffering, and loss to face a new day.

> I know that my redeemer lives, and that in the end he will stand on the earth.
>
> —Job 19:25

WEEK 32

SERIES: ENOUGH

Enough to build a Heavenly Life!

Colossians 3:5–11
By Dr. Bill Elliff

Introduction

Dual citizenship is a fascinating situation where a person can have all the rights and privileges of a citizen in more than one nation. How can you gain citizenship in a country that is not your native country? It can occur when:

- at least one parent is a citizen of a foreign country.
- your birth takes place in another country's territory.
- you marry a native citizen in their country.

What is the best description of a true follower of Christ? It is a person who carries dual citizenship. He belongs to the kingdom of this world and the kingdom of heaven. One nation is amazingly superior to the other, but Christ followers are citizens of both, nonetheless. And they can function fully in either.

This dual citizenship is what gives you the ability to be conformed to the image of God and overcome sin. If you are in Christ, you are a powerful person who has been transferred into a perfect world. You no longer have to live merely by the power and philosophy of this world.

But how is this accomplished practically? We now live in the heavenlies, but how do we become heavenly in our behavior? Read Colossians 3:5–11.

Looking for More in All the Wrong Places

Sin always happens when we look for more in all the wrong places. In verse 5, Paul describes the progression of sin takes our lives.

1. **Covetous:** we want more.

2. **Evil desire:** we want more of wrong, evil things.

3. **Passion:** we become consumed and willing to do anything to gain the "more" that we desire.

4. **Impurity:** we begin thinking uncleanly, dirtying our minds with thoughts and lust in this direction.

5. **Immorality:** we engage in unlawful behavior of any kind. *Immorality* is not just a sexual word.

6. **Idolatry:** we worship any false god. Examples include:

   A. **Hedonism:** I want more pleasure from this world.

   B. **Materialism:** I want more stuff from this world.

   C. **Fame:** I want more recognition from this world.

   Think about the sin or habit that you have the greatest struggle with and walk through the progression we've just mentioned. Do you want more than what Christ is providing? Has that want led to desire of evil things? Have you become more passionate in that desire? Has this led to impure thoughts and immoral or unlawful actions? And now, do you find yourself idolizing that sin and letting it take God's rightful place?

   To live a heavenly life, you must recognize this progression, but a further step is needed.

Overcoming Sin

Sin must be murdered, or it will murder you. Paul says in verse 5 that we must "put to death all that is earthly." This is a strong, violent, aggressive term. We are to murder, execute, and get rid of sin. It stresses a deliberate and determined action.

This implies continuous attention. It means dealing brutally with sin until it's dead to us. But why is it necessary to "put to death all that is earthly?"

1. **Because sin ruins lives and brings judgment.** Sins are things in which we "once walked" (v. 7) and which caused the "wrath of God" to be upon us. As believers, we are no longer under God's wrath. Now, as believers, why would we indulge in the very things that God hates and judges?

Do you realize that the very sins you are looking to in this world are not solving the "wanting more" problem in your life? In fact, sin is killing you, ruining your life and the lives of others, and it is worthless.

2. **Because you can.** Christ commands us to do three things to rid ourselves of sin that He couldn't ask of us if it couldn't be done. These are:

A. Put it to death (v. 5).

B. Put them all away (v. 7).

C. Don't lie (v. 8).

Now, why does God say this so simply? He doesn't give the motivation, but just says, "Do it!" He has already told us the motivational key in the first two verses of Colossians 3. We have died and now live in heaven. We live in two nations. We are to keep looking around in heaven. As we do, the things of this earth will seem worthless and easy to relinquish.

Amazing Transformation

As you put to death all that is earthly, something amazing happens. When the earthly falls away, the image of God emerges. Paul reminds us in verse 10 that we are to put on the "new self who is being renewed to a true knowledge after the image of its creator." Look at this progression into God's image:

1. **We keep looking around us in the heavenlies and gain "true knowledge"** (v. 10). We see that Christ is enough. We see the beauty of the new kingdom versus the ugliness of the kingdom of this world.

2. **We put to death all that is earthly.** We gladly lay down our sin.

3. **As we lay down our sin, the image and likeness of Christ emerges!**

Conclusion

Do you know how to get an old bone away from a dog? Don't reach down and pull it away. You will pull back a handless arm! The solution is simple: place a steak beside the old bone and the dog will gladly relinquish that which is worthless for what is more valuable.

Turn your eyes into the heavenlies. Keep your focus there, and you will find yourself gladly choosing the "more" that only Christ can give!

ADDITIONAL SERMONS AND LESSON IDEAS

Let the Fire Fall

1 Kings 18:1–39
By Dr. Adrian Rogers

Introduction (1 Kings 18:22)

1. The time of 1 Kings were dark days in Israel: days of apostasy, apathy, and horrible sin.
2. The prophet Elijah told the people to make up their minds and decide whom they would follow: either the Lord God or the false idol known as Baal. All of the people gathered at Mount Carmel, where they built an altar and placed a sacrifice upon it. Elijah then directed the people to pray, and the God who answered with fire, Elijah said, "Let him be God."
3. We, too, need revival fire (Matt. 28:20; 2 Chron. 7:14)

Let the Fire Fall

1. The enemies of revival (1 Kings 18:3–22)
   A. The compromisers represented by Obadiah (1 Kings 18:3–6).
      i. Obadiah was looking for grass to feed the herds when he should have been praying for rain. He was trying to prop things up. Obadiah was trying to get by without repentance.
      ii. Are we compromisers today?
         a. Was there ever a time when you loved Jesus more than you love Him now?
         b. Do you still have the joy of your salvation?
         c. Do you remember specific times when your prayers were being answered, but now your prayer life is weak?
         d. Is there anything about your life that is different from that of the world?

     e. Do you love to feed on the Word of God?

     f. Do you think that you've done all that God wants you to do?

B. The corrupt represented by Ahab and Jezebel (1 Kings 18:17–18). See 1 Kings 16:30 and 1 John 4:4.

C. The confused represented by the people (1 Kings 18:19–21).

     i. What is there in you that is so different that it would bring conviction to those who straddle the fence spiritually?

     ii. What is there in you that would cause your neighbor to ask, "What does this mean?" (Acts 2:12)

D. The competition represented by the priests of Baal (1 Kings 18:22). See 1 John 4:4.

2. The elements of revival (1 Kings 18:30–37)

A. The solidarity of God's people (1 Kings 18:30–31). See Psalm 133:1.

B. The separation of God's people from the world (1 Kings 18:32). God wants a holy people (James 4:4).

C. The sacrifice of Jesus Christ (1 Kings 18:33). See Revelation 12:11 and John 12:31.

D. The supernatural power of God (See 1 Kings 18:33–35). See Isaiah 44:3.

E. The strength of believing prayer (1 Kings 18:36–37). See John 12:28.

3. The evidence of revival (1 Kings 18:38, 39)

The fire fell

1. Fire consumes (1 Kings 18:38).
2. Fire convicts (1 Kings 18:38).
3. Fire converts (1 Kings 18:39).

This sermon aired on Love Worth Finding *May 16, 2010 and May 23, 2010.*

Life's Crossroads

Numbers 13
By Duane Floro

Introduction

The Israelites found themselves so close to reaching their prize. They had traveled far and experienced much along the way. However, the prize was not possession of a land; instead, the prize was the Israelites being possessed by their God. Times of decision are dependent on our faith that helps determine our direction. I remember a "crossroad" experience in my life where I sought the Lord's leadership. In the midst of seeking to obey Him, I heard the Lord say, "I have heard you, I will allow you to choose, I have much to teach you on either path." It is not a place, but a person: the Lord Himself.

Crossroads Stretch Us

1. **We better understand God.** Moses found the Lord to be "The Great I Am."
2. **We better understand His purposes.** For the Israelites, it is the message of "redemption."

Crossroads Send Us

1. **We experience the journey personally.**
2. **We leave the bondage for the liberty.**

Crossroads secure us

1. **He continues to conform us into His likeness.**
2. **He promises to bring us into His presence for eternity.**

Conclusion

Crossroads should not paralyze, but should mobilize the people of faith toward God's wonderful plan to the prize of His land of promise.

WEEK 33

SERIES: ENOUGH

Enough to build a Heavenly Church!

Colossians 3:12–17
By Dr. Bill Elliff

Introduction

What in the world is this thing called "the church?"

- A social club?
- A religious clique?
- A hospital where we try to get healthy?
- A seminar to learn a few how-to's?
- A religious exercise to appease God?

In fact, the church is a microcosmic picture of heaven, designed to entice others to enter. Each church is to be a light in the middle of a crooked and perverse generation to illustrate that there is a better community. God has called us to experience and enjoy heaven in these communities now so others can join us.

Read Colossians 3:12–17

The New, Heavenly Community

The church is not a random group of people who have decided to join in a community. Paul uses three important words to describe us. God has called us:

1. **Chosen (Col. 3:12):** It is God's intent and design that have brought us together. For distinct reasons, God desires each of us to be a part of this community.
2. **Holy (Col. 3:12):** You are different. We are new people with Christ in us and we have the capacity to live differently.

3. **Beloved** (Col. 3:12): We are people who are loved and have love. The church has a new, God-given capacity to love like no other community on earth.

Equipped for a Purpose

God has called us to enjoy heaven now because of our new status within His church. Every day, we set our mind on things above, look into heaven, and pray that God's kingdom will come and that God's will be done on earth as it is in heaven.

The Earthly Community

We become an earthly community that is part of God.

1. **We are clothed in His love** (Col. 3:12–14). Every day, we ask a simple question: "What am I supposed to wear today?" Different occasions demand different outfits. God's love is what everyone in the church is to put on; it will cause them to experience and illustrate heaven. This is the list of the clothing of a follower of Christ:

A. **Compassionate hearts: we are to put on deep understanding of the needs and sorrows of others.**

B. **Kindness: we treat each other with goodness and grace.** Compassion is the feeling, but kindness is the action.

C. **Humility: we are to clothe ourselves with an accurate view of ourselves and others.**

D. **Meekness: we treat others as we want to be treated, because we are clothed in humility.** Be gentle with each other!

E. **Patience: we "suffer long," and we are willing to endure a lot with others—even those who hurt us.**

F. **Forbearance: we bear complaints for a long time without retaliation.**

G. **Forgiveness: we make the choice to release a debt by faith for the glory of God in this community because we have been forgiven.** We are never more like heaven than when we forgive.

H. **Love: we are bonded by His love that unites us and makes us perfect.** This is the ultimate affection of heaven!

2. **We are ruled by His peace (Col. 3:15).** Peace is to act as an umpire when there is an infraction. In heaven, nothing disturbs this peace! We can enjoy peace with each other as we live in the heavenlies and bring this peace down to earth.

3. **We are enriched by His word (Col. 3:16).** In this holy community, we can let the Word of God be at home in us. It brings all the riches of wisdom and knowledge to every situation and relationship. We are to "teach and admonish one another." Why is this community so wonderful? Because the Word of God moves, directs, and refreshes us.

4. **We are overwhelmed by His songs (Col. 3:16).** In such a loving community, we are so overwhelmed by the love of God that we can't help but sing with gratitude.

This is what God wants the church to enjoy each day! It is what you have been chosen and set apart for. But this is not only for our glorious enjoyment, but for a greater purpose.

A Picture of Heaven

God has called us to enjoy heaven now, so others can join us! Paul reminds us that we live in this heavenly community with heavenly relationships for a higher agenda. "Whatever we do," he says, "do all in the name of the Lord Jesus" (Col. 3:17).

A national ambassador is one who represents a different country. He is directed to do everything in the name of that country and for the good of that country. He is to be so effective that those he reaches would even desire to live in that country.

As we walk in these heavenly relationships in the church, we are ambassadors for our King. Our new nation should be a picture of heaven so enticing that others say, "I would love to be a part of that community."

Conclusion

What would it take for this picture of heaven to be lived out in our church? We cannot change the whole church, but we can begin by cooperating with

God in our own lives. We must fix our eyes on heaven each day, letting God's kingdom come into all of our relationships.

The lives of others are at stake. God has called us to enjoy heaven in our relationships so that the world can be drawn to this eternal community!

ADDITIONAL SERMONS AND LESSON IDEAS

Running from God

Jonah 1:1–3
By Phil Newton

1. **Introduction:** A prophet of Israel would be called to preach a message of judgment in the midst of his enemies.
2. **The prophet rejected his obligation of the divine call.**
3. **God does not take the prophet's life, but preserves him in the most unusual way.**
4. **An entire, wicked metropolis would humbly bow in repentance before the simple message of the prophet and plead for the mercy of God.**
5. **The success of the prophet's message is met with unmeasured despondency.**

But the book of Jonah, though full of surprises, is not a book *about* surprises. Nor is it a book about a great fish, nor a reluctant prophet. It is chiefly a book about God. Jonah helps us to understand the greatness of God's mercy and the extent of His missionary heart.

1. **The privilege of God's messenger (1:1):** God spoke to Jonah with the same authority with which He spoke to Isaiah. He gave the prophet a message, and he had the responsibility to faithfully deliver that message without diluting or changing it.

The normal pattern for prophets was to deliver oracles to their own nation, but the obligation of the prophet was to go and speak wherever God demanded. In this case, the Lord sent His messenger to Nineveh.

2. **The mercy shown to the wicked (1:2)**

A. **God's discovery:** Nineveh's wickedness drew the attention of the living God. God's discovery of sin is the uncovering of sin. The omniscient God knows the depth of our sin. But when a people's wickedness "has come up before [God]," then you know that He has uncovered it so that a people might understand their wretchedness before God.

B. God's action: As God discovered Nineveh's sin, He also sent His messenger to call them to repentance. The book of Jonah is a story of God's action to save unworthy and uninterested sinners.

3. **The folly of running from God (1:3):** So begins the foolish journey of Jonah in his attempt to side-step the divine will. This tells us much about Jonah. But perhaps more importantly, it tells us about ourselves. For at the root of our own lives, we have some Jonah-like tendencies.

A. Character of man disclosed: God speaks through His word to us, and we immediately run through a hundred excuses for why we cannot do what God has imposed upon our lives!

B. Character of God revealed: "But Jonah" is not the end of the story! Instead, we see the patience of God addressing the unwillingness of Jonah and making him *willing* to go to Nineveh in obedience to God. God wins out, as He always does. In the process, He drenches the paths of our lives with His truth and grace.

Conclusion

Do you find yourself trying to run from God? Where will you flee from His presence? Or better yet, why would you even attempt to flee the presence of God? May you know the joy and utter delight of walking in obedience to the living God through Jesus Christ the Lord.

Preached at South Woods Baptist Church in Memphis Tennessee, February 7, 1999.

To Serve Like Jesus

John 13:1–12
By Duane Floro

Introduction

Prior to Jesus' journey to the cross, He sat down with His disciples for dinner. While the meal was being served, Jesus stood up to wash the disciple's feet. We know this story because of the response by Peter, but the greater truth seems to be in a towel and a basin.

The Towel and Basin

The end of verse 1 states that "Jesus wanted to show them the full extent of His love" because:

1. **His Time:** "Jesus knew that the time had come" (v. 1)
2. **His Opposition:** "the devil had already prompted Judas...to betray Jesus" (v. 2)
3. **His Purpose:** "He had come from God and was returning to God" (v. 3)
   In verse 12, He explains His actions to the disciples, saying that this is:

1. **A model to follow:** "wash one another's feet."
2. **An identification to the world:** "you should do as I have done."
3. **A blessing to all who do this:** "Now that you know these things, you will be blessed if you do them."

Conclusion

For such a time as this, in the face of all your opposition, Jesus has given you a *purpose* to glorify Him as you serve like Jesus!

WEEK 34

SERIES: ENOUGH

Enough to build a Heavenly Home!

Colossians 3:18–21
By Dr. Bill Elliff

Introduction

All kids have a fear of something. Ours have a fear of cleaning their rooms. Around our house, we call cleaning day the "day of reckoning." That is the moment when their bedrooms have gone beyond the scope of recognition, all semblance of order has passed, and I am really fed up. I have a simple system. It's worked now for over 33 years. I enter their room—with a minimum of grace and maximum of truth—with two trash bags in hand.

"Today, my child, is the day," I calmly say. "This trash bag is for trash. The other bag is for garage sale items. Everything, except for a very few items that I deem worthy of saving, will go into one of these bags." We push everything into the middle of the room, sit down, and go through it together. Together we bring about order to their rooms.

God loves order, too. When He brings order, it's absolutely breathtaking. He brought order out of emptiness in creation. He built the first home and it was beautiful and productive, but sin brought disorder, and now God longs to bring that order back into our home.

When you peer into heaven, you see perfect order in the heavenly home, and this is exactly what God wants to bring to earth in your home!

Order from Chaos

Read Col. 3:18–21. God wants to bring heavenly order to earthly chaos. Chaos fills many homes: competition, selfishness, anger, disrespect, unforgiveness, bitterness, and hopelessness. But when you look up into God's family in the heavenlies, what do you see?

1. **Sacrificial Love:** In heaven, there is the perfect Groom, Jesus Christ. He is a strong leader who is perfect in His love and willing to do anything to care for His bride.

2. **Empowering Roles:** In heaven, there is a perfect bride, the church. She is perfect in her adoration of her husband. She honors Him and lives, with all of her gifts, to magnify Him and submit to His leadership.

3. **Grace-filled Training:** In heaven, there is a perfect Father who continually trains His children with the perfect balance of truth and grace.

4. **Humble Obedience:** In heaven, every child recognizes his absolute need of his Father and instantly, gladly obeys everything He says.

Can you see into the heavenly home? It is the precise example of what God wants to bring into your earthly home. But how can this happen?

It Always Starts with You

God wants to bring heavenly order to earthly chaos through you. You may be saying, "My home is anything but that, but I'm just waiting for my spouse/parents/kids to start!" This statement is a silly word game, a sign of spiritual immaturity, and a recipe for continued and endless disaster.

We should be saying, "I don't know about my spouse, but I'm going to do everything I can to bring God's kingdom order into our home." Each member of the family has roles that, if followed, will bring godly order.

1. **Husbands should become loving, understanding leaders.**
   A. *Love* is the husband's divine calling to bless his wife and glorify God by continually choosing against his own desires to save, protect, and develop his wife.
   B. "Do not be embittered" means that the husband must continue to forgive his wife. Harbored hurt always leads to bitterness.
2. **Wives should become respectful, aggressive helpers.**
   A. "Be subject" implies the divine calling of a wife to embrace and support God's divine order for the home and to put her husband in the best possible position to lead through her honor and service.

This doesn't mean that wives are not to speak the truth in love, but beneath every speech should be the desire to do everything to help the husband be a great leader, thus showing the greater picture of Christ and His submissive bride, the church.

When is submission not in order? When a husband asks his wife to violate a clear, stated command of Scripture. But, even if there are occasions where a wife must stand against her husband's leadership, this should be done in such a way in which the husband knows with all his heart that his wife longs to help him be a great leader!

B. *Fitting* **is the word used of a nice outfit that complements the wife well and makes her look amazingly attractive.** Submission and respect adorn a wife like no earthly clothes.

3. **Children become humble, obedient learners.** Children are to do what they are asked to do with the right attitude, when their parents ask them. Children are to obey "in everything" because this is "well-pleasing to the Lord." An obedient spirit indicates a humble heart that recognizes the difficult responsibility a parent carries.

4. **Fathers become grace-filled, patient trainers.** Why does Paul only mention fathers? Because fathers play a mighty role in displaying heaven as they illustrate the nature and character of God.

A. **Fathers should never** *provoke* **the children,** which means to rouse to needless irritation.

B. **Fathers should not** *discourage* **their children** in a way that causes them to lose heart or feel that there is nothing they can do to please their dads. We can discourage by:

i. **Continually using the past**

ii. **Never really forgiving**

iii. **Not letting up in a conversation**

iv. **Repeating a command or rebuke over and over again**

v. **Making demands that are unreasonable**

vi. **Not listening**

vii. **Not balancing discipline with affirmation**

viii. **Comparing to other siblings**

ix. Not giving sufficient expressions of love

x. A sinful, merely earthly dad is domineering and ungrateful.

This brings hell, not heaven, into the home.

Conclusion

A child's building blocks can either be a chaotic mess in the middle of a room or be joined together to create a beautiful structure. God has given us the building blocks for our homes, and they are perfectly joined together—each in their proper place in heaven. If we will cooperate with Him, He will make our homes heavenly!

ADDITIONAL SERMONS AND LESSON IDEAS

Found Out!

Jonah 1:4–9
By Phil Newton

Introduction

Do others know you as you really are? Perhaps that is an uncomfortable question. Many people work diligently to mask the real person within.

Jonah had done a great job of hiding his relationship with God. But in the revelation of God in the stormy sea and in Jonah's confession, Jonah's mask was removed. The revelation of God exposed his heart. as it also exposes our own hearts.

1. **The backslider: identity concealed (1:3, 4).** Jonah, the believer, was a back-slidden man. Backsliding comes in two forms. First, the Bible uses this term, or similar ones, to describe the person who makes a pretense of true religion but gives way to sin. The second form of backsliding involves the believer who has first entered into a genuine relationship with the Lord but for some reason has grown cold in his Christianity and has allowed the patterns of his old life to slip into the forefront of his life.

   A. Sleep of despair. The Christian backslider can never be comfortable with his condition. The man who has truly known the grace of God in his life finds himself in the most miserable of positions: being at odds with the God who has shown him grace through Christ.

   B. Mistaken identity. The last thing Jonah wanted was for the men on the ship to discover that he belonged to Jehovah and that he was running away. A backslidden prophet is nothing to be proud of.

   C. Plight of prayerlessness. One thing the backslider does not want to do is pray. Yet this was the very thing which the ship captain called upon Jonah to do.

2. **The world: identity revealed (1:5).** Standing in sharp contrast to Jonah is the picture of the world as seen through the lives of the ship's crew.

A. **Fear of death**

B. **Errant theology.** The unbeliever has an errant theology. His whole understanding of God is twisted, distorted, shaped by his culture, or even by his own way of thinking.

C. Inadequate religion. The religion of the sailors did not work. They tried everything they could. They exercised all the religious practices they knew. But nothing worked. Their religion proved inadequate for the crisis they faced.

3. **The Lord: identity unveiled (1:9)**

A. **God of the storm.** The word used, *hurled*, is the same used to describe a soldier throwing his spear accurately at its target. And God did have a target: His rebellious child, Jonah.

B. Transcendent Creator. Jonah wanted the sailors to know that his God was not just another local, tribal deity. This was not an ordinary god made of stone or sticks! He is a God who is beyond us, "The Lord God of heaven."

C. God of His people

Conclusion

Have you been found out this day? Has the Spirit of God exposed your own heart being in rebellion against God? He takes no prisoners. Either you belong to Him, or you are under His judgment.

Preached at South Woods Baptist Church in Memphis Tennessee, February 14, 1999.

Understanding Biblical Faith

Hebrews 11
By Duane Floro

Introduction

I enjoy movies with the sole champion in the middle of the arena surrounded by the opponent. The music builds and the audience holds their breath awaiting the hero's action. We may think, "If I were the one before the crowds, I would make the right choice." However, most of us live the majority of our days witnessed only by a few. What then will guide our actions?

The Definition: Hebrews 11:1 Faith is:

1. "confidence in what we hope for. . ."
2. ". . . assurance about what we do not see."
3. Remembering that the "object" of our faith is significant.

The Details: Hebrews 11:3–6: Three Examples of "Biblical Faith"

1. From the beginning, God was the Creator (v. 3).
2. From the beginning, the offering that confirms trust (v. 4).
3. From our lifestyle (v. 5).
4. Two principles: ". . . must believe that He exists;" and (2) ". . . He rewards those who earnestly seek Him" (v. 6).

The Demonstration: Hebrews 12:1–3: The Evidence that we have Grasped This

1. Rid oneself of that which hinders.
2. Focus on Jesus.
3. Do not stop now!

Conclusion

May we live out our faith for an audience of one—the One who loves us so.

WEEK 35

Entering the Kingdom

Matthew 5:1–5
By Dr. Bill Elliff

Introduction

I had an uncle who was old and gruff. It seemed that he didn't like anyone, but for some reason, he liked me—although I was afraid of him. He took me to the toy store once, and invited me to get whatever I wanted. I was shocked. But, as I thought about it, I knew that his offer couldn't possibly be real (because of what I thought I knew of him). So, I made one of the most serious errors of my early life and chose a thirty-nine cent water gun. For years, I've kicked myself. I had all the riches of a toy store offered from one who loved me, but I walked away with almost nothing!

You don't know what you're missing. Do you realize that there is a whole kingdom waiting for you with all its riches? But it may be that, because of fear or disbelief, you have never entered and received all that the King has to offer.

What does it take to enter the kingdom of God? No one knew better than Jesus. In the beginning of the Sermon on the Mount (which is the manifesto of the new kingdom), He tells us.

Entering the Kingdom

Read Matthew 5:1–5. To enter the forgotten kingdom, we must see our need so greatly that we gladly bow.

1. **We must see our need (Matt. 5:3).** What does it mean to have "poverty of spirit?" Obviously, it does not mean that we are materially impoverished. It implies that we understand our need—our total depravity and desperate emptiness without Christ. Romans 9:3–12 is a tremendous, compelling statement of our need. But we don't believe this. We think we're rich, sufficient, and completely capable of building our own kingdom.

Read Revelation 3:17, 18, which is Christ's wake-up call also to recognize our need. What is the difference between a man who recognizes his spiritual poverty and one who doesn't?

Jesus told the story of a Pharisee and a tax collector in Luke 18:9–14. The Pharisee wrapped his robes around himself and was thankful that he was good. He had need of nothing. The sinful tax collector could not even lift his eyes to heaven, but kept beating his breast and saying, "Lord, be merciful to me, a sinner." Jesus then reminded them that only this man went home right with God. Why? He recognized his spiritual poverty.

You'll never be interested in entering the kingdom until you first see your need.

2. **We must see our needs so greatly (Matt. 5:4).** Next in the progression is mourning. This does not mean grieving from the loss of a loved one. God does comfort those who are mourning, but that is not the context of this passage. Look at the progression. Blessed are those who see their need so greatly that they mourn.

Do you know that we are commanded to mourn? James 4:9 says, "Be wretched and mourn and weep. Let your laughter be turned to mourning and your joy to gloom." This verse is in the context of a call for repentance and holiness. But it begins by seeing our sin and need so greatly that we mourn.

In Paul's letter to the Corinthians, he rebuked them for allowing a sinful man to continue his fellowship with the church without the church warning him of his sin. Paul encouraged them to take action. The Corinthians did, and the man repented. In Paul's second letter to the Corinthians, he reminds them to restore the man. In 2 Corinthians 7:9–11, Paul explains that he was glad that his rebuke brought a godly sorrow that led to repentance without regrets.

Have you ever had repentance with regrets? You hear a sermon and feel somewhat sorry for your sin. You walk away, determined to do better, but there is a string going out of the bottom of your clothes tied to that pet sin. You look back over your shoulder thinking, "I am going to turn from that sin, but I really, really love it!" That's repentance with regrets, and it never lasts.

What does it take to enter the kingdom? It takes that Spirit-wrought conviction that you regret your sin so deeply that you are ready, without reservation, to turn gladly from an independent life.

All of this, though, is merely the preparation to enter the kingdom.

3. **We must see our sin so greatly that we gladly bow (Matt. 5:5).** Jesus says that the real blessing comes to those who are meek. What is meekness? Meekness is the submissive spirit. It is the spirit of one who is willing to be governed by another. Those who are not meek are proud, unbroken, and completely convinced that they can handle life by themselves. The meek are exactly the opposite.

Look at the progression of these beatitudes. Blessed are those who recognize their spiritual poverty. They see this so greatly that they are broken and mourning and anxious for Christ. And then, in meekness, they gladly turn to the King and say, "Rule me! I am so sick and tired of my own life that I am gladly willing to let you be in complete control!"

What is the kingdom of heaven? It is the place where the King rules! And only those who submit to the King will enter His kingdom.

Conclusion

Jesus makes an amazing statement in Luke 12:32*b*: ". . .your Father has chosen gladly to give you the kingdom." He is not hiding the kingdom from us, nor is He anxious to withhold anything. In fact, He is most greatly glorified when we receive and experience all that the kingdom affords. But He waits for us to see our need so greatly that we humbly bow!

ADDITIONAL SERMONS AND LESSON IDEAS

Divine Pursuit

Jonah 1:10–17
By Phil Newton

Introduction

Patiently, deliberately, the "Hound of Heaven" pursues the rebel until he knows the rest of redemption in Him. Yes, the sinner comes, willingly and freely, but only because "the Hound of Heaven" has first done the secret work of bringing the sinner to Himself. Just as the Lord pursued a rebellious Jonah and pagan sailors in a raging sea, He pursues sinners until they know the peace of being reconciled to God through faith in Christ.

1. **He arrests our rebellion.** Whether a man is a religious rebel like Jonah or a pagan rebel like the sailors, he is a rebel nonetheless. So how does the rebel turn from his rebellion? It comes about by a divine work, arresting our rebellion and bringing us into a right relationship with God through Christ.

   A. **Fear of God (1:5).** Then the Sovereign Lord enters in! Men who had "no fear of God before his eyes" were seized with a fear of God! First, it was the great storm that frightened the men (1:5). But then they came to discover the reason for the storm, that it was sent by the Lord because of the rebellion of Jonah. They understood for the first time in their lives that there is a God in heaven who rules over the affairs of men, that all of creation exists at His pleasure. This was no ordinary fear caused by bad weather. It was a fear that gripped their souls. It was a fear of standing before an angry God without a mediator.

   B. **Admission of guilt (1:7–10).** The Lord God brought Jonah face to face with the guilt of his sin. No more excuses. No more running. Though God might justly take Jonah's life in the angry jaws of the sea, Jonah will hide no longer. He comes clean before God.

2. **He brings us to desperation** (1:5, 11, 14, 15). As long as a sinner thinks that he can save himself by his own effort, he will not look Godward. Man naturally has a self–dependence, especially when it comes to eternal things. That is symptomatic of the fall.

   A. **Sense of hopelessness.** Until a person sees that he cannot save himself from God's judgment, he will have no motivation to flee to the Lord for refuge from the storm of God's wrath. That is why conviction of sin becomes so intense by the work of the Holy Spirit. He presses the reality of our separation from God so that we realize that our hands are empty and useless in putting us into a right relationship with God.

   B. **Death to self.** Surely we see a death taking place in the rebellious Jonah! Not that Jonah died physically when he spent three days in the fish's belly; Jonah died to his own self-will as he resigned himself to be cast overboard on behalf of the crew.

3. **He reveals Himself:**

   A. **As Sovereign Judge** (1:4)

   B. **As Merciful Redeemer** (1:15, 16)

Preached at South Woods Baptist Church in Memphis Tennessee, February 21, 1999.

The Call from Without

Acts 16:6–10
By Dr. Jimmy Draper

Introduction

The cries of a lost world resound with a deafening, thunderous roar. Never have so many enjoyed so much of the things this world has to offer; yet the despair and hopelessness in the human heart is greater than ever before. The lostness of mankind clamors for our attention today.

We Must Hear the Call (vv. 6–9)

1. The preparation for the call (vv. 6–8): God has a vision for you, but you must be faithful in fulfilling it.
2. The presentation of the call (v. 9)
   A. The Macedonian man realized he had a great need.
   B. Within the heart of each individual in the world is a longing that only Christ can satisfy.

We Must Heed the Call (v. 10)

1. Paul was not praying about whether or not to go, but where to go when he did!
2. The phrase "preach the gospel" is summed up with one word in the Greek language: *evangelion*. It literally means "to evangelize."

Conclusion

What is the gospel? God has acted for the salvation of the world in the incarnation, death, and resurrection of Jesus Christ. We must hear the call. We must heed the call.

WEEK 36

Passion for the Kingdom

Matthew 6:33
By Dr. Bill Elliff

Introduction

Imagine this scene: It's the first Saturday of the college football season. Fans have gathered by the tens of thousands. The teams have practiced for hundreds of hours. Thousands of dollars have been spent. The coin is tossed. The teams enter the field and line up. The referees are ready. But there's one thing missing: a football. Anything you attempt can be worthless if you forget the most important thing.

What is the most important thing in this life? Wouldn't it be tragic to reach the end of life and realize that you've missed the main thing? Jesus reminds us of what is most important.

The Most Important Thing

Read Luke 12:15–34. We have forgotten the singular thing that matters and lasts. What if there was a lost treasure that would:

- Bring you perfect love
- Fulfill every longing of your heart
- Satisfy you completely
- Never run out
- Change the lives of those around you
- Be the most important thing in the world

That treasure is the Kingdom of heaven. But for most, it is forgotten, never experienced, or hardly noticed. How could this happen?

1. **Some have never entered.** This man in Luke 12 didn't know. He thought that life merely consisted of this material world. There are millions of people in the world just like him!

Have you entered the kingdom? Are you helping others enter? Only as we enter the kingdom will begin to experience its riches.

2. **Some have been distracted.** Tinnitus is a disease that causes constant ringing in the ears. Sometimes it's so loud that it's almost all one hears. It overwhelms other noises and becomes the focus. There are many things in this world that cause spiritual tinnitus.

A. **Love of power and reputation**

B. **Love of pleasure**

C. **Love of material possessions**

D. **The noise of busyness and activity**

All of these noises drown out the still, small voice of God, calling you to experience His kingdom. Hours and even days go by and you never look at, think about, or give yourself to the most important thing in the world—the only thing that matters and lasts. See the parallel in Matthew 13:22.

Have you entered the kingdom? And, is your mind set there? Are you passionate about it? Are you experiencing and expanding it, or have you forgotten it altogether?

Passionate Kingdom Expansion

To experience and expand the kingdom calls for radical passion, but yields radical reward.

1. **Radical passion**

A. **"Seek" implies earnest, unrelenting searching**

B. **"First" implies that it's done above all else.** What do you seek first?

C. **"The kingdom" tells us what we are to pursue.** We are to look up into God's kingdom and see what is there, and go after that. We are to pray that His "kingdom would come and will be done on earth as it is in heaven" (Matt. 6:10).

D. **"And His righteousness"** implies that our goal is pursuing all that is right, which is found in the kingdom.

2. **Yielding radical rewards**

A. **"And all these things"** is not some things but all things. This literally means that everything that you need will be added.

B. **"Will be added" indicates that it is a fact.** God has promised that He will give the riches of His kingdom. If you pursue His kingdom, you will be rewarded.

C. **"To you" is a wonderful reminder that it is personal.** God will give to *you* what you long for and desire.

Are you pursuing with a passion the kingdom of God? If so, it will yield incredible rewards!

Conclusion

There once was a man who collected widgets. He bought them from all over the world. He became known as the great widget collector in history. Articles were written about him. His house could not contain all the widgets he had collected, and so he built a massive widget museum.

One day the man died. A long obituary contained the story of his widget passion. But on the other side of the grave, the man stood before his Creator with empty hands. He realized that all of his time and energy and money had purchased nothing for the billions of years of eternity. All of his widget fascination had yielded not a single eternal result.

Anything is worthless if you've missed the most important thing. What about you?

ADDITIONAL SERMONS AND LESSON IDEAS

Lessons from the Belly of the Fish (Part 1)

Jonah 1:17–2:9
By Phil Newton

Introduction

At the moment when we think that all hope is gone and that God has truly left us alone, He breaks into our lives. As we investigate Jonah's experience and prayer, we find that he discovered more about the Lord in the darkness of the fish's belly than he had ever known before. In the slimy darkness of the fish's innards, Jonah begins to see what he had never understood. It is in the darkest moments of life that God often sheds the greatest light on His character.

1. **Jonah learned that God is the Sovereign Lord (1:17).** The title which we use so often, *Lord*, implies sovereign ruler. Sovereignty is bound up within the nature of God. God cannot *not* rule.

   A. **Over creation (Ps. 8:3–4a; 19:1; 24:1, 2).** The book of Jonah illustrates this. How did the storm begin to rage upon the sea and then instantly cease when Jonah was cast overboard? How did the intensity of the storm increase when the sailors tried to evade its grip? How did a fish swallow a man sinking into the depths of the sea? Behind it all is the working of a mighty Sovereign over His creation!

   B. Over life. Jonah also saw that divine sovereignty was exercised over his life. Getting Jonah into the fish was one thing. Protecting him for three days, changing his heart, then getting him back on his mission to Nineveh was another!

2. **He learned that God is a Faithful Father (2:1).** Though Jonah had been unfaithful and rebelled against the Lord, God remained a faithful Father. God never left Jonah.

A. **Shows compassionate love.** Fellow Jonahs, have we not called out to God in much the same distress? And, like Jonah, have we not found the Lord to be a compassionate Father, demonstrating true love for His children?

B. Exercises restorative discipline. But did not God bring great distress upon Jonah? Indeed, He did. That, too, was an illustration of God's fatherly love for His children. For we find in the storm, and even in the great fish, the reality of divine chastening for those who belong to Him. Discipline is evidence of a faithful father (Heb. 12:5–13).

3. **Jonah learned that God is the Merciful Redeemer (2:4–9).** Mercy is shown to pagan sailors, not only physically but also spiritually. Mercy is shown to the wicked people of Nineveh. And mercy is shown to the rebellious prophet.

A. **Mercy to the hopeless.** Mercy describes God's attitude toward the undeserving and hopeless.

B. **Grace to the sinner.** Grace implies the content of His action in accomplishing something for the undeserving and hopeless. We find Jonah praying to God in reference to His temple. The temple was significant because God had chosen that place to reveal Himself to His people, and it was the place where He established a mercy seat upon which an atoning sacrifice would be offered each year to propitiate the divine wrath.

C. **Forgiveness to the believing.**

Preached at South Woods Baptist Church in Memphis Tennessee, February 28, 1999.

God's Cure for Barren Churches

Psalm 126:6
By Junior Hill

Introduction

The church of the Lord Jesus Christ is very much alive. The truth of the matter is, many of our churches are desperately sick. They have a religious illness, a Laodicean fever that has reduced them to spiritual barrenness—having a form of godliness and yet denying the power thereof.

The Broken Sower (v. 6a)

1. **The picture presented** is that of man walking out across barren fields, and as he looks upon the dry and scorched earth before him, he no doubt remembers how it once bloomed and blossomed with harvest.
2. **God's plan for healing broken churches** is to be broken in spirit, for "the Lord is nigh unto them that are of a broken heart; and saveth such as be of a contrite spirit" (Ps. 34:18 KJV).

The Blessed Seed (v. 6b)

1. Some churches merely ignore it.
2. Other churches merely imitate God's cure.
3. Some churches obediently implement God's remedy.

The Blissful Soul Winner (v. 6c)

1. **No longer is he bowed over, burdened, and broken.** No longer does he weep over those dusty, dry fields.
2. **It's harvest time now.** Across those fields we see him coming, leaping and rejoicing—laden with sheaves, which God has given him in response to his faithful labor.

Conclusion

The God of heaven has given an unfailing formula for victory over barrenness, and praise His holy name, it works for everyone!

WEEK 37

Proclaiming the Kingdom

Matthew 4:17–23; 10:7–8
By Dr. Bill Elliff

Introduction

Rich Warren's book *The Purpose Driven Life* has become one of the best selling non-fiction books of all time. It seems that this book touched the ultimate nerve, because everyone longs to know his or her purpose in life. The question most people ask more than any other question is, "What is God's will for my life?" What am I supposed to do on this earth?

Jesus, the perfect man, knew the answer to that question, for His life and for ours, and He demonstrated it clearly. If we listen to Him, we will discover it too.

Life's Purpose

Read Matthew 4:17–23; 10:7–8. We have one job: to relentlessly proclaim and demonstrate the immediacy of the kingdom.

1. **We are to proclaim the immediacy of the kingdom.** To *proclaim* is to announce in an official capacity or to herald news. It was a word used when a new king had begun his rule, and thus a new kingdom had begun. It was not the proclamation of something that might happen, but of what had happened—what was true.

   Jesus came proclaiming that the kingdom of God had come and that it was available to all, although He knew some would not believe it.

   The parable of the soils (Matthew 13) illustrates that Jesus felt His job and ours was to proclaim the message. The response would be up to God, and would also hinge upon the condition of the soil.

Do you realize that this is your singular job? To proclaim and announce with authority that the kingdom of God has come?

2. **We are to demonstrate the immediacy of the Kingdom.** Jesus not only proclaimed the kingdom, but also demonstrated it. Everywhere He went, kingdom activity was accomplished, and lives were changed. He was saying, "The kingdom is here—and this is what it looks like!"

This is why our good deeds are so important. God wants our spiritual activity to bring the kingdom of heaven down to earth so people can see and feel its value. Matthew 5:16 reminds us that, when this light shines, people will see the kingdom.

Do you realize that this is your job? Both of these components are important because :

- Proclamation without demonstration is unbelievable. Demonstration validates what we are proclaiming.
- Demonstration without proclamation is misleading. If we don't tell others why this is happening, they will think it is our work, not God's.

3. **We are to proclaim and demonstrate the kingdom relentlessly!** We are to proclaim and demonstrate the kingdom everywhere, all the time, as we go.

In Matthew 28:19, 20, Christ uses these same words and gives us our purpose. As we go, we are to make disciples and train them to make disciples on their own.

Paul's final words to his young disciple, Timothy, in 1 Timothy 4:1–8 remind us that our main job is to make this proclamation, and that it can be done. Paul was faithful to the end, and we can be, too!

Conclusion

The two most important questions any businessman can answer are these:

- What's your business?
- How's business?

One day, we will stand before God to give an account of our lives. We must understand what our purpose, our business is—to proclaim and demonstrate relentlessly the kingdom of God—and do it well for His glory!

And there's a reason for us to settle these questions—if people never hear about the kingdom and see a demonstration of the kingdom, they can never enter the kingdom

My son, David Elliff, was a missionary in Southeast Asia. One day, he came to his ministry building and there was a crowd outside the neighbor's house, and everyone could see a woman who had hanged herself on the door of her house. He sent me an email with the following words:

> Tonight I saw a dead person. A 23-year-old girl who hung herself with an extension cord. It rocked me to my core. Over and over that vision has come back into my mind. From that vision so many words scream in my head; hopeless, lost, suffering for eternity, un-reached, too late, separated from God, lost opportunity.

> I watched as those around walked over to look at the still hanging body. Some had sad faces, but many looked unfazed. Children peered into the house and then ran away talking excitedly about what they had seen. Death is a way of life. It is just another cold body. And without Christ, that is exactly what you have. Another cold body. There is nothing to look forward to, nothing to console or comfort, simply another person who departed from the earth.

> That image keeps replaying in my head. In a way, I hope the immense feelings after seeing that dead stranger stay with me for the rest of my life. What I saw today was not just one person hanging there, but a whole nation hopelessly going to hell unless we tell them about Christ.

ADDITIONAL SERMONS AND LESSON IDEAS

Lessons from the Belly of the Fish (Part 2)

Jonah 2:1–9
By Phil Newton

Introduction

Life is full of lessons, but few lessons can be more profound than the lesson of repentance that Jonah learned in the belly of the fish. The silver lining of the story of Jonah is that God restores his child to continued fellowship and usefulness in repentance and renewed obedience.

1. **Why repentance is necessary**
    A. **Nature of the redemptive relationship (2:1 "His God").** Since you are in relationship with the Lord, there are responsibilities on your part for the ongoing development of this relationship.
    B. **Relationship offended (1:1–3).** Jonah belonged to the Lord and, therefore, had the joyful responsibility of obedience to the Lord. He chose to do otherwise. Such a choice is sin.
    C. **Relationship acknowledged (2:1).** Jonah was not praying as an "outsider" to the faith. He knew the Lord. He had enjoyed sweet communion with the Lord in previous days. It was the reality that his relationship with the Lord continued which brought him ultimately to repentance.

    The burning ember of spiritual life remains, even when covered by the cold ashes of sin.

2. **What leads to repentance? God had never left Jonah.** Jonah was the one on the run. Yet the steady persistence of the Lord pursued the cold-hearted prophet until he was brought to repentance from his damaging sin.

    What did the Lord bring about in Jonah's life to bring him to repentance?

    A. **Desperation of soul (2:2).** Here was no casual prayer. Instead, we find a man praying in desperation (Ps. 4:1;5:1, 2; 6:2, 3;13:1). The purpose in times of desperation is to drive us to the Lord in prayer.

B. Affliction through discipline. We all must admit that Jonah would not have had such a sense of desperation nor such a heart-wrenching cry to God independent from the hand of divine discipline.

C. Preservation by God. Above all else, the thing which brought Jonah to repentance was that he saw the Lord in his afflictions and in his preservation.

When our spiritual lives begin to chill out, when our discipline before the Lord grows weak, when the attitude of our heart turns inward in self-centeredness, and when the flame of divine love dims, our great need is to see the excellence and glory of God. We do so through the reading of Scripture, through hearing the Word proclaimed, and through God-centered worship.

3. **What happens in repentance?**

A. Look to the Lord. ("Then Jonah prayed to the Lord. . . . I called out. . . to the Lord. . . my prayer came to Thee, into Thy holy temple.") Prayer looks away from the world and puts the whole focus of life upon the Lord.

B. Return to obedience (2:9)

C. Guard against sin's reoccurrence (2:9). Jonah establishes some signposts to help him deal with his own weakness of sin.

i. He would remember the vanity of idolaters.

ii. He would maintain the practice of continuing to offer sacrifices unto the Lord.

Preached at South Woods Baptist Church in Memphis, Tennessee, March 28, 1999.

False Gods Give No Answers

1 Kings 18:20–29
By Dr. Dwight "Ike" Reighard

Introduction

On April 14, 1912, the Titanic was crossing the Atlantic Ocean on a journey to America. At approximately 11:40 p.m., the Titanic struck an iceberg that created a 300-foot gash in the ship's starboard side. History tells us the truth—the world's "safest" ship was not safe after all.

We Christians had better get our message across before America sinks beneath the dark waters of her sin. Icebergs of iniquity are all about us, and America is about to sink!

We Must Determine: Are We with God, or Against God?

1. The problem is obvious.
2. The prescription is optional.

Our Choices Will Reveal the Difficulty of Life's Challenges

1. Doing the right thing is often the hardest thing to do.
2. Doing the right thing is often the most unpopular thing to do.
3. America's false gods:
   A. God of Sex
   B. God of Materialism
   C. God of Recreation
   D. God of Music
4. False god will give you no answers
   A. In the 1920s, it was education.
   B. In the 1930s, it was economics.
   C. In the 1940s, it was world politics.
   D. In the 1950s, it was science.

E. In the 1960s, it was sociology.

F. In the 1970s, it was unrestraint, doing your own thing.

G. In the 1980s, it was greed, money, and career.

H. In the 1990s, it was false gods.

5. Our greatest challenge will result in dealing with the consequences

A. We must repent.

B. We must restore.

C. We must recommit today.

D. We must share the true gospel.

WEEK 38

Jehovah!

Exodus 3:13–17
By Dr. Kent Spann

Introduction: What's in a Name

There are all sorts of name books that give you the meaning behind names. While it is interesting to discover the meaning of one's name, in our culture there is little significance put on the meaning of the name.

In Hebrew culture, however, a name was significant. A person's name signified something. That is why we find God changing the names of Abraham and Jacob. He inspired Old Testament prophets to give their children certain names to symbolize what He was doing in Israel. In the ancient world, knowing another's name was a special privilege that offered access to that person's thoughts and life.

What is His Name?

In Exodus 3:13, Moses asks the name of the God that is sending him to Israel. Why would Moses ask what His name was? Wasn't the name of God known? In this context, Moses was not necessarily asking what God's name was; he was asking, "What does your name mean?" He was asking, "What kind of God are you?"

A name meant something. The people of Israel, having lived under tyranny now for all these years, needed to know what kind of God was saying that He would deliver them. They had seen all of the gods of Egypt. They elicited no courage or confidence, as they were nothing more than wood and precious metals.

God answers Moses in 3:14 by telling him the name: His name. God reveals in the passage the name that He would be most commonly known by. This name is used 6,823 times in the Old Testament. It is the name *Yahweh*.

Not only was it the most commonly used name for God in the Old Testament, it was the most revered. Rabbinical writings have distinguished Yahweh by various euphemistic expressions, as "The Name," "the Great and Terrible Name," "the Peculiar Name," "the Separate Name," "the Unutterable Name," "the Ineffable Name," "the Incommunicate Name," "the Holy Name," "the Distinguished Name."[1]

The name Yahweh is actually a four-letter word in Hebrew. It is made up of four consonants: YHWH. Later Jewish scholars, called Masoretes, added vowel signs from God's other name, Adonai. That gave us the name Jehovah, which is the word we most commonly use. In our English text, you know when the name Yahweh or Jehovah is being used, since it is in reference to the Lord in small caps.

What was Jehovah or Yahweh saying about Himself through His name?

1. **I AM the living God.** On April 8, 1966, an issue of *Time* magazine was released with a front cover that read "Is God Dead?" Perhaps some of the Israelites after all those years of captivity wondered if God was alive. They had cried out to Him but nothing had happened.

We are prone to wander down that path sometimes, especially when things are not going right, prayers aren't answered, troubling events take place, or tragedy strikes our lives.

We can act like God is dead. He is not. He is alive. He is Yahweh. He is Jehovah.

2. **I AM, the self-existent God.** Sigmund Freud said that man created God. How would God answer Freud? "I AM WHO I AM" (Exod. 3:14) The name I AM is based upon the Hebrew verb "to be" (*havah*). God is saying that He is the one who always was, who always is, and who always will be. The angels in heaven declare Him to be the self-existent God. See John 14:6; Colossians 1:16, 17; Revelation 1:8; 4:8.

He is the uncaused cause. He has no beginning and no end. He doesn't derive His existence from anyone or anything. He did not become. There is no other power or force behind Him. He doesn't derive His authority from any other. There is no reality outside of God. He, therefore, is the source of life.

3. **I AM the preeminent God.** No doubt the Israelites had heard the names of many gods while in Egypt. They had a pantheon of gods. God declares loud and clear that He is the only God. See Isaiah 43:10.

That is why God forbids and detests idolatry of any kind, because it is our declaration that God is not preeminent. It doesn't matter what the idol is: money, sex, fame, other religion's gods, knowledge, sports, etc. Nothing must supersede God.

4. **I AM the unchanging God.** People change with the wind and the crowds. Time changes us. Events change us. Relationships change us. God never changes. See Psalm 102:27; Hebrews 13:8; James 1:17.

In our changing world full of instability, one thing is sure and secure: God never changes!

5. **I AM the ever-loving God.** Yahweh is the name of covenant relationship. He is reminding them that He loves them because He is in a special relationship. He hasn't forsaken them or forgotten them.

6. **I AM the personal God.** God is intricately involved in His creation and our lives. See Jeremiah 29:11.

7. **I AM the all-sufficient God.** He didn't tie Himself to one thing as the Egyptian gods would. They had a god for everything—sun god, afterlife god, etc. Each did a different thing for the people. Not Jehovah. He simply says, "I AM." "I AM all that you need."

Conclusion

What should be our response to this great God?

⟶ Believe Him.
⟶ Revere Him.
⟶ Obey Him.

Endnotes

Herbert Lockyer, D.D., *All the Divine Names and Titles in the Bible*, (Grand Rapids: Zondervan, 1975), 17.

ADDITIONAL SERMONS AND LESSON IDEAS

Re-commissioned

Jonah 2:10–3:4
By Phil Newton

Introduction

Do you always obey God the first time you see a truth or hear the command of God proclaimed? I dare say that we might like to do so, but on many occasions, we find ourselves being defiant, stubborn, or fearful of following after the Lord. He graciously brings us along so that we might ultimately know the wonder of His grace.

1. **God's prerogative.** Can we tell God what to do? Many times people try to tell God what He must do or how He must act. But that is certainly not our prerogative. Jonah found that he was not in a position of telling God how to do things.

   A. No obligation (2:10). Perhaps we first see this when we understand the reality that God is not obligated to us, even when we consider that we have humbled ourselves before him. It is his right alone to forgive, since it is before him alone that we have sinned. Did the Lord have to eject Jonah from the fish?

   While God is under no obligation to us, he shows abundant mercy to us.

   B. Cooperation (1:17). It seems that the wind, the storm, and the fish demonstrated much better obedience than Jonah! All of nature works in harmony with the divine purposes. Nature does not have a mind of its own; it functions to serve the great purposes of God.

   In a similar fashion, Jonah was subdued by this same divine purpose. The only reason that Jonah chose to do right was that the Lord God brought about Jonah's cooperation.

B. Second time (3:1). How sweet it must have been in the ears of Jonah to hear the words of the Lord "the second time." He is the God of the second time.

C. No grudges (3:2). Jonah knew that he had been forgiven by the Lord. See Psalm 130:3, 4. Forgiveness does not mean that God ignores the sin as long as the sinner does not step out of line. Forgiveness implies that the Lord puts the sin completely away, so that the one forgiven is never held guilty for the sin again.

2. God's child responds

A. Attention (3:3). When the child of God has been humbled by the disciplining hand of the Lord, he is brought to a new capacity of hearing the Word of God.

B. Obedience (3:3). You almost wonder if the Jonah you find in the first chapter is the same Jonah you see in the third chapter! No more fleeing. No more hiding. No more excuses. No more silence in the face of trials. Just obedience. Jonah had made his mind up to obey the Lord.

C. Message (3:4). Jonah's re-commissioning brought him a new message and new sense of spiritual power.

Had he gone to Nineveh initially, he may not have been ready. As Sinclair Ferguson observes, "Jonah was not really fitted to be the evangelist of the Ninevites. He had no comprehension of their condition, nor had he any true sympathy for them. . . . . It is clear, however mysterious it may seem, that God used even the result of Jonah's disobedience to equip him for service"[1]

Preached at South Woods Baptist Church in Memphis, Tennessee, April 11, 1999.

Endnotes

[1] Sinclair Ferguson, *Man Overboard: The Story of Jonah*, (Wheaton, Ill.: Tyndale House Publishers, 1982), 69.

Bringing Our Friends to Christ

Mark 8: 22–24
By Dr. Richard G. Lee

Introduction

Do you have a friend who is without Jesus? He or she may be a relative, a coworker, or a lifelong friend who has never met Jesus as personal Savior.

A Friend Like You

It will probably take a friend like you to reach this person for Christ. Notice the lessons that the Lord Jesus teaches here.

1. His friends brought the blind man to Jesus
2. His friends believed God for his healing (v. 22)
   A. Never underestimate the power of our prayers.
   B. Never underestimate the power of our witness.
3. His friends cared for his needs (v. 23)
   A. We must care for others, even when they believe wrongly.
   B. We must begin where our friends are in leading them to understand Christ.
   C. We must always lead them all the way to the cross.

4. His friends never gave up on him (vv 23–25)

Conclusion

We should never give up on our friends, because Jesus loves them. He is not willing to give up on them. Why should we? Jesus touched the blind man's eyes, and he began to see—but he needed a second touch to come to full sight.

WEEK 39

SERIES: HE IS JEHOVAH

Jehovah Jireh

Genesis 22:1–14
By Dr. Kent Spann

Introduction

Every person faces some kind of test in his life. It might be a test on the job. Maybe your boss gives you an assignment to see if you can complete it successfully. If you succeed, you will be given a raise. In a relationship, it might be a test of time and separation to see if two people are meant for each other. If you are in college or school, there will always be a test which shows the professor just how much you have learned. Some tests are minor; others are major. Some tests have great impact on us while others have very little.

What if the test that faced you was God asking you to sacrifice your only son to him? In the Bible, there is the account of a man who was asked to do that very thing. Turn to Genesis 22:1, 2. This was not a temptation experience where the devil was tempting Abraham. This was a real test from God. The word *tested* generally means prove, test, put to the test, rather than the current English idea of "enticing to do wrong." God tests us to prove the quality of our faith.

What's a Person to Do? (Genesis 22:3–9)

What would you do if you were asked to sacrifice your only son? What does Abraham do with Isaac?

1. **He obeyed God (22:3).** Here we see Abraham's act of obedience. What we don't see is the agonizing that must have gone on within Abraham's heart. The Scriptures do not record that, but human experience would tell us that there was an internal struggle, which is a key component of tests.

Whatever Abraham's struggle was, when it was all said and done, he stepped out in obedience. Warren Wiersbe says:

Our faith is not really tested until God asks us to bear what seems unbearable, do what seems unreasonable, and expect what seems impossible.

2. **He trusted God** (22:4–10). Abraham trusted God before he knew what was going to happen. He didn't understand, but he did trust God. After all, it was Isaac, the promised heir, who was to be sacrificed.

A. He confessed his faith in God.

   i. He confessed to his servants that he would return (22:5).

   ii. He confessed to Isaac that God would provide (22:8).

B. He practiced his faith in God. He didn't just talk the talk of faith, he lived the life of faith.

   i. He went up to the mount (22:6, 7).

   ii. He built the altar (22:9a).

   iii. He laid his son on the altar (22:9b).

What made Abraham's faith so special is that it was a real faith. He didn't have the Scriptures to derive His understanding of God. He didn't have thousands of years of recorded history to gain strength and courage from. He had a primitive knowledge of God, and yet he believed that God would provide. That is why Romans 4 speaks of his faith, as does Hebrews 11:17–19.

What Does God Want? (Genesis 22:10–12)

The drama intensified. Abraham raised the knife. His arm began to move down to drive the knife into Isaac's chest when suddenly the voice of the angel rang out, "Abraham, Abraham." His arm stopped. Abraham passed the test.

What did God want? The same thing He wants from us: total surrender!

Dr. Adrian Rogers tells of a conversation with Romanian pastor Josef Tson, who suffered during the Communist reign in his country.

As Joseph and I rode along in his car, I said, "Josef, tell me about American Christianity." He said, "Adrian, I had rather not." I said, "No, I want to know."

He then said, "Well, Adrian, since you have asked me, I'll tell you. The key word in American Christianity is commitment." I said, "That is good, isn't it, Josef?"

He replied, "No, it is not. As a matter of fact, the word commitment did not come into great usage in the English language until about the 1960s. In Romania we do not even have a word to translate the English word commitment. If you were to use commitment in your message tonight, I would not have a proper word to translate it with."

Josef continued, "When a new word comes into usage, it generally pushes an old word out. I began to study and found the old word that commitment replaced. Adrian, the old word that is no longer in vogue in America is the word surrender."

"Josef," I asked, "What is the difference between commitment and surrender?" He said, "When you make a commitment, you are still in control, no matter how noble the thing you commit to. One can commit to pray, to study the Bible, to give his money, or to commit to automobile payments, or to lose weight. Whatever he chooses to do, he commits to it. But surrender is different. If someone holds a gun and asks you to lift your hands in the air as a token of surrender, you don't tell that person what you are committed to. You simply surrender and do as you are told."

He said, "Americans love commitment, because they are still in control. But the key word is surrender. We are to be slaves of the Lord Jesus Christ."[1]

God wants total surrender (Luke 9:23–25).

God's Provision (Genesis 22:13, 14)

There was unfinished business: Abraham had gone to the mountain to offer a sacrifice. The problem was that Abraham had brought no sacrifice other than Isaac. It was at that moment that Abraham looked up and saw the ram (22:13). God provided the sacrifice. God always intended to provide the sacrifice.

Abraham names the place to commemorate it Jehovah Jireh, which means "The Lord Will Provide."

What did Abraham learn that day, and what do we learn?

1. **God will provide what we need.** When you take the meaning of the place where Abraham went, Moriah, which is related to the word Jireh, and the name given to God, we learn that God sees our needs before we do. He already has made provisions for them. Lockyer says that His pre-vision means His pro-vision.

   A. **Where does the Lord provide for our needs? In the place of His assignment.**

   B. **When does the Lord provide for our needs? Just when we really need it.**

   C. **Whose needs does the Lord provide for? Those who trust and obey.**

2. **God reveals Himself to us through his provisions.** Abraham learned what kind of God Yahweh was through that experience. If he had not gone through this experience, he would not have known God as Jehovah–Jireh. We say that we want to know God more intimately, but are we willing to go through the experiences that will draw us close to Him? Are we willing to travel the roads required to know Him?

   Paul said, "And my God shall supply all your need according to His riches in glory by Christ Jesus" (Philippians 4:19).

Conclusion

Our God is able and willing to provide. We often miss out on His provision because we are unwilling to totally surrender to Him. Trust and surrender, for there is no other way!

Endnotes

[1] Adrian Rogers, *The Incredible Power of Kingdom Authority* (Nashville: B&H, 2002), 60–61.

ADDITIONAL SERMONS AND LESSON IDEAS

The Awakening (Part 1)

Jonah 3:5–10
By Phil Newton

Introduction

The entire course of the world has been affected by spiritual awakenings. The consciousness of communities toward the things of God are elevated, a fear of God sweeps through like a tornado wind, and many are brought to a genuine knowledge of Christ in a short period of time. Work that might have taken years to accomplish takes place in a matter of days. We find Jonah in the midst of such a surprising awakening

Nineveh was home to superb artisans and builders who constructed an elaborate city with 200 foot-high walls, and wide enough for three chariots to pass simultaneously. The scientific minds of the Ninevites, coupled with their military prowess, produced the most feared people on the face of the earth in the ninth and tenth centuries BC. Their disregard for human life was notable. They would cut the noses off of those whom they conquered, and would literally skin many of the conquered while alive. The least likely place that a spiritual awakening would take place in the early part of the eighth century BC was Nineveh.

The book of Jonah offers a telling example of God's work to awaken unbelievers. How did this awakening come about?

1. **Awakening message.** Central to every spiritual awakening that we have recorded in history is the proclamation of God's Word.
   A. **Content of the Message.** Jonah preached, "Yet forty days and Nineveh will be overthrown." Was this the entire message that he preached? Most commentators think that Jonah probably said more, but this summarized his message.
      i. **He likely told them of his calling, his running from God, and the divine judgment which he faced.**

ii. He surely reproved them for their wickedness.

iii. Jonah's preaching applied the *law of God* to the actions of the Ninevites.

Does the preaching of Jonah parallel any of the other great awakenings in history? In the first Great Awakening of the eighteenth century, we find men like George Whitefield, Gilbert Tennent, his brother William, and Jonathan Edwards, preaching the severity of divine judgment against sinners.

Most sinners will not give thought to God until they begin to feel the flame of divine wrath leaping toward them.

B. Intent. The message of Jonah appeared to be only one of gloom, but the fact that the message was delivered was an evidence of the divine intent to show mercy. Why warn the Ninevites of judgment to come? Why give them forty days to consider their ways and anticipate the burning anger of God? Jonah did it to see if they would repent.

C. Urgency. Just ask the typical person if he deserves to go to hell and face an eternity of divine wrath. What will he say? "Me? Deserve hell? Oh, I'm not that bad!" But how bad is our sin? We may retreat and say that our sin was not as bad as that of Nineveh. Yet Jonah warned them, "Yet forty days and Nineveh will be overthrown."

How many days do you have?

The urgency in Jonah's message is something which we have lost in our own day.

Conclusion

Jonah's message was not complicated, nor was it entertaining to the ears. But it found a lodging place in the minds and hearts of the people of Nineveh. Does this same message, viewed from the light of Scripture, find a welcome in your heart this day?

Preached at South Woods Baptist Church in Memphis, Tennessee, April 18, 1999.

My Mission in the Marketplace

Romans 10:9–14
By Rick Warren

Introduction

When you speak with people who make their lives count, you'll find that they have a life mission.

The Christian's Mission

1. **You are a witness.** The moment you become a Christian, God gives you a new mission. In Acts 20:24 (TLB), Paul says:

> Life is worth nothing unless I use it for doing the work assigned me by the Lord Jesus [*that is his mission, and then he tells us what it is*]— the work of telling others the Good News about God's mighty kindness and love.

Witnessing is simply sharing what God has done in a person's life.

2. **You are sent by the Lord (John 17:18).** You don't become a missionary by crossing the sea; you become a missionary by seeing the cross.

The Importance of Our Message

1. **We have a life-saving message.**
2. **People are hungry to hear it.**

New Testament Times

Three things were true:

1. **Problems were great.**
2. **People didn't know what to do.**

3. People didn't know where to go for help.

Do you know anybody like that? The world is full of people like that! The world is far more ready to receive the good news than we are ready to share it.

Being a Missionary in the Marketplace

How can you be a witness at work?

1. By the quality of your work (1 Cor. 3:13).
2. By your positive attitude (Philip. 2:14, 15).
3. By telling the good news (Col. 4:5).

WEEK 40

SERIES: HE IS JEHOVAH

Jehovah-Nissi

Exodus 17:8–16
By Dr. Kent Spann

Introduction

Have you ever really been surprised? Have you ever been totally caught off guard? We call it being "blindsided" because we don't see it coming.

Israel is on her way to the Promised Land when she arrives at a place called Rephidim. The Hebrew word *rephidim* means "rest" or "sustains." That is an interesting name for the geographical place, especially when you read the remainder of the story. Rephidim was anything but restful for Israel.

While at Rephidim, the Israelites are attacked by the Amalekites. The Amalekites were an ancient wandering Tribe. They were descendents of Esau and thus direct descendents of Isaac, but they were bitter and hostile enemies of Israel.

How did they attack? According to Deuteronomy 25:17–19, they attacked those lagging behind. Israel had to be surprised. They had done nothing to provoke the attack.

Warren Wiersbe says, "There's no record that the Jews ever had to fight any battles in Egypt, but once they were delivered from bondage, they discovered they had enemies."

You may be surprised to know that, as a Christian, you have real enemies who hate you and want to see you wiped out or destroyed. Who are the Christian's enemies?

⌒ The Devil (1 Peter 5:8: John 10:10)
⌒ The World (1 John 3:13; Luke 21:17; John 15:18–20)
⌒ The Flesh (Galatians 5:17)

Prepare for Battle (Exodus 17:9–12)

Remember that the Israelites were not veterans of war. They were slaves. This was their first battle. The Amalekites, on the other hand, were seasoned warriors. They were militants. What was the strategy? See 17:9, 10.

1. **Joshua and the Israelite army would engage the Amalekites in battle (17:9*a*, 10*a*).**
2. **Moses would go up on a hill overlooking the battlefield (17:9*b*, 10*b*).** What was the significance of Moses lifting up his hands? Was it, as some say, like the commander of an army directing his soldiers? If that were the case, then Moses would need to be on the field of battle. What was Moses doing? He was praying and interceding. One commentator says, "The lifting up of the hands has been regarded almost with unvarying unanimity by Targumists, Rabbins, Fathers, Reformers, and nearly all the more modern commentators, as the sign or attitude of prayer."[2]

Moses was fighting too, just on a different field of battle. Whether or not Moses fully understood the fact that this was a spiritual war with unseen forces aligned against him is uncertain, but something bigger than just a physical battle was going on. He surely knew, because he went onto the mountain to pray.

How important is God's intercession in this battle? As long as Moses lifted up his hands, Israel prevailed; but when he lowered his hands, the enemy prevailed (17:11). Christian missionary martyr Jim Elliot said, "That saint who advances on his knees never retreats."

Moses was willing to pray, but the work was tiring (17:12). True intercession is intense and tiring work. Thankfully, when Moses grew weary, Aaron and Hur were there to assist him. We all need Aarons and Hurs in our lives.

As Christians, we have to engage in the battle (1 Timothy 1:18; 6:12). We can't run and hide. But the most important thing we do is pray (Ephesians 6:18). Samuel Chadwick, a great English preacher, said, "The one concern of the devil is to keep us from praying." Why is that? The reason is that prayer is where the victory is won.

A Revealing Victory (Exodus 17:13–16)

Israel won their first battle. But there was something more important going on. They were going to learn about God. God tells Moses to write something important (17:14). The message was clear: God would defeat the enemies of His people.

In response to God's message, Moses built an altar, or a memorial, and he gave it a name, one of the names of God (17:15). He called it Jehovah-Nissi. The Hebrew word *nissi* means "signal pole," "standard, ensign, or banner." Moses was declaring that the Lord is our Standard, and that we march under His banner or His flag.

What did God reveal in Israel's victory? What does God reveal to us when we win the victory? That He is Jehovah-Nissi. What does that mean?

— When we go to battle, we go with God's presence.
— When we go to battle, we go with God's power.
— When we go to battle, we go with God's provision.

When (not if) we are attacked by the enemy, we need to remember that He is Jehovah-Nissi. God is the source of our victory when we are engaged in battle by the Devil, the world, or the flesh.

Conclusion

In the First Battle of Bull Run in the Civil War, Gen. Thomas Jonathan Jackson was leading the Virginia troops of the Confederacy. The Confederates were being routed by the Union forces. One man from another division saw Jackson mounted on his horse, leading his troops, and pronounced, "There stands Jackson like a stone wall! Rally behind the Virginians!" They did so, and the Confederacy won a decisive and surprising victory at the outset of the war, dashing the Union's hopes for a quick victory. And Thomas Jonathan Jackson was thereafter known as Stonewall Jackson. That day, he was the "banner" for the Confederate troops. Although shots were flying all around them, they saw Jackson, standing before them, as impregnable as a stone wall, and rallied behind him. Similarly, the Lord is our banner. Although demands and accusations may be flying all around us, we are to look to the Lord who stands before us and rally behind him.

Sammy Tippit, an evangelist from San Antonio, Texas, writes:

> Our banner must not be our ministries, our denominations, our pro-grams or our methods. Our banner must be Jehovah-Nissi. Moses built an altar and called it Jehovah-Nissi. Perhaps you need to build an altar in your heart and call it Jehovah-Nissi. Allow Him to be your rallying point. He alone gives victory. If you find yourself discouraged in the midst of spiritual battles, then you will always be able to return to that altar and find the source of victory."[2]

Let's go to battle under the banner of our Lord!

Endnotes

[1] C. F. Keil, and F. Delitzsch. *Commentary on the Old Testament*, vol. 1, (Peabody, MA: Hendrickson, 2002), 372.

[2] Precept Austin, *http://www.preceptaustin.org/jehovah_nissi1.htm* (accessed March 28, 2011).

ADDITIONAL SERMONS AND LESSON IDEAS

The Awakening

Jonah 3:5–10
By Phil Newton

Man's heart is so dark, so filled with hatred for God, so numbed by his own love for sin, that he ignores the restraint of God's law. He does not hear the life-changing message of Christ that is proclaimed all around him. His interest is that of going his own way. In that vein, man continues to reap the consequence of a life without God. He has failed to hear the voice of God speaking through Scripture, revealing the only hope for sinful men.

A divine intervention must take place for sin-deadened men to respond to the gospel. Something happened in Nineveh that cannot be explained in terms of Jonah's ability or the receptivity of the citizens. The wind of God swept through the city, awakening the lifeless souls of men to the reality of divine judgment.

1. **Awakening message.** Review the previous message.
2. **Awakening response.** Action took place when Jonah began preaching in Nineveh. The text reminds us that Jonah had only gone one day's journey into the city—about sixteen miles—before there was such a movement of Ninevites turning to God and repenting of sin that it can only be described as an awakening. The term often used to describe "awakenings" is the word "revival."

   Let us consider these normal elements of an awakened soul who finds rest in Christ.

   A. **Believe God (3:5).** The thing that produced faith in the Ninevites was their "fear of God's wrath" (3:9). Others have been overwhelmed by the *love* of God in Christ for you. How you came to the place of trusting in Christ alone is not the issue; rather, that you, by God's grace, have believed savingly in Jesus Christ alone.

B. Turn from sin (3:5–9). We see that they were not just repenting of sin in general, but of specific sins in their lives. That is a good evidence of the genuineness of faith.

Scottish pastor Hugh Martin has given a wonderfully clear explanation of true repentance:

> The principle is this: true repentance is a change of mind, of heart, of disposition: it is the making of a new heart and of a right spirit. It originates in regeneration; in our being born again; in our obtaining a new nature and becoming new creatures in Christ by the Spirit. And it flows forth, in unmistakable manifestations, in a new course of conduct; in a reformed life; a life aiming at new ends, conducted under a new rule, and aspiring to attain to a new standard. Repentance, springing from a true fear of God and a true sight of sin, manifests itself in a dutiful obedience to God's law and a jealous abstinence from sin. True and saving repentance is not a mere shaking off the evil fruit from the tree, and tying on fruit of a better appearance. it is the changing of the tree's very nature; and good fruit is then naturally brought forth, and not artificially appended.[1]

B. Plea for mercy (3:8, 9). The pleas to God in the city of Nineveh came with a sense of urgency (3:8, 9). So now they appealed to the mercy of the Lord God to be shown to them. Only God, in mercy, could avert the destruction and give them life.

Preached at South Woods Baptist Church in Memphis, Tennessee, April 25, 1999.

Endnotes

[1] Hugh Martin, *A Commentary on Jonah*, (Edinburgh: The Banner of Truth Trust, 1978, from 1870 edition), 271.

Bring Them In

John 1:35–51
By Dr. James Merritt

Introduction

We see in this text that every Christian has what is necessary in his or her hands, head, and heart to bring people to Jesus.

Commitment to Jesus (vv. 35–37)

1. Soul winning is a matter of following the Lord Jesus Christ.
2. Soul winning is a matter of obedience.

Communion with Jesus (vv. 38, 39)

After the disciples had made a commitment to follow Jesus, notice that they then took some time to fellowship with Jesus. Fellowship always comes before fishing. Worship always comes before witnessing.

Confession of Jesus (vv. 40, 41)

1. **The disciples were so full of Jesus that they had to go tell somebody about Him.** Notice how these disciples confessed the Lord Jesus:
   A. They were seeking.
   B. They were speaking.
2. **They witnessed with their lives as well as with their lips.** When there is commitment to Jesus, communion with Jesus, and confession of Jesus, there will also be conversion.
3. **Conversion by Jesus**
4. **Personal presentation**
5. **Positive declaration**
6. **Persuasive confrontation**
7. **Powerful transformation**

Conclusion

The wonderful thing about salvation is this: It doesn't deal with the symptom; it always deals with the problem.

WEEK 41

SERIES: HE IS JEHOVAH

Jehovah Rophe

Exodus 15:22–26
By Dr. Kent Spann

Introduction

Have you ever taken a trip that didn't turn out right? Have you been on a vacation where everything went wrong, or taken a cruise during the worst storm of the year? What about when you finally made your trip back home and ended up stuck in the terminal of an airport because of inclement weather? Israel had one of those kinds of trips.

The Journey to Marah (Exodus 15:22–23)

Israel's journey from Egypt turned out badly when they arrived at Marah. They were in the desert of Shur, which is barren and sandy. This is their first experience of the real wilderness. Dry and thirsty, they arrived at Marah where there should have been water. There was—bitter water. In Hebrew, *marah* means "bitter."

In our lives, we are not literally travelling on a road to Marah, but we are travelling on the road of life. Along the way, there will be places of "bitter water." It is the abusive spouse that makes life bitter. It is the news that a couple can't have children. It is the devastating words that your spouse is leaving you. It is a parent watching his young child suffer horribly and then die. It is a prayer that God doesn't answer. Whatever the experience, it leaves a bitter taste in our mouths.

Facing Marah (Exodus 15:24)

What is Israel's response to the bitter waters? They start grumbling (15:24). Now, the waters are not the only things that are bitter—so are the people. They are grumbling against Moses, their leader, and ultimately against God.

How could they become bitter in light of what they had just experienced? The same way we do. We fail to come to God, seek Him, and trust Him. Martin Luther said, "When the supply fails, our faith is soon gone."

Our churches are full of bitter people wounded by life, by people, and even by God (though they wouldn't say that). Churches, including this one, are full of people who have come to the waters of life thirsty—only to be hurt, wounded, disappointed, etc.

Bitterness is poisonous, not only in the life of the individual, but also to all they come in contact with (Hebrews 12:15).

Healing for Marah (Exodus 15:25–26)

Moses, the leader of Israel, is faced with a grumbling and complaining group. What does he do? He does the right thing: he cries out to the Lord. God told Moses to throw a piece of wood or a tree into the water. The water became good to drink.

God powerfully revealed Himself at Marah, both to His people then and to us today (15:26). The phrase "I am the Lord, who heals you" is *Jehovah-Rophe*. The Hebrew word *rafa* means to heal.

1. He is the God who heals our circumstances.
   A. Sometimes, He changes our circumstances altogether.
   B. Sometimes, He does something to sweeten the circumstance.
   C. Sometimes, He gives you more satisfaction with the divine will.
2. He is the God who heals our hearts.
   A. He heals our emotions.
   B. He heals our attitudes.
   C. He heals our desires.
3. He is the God who heals our minds.
   A. He heals the way we think.
   B. He heals the way we perceive things.
4. He is the God who heals our bodies.
   A. He can heal us by preventing the disease. Have you ever thought about how many diseases God has protected you from? Your good health is God's work of healing.

B. He can heal us by curing the disease.

C. He can heal us by giving us temporary relief from the disease.

D. He can heal us by taking us to heaven (Revelation 21:1–4).

5. He is the God who heals our sins.

We are born sick, not with a physical sickness, but with a spiritual sickness (Psalm 51:5; Romans 3:10–18). All that we see today—the war, hatred, disease, famine, violence, drugs, alcoholism, abuse, immorality, etc.—is the result of sin.

All of our attempts as man to heal our sin problem has failed miserably. Only Gd can heal our sin-sickness. And how does He do it? He heals us just like he did at the waters of Marah, with a tree—the cross of Christ.

Conclusion

In 2006, Yoko Ono placed a full-page ad in the New York *Times* calling for December 8, the anniversary of John Lennon's death, to be made a global day of healing. She wrote, "One day we will be able to say that we healed ourselves, and by healing ourselves, we healed the world."

We cannot heal ourselves, and we certainly cannot heal our world. There is only one that can heal us and our world. His name is Jehovah-Rophe.

> He himself bore our sins in his body on the tree, so that we might die to sins and live for righteousness; by his wounds you have been healed.
>
> —1 Peter 2:24 (NIV)

ADDITIONAL SERMONS AND LESSON IDEAS

Theology *Un*-applied

Jonah 4:1–4
By Phil Newton

We could label the fourth chapter of Jonah "The Pouting of Jonah." We would imagine that Jonah would be elated at the response of the Ninevites to his preaching. Yet he only pouts, complains, prays in anger, and desires to die! What was his problem? Jonah had plenty of theology in his head, but all too little had penetrated his heart.

1. **Theological aptitude.** We must understand that Jonah was a good theologian. However, Jonah had a theological problem common to all men. Though we know some truths about God, we want God to somehow fit into our own slant. Let us see Jonah's theological convictions.

    A. **Revelation of God** (4:2). Jonah's knowledge of God displayed a grasp of His compassion. He knew these truths of God concerning His compassionate treatment of sinful men. See Psalm 103.

    B. **Experience of God.** But Jonah didn't only know these things; he had experienced this knowledge of God on a first-hand basis. He knew what it was to face the reality of not deserving anything from God then, by divine mercy, to be delivered from bondage, given new life, and restored into God's favor.

2. **Self-justification.** At issue in our text are two very significant matters. First, what Jonah *knew* about the Lord by means of revelation should have framed his theology. Second, what Jonah *wanted* the Lord to be had an undue influence on the shape of his theology.

    A. **Misshapen theology** (4:2). Though he could articulate a good theology, there was something wrong at its base. Jonah conveniently sought to twist and rearrange his theology in order to fit his views toward the Ninevites. Jonah thought that, for the Ninevites to repent, being a wicked, pagan people, it would tarnish the glory of God. So Jonah was acting as the protector of God!

B. Anger, bias, nationalism. The last thing he wanted to happen was for these pagan idolaters to receive the same mercy, grace, and compassion that the Lord had been showing to Israel for hundreds of years. The Lord belonged to Israel! Or at least Jonah thought this was true.

Jonah was more concerned about Israel keeping God to themselves than in God's glory and redemptive work being spread throughout the world.

3. **Fear of theology.** As long as Jonah could keep his thoughts about Yahweh under control, then he was okay.

A. Right theology, wrong conclusions (4:3). Jonah made some faulty conclusions, even though he had a fairly good theological understanding of the Lord.

    i. **He was mistaken to think that the Lord could go against His nature.**

    ii. **He was mistaken to think that others are less important than he himself was.**

    iii. **He was mistaken to think that God's warnings offer only judgment and never hope.**

B. Correcting question (4:4, 9). Twice in this chapter, we find the Lord asking Jonah a simple question: "Do you have good reason to be angry?"

Jonah was angry with God for being God. Do you ever find yourself being angry with God for being God?

Conclusion

What if Jonah had only put into practice what he had known in his head about the Lord? He had a reasonably good theology—that is, until he began to twist it to fit his own plans, prejudices, and biases. The story of Jonah provides us with a good case of theology un-applied.

Preached at South Woods Baptist Church in Memphis, Tennessee, May 2, 1999.

Being Like Jesus

Matthew 9:32–38
By Dr. Larry L. Lewis

Introduction

To be like Jesus, we must understand how He felt and acted, and what He said and did. Matthew 9:32–38 gives us a portrait of Jesus.

What Jesus saw: "When he saw the multitudes" (v. 36)

Everywhere Jesus went, great multitudes followed Him. He saw them not as a hindrance, but as an opportunity for witness and ministry.

1. **He saw their needs.** America is filled with people in need: the homeless, jobless, and hopeless.
2. **He saw their lost condition.** He saw them as "sheep having no shepherd" (v. 36). He knew that they were without God and without hope in this world and eternity.
3. **He saw their potential.** He saw every one of them as a precious soul with unlimited potential.

What Jesus felt: "He was moved with compassion" (v. 36).

"Moved with compassion" literally means that He became sick inside.

1. **How desperately we need people who will weep over their cities and communities.**

Reproduced with permission of the North American Mission Board, Alpharetta, Georgia. All rights reserved.

WEEK 42

SERIES: HE IS JEHOVAH

Jehovah Shalom

Judges 6:1–24
By Dr. Kent Spann

Introduction

We live in a culture of fear. The fear of terrorist attacks is now the norm since 9/11. Kids fear violence, not just on the streets, but in their schools and homes. The uncertainty of the United States economy hasn't helped, either. Bishop Fran Griswold in 2003 said, "The only sense of community we have now is shared fear or anxiety."[1]

Israel during the time of the Judges could certainly relate. Turn to Judges 6. The Israelites found their world in chaos. The Midianites were oppressing them. The Midianites were descendants of Abraham and Keturah (Genesis 25:1–2) whom Israel defeated during the wilderness wanderings (Numbers 22:4; 25:16–18). A nomadic people, their basic tactic was hit and run. They waited until the crops were ready to harvest and then, like a bully, they swooped in and took what they wanted. Israel was the victim. Israel's only recourse was to cry out to the Lord (6:6).

God's Rebuke of Israel (Judges 6:7–10)

Perhaps the Israelites were asking why this was happening to them. Maybe they were accusing God of disowning or abandoning them. In Judges, God sends a prophet to explain why all of this has happened to them: they were worshipping other gods. Israel thought that God had forsaken them when it was the opposite. They were being terrorized by the Midianites, because they were living outside of the will of God.

Here is a life truth: when you live outside of the will of God, expect turmoil.

Meanwhile. . . (Judges 6:11–22)

God was at work setting in motion His plan to deliver His people. He was calling out to Gideon to lead the people into battle.

1. **The Lord's Mighty Warrior (6:12).** The Lord's greeting must have startled Gideon. He probably looked around to see who was being greeted with this name of valor, because he sure didn't think of himself that way.

   God was talking to Gideon, addressing him not as he was, but as what he would become. He would be that mighty warrior. That is a powerful truth for us to remember as we live life before God: He doesn't see us as we are in our failure, but as we will be by His grace!

2. **Gideon's response to the promise of God's presence (6:13).** We would say, "Excuse me, Lord, but how can you say that you are with us when we are being invaded and conquered by the pagan Midianites? We don't see you doing the things you did in the early days."

   Sometimes it is hard to reconcile the promises of God with our circumstances. It is hard for us to see the hand of God, especially when we are living in sin.

3. **God's response to Gideon (6:14).** God doesn't outright answer the question, and yet He does answer. The fact that God was there calling out to Gideon was evidence that He hadn't forsaken them.

4. **Gideon's Response to God's Call (6:15).** God calls Gideon a valiant warrior; Gideon calls himself weak and lowest on the totem pole. He basically says to God, "Lord, do you realize who you are dealing with?" What was Gideon doing? He was making excuses why he couldn't do what God called him to do.

   Does Gideon's story resonate in your heart? It does because you have done the same thing. God has called you to a task or an act, but you have made excuses not to do those things. You let fear keep you from stepping out. You let your inadequacies keeping you from stepping out.

   God specializes in using the weak and inadequate (1 Cor. 1:26–29). Hudson Taylor, founder of the China Inland Mission, said, "All of God's great

men have been weak men who did great things for God because they reck-
oned on His being with them; they counted on His faithfulness."

5. **God's Response to Gideon's Excuse (6:16).** Gideon thought that the Lord
expected Gideon to get it done. God reminds Gideon that it isn't going to
be him that gets it done but God through Gideon.

6. **Gideon's Struggle of Faith (6:17–22).** Gideon struggles to believe what
God is telling him, so he asks for a sign. At this point, he just needs to be
sure that this is the Lord speaking to him, that it is really God calling him.

God graciously performs the miracle, and it is at that point when Gideon
realizes with certainty that he has been dealing with the Lord (6:22).

7. **God's Blessed Peace (6:23–24).** Gideon was fearful; God promises His
peace. The opposite of peace is fear, worry, and anxiety. Fear paralyzes us.

Gideon comes to a new realization about God: He is Jehovah Shalom
(6:24). In response to God's blessed assurance of peace, Gideon builds an
altar and names it Jehovah-Shalom, which in Hebrew means *The Lord is
Peace*. Shalom is a common Hebrew greeting. It is the equivalent of our
"hello." Shalom means peace.

God of Peace

What did Gideon really need? Peace. What do we really need? Peace.

1. **We need peace with God.** Gideon needed peace with God because he was
afraid in God's presence. He knew that he was a sinner and God was holy.
Israel needed peace with God, because sin and disobedience always leads to
fear. For examples, see Genesis 3:8–10 and Isaiah 57:20–21.

Men have been seeking peace with God since the fall of man. Only God
can provide the peace we need, and He did it through Christ (Isaiah 53:5;
Romans 5:1).

Herbert Hoover understood this truth as shown by his statement, "Peace
is not made at the Council table or by treaties, but in the hearts of men."

2. **We need peace from God.** Gideon also needed peace from God if he was
to accomplish the task of defeating the Midianites. The circumstances were
overwhelming, and he was inadequate for the task.

Now I want you to notice that peace from God certainly doesn't mean the absence of conflict. God was calling Gideon to battle. A battlefield is anything but peaceful. Jesus spoke of the peace He had as He faced the cruel cross (John 14:27).

We equate peace with the absence of conflict. Therefore, we are avoiding conflict. We change a job, bail out of a marriage, change schools, thinking that those actions will bring peace—but they won't. Peace is not found in a change of circumstance or venue; peace is found within a person. See 2 Thessalonians 3:16; Isaiah 26:3; Romans 8:6. When our peace is anchored in a relationship with God, then nothing can take away our peace, not even the turmoil of the world.

Conclusion

In his book *Peace Child*, Don Richardson records the moving account of how the Sawi people of Irian Jaya came to understand salvation through Jesus Christ. For many months, Don sought some way to communicate the gospel to this tribe. Finally, the answer came to their prayers. All demonstrations of kindness expressed by the Sawi were regarded with suspicion, except one act. If a father gave his own son to his enemy, his sacrificial deed showed that he could be trusted! Furthermore, everyone who touched that child was brought into a friendly relationship with the father. Don shares that Jesus was God's Peace Child. All who touched Him would be brought into a friendly relationship with God.

It was true for the Sawi people, and it is true for you, my friend.

Endnotes

http://www.freerepublic.com/focus/f-news/845190/posts

ADDITIONAL SERMONS AND LESSON IDEAS

When God Makes His Point

Jonah 4:5–9
By Phil Newton

God's purposes were abundantly accomplished in Nineveh. Thousands were converted; judgment had been averted. God's glory was manifested in His mercy, shown to the wicked Ninevites. You are almost left with the idea that the book of Jonah is primarily about Nineveh, but then you see the focus move from the masses in Nineveh to one lonely figure underneath a makeshift shelter. Jonah had done his duty, but God is never satisfied with His children merely performing duty. He is out to change our character, behavior, and world-view, and to shape us in His own image.

How was this accomplished in Jonah's life? How did God make His point with Jonah?

1. **The Lord exposes areas requiring discipline.** What needed to be changed in Jonah?

    A. **Ignoring reality (4:4).** When God asks such a question, there is something in the person's life that must be addressed. But Jonah ignored the reality of his own sin. He offered no response to the divine question.

    B. **Priority on what is temporal (4:5–8).** One of the most significant areas we find afflicting Jonah was his priority on the temporal events. He was overly concerned about his comforts rather than the eternal souls of the people of Nineveh.

    C. **Nursing attitudes (4:5).** Jonah was stewing over the favor being shown to the Ninevites. He nursed his secret (if we can call it secret!) attitude of bitterness, anger, and vengeance.

    D. **Dulled hearing (4:8–9).** Jonah was so consumed with his own interests, comforts, and desires, that he was insensitive to the voice of the Lord speaking to him. He was dulled in his hearing.

E. **Escapism mentality (4:8).** Jonah had earlier run from the word of the Lord. Now he just wanted to die. He did not want to face the realities of life. He was engaging in escapism. Refusing to deal with your sin, resisting efforts of reproof, and stubbornly refusing repentance are all examples of practicing escapism.

2. **The Lord applies the grace of discipline.** In what ways does the Lord discipline us?

A. **By asking people searching questions (4:9).** The purpose of God's questions is to cause Jonah to think. If only he could get a good look at what he was doing, it would seem that Jonah might turn from his soured attitude.

B. **In gentleness and kindness (4:6).** The text tells us that the Lord gave this plant "to deliver him from his discomfort." "The kindness of God leads you to repentance" (Rom. 2:4).

C. **Through distressing circumstances (4:8).** This "scorching east wind" refers to the hot Mediterranean sirocco winds. It is compared to the heat of an oven, blowing across the desert floor, torturing all in its path. It was a messenger sent to awaken him, to help him understand the foolishness of his complaints, to enable him to see the perverseness of his desires for Nineveh.

D. **With living parables (4:10–11).** "Jonah, you have had such great compassion on a plant that is here one day and forever gone the next. Should God show less compassion for those whom He has created and nurtured, who have eternal souls?"

Living parables may come to us through the circumstances of life, through observations in creation, through lessons in our families, through situations arising on the job.

Conclusion

If we keep in mind that discipline is not simply the concept of performing punitive acts, but a means of training children into maturity, it will encourage us to realize that God is training us.

Preached at South Woods Baptist Church in Memphis, Tennessee, May 16, 1999.

Why We Cannot Remain Silent

Mark 16: 15; John 14: 6, 21
By Dr. Bill Bright

There are five concepts concerning witnessing that will affect the lives of every Christian.

1. Christ has given a clear command to every Christian.
   A. Jesus Christ's command to the Christian community (Mark 16:15).
   B. This command is the duty and privilege of every man and woman who confesses Christ as Lord.
2. Men and women are lost without Jesus Christ.
   A. Jesus is the only way of salvation (John 14:6; Acts 4:12).
3. Rather than being "not interested," the people of the world are looking for God.
   A. When properly approached in the power of the Holy Spirit, the majority is truly hungry for the gospel.
   B. The vast fields of human souls are ripening all around us and are ready now for reaping.
4. We Christians have in our possession the greatest gift available to mankind, the greatest news ever announced.
   A. People want to hear the good news.
   B. When you present the good news with love in the power of the Holy Spirit, you will usually see a positive response.
5. The love of Jesus Christ for us, and our love for Him, compels us to share Him with others.
   A. Jesus measures our love for Him by the extent and genuineness of our obedience to Him (John 14:21).

Reproduced with permission of the North American Mission Board, Alpharetta, Georgia. All rights reserved.

WEEK 43

SERIES: HE IS JEHOVAH

Jehovah Tsidkenu

Jeremiah 23:1–6
By Dr. Kent Spann

Introduction: Unrighteous Everywhere (Jeremiah 23:1)

Up to this point, Jeremiah has been addressing the unrighteousness in Judah. In Jeremiah 21–22, he denounces the last five kings of Judah. Sadly, unrighteousness was not just out in the streets; it was in the pulpits of the land. The "spiritual" leaders of the land were unrighteous.

This can be likened to America today. (The preacher should come up with a list of things that show how unrighteousness is everywhere.)

Unrighteousness Brings the Judgment of God (Jeremiah 23:2)

Scripture teaches over and over again that righteousness always brings the judgment of God. Why does unrighteousness bring God's judgment? Simply stated, it is because God is righteous. It is who He is (Psalm 11:7; 48:10; 71:15; 116:5; 119:137), and it is how He acts (Jeremiah 9:24; Psalm 71:19).

God's righteousness has two implications for us.

1. **God demands righteousness (Deut. 6:25; Isa. 5:7; Matt. 5:48).**
2. **God defines righteousness (Psalm 50:6).** "Be perfect, therefore, as your heavenly Father is perfect" (Matthew 5:48; NIV).

We try to dumb down righteousness. We define it by others, by ourselves, by the government, the church, etc. We dumb down righteousness so that we can justify our own actions. Jesus told a parable about that in Luke 18.

Only God defines righteousness.

The Big Problem

Trying to justify our own actions creates a big problem. In order for us to be right with God, we have to have "perfect righteousness" (Matt. 5:48). The big problem is that we are not righteous (Rom. 3:9–18), nor can we become righteous on our own. What about our righteous deeds? Isaiah 64:6 makes it clear what God thinks of our righteous deeds.

The big problem is that we are absolutely unrighteous!

How Can we be Right with God?

If God demands perfect righteousness, but we are absolutely unrighteous, how then can we be right with God? That is the most important question that a person can ask. The answer to that question is troubling: We can't be right with God because we are all wrong with God.

God has to take care of the problem, which is precisely what He says He is going to do in Jeremiah 23:3–6.

1. **He is going to raise up one who is righteous (23:5).** God says that He is going to raise up a righteous branch. That righteous branch is Jesus Christ (1 John 2:1; Hebrews 4:15).

2. **The righteous one will become our righteousness (23:6).** Here we are introduced to one of the names of Jehovah. *Tsidkenu* is the transliteration of the Hebrew word. The word is *tsedsk*, which means straight, right, or conforming to an ethical or moral standard. Christ will be our righteousness.

   A. **Our sin was imputed to Christ so that He became sin for us** (Isaiah 53:5; Galatians 3:13; 1 Peter 3:18).

   B. **Christ's righteousness was imputed to us so that we have the righteousness of Christ** (2 Cor. 5:21; Rom. 5:12–19).

   C. **Because we have the righteousness of Christ, we are justified or right before God.** God through Christ first constitutes us as righteous and then declares us as righteous. It would be like Bill Gates depositing one billion dollars into your bank account and then declaring you wealthy.

Spurgeon described it this way:

When we believe in Christ, by faith we receive our justification. As the merit of his blood takes away our sin, so the merit of his obedience is imputed to us for righteousness. We are considered, as soon as we believe, as though the works of Christ were our works. God looks upon us as though that perfect obedience, of which I have just now spoken, had been performed by ourselves—as though our hands had been bonny at the loom, as though the fabric and the stuff which have been worked up into the fine linen, which is the righteousness of the saints, had been grown in our own fields. God considers us as though we were Christ—looks upon us as though his life had been our life—and accepts, blesses, and rewards us as though all that he did had been done by us, his believing people.[1]

Author and theologian John Stott said the following: "The concept of substitution lies at the heart of both sin and salvation. For the essence of sin is man substituting himself for God, while the essence of salvation is God substituting himself for men."

A twelve year old girl lay dying. Her mother asked her, "Are you afraid, my darling, to go and meet God?"

"Oh no," she replied, "I am not afraid; I look to the justice of God to take me to Heaven."

The mother thought her child must be wandering so she said, "My darling, you mean His pity, His love."

"No, mother," she replied, "I mean His justice. He must take me to Heaven, because Christ is my Righteousness, and I claim Him as my own; I am as He is now in God's sight, and God would never reject His own child."[2]

Conclusion

So what could get in the way of so wonderful a salvation? Dr. Gestner said, "Christ has done everything necessary for his salvation. Nothing now stands between the sinner and God but the sinners' good works."

In other words, pride will keep you from heaven. In June of 2006, Warren Buffet, the world's second-richest man at the time, announced that he would donate eighty-five percent of his forty-four billion dollar fortune to five charitable foundations. Commenting on this extreme level of generosity, Buffet said: "There is more than one way to get to heaven, but this is a great way."[3]

There is no other way to heaven. God's righteousness demands Christ's righteousness!

Endnotes

[1] Charles Haddon Spurgeon, "Jehovah Tsidkenu: The Lord Our Righteousness."

[2] Herbert W. Lockyer, *All the Names of God*, (Grand Rapids: Zondervan, 1975), 55.

[3] Associated Press, "How Do You Spend $1.5 Billion a Year?" *www.cbsnews.com* (June 27, 2006).

ADDITIONAL SERMONS AND LESSON IDEAS

Bearing with One Another

Romans 15:1–6
By Rev. Brian Bill

I have good news and bad news. The good news is that everyone who has received Jesus Christ is going to heaven. The bad news is that we're traveling there together.

In his book *People I Could Do Without*, Donald Smith writes that our pent-up irritation can either cause us to go on a "reactionary rampage" or to respond with a "silent seethe."[1] While it's difficult to put up with people who drive us crazy, we must learn to bear with them.

In this section of Romans, Paul is writing to two distinct groups of people in the church at Rome: the weak and the strong. And each group grated on the other.

In dealing with those who bug us, instead of shutting down or blowing up, we must:

1. **Put up (15:1).** The word, *bear* means to "endure patiently and to be indulgent." We're challenged here to restrain our natural reaction towards odd or difficult people by just letting them be themselves without thinking that they need to become just like us.
2. **Build up (15:2).** The phrase *build up* is a construction term. When we blast away at people, we willingly or unwillingly participate in the process of tearing them down. God longs for builders in the body of Christ (1 Thess. 5:1).
3. **Look up (15:3).** If you find yourself getting really mad at people, then it's probably because you're not looking up enough (Matt. 17:8). Friend, look up at Jesus and remember that He puts up with you *and* He puts up with the person who is bugging you.
4. **Grow up (15:4).** If we're going to bear with the porcupine people in our lives, we must also take responsibility to grow up in our faith by soaking up the Scriptures (1 Peter 2:2).

5. **Stand up (15:5).** Since God bears with us, we must be willing to stand up with those who are different from us. God's heart is for the church to be united and to stand together (Acts 4:32).

6. **Speak up (15:6).** The reason why we are to bear with one another is so that we can bring glory to God. To glorify is to cause people's attention to focus on God so that they acknowledge Him as important.

If we want the body of Christ to be built up, here are some exercises we can add to our spiritual workouts:

1. **Pray for problem people for two weeks.** Your relationship with people who irritate you will radically change if you pray for them by name.

2. **Let go of grudges and forgive faults.** Release your grip on a grudge, or it will strangle you. The longer you hold on to it, the more it gets hold of you.

3. **Perform an act of service.** Loving feelings tend to follow loving actions. If you wait for the feeling, you may be waiting a long time.

God blends our personalities, idiosyncrasies, gifts, talents, and experiences into something beautiful that He calls the church. And that's good news.

Endnotes

[1] Donald G. Smith, *People I Could Do Without*, (Lafayette, CO: White-Boucke Publishing, 2007).

The Sin of Silence

2 Kings 7:9

Rudy Hernadez

In the background of the text, Samaria is under siege by Ben-Hadad, King of Syria. Four lepers outside the gate were used by God to break the famine.

Searching men (7:3–4)

1. They were hungry for food.
2. They were hungry for health.
3. They were hungry for trust in others.
4. They were hungry for life.

Successful people

1. They were motivated by a personal need.
2. They were driven by common sense.
3. They were directed by divine intervention.

Satisfied people

1. They yielded to faith and feasted on the findings.
2. They yielded to greed and hoarded the bounty.
3. They yielded to conviction and acknowledged their sin.

Sharing people

1. They were apprised of their victory.
2. They were awakened to their sin.
3. They were challenged by their responsibility.

We have a crisis, and we must attend to it. We have a crowd and we must minister to it. We have a cross, and we must communicate it. We have a crown, and we must share it. We must get up (get awake), listen up (get attentive), sign up (get committed), gear up (get ready), brush up (get trained), and team up (get organized). Finally, we must speed up (get going).

WEEK 44

Alive and Six Who Said So!

1 Corinthians 15:1–8
By Calvin Miller

Introduction

Beyond the shroud, beyond the blood and bandages, beyond the spices and the close, dank air, He stood alive once more. The Greek word for this is *anastasis*; the English derivative is the proper name *Anastasia*. Both words mean "to stand again." Dead men lie; living men stand. The proper sequence is to stand, then lie, and then lie forever. But Jesus stood, lay, and then stood again, alive forevermore. And for six weeks after He was laid in a cold tomb, He stood again upon the earth.

He's Alive!

The resurrection is not to be doubted. In 1 Corinthians 15:3–8, Paul publishes the first list of resurrection witnesses ever to be set down in ink. Here is the list, the first list ever to be compiled, of six who said that they actually saw the dead Christ alive again. The first to see Christ was Peter, and the last was Paul.

Appearance one was Peter. Why first? Because he had a lot of corrective confession to take care of. He had last seen Jesus alive on Maundy Thursday at the Savior's trial where the apostle had denied, even to the point of profanity, that he even knew Christ. He needed a brighter, more confident, sunlit morning to correct his treachery.

Appearance six was Paul. Why last? Well for one thing, Paul's appearance came a couple of years after everyone else's. Paul, in the meantime, had held the coats of those who had stoned Stephen. He had some apologizing to do, too. These two men, who were the two most responsible for the beginning of the Christian enterprise, were the book-ends of this first list of witnesses. Peter would get a good chance to repent when Christ served him a hot fish breakfast by Galilee in

John 21. Paul got his chance to say "Yes Lord!" on the Damascus road. Between number one and number six, there were four more in Paul's list of witnesses.

Appearance two came, as you would expect, to the twelve, only there were only eleven of them left. Appearance number two must be divided into two parts, for the appearance to the twelve occurs twice right after Jesus arose (John 20:24–31). Appearance Two-A was just to the ten (minus Thomas), and appearance Two-B was to the eleven a week later with Thomas. Perhaps Paul counts it as one appearance because it was relatively to the same observers.

Appearance three was to over 500 brethren at once. If you want to strengthen the case that He really is alive, He's got to quit showing up just in little cameo appearances. Is there an Epic Appearance with a cast of thousands? Yes, at least of half a thousand. If only a few people see Him, it might be only a hallucination; but if hundreds see Him at the same time, it is an honest apparition, or a real appearance. It was Abraham Lincoln who said, "You can fool all of the people some of the time, and some of the people all of the time, but you cannot fool all of the people all of the time." This is certainly the case of Christ's third appearance. Here is Christ on the front of the New York *Times*! Here is Christ on a billboard! The neon sign appearance is this appearance! Historically high and lifted up! Jesus is alive!

Appearance four is to James, his half-brother. This is the same James who, in Mark 3:31–35, had likely gone with his family, his mother and brothers, to get Jesus off his berserk (as James saw it) preaching tour. At that early time in Jesus' earthly ministry, apparently James didn't believe that Jesus was the Messiah. What changed his mind? Who knows? But legend says that it was this rather confrontational appearance that did it. The story circulated widely that Jesus came to his doubting brother by walking into the old Carpenter shop that Jesus had earlier abandoned. Then James, who had afterwards taken over the family business, saw Jesus alive again and came to faith in the living Christ.

Why does this skeptic get special treatment? Is it just because he's in the family? No, I think not. I think it is because James, like Thomas, is not a disinterested skeptic. It is because James was crying out to believe that Jesus really was alive. Aching skeptics are the special target of God's love. Hence, resurrection appearance number four.

Appearance five is to the disciples again. Maybe it was the Olivet, Great Commission appearance that Paul has in mind for this one. If so, it is one of the most consequential of all appearances—the mandate of world redemption.

Conclusion

There is a story I have heard in several versions that tells of a little boy whose doting parents had spoiled their son into "brathood." On one occasion, the boy was found carrying a paper sack filled with the most pitiful kind of stirring. He had captured a lot of tiny birds, and their imprisoned wing-beats were slapping hopelessly against the manila walls of their paper prison. Their pitiful chirping sounded small and hopeless.

He met an old man as he walked along. "Whatcha got in that sack?" asked the old man.

"A sack full of sparrows!" said the boy.

"What are you going to do with them?" asked the man.

"I am going to take them out of the sack one by one and tease them—pull a feather out now and then, and then release them to the cat for his dinner."

"How much would you sell the whole sack for?"

The little boy thought a moment and decided to put a lot of capital on the venture. "I'll take two dollars for the whole sack."

"Done," said the old man, and he reached into his pocket, pulled out the two dollars, and gave them to the lad. The boy handed him the sack.

In but a moment, he untwisted the coiled neck of the bag and pulled it open, and the imprisoned birds exploded into the freedom of the open sky.

And so it happened one day that God met Lucifer with a huge bag. Inside the bag there were the sounds of human desperation begging for life.

"Whatcha got in the bag?" asked the Father.

"The people. . . all of them!" smirked Lucifer.

"And what will you do with them?" asked God.

"I will take them out and torment them one by one and, when they are all worn out with trials, I will throw them into hell."

"What would you take for the whole bag?" asked God.

"Only your Beloved Son!"

"Done!" said the Father, and He opened the bag.

And right after that, He opened the Tomb!

And how do we know for sure that Jesus walked out of it! Simple math! There were six who said so.

ADDITIONAL SERMONS AND LESSON IDEAS

Giving God Your Best

Malachi 1:6–14

By Rev. Brian Bill

It isn't easy to listen, is it? That's probably how Malachi's listeners felt. Let me remind you of the situation Malachi is addressing. The Jews had returned to their land after living in modern-day Iraq for seventy years. The temple had been rebuilt, and the worship of God had been reestablished. While outwardly everything seemed okay, on the inside a cancer of complacency had been eating away at their commitment. Their worship had become wimpy, their leaders had morphed into lightweights, their relationships had ruptured, their offerings were anemic, and they had stopped serving. As God's final spokesman at the end of the Old Testament, Malachi comes on the scene to challenge them—and us—to give God our best.

1. **Embrace an authentic faith** (1:6, 7). There are two sides to the Father's love. One side is tender and the other a bit tougher. He is relational in His giving, and He is resplendent in His glory, and as such, we must honor Him, which means to consider Him weighty.

2. **Give God priority over possessions** (1:8–9). The priests were accepting, not just the second best from the people; but worse than that, they were bringing God sick sheep and gross goats. They were offering the ones that weren't worth anything. God is not interested in substandard sacrifices (Lev. 22:2, 19, 20).

    There are three standards for sacrifices in Scripture.

    A. Give the best (John 12:3–5).

    B. Give to God first (2 Chron. 31:5).

    C. Giving should cost us something (2 Sam. 24:24).

3. **Grasp the greatness of God** (1:10–14). God would much rather have us shut down the church than to come to Him with pathetic leftovers. Every time God mentions sacrifice, He follows it with the phrase, "I will be great"

or "I will be feared." Sacrifice is directly linked to the greatness of God. When we offer Him little or nothing, we are really saying that God doesn't matter much to us.

Instead of counting it a privilege to minister on God's behalf, they exclaimed, "What a burden!" They even "sniffed at it contemptuously," which means that they "puffed" or "blew" in exaggerated exasperation. I imagine God looking at us and wondering why we get so bored with Him (see Micah 6:3; Isa. 1:12, 13).

If you ever get a glimpse of the greatness of God and what Jesus has done for you, you'll never play church again and you'll give God your best for the rest of your life.

The Obvious Priority of Evangelism

Matthew 18:11
By Dr. Bailey E. Smith

There is only one reason that Jesus died, and it's because there is a literal hell. There is no one who can be Savior and Redeemer other than He who graced Golgotha's crest: Jesus Christ.

The Real Thing of Evangelism

1. **We must acknowledge these truths:**
   A. **Hell is hot.**
   B. **Heaven is sweet.**
   C. **Judgment is certain.**
   D. **Salvation is only in Christ Jesus.**

   Only when we understand these things can we lead the world from darkness to light, death to life, and despair to joy.
2. **We must all be clear about the real purpose of evangelism: winning every lost person to a saving knowledge of Christ.** People are not more difficult to reach today than they were fifty years ago, but too often Christians are lazier then they were fifty years ago. Let's knock on the doors for the One who is the door to life abundant and life everlasting. No one is going to tell them unless we do.

The Realistic Task Before Us

Because our world is lost, the task before us demands an all-out effort in at least two areas:

1. **Reaching the lost.**
2. **Motivating Christians to be consistent soul winners.**

Sometimes it is easy to get the idea that churches are making A's in everything that doesn't matter. We have excelled in all that is unimportant, but in the one thing Christ has told us to do—to win, teach, and baptize—we have flunked out.

WEEK 45

COMMUNION SERMON

To Contemplate The Cross

I Corinthians 11:11–18
By Dr. Calvin Miller

Introduction

When we really celebrate communion, we discover a Christ who is not just the Lord of a little ritual. He is a Christ who suffers, who dies, and who bleeds His love and weeps His last moments away pleading for His church to be one. In light of this call to unity in love, Paul writes to these Corinthians, "I find you filled with unforgiveable divisions." See 1 Corinthians 1:11–18.

Paul reiterates his concern about this division with a couple of things on his mind.

First, they had picked out personal heroes.

In championing their individual favorites, they had forgotten that there is only one Hero of the Faith. One flick of our radio dial today and we can hear any number of preachers; nearly all are heroes to someone. Our lists of heroes do not always match. Paul is saying here that only Jesus has the unquestioned right to heroism in the church. When we become divided over any other personalities of the preached gospel, we seriously err!

Second, they showed favoritism.

Let us reconstruct the early church that Paul is speaking to. In that church, there were a few very wealthy patrons. Cowering behind the wealthy at these dinners were the poor slaves of the Roman Empire. These slaves had little. When they huddled in the corner with their crusts of nothing while the wealthy patrons of the church walked by to get their food, those who were wealthy were scared to death that the poor would run ahead and eat the food they had brought to church to eat themselves. No wonder Paul cried out his rebuke: "Do you despise the church of God and shame those who have nothing?" (1 Cor. 11:22).

Here we must introduce the word that we use too fast and loose. The word *communion* means "to be one with—to make one of the two!" Yet, when the church comes together with an obvious socio-economic distrust, the church remains two. Communion declares, "There are no special people of favor in this world, except that in the cross all people have been made people of special favor!"

What is it that this wonderful, broken body of Jesus does? What is the accomplishment of His beautiful, yet heinous, horrible, yet wonderful, spilling of the blood of Christ? What is the great interpersonal healing hidden in the cross? When you are tempted to get short with people, remember His dying love. Do people annoy you? Think about God's marvelous cross-love.

The cross on which Jesus died is linked by our own cross in Galatians 2:20, "a cross on which I crucify myself," understanding that my life is not my own. I am in debt to all people. Elton Trueblood once said:

> Once a Christian has become a member of Christ's company he must be ready to give up some of his personal freedom, much as any soldier—and even as any Communist—does. He may, for example, no longer be the sole arbiter of his own time and energy; and he cannot be free to use all of his money on his own self-indulgence.[1]

When we speak of taking up the cross, we speak of sacrifice! Sacrifice our sacrifice, His sacrifice! If you are going to be in the company of Jesus' disciples, you must be prepared to sacrifice personal freedom or time or money or life. We ought to ask ourselves, "What does it mean to be a part of Jesus' community?" Jesus said, "You are going to make sacrifices if you are going to follow me. You are going to take up your cross, and you are going to walk after me daily."

We are not only to think of the cross when we have communion. It is literally to stay out in front of our minds and hearts as we live! Every moral consequence! Every moral action! All must be brought to the cross and made to bow and cry out, "Lord Jesus, is this worthy of the blood you have spilled on my behalf?"

To touch the person of Jesus Christ is to remember what He did and the cost of it. When you do remember, you will be compelled to declare, "I have nothing but the highest adoration for such a Christ."

When the church comes together, it comes together to celebrate the cross. It is harder in Protestant churches to see the plainness of our glory. Walking into a Catholic church and seeing a crucifix Sunday by Sunday prompts people to remember that the church gathers to celebrate the death of our Lord Jesus Christ.

And such a celebration is always to occur in illumination of our inner lives and motives (1 Cor. 11:28)! "Examine yourself! Examine yourself!" cries the apostle. "If you can taste the wine without thinking of the blood, if you can taste the wafer without thinking of His body, you have sinned a great sin. You literally eat and drink damnation to yourself!"

We are to examine ourselves. We must ask what the cross means and how the suffering of Jesus Christ is related to wash day and our gathering of rosebuds. We know, however, that it means we are in communion with Christ. Being one with Him, we must pick up our cross and follow Him, living a crucified life! Only in such living can we paint a valid picture of who Jesus is.

When I think about the cross of Christ and all it means to be one in communion with Him, I understand that it really is possible to draw a picture of God! But if you are going to draw a picture of God properly, you must take upon yourself the cross of Christ! Luke 9:23 says that we do not do that for a lifetime. We do it momentarily. We must take up our cross daily. Every day we live, we must live under the Lordship of the Christ who died.

I think that I know what Jesus meant when He said, "Life is to be a daily taking of our cross." And I understand what Paul means in the last of this beautiful passage when he says, "Learn to serve each other." The greatest service Jesus could do, He did when He hung by His hands and died in the April wind. The greatest service we can do for Him is when we sacrifice our plans and agenda and say, moment by exulting moment, "Lord, Lord Jesus. You have, in blood and brokenness, showed me what it means to live and die for others. Thus I do take up my cross!"

Endnotes

[1] Elton Trueblood, *The Company of The Committed* (New York: Harper & Row, 1961), 40

[2] Ibid.

ADDITIONAL SERMONS AND LESSON IDEAS

Hannah: A Woman of Faith

1 Samuel 1:1–2:11
By Rev. Brian Bill

A mother was talking to an old friend and said, "I remember before I was married that I had three theories about raising children. Now I have three children and no theories." The Bible doesn't really deal in theory, but instead provides principles and practices for us to follow. If you're a mom and looking for a model to mimic, may I suggest that you hold on to the Old Testament woman named Hannah?

Hannah portrays five defining traits of a woman of faith.

1. **Women of faith exhibit real problems (1:1–8).** The Bible is filled with real people with real problems, who face them with real faith. Hannah was barren and as a result was spiritually disturbed, socially disgraced, and emotionally depressed. On top of that, her rival Penninah felt the need to needle and harass her.

2. **Women of faith express vibrant prayers (1:9–18).** Hannah had problems, but she didn't shut down or lash out at those around her. She expressed her faith in prayer. God uses our problems to get our attention and to teach us (Ps. 119:71). Her weeping led to worship, as her tears mingled with her prayers. It is significant that verse 12 says, "She kept on praying to the Lord." This wasn't just a quick popcorn prayer. This was a repeated request, bathed in tears.

3. **Women of faith experience God's provision (1:19, 20).** A short time later, Hannah conceived and gave birth to a son, naming him Samuel. His name sounds like the Hebrew for "heard of God." Every time she said his name, she was reminded of his origin and destiny.

4. **Women of faith excel at keeping their promises (1:21–28).** Many people make promises to God, only to forget them once time passes. Not so with Hannah. She fully intended to keep her promise, because she knew that

Samuel did not really belong to her anyway. Hannah not only dedicated herself to her child, she also dedicated her child to the Lord and brought him to the house of the Lord.

5. **Women of faith explode with praise (2:1–11).** Hannah then breaks into praise because she was thrilled to be able to parent a prophet! Notice that she doesn't brag about how handsome Samuel is, or how smart he is, or how neat it is that he can say prayers at his young age. She overlooks the gift and gives praise to the Giver.

Conclusion

Hannah is an example of a woman of faith. She endures years of silent suffering because of her barrenness and the cruel harassment at the hand of Penninah. She goes to the place of worship, knowing how painful it is. She faithfully worships, pouring out her tears and petitions. And when God answers her prayers, she not only keeps her promise, she explodes with praise.

Mothers, make it your mission to give your children to the Lord for a lifetime of dedicated service. Hold on to the model of Hannah, no matter what child rearing theories abound.

The Strangest Thing About God

Hebrews 2:14–18
Dr. Mark D. Roberts

Begin your sermon with a story about a time when your expectations for someone were completely turned upside down.

The Strangest Things About God

1. God hears all prayers at once.
2. God puts up with our imperfections.

The Strange Truth of Hebrews 2:14–18

God's response to human need and suffering:

1. To become human in Jesus in every respect (except for sinning).
2. To take on our human limitations and suffering (Heb. 2:17).

The Example of Aslan

Aslan's willingness to become vulnerable, even to die, in *The Lion, the Witch, and the Wardrobe*. It is a beautiful picture of Christ's own incarnation and condescension.

No Quick Fix

Part of what is strange about God's choice to save is that it offers no quick and simple solution.

Good News! Jesus is Able to Help

1. Because Jesus experienced what we experience, He is able to help us (Heb. 2:18).

2. Jesus knows how it feels to be human: to love, to hurt, to suffer, to be tempted, and to be rejected. Thus, He is able both to understand and to help.

3. The strangest thing about God is also the most wonderful thing about God!

Scripture quotations from the NRSV.

WEEK 46

RIGHT TO LIFE SUNDAY

Raising the Children We Cherish

Proverbs 4:1–10
By Dr. Jerry Sutton

Introduction

A key component of the right to life movement is the underlying assumption that children are valuable. In fact, Psalm 127:3 tells us that "children are a gift from the Lord." If children are a valuable gift from the Lord, what obligation does that bring to parents? In Paul's words, "parents are commanded to raise their children in the nurture and admonition of the Lord." Another translation is that parents are to "bring them up in the training and instruction of the Lord" (Eph 6:4).

Apart from Jesus, the wisest man in history was Solomon. He discusses parenting in Proverbs, and in fact refers back to what he learned from his father David. What instructions did Solomon receive from his father? And what life skills did he attempt to pass on to his children?

Proverbs 4:1, 2 records Solomon's word to his own sons. "Listen, my sons, to a father's discipline, and pay attention so that you may gain understanding, for I am giving you good instructions. Don't abandon my teaching."

The foundation here addresses issues of discipline by the parent, attention by the child, and the payoff, which is the child's understanding. The admonition is "get this" and do not lose it. Do not abandon my teaching!

My contention is that the same words need to be communicated with our children today. We must discipline our children. We must instruct our children. We must strive to give our children our understanding of how the world works. And we need to admonish them not to abandon what we have taught them.

Notice, in verses 1–10, how Solomon describes for his children what David taught him. He gives a principle in the form of a command, and then identifies the payoff for embracing the principle.

Pay Attention and You Will Gain Understanding (4:1)

You can hear without gaining understanding, but you cannot gain understanding without hearing. Solomon knew to challenge his sons to pay attention, be perceptive, and grasp what is being said.

Many opportunities are lost because we fail to pay attention. How many times has a door been opened for us but we missed it because we were not alert? If we want to gain understanding, we must pay attention!

Keep the Commands and You Will Live (4:4)

This refers not simply to a father's commands to his children, but to every command that the Lord has given. Recall the Great Commission's demands. The single phrase is "make disciples!" The key imperative verb is "make." The "going," "baptizing," and "teaching" are participles modifying the command to "make disciples." And on closer inspection, the final command is not simply to teach, but to "teach them to obey everything I have commanded you" (Matt. 28:18–20).

One of God's principal concerns is that we keep His Commands. This is the pathway to life!

Don't Abandon Wisdom and She Will Watch Over You (4:6)

Wisdom is the ability to see life from God's perspective and to make decisions accordingly. The challenge for so many believers is that they reach a level of maturity but then begin to coast. In short, they abandon wisdom and then are surprised when life turns sour. We must constantly remind our children (and ourselves) that being wise is more than what we know; it is what we do.

Love Wisdom and She Will Guard You (4:6)

The Lord has so structured life that, when we live wisely, safeguards are in place that keep us from the danger of destructive temptation. God's desire is that we cultivate such a love for wisdom that we will automatically run in its direction. If we allow wisdom to be our constant companion, the Lord will be our constant protector.

Cherish Understanding and She Will Exalt You (4:8)

Verses 1, 5, and 7 emphasize the importance of gaining understanding. It comes from paying attention and placing a priority on its content. Knowing God's ways, God's values, and God's priorities is crucial. Those who pursue knowing the heart of God should not be surprised when God blesses them. In this place, it is being exalted or promoted. Recall that being exalted does not come from another person but from God's decision (Ps. 75:6–7).

Embrace Understanding and She Will Honor You (4:8–9)

That last phrase means that she will bring you honor. To embrace understanding means to wrap one's arms around it as a cherished friend. What the Lord is saying to us is that we need to value and embrace understanding as a top priority! Where do we find understanding? From the truth of God's Word. James admonishes us to be doers of the Word and not hearers only! If we make gaining understanding a top priority, God will bring us honor! Solomon describes this honor in terms of an ornament and a crown.

Accept My Words and You Will Live Many Years (4:10)

This is a parallel passage to Ephesians 6:2, "Honor your father and mother— which is the first commandment with a promise—that it may go well with you and that you may have a long life in the land."

These seven principles and their payoffs are the foundation of what every child needs to know. And the responsibility to teach these things rests with the parents.

Conclusion

So, for you who are parents, will you (in the words of Paul) commit yourself to raise your children in the nurture and admonition of the Lord?

ADDITIONAL SERMONS AND LESSON IDEAS

God's Answers to Our Questions

Job 38–42

By Rev. Brian Bill

I was on the wrestling team in high school. I wasn't that good. In fact, during our homecoming match my senior year, even though I was captain of the team, I got pinned in seven seconds!

After being pummeled with some questions by his friends, Job has some questions for God, and he asks them throughout the book. In chapter 38, God answers Job with some questions of His own. Actually, He challenges Job to a wrestling match. The phrase "brace yourself like a man" is an image taken directly from the ancient sport of belt-wrestling. Job is invited onto the mat with the Almighty and ends up going two rounds with Him.

God is not out to crush Job, but to make him contrite. He's not interested in humiliating Job, but instead wants to humble him.

Round One (Job 38–39)

In chapter 38, the Almighty has Job gaze at the heavens, and in chapter 39 he's directed to observe some animals. I count sixty different questions that are asked by the Almighty in these chapters. After each question, if you listen carefully, you can almost hear Job whisper, "I'll pass on that one."

Round Two (Job 40–41)

Not surprisingly, round one goes to God. Unfortunately for Job, the bell for round two goes off in 40:7, 8, and God continues His questioning. While Job is silenced, he is not yet convinced, so God grabs his belt again and puts him on his back.

God then asks Job to consider two great creatures, the Behemoth and the Leviathan. If no one can control what God has created, how can Job control the Creator?

Job's response to the Almighty in round two is found in 42:3: "Surely I spoke of things I did not understand, things too wonderful for me to know."

Job doesn't get all of his questions answered, but he does get to know the Almighty. He finally breaks down and throws in the towel in 42:5–6. When we really see God, we can't help but be changed. Job repented of thinking that he had the right to judge Jehovah.

Ultimately, the only answer God gave to Job was Himself. This has been called the first rule of the Christian life: He is God, and we are not.

Here are some lessons we can draw from Job.

1. The time to prepare for suffering is before suffering comes.
2. We need a new view of God and a new view of ourselves.
3. God's good will for each of us includes suffering (1 Peter 4:12).
4. We can and must praise and worship God even when we are in pain (Job 1:20).
5. God is not obligated to answer our accusations, but we are obligated to answer Him.
6. God's silence is not the same as His absence.

Maybe we should think twice about entering a wrestling match with God.

When Welcome Isn't Easy

1 Peter 4:8–11
Dr. Mark D. Roberts

As a pastor, sometimes I have been "The Complaint Department." (Tell a time when you were you were the complaint department.)

Be Hospitable Without Grumbling

1. 1 Peter 4:9 calls us to be hospitable "without complaining." The Greek word for "complaining" is *gongusmos*, meaning "murmuring" or "grumbling."
2. Why would Peter add "without grumbling?" Because he knew that sometimes welcoming people isn't easy. We can only be hospitable to those who bug us on the basis of "the manifold grace of God" (1 Pet. 4:10).
3. Churches are often greenhouses for grumbling and complaining. If we were to take 1 Peter 4:9 to heart and do it, it would change our churches and empower our witness.

But isn't there a time for complaining?

There are times when it is right to communicate negative information (for example, Matt. 18:15). But complaining is not only unbiblical, it also hardens our hearts to others and even to God.

The Challenge of the Uncomplaining Life

For many, the uncomplaining life will not come easily. But, by God's grace, it will transform our attitudes, our relationships, and our ability to embody the grace of God as His people.

(Scripture quotations from the nrsv.)

WEEK 47

INDEPENDENCE DAY MESSAGE

God and Nations

Psalm 75:6–7
By Dr. Jerry Sutton

Introduction

All over the world, we are seeing kingdoms and regimes fall, and watching new ones emerge to take their place. In light of these developments, it is wise to seek understanding from God's Word. Hear Psalm 75:6, 7: "Exaltation does not come from the east, the west or the desert, for God is the judge: He brings down one and exalts another."

In light of events unfolding in the world today, what can we, the people of God, conclude? Instead of being fearful or anxious, we can have great confidence that God Himself is in control.

Scriptural Proof that God is in Charge

1. **God is the judge.** God is the only one in the universe with absolute knowledge. He is the only one who is absolutely just. And He is the only one who is all powerful. Scripture teaches us that this God, our God, is the judge of all the earth.

   Not only will He judge the saints at the Judgment Seat of Christ and the lost at the Great White Throne Judgment, but He remains the all-powerful judge today. He decides the fate of nations and their rulers.

2. **All human kingdoms are temporary.** Through history, kingdoms have emerged and then collapsed. Some last longer than others. Some thought the Greek Empire would last forever. It fell. Others thought the Roman Empire would last forever. It fell. Hitler bragged that his Third Reich would last a thousand years. It did not last a thousand weeks! Why? Because all human kingdoms are temporary. Only God's kingdom will last for eternity.

As much as we love our nation, the United States, we must understand that it too will someday come to an end. Why? Because all human kingdoms are temporary. Yet, we can take comfort in the fact that God Himself decides how long it will endure!

3. **God chooses when to remove leaders and when to remove nations.** Psalm 75:7 tells us, "He brings down one and exalts another." This was clearly demonstrated when God decided to remove Saul and replace him with David in ancient Israel. Recall how the Apostle Paul expressed his own concern about God placing him on the shelf, becoming a castaway, because of the prospect of compromise. He guarded his own heart so that something like this would not happen.

4. **God chooses which nations to exalt and which leaders to bolster.** Again, Scripture says, "He exalts another." So can you and I do anything to sway the heart of God? Consider this. Proverbs 14:34 tells us, "Righteousness exalts a nation, but sin is a disgrace to any people." When a nation as a whole, or a large portion of people in a nation, insist on living righteously, God, I believe, knows that desire! Yet, when they turn away from the Lord, it should be no surprise that a nation falls.

Another critical verse for us to consider is 2 Chronicles 7:14. If there is a human element in the rise and fall of a nation, it is when God's people in that nation seek the Lord. God help us seek Him!

I believe the future of our nation is dependent not on our mighty military, not on homeland security, or even which political party is running the nation. It is directly dependent, I am convinced, on the people of God praying and living righteously.

The hard question to answer is, how about you? If righteous living provides security for our nation, if it is up to you, how secure are we?

God said this to Ezekiel, "I searched for a man among them who would repair the wall and stand in the gap before Me on behalf of the land so that I might not destroy it, but I found no one" (Ezek. 22:30). The result? The wrath of God was poured out on that nation!

Conclusion

If we consider the testimony of Proverbs, 2 Chronicles, and Ezekiel, we must conclude, at least partially, that the security of our nation is directly dependent upon the holiness, steadfastness, and intercession of the people of God. Heaven help us to live righteously, be steadfast, and to intercede!

ADDITIONAL SERMONS AND LESSON IDEAS

How to Handle Conflict

Matthew 5:21–25
By Rev. Brian Bill

Introduction

A couple of years ago, I took our lawnmower blade in for its yearly sharpening. I found out that I had the blade on upside down the entire year. I wondered why our lawn hadn't looked very lush.

In order for the lawnmower to work properly, the blade must be put on correctly. Most of us know what we're supposed to do, but we don't always do it correctly. This is especially the case when it comes to handling conflict. One person said this about Christians who quarrel: "Where two or three come together in Jesus' name, there will eventually be conflict."

In Matthew 5:23, 24, we read some words that are simple to understand and yet so sharp that they're bound to cut us:

1. **Anger can wipe out our worship.** Being reconciled is more important than being religious.
2. **Peacemaking is very personal.** The pronouns change in this passage from the plural "you all" to "you" singular.
3. **Friction in the family must be dealt with.** The word "brother" is used four times in verses 22–24.

Steps for Handling Conflict

Verse 24 lays out four steps for us to take when we have tension in a relationship.

Leave Abruptly

We need to pause in our praise until we're at peace, because God is more pleased with correct relationships than He is with correct ritual.

Go quickly

We're to leave the place of reverence to go find the place of reconciliation with the one we've wronged. The priority in peacemaking is to resolve everything right away.

Matthew 18:15 says the same thing, only we're told to go if we've been the one sinned against. Whether you have been wronged or you're in the wrong, it's always right to go. Ideally, we should run into the person we're in conflict with, because if they're doing it right, they'll be coming to us. But even when they don't show, we are still required to go.

Be reconciled

Let's personalize the priority of peacemaking by saying this phrase together: the pursuit of reconciliation is always my responsibility.

The verb tense changes here, suggesting an intense effort. Remember, the goal is reconciliation, not revenge.

The Peacemakers ministry offers "Four Promises of Forgiveness" that are very helpful.[1]

1. **I will not dwell on this incident.**
2. **I will not bring this incident up and use it against you.**
3. **I will not talk to others about this incident.**
4. **I will not allow this incident to stand between us or hinder our personal relationship.**

Come worship

Reconciliation is important enough to interrupt our worship of God because unresolved conflict has already interrupted our worship. A right relationship with God depends on our willingness to maintain a right relationship with one another.

Conclusion

When the blade of the Bible is put on correctly, it's always sharp. It can be painful (Heb. 4:12), but it also leads to peace.

Endnotes

[1] Peacemaker Ministries, "Four Promises of Forgiveness," *http://www.peacemaker.net/site/c. aqKFLTOBIpH/b.1172255/apps/s/content.asp?ct=1464677* (accessed January 29, 2011).

A Preacher's Four Orders

2 Timothy 4:1–5
By Dr. Dean Register

In the New Testament, Jesus began His ministry by preaching (Matt. 4:17). After the resurrection, the apostles spread the message of Jesus throughout the Roman Empire by preaching. In Paul's final letter to Timothy, he presents a portrait of a preacher's four orders.

1. A preacher is ordered to proclaim God's Word.
   A. Paul used the Greek word *preach* (*kēryxon*) to convey an announcement.
   B. A preacher is under orders to announce the message of his Sovereign.
   C. A preacher is charged with proclaiming God's Word instead of human opinion.
2. A preacher is commanded to carry out the assignment with discipline.
   A. He must discipline his heart to proclaim the gospel, whether he feels like it or not.
   B. He must correct error, rebuke iniquity, and encourage faith.
   C. He must fulfill his assignment with patient teaching.
3. A preacher is warned that many will not embrace God's truth.
   A. Many will reject sound doctrine.
   B. Many will develop "itching ears" and hear only what they prefer.
   C. Many will turn away from God and turn toward myths.
4. A preacher is charged to rescue the perishing.
   A. He must keep his mind focused on Christ's mission.
   B. He must engage in reaching the lost.

Conclusion
A faithful preacher is a powerful tool in the hand of God.

WEEK 48

THANKSGIVING SERMON

Ninety Percent of All Lepers

Luke 17:12–19
By Dr. Calvin Miller

Introduction

C. S. Lewis said that ancient man approached God out of a strong feeling that he was approaching a judge. "For modern man, the roles are reversed," says Lewis. "Modern man is the judge and God is in the dock."[1] Maybe this is why we feel that we have no obligation to thank Him. I suspect that this is what lies behind the reason that we are developing a culture without a sense of thankfulness. But for me, our thanklessness smacks of a lazy atheism. Remember, one old definition of an *atheist* is someone who sometimes feels gratitude, but has absolutely no one to thank for it!

There are two sides in the issue of all self-righteous abundance: the thankful and the thankless. The thankless tend to act as though they are responsible for their circumstances and are entirely self-made. The thankful see the providence of God in all they hold. The thankful believe that it is not how much we have or don't have in life, but what we view as the source of what we have or don't have that is important.

I once sat down with a missionary couple in Costa Rica who obviously were living on a shoestring. I studied the very meager table as we sat down. As the host said grace, his prayer swelled with such gratitude over God's abundance that I was tempted to open my eyes to peek and see if there was something on the table that I had missed. But I had missed nothing. It was not what was on the table that really produced gratitude; rather, his Christian gratitude was a way of life.

I have sat down with a great many people who fed me more sumptuously, but their sign to begin eating was not a bowed head, but the green light signal of a fork which the host picked up.

But back to the lone Samaritan leper whose thankfulness mandated a bent neck and said, "God, You are the Giver of this feast." The 90 percentile lepers are those who begin to eat when the host picks up his fork. All of this goes to prove the old cliché: "gratitude really is an attitude." Gratitude has absolutely nothing to do with what we have. Gratitude is a lifestyle. It rehearses praise so continually that God is always the Giver, and lepers are cleansed by His giving.

Is Jesus sorry that He cleansed the ingrates? Of course not, it is God's nature to cleanse, to heal, and to give. But He does ask a very profound question in Luke 17, "Where are the other nine?" It's a fair question! If ten lepers are healed and only one comes back, where are the other nine?

Let us live, therefore, in a constant attitude of God's abundance and reverence, as urged by the writer of Hebrews (12:28). Now, I know that God does not always provide us all the abundance that we want. But Psalm 37:25 says, "I am old but have been young and I have never seen the righteous forsaken nor his seed begging bread." My suspicion is, this week most of you will sit down to a very fine meal. I hope that, as you do, Psalm 100:4 will come to you, "Enter his gates with thanksgiving, and enter his courts with praise." God is the keeper of your feast. He is the maker of your feast.

Tony Campolo said that, as he was eating a meal in Haiti, he started to pick up his fork and eat when he glanced to the window, which was near his table, and saw the faces of little hungry Haitian children, faces pressed against the glass, watching him eat, mesmerized. "For a moment," his said, "I had the awful feeling of guilt and sat poised, not knowing whether to eat or not." Then the waiter stepped over and said, "Sir, don't let this bother you," and pulled the blinds. "I laid down my fork, unable to eat that meal." But he said, "It's so like the American culture to forget to thank God for what we have, to pull the blinds and forget that we are part of the 6% of the world who have enough continually to eat again and again and again. 'Enter his courts with praise; enter his gates with thanksgiving.'"

While you eat your turkey next Thanksgiving, consider this: six hundred people will die of starvation while you're eating that turkey. On Thanksgiving Day, twelve thousand people will die of starvation. Eight hundred million people in this world have not had enough to eat today. One out of every ten babies born this week will die within the first week. Twenty-five percent of those babies will never reach the age of five years. I now understand what it means to be a nation upon whom God has rained His blessings. I understand how Malcolm Muggeridge must have felt when he watched Mother Teresa take a baby from the dustbin who someone had cast aside, believing it dead, and then suddenly chirping, "See, there's life in it!" Most of the world is not dying under nuclear annihilation; rather, by the thousands, many do die whimpering in the night. And T. S. Eliot's lines haunt us, saying, "This is the way the world ends / Not with a bang but a whimper!"

We all sometimes complain that God is unfair. But I remember that gratitude is an attitude. Habakkuk 3:17 shouts our obligation to praise, whatever our financial circumstances. There's no use whimpering. Harold Kushner said he used to have an old teacher who said, "To say life is unfair is like saying a bull won't charge a man who happens to be a vegetarian."

Conclusion

Jesus' lone leper is a picture of great gratitude, a picture of grace. Those of us who have been redeemed by a living Lord Jesus cannot help but say, "Thank you, God. Thank you for eternal life, thank you for our daily bread." Break from that crowd of thankless lepers long enough to remember Somalia. Somalia is a land where there aren't any title holders any more. There are no grain fields. Everyone there lives in extremes. Life is waiting on the United Nation grain trucks.

This Thanksgiving, enter His courts with thanksgiving and enter His gates with praise. "Were there not ten lepers healed? Where are the other nine?"

Then answer, "Lord, I do not know where the other nine have gone. I only know that I have received healing, and to not praise you is a sin that I must not condone. I have been loved, I am clean. I must enter your gates with thanksgiving, I must come into your courts with praise."

Endnotes

[1] Calvin Miller, *A Hunger for Meaning* (Downers Grove, IL: InterVarsity Press, 1984), p. 114.

ADDITIONAL SERMONS AND LESSON IDEAS

Worshipping When You Don't Want To

Habakkuk 3:17–18
By Rev. Brian Bill

It's sometimes hard for us to jump right into singing when all we feel like doing is sighing (see Ps. 137:1–5).

Shane Hipps has written an intriguing article in *Leadership Magazine* called "Praise That's Premature?" He suggests that, when we sing only happy songs, it becomes a kind of pep rally to inspire excitement about who God is. Because grief is an unpleasant emotion, we tend to deny our suffering in favor of celebration: "Authenticity and integrity in worship means expressing both lament and praise. Each element completes the other."[1]

The prophet Habakkuk knew something about how hard it is to worship when our heart is just not in it. In the first two chapters, we see how important it is to express our honesty.

- Declare your questions (1:3)
- Describe your complaints (1:13)
- Deepen your commitment to God (2:1)

It's possible to praise God even when we're in pain, and to love Him when we experience loss. In fact, the most authentic times of adoration often come when we feel the most awful. Chapter 3 records the process of moving from pain to praise.

1. **Revere** (3:2–4). When filled with grief, gaze on the glory of God.
2. **Review** (3:5–15). Go back and remember what God has done in your life and in the lives of His children in the past.
3. **Rest** (3:16, 17). Habakkuk decided to rest in God's timing, even though he didn't like what was about to happen. Instead of rebelling, let's rest in Him.

4. **Rejoice (4:18).** Disappointment does not have to lead to despair. Even though there will be no food and no flocks, Habakkuk remained determined to rejoice.

5. **Rely (3:19).** God's sovereignty should always have a strengthening impact on us. A deer is swift and surefooted and can scamper up hills and mountains to find safety and freedom, even on rocky paths and difficult ground.

Hinds' Feet on High Places by Hannah Hurnard is an allegory of the Christian life. It's the story of a young woman named "Much-Afraid," and her journey away from her fearing family into the High Places of the Shepherd, guided by her two companions Sorrow and Suffering.[2]

Have you made it to the high places? Don't discount the importance of being accompanied by sorrow and suffering. With God, we can rise above our circumstances.

In chapter one, Habakkuk is low. In chapter two, he climbs up to the watchtower to wait for God's answer. And in chapter three, he is walking on the heights. He has steadily progressed on an upward arc toward God. Are you ready to move from pain to praise? The way to progress is to revere, review, rest, rejoice, and rely.

Habakkuk's name can mean "wrestling," but it also means "embrace." We see both in this little book, as he moved from fighting with God to faith in God; from wrestling to worship. Are you ready to do the same?

Endnotes

[1] Shane Hipps, "Praise That's Premature?" *Leadership Journal, http://www.christianitytoday. com/le/2007/spring/17.64.html* (accessed January 29, 2011).

[2] Hannah Hurnard, *Hinds' Feet on High Places* (Uhrichsville, OH: Barbour Publishing, 1977).

A Terminal Condition

Romans 3:21–27

By Dr. Dean Register

I suffer from a terminal condition. I was born with it, and I have battled it for many years. Not only am I infected, but my Dad and Mom were also infected. Tragically, my children and grandchildren have the same terminal condition. It is a malignancy in my soul that the Bible calls *sin*. In the third chapter of Romans, Paul tells us three vital truths about this condition.

1. The reality of sin
   A. Everyone is infected.
   B. Sin is in both disposition and deed.
      i. As disposition, sin invades our attitudes and thoughts.
      ii. As deed, sin performs rebellion toward God and acts of injury toward others.
2. The results of sin
   A. Sin distorts our relationship with other people.
   B. Sin defiles our relationship with God.
   C. Sin destroys all things.
   D. Sin, when it is finished, brings forth death (James 1:15).
3. The Remedy for Sin
   A. The remedy is offered freely by God's grace.
   B. The remedy is received freely because of Jesus' atoning sacrifice.
   C. The remedy excludes meritorious boasting.

Conclusion

If we never take sin seriously, we will never rejoice in salvation deliriously. We can't cure ourselves of a terminal condition. We can't excuse our sinful sickness. There is One, however, Who can and does cure us. Through faith in His sacrifice, we are healed and sealed (1 Peter 2:24).

WEEK 49

A Theology of Time

Galatians 4:4–5
By Dr. Jerry Sutton

Introduction

I find it intriguing that Jesus Himself, in one of His post-resurrection appearances, explained to His disciples, "It is not for you to know the times or the seasons" (Acts 1:7). These two words depicting time are different. The first word, "times." refers to the unfolding of chronological time. The second word, "seasons," refers to unique opportunities and unique moments in the unfolding of time.

When Paul penned Galatians 4:4, he used the word for the unfolding of chronological time. "When the fullness or completion of time had fully arrived, God sent forth His Son." This is Paul's first mention of the Incarnation.

What Paul Tells us about God

1. **God had a plan.** Jesus was not created in Mary's body, He was delivered to the world through her body. God sent His Son! Jesus, the pre-existent one, entered into time through the agency of Mary's body. The "sent-one" was born through the agency of Mary's body! And on top of that, He was born under the law. He was Jewish by genetic composition.
2. **God had a purpose.** In fact, Paul relates two purposes in our text. First, Jesus came to redeem those under the law. Second, He did this so that those under the law might receive the adoption as sons. The good news is that Jesus did not stop with bringing salvation to God's chosen people, the Jews. Jesus Himself taught us that the Gospel is to be preached in the entire world, from Jerusalem to the ends of the earth.

The point I want to make is that God entered into time in the person of His Son, to redeem lost humanity. That was the purpose of Jesus' mission.

3. **God has given a promise (Galatians 4:4, 5).** Specifically, God's promise is redemption and adoption. These two promises refer to "being bought back" and "being brought in." It depicts moving from death to life. So here in Galatians we see that God had a plan, a purpose, and a promise.

As we examine the gospels and their descriptions of the story of Christmas, we discover in Matthew's account (Matt. 2:4–6) that Herod was keenly aware and fearful of what was unfolding in time. He wanted to know the *what* (Messiah's birth) and the *where* (location). This, the religious leaders note, was written in prophecy.

Luke's Gospel is even more specific with respect to the importance of time. In Luke 2:1, he refers to the fact that Caesar Augustus sent out a decree "in those days." In 2:6, Luke observes that "while they [Mary and Joseph] were there [Bethlehem], the time came for her to give birth. Literally, "the days were fulfilled."

Now, my point in noting this is that God Himself is superintending the unfolding events of history. From eternity, He entered the constraints of time in order to secure for us life in eternity.

Conclusion

In light of this, here are four principles for you to consider:

1. **God is the author of time.** He created it. He is outside of it. He understands everything that has or will occur in the realm of time. He is the author and creator of time.

2. **Those of us who know Him need to maximize our time.** See Eph. 5:15, 16 and Psalm 90:12. We can waste or invest the time we are given. Let's invest it wisely.

3. **Decisions in time are locked in for eternity.** Let's make the right decisions!

4. **Only in the present does time touch eternity, so let's live in such a way that our lives make a difference!**

ADDITIONAL SERMONS AND LESSON IDEAS

Leaving a Legacy

Psalm 71:17, 18
By Rev. Brian Bill

An elderly man was filling out an application for a retirement village and very carefully and deliberately answered all the questions. After filling out his current address, he came to the word *zip* and printed: "Normal for my age."

No matter how old you are or how much zip you have left, it's not time to let go. If you're in the golden years of life, you have more to give because, as we grow older, our responsibilities grow with us (Ps. 92:14).

The character of our children tomorrow depends on what we put in their hearts today. If we expect the younger generation to grow spiritually, those of us who are older must pass on what we possess.

This is not easy to do because we live in a culture that promotes youthfulness and denigrates the elderly. The Bible calls us to instead honor the aged (Lev. 19:32).

There are two main lessons in Psalm 71:17, 18.

1. **Know God in your youth by learning from Him (17*a*).**
2. **Show God in your later years by leaving a legacy (17*b*–18).**

If you've witnessed the wonder and works of God, then proclaim God's power to others, and do it with a sense of life-and-death urgency.

David declared God's marvelous deeds, His power, and His might to the next generation, because he knew he was going to pass away. He was determined to pass along God's actions and God's attributes (Ps. 9:1; 26:7; Is. 46:4). What will you pass along?

Demographers have recently identified a new life-stage between adulthood and true old age called "the third age," "midcourse," or "my time." I'd like to suggest another term and call it "prime time for proclamation." Biblically understood, a longer life is an opportunity for extended ministry.

David wants to stay alive long enough to leave a legacy: "till I declare your power" (Ps. 71:18).

How would you complete this sentence: "God, allow me to say alive until I..." What is it that you have not yet done for the next generation? Do it today.

1. **If you're younger, seek out the wisdom of the older.**
2. **If you're older, seek out the younger.** Have you done everything you can do in your family to declare God's deeds to the next generation? If you're still alive, it's not too late to leave a legacy.

   According to a report from "America's Senior Volunteers," just seventeen percent of adults age 55 and over who were not directly asked to volunteer actually end up volunteering. Among those who were personally asked, however, eighty-four percent volunteered.[1] If you're a senior saint, consider yourself "asked" by the Almighty to serve God's purposes in your generation.

   Before passing on, make sure you pass on a legacy.

Endnotes

[1] Experience Corps, "Fact Sheet on Aging in America," *http://www.experiencecorps.org/images/pdf/Fact%20Sheet.pdf* (accessed January 29, 2011).

How to Stand When Others Don't Understand

Mark 3:20–30
By Dr. Dean Register

Sooner or later, we all face a situation that requires us to stand upon a conviction, a virtue, or a truth when others don't understand. Jesus was often misunderstood and maligned. He heard the slurs and rumors. He endured the lies spoken about Him without sacrificing truth on the altar of His critic's comprehension. He demonstrated how we can stand when others don't understand.

1. Know to whom you belong (vv. 20, 21).
   A. Jesus' family misunderstood His mission and tried to "take charge of Him."
   B. His family misunderstood His preaching and thought He was "out of His mind."
   C. Jesus knew He belonged to the Father regardless of His sibling's confusion.
2. Face criticism courageously (vv. 22–27).
   A. Religious leaders accused Jesus of being "possessed by Beelzebub."
   B. The accusation was a character assassination, because Beelzebub was another name for Satan.
   C. Jesus didn't flinch from their criticism, but exposed their fallacy.
   D. Jesus courageously discredited their charge.
3. Trust the Holy Spirit to lead you (vv. 28–30).
   A. Do not resist His counsel
   B. The Spirit's role is to "guide you into all truth" (John 16:12)
   C. Embrace His forgiveness and point others to His forgiveness.
   > Jesus never sinned in the face of confusion and conflict, and He shows us how to stand when others don't understand!

WEEK 50

SERIES: A THEOLOGY OF CHRISTMAS

A Theology of Intention

Luke 1:76–79
By Dr. Jerry Sutton

Introduction

One of the pivotal personalities in the story of Christmas is John, the son of Elizabeth and Zachariah. At John's birth, his father gave a prophetic declaration concerning his role as the Savior's forerunner and herald.

The prophetic utterance provides a clear statement of John's own mission as well as the mission of Jesus. In fact, the prophetic words give clarity to God's intentions at the very first Christmas season.

What Does God's Word Teach Us?

1. **John was sent by God (1:76–77a).** Prior to John's birth, God had already planned his life's mission. Our text tells us that he would be called a "prophet of the Most High." His assignment would be to "go before the Lord to prepare His ways." John's task would be to point people to Jesus! One more description of his assignment is that he will give His (God's) people knowledge.

    Scripture is clear that John had a mission assigned to him from before his birth. John was sent. It was a demonstration of God's intent!

2. **John was sent to point people to God's Salvation (1:77b).** Zachariah further articulates that the avenue to this salvation is "through the forgiveness of their sins." If we were to expand on this from Romans, we would point out that this is tri-dimensional. When I receive Christ, I am saved from the penalty of sin. Progressively, as I mature, I am increasingly saved from the power of sin. And ultimately, in Heaven, I will be saved from the presence of sin.

Yet the principal issue is this: have you trusted Christ to save you? Have you experienced that initial forgiveness of sin? This is God's intention for you!

So, why is it that God would send John to point people to His salvation? Why is it that God would do anything at all other than bring judgment on the magnitude of humanity's sin? Simple!

3. **Sending John points out God's Sensitivity (1:78).** Zachariah declares that all of this has happened because of God's "merciful compassion." These two words are variously translated "heart of mercy," "tender mercy," or "bowels of mercy." Mercy is at the very heart of the God who created and subsequently sustains and runs the universe. The reason that God would do all He has done to secure our salvation is that He is a merciful God with a tender heart!

No wonder Jesus said "Come to Me, all who are weary and heavy laden, and I will give you rest." (Matt. 11:28). Or consider what He said in Matthew 22:37, "O Jerusalem, Jerusalem, who kills the prophets and stones those who are sent to her! How often I wanted to gather your children together, the way a hen gathers her chicks under her wing, and you were unwilling." He wanted, but the hearers were unwilling!

4. **God Himself will be the sunrise for our darkness (1:78*b*, 79).** Zachariah declares, "the dawn from on high will visit us, to shine on those who live in darkness and the shadow of death, to guide our feet into the way of peace."

God will take the initiative to visit earth, to shine light on darkness and on those who live in the shadow of death. He will guide us to peace, so here is the God who will visit, reveal, and guide. The conclusion is that He wants us to experience His peace! In this matter, God is purely intentional!

Keep in mind that Zachariah gave this prophetic word at the birth of his own son, before Jesus ever arrived on the scene!

Conclusion

This teaches us three things about God's intentions toward you:

1. **God knows you.** If He knew John prior to his birth, then He knew you. He knows everything about you. He knows your strengths, weaknesses, flaws, hurts, and fears. He knows you!

2. **God loves you.** In the deepest recesses of God's heart, we find love. The object of God's love is you. He cares about you. He sent His Son, Jesus Christ, to die for you! In fact, John the Apostle tells us, "For God so loved the world, that he gave His only begotten Son that whosoever believes in Him should not perish, but have everlasting life" (John 3:16). That's a lot of love! And God demonstrated that love by sending His Son, Jesus, to the cross!

3. **This God who knows you and loves you has a purpose for you.** You are not an accident. You are not insignificant. God has intentions for you, and they are for your own good!

He wants you to be saved. He wants you to have your sins forgiven. He wants to do for you what He has done for so many others. He wants to deliver you out of darkness. He wants you to experience His peace. That is His intention!

ADDITIONAL SERMONS AND LESSON IDEAS

Caregiver Guidelines

Job 2:11–13
By Rev. Brian Bill

Have you ever wondered what to say when you're face-to-face with another person's pain? Ever been speechless when speaking to someone who is suffering? Perhaps you've been on the receiving end of some insensitive comments like these:

- "I know just how you feel."
- "God must have needed him in heaven."
- "God told me that He'll heal you."
- "Time heals all wounds."
- "God must be trying to teach you something."
- "If you do what I did, then you'll feel better."
- "My Aunt Mildred had the same problem . . . ."

Our maxims and cute sayings in the face of suffering are not only empty, they can also be excruciating. Let's resist trying to package people's pain. Let's also cut out the clichés and jettison the jargon.

In Job 2:11–13, three friends come to comfort Job, and do a good job as caregivers, at least at the start. From Job's three friends, we can take some important lessons on how to respond appropriately in situations where another is suffering.

1. **Hear the hurting.** Eliphaz, Bildad, and Zophar "heard about all the troubles that had come upon him."
2. **Sacrifice your schedule.** The next thing they do is "to set out from their homes."
3. **Partner with people.** They "met together by agreement." It's a good idea to take someone with you when you hear of a need.

4. **Go with grace.** Their goal was to go "and sympathize with him." This is the word nud in Hebrew, which means to rock back and forth.

5. **Come with comfort.** This is a similar idea and carries with it the idea of coming alongside.

6. **Expect a change in appearance.** "When they saw him from a distance, they could hardly recognize him."

7. **Exhibit your emotions.** When they saw Job in his distress, "they began to weep aloud."

8. **Respond with rituals.** After weeping aloud, they "tore their robes." That was a cultural way of demonstrating that they were all torn up on the inside.

9. **Honor with humility.** In that culture, pouring dust on the head was a sign of humility. It's the idea of looking for ways to enter into someone's pain.

10. **Sit with the sufferer.** "Then they sat on the ground with him." It's important to get on the person's level and get as close as possible.

11. **Take the time needed.** They were in no hurry to leave, being there for "seven days and seven nights." While we shouldn't overstay our welcome, it's important to spend time with people when they're in pain.

12. **Be silent in the face of suffering.** "No one said a word to him, because they saw how great his suffering was."

When you see someone suffering, *show up and shut up*. Don't stay away and, when you come, silence may be better than speech. We may have some insight, but we don't have all the answers.

How To Be A Good Friend

Luke 10:25–37
By Dr. Adrian Rogers

In this passage in Luke, Jesus gives us the parable of the Good Samaritan. This is the background to the parable:

➤ An insincere lawyer tested Jesus by asking Him a dishonest question.

➤ The lawyer was religious, but he had no relationship with the Savior. He knew something about the law of God, but he had no real life in his heart.

➤ This man had no problem with the idea of loving God, but he did not want to love anyone he didn't have to love (1 John 4:20).

1. The parable of the Good Samaritan is a story of criminal inhumanity (Luke 10:30). The man who fell among thieves, was beaten and robbed, is a picture of humanity going away from God, battered and robbed by the devil.

2. The parable of the Good Samaritan is a story of casual indifference (Luke 10:31). The priest represents religion with its rituals.

   A. The Levite represents religion with its rules.

   B. The life of the apostle Paul attests to the fact that religion cannot save (Phil. 3:5–8; Gal. 3:10).

   C. The priest and the Levite, rather than being a part of the solution, became part of the problem because they did nothing. They committed the sin of omission.

3. The parable of the Good Samaritan is a story of compassionate involvement (Luke 10:33–35).

4. The Good Samaritan is a picture of the Lord Jesus.

   A. Jesus has genuine compassion (Luke 10:33).

   B. Jesus has gracious compassion (Luke 10:33, 34).

   C. Jesus has gentle compassion (Luke 10:34).

This sermon aired on Love Worth Finding *on November 11, 2010.*

WEEK 51

SERIES: A THEOLOGY OF CHRISTMAS

A Theology of Capacity

Luke 2:8–11, 13–14
By Dr. Jerry Sutton

Introduction

One of my favorite episodes in the Christmas story involves the appearance of the angels to the shepherds. The fact that God's glorious angels appeared to lowly shepherds is a striking picture of God's special consideration for humanity. Yet, what is most striking for me is the message of the angels "Do not be afraid; for behold, I bring you good news of great joy which shall be for all people; for today in the city of David there has been born for you a Savior, who is Christ the Lord" (Luke 2:10, 11).

After giving instructions on how to find the infant Savior, a great heavenly host declares, "Glory to God in the highest heaven, and peace on earth to people He favors." Some translate that last word, *eudokia*, to mean "men of good will" or "men with whom He is pleased." Others translate it as "good will toward men."

What this Angelic Message Says to Us

1. **We hear the angel's prohibition (2:10).** The angel said, "do not be afraid." The verb tense is such as to say, "stop being afraid." Fear is unnecessary. I am not here to hurt but to help. I am not here to attack you but announce to you something that is for your benefit and your blessing!

   So at the outset, there is a prohibition, there is no need to fear! As we respond to God's Word, there is no need for us to fear. He invites us into His family! There is no need to run and hide; rather, we are to heed and respond to the invitation.

2. **We hear the angel's proclamation (2:10*b*–11, 14).** The angel preaches "good news" to the shepherds. In fact, our word *Gospel* means "good news." The practice of sharing the good news is *evangelism*, which comes from the same root word. The good news is that God has sent His Savior to the world in the form of a baby. He sent Jesus Christ, the Messiah, the Son of God!

Notice the recipients (1:10), "for all the people." Some argue that this word "all" does not mean all people, but all of a certain group. Yet that is not what our text says. When the shepherds hear the angel's proclamation, they heard that this good news was for all people. No one is excluded.

Notice also the results (1:10*c*, 14). The good news upon its reception will produce a three-fold result. First, it will produce "great joy" (1:10*c*). Joy is not the same concept as happiness. Happiness depends on what happens. It is circumstantial. Joy depends on Jesus, and it is relational. It is that inner peace and contentment that we have when we know that God has everything under control and that our lives, which are in His hands, will experience His blessing. This good news will result in great joy!

A second result (1:14) is that it will bring glory to God. The angels declared, "Glory to God in the highest heaven." Our God is good, great, and gracious! The message from the angel is that it will give glory to our God!

A third result is that it will produce "peace on earth." One promised result is that, whenever the Gospel, the good news, is received, God's peace will reign. If there is no peace in the world, at least there can be peace in our hearts. Recall Paul's admonition about prayer: "Be anxious for nothing. . . and the peace of God which surpasses understanding will guard your heart and minds in Christ Jesus."

So, here is the message and promise of Christmas. Permit me to refocus on one key concept. The angel said that good news would be "for all the people." Why should we conclude that the Gospel is for all people and not just a predetermined few?

What does Paul say on this matter? As one of the last epistles written by Paul, he writes to Timothy, "This is good, and it pleases God our Savior, who wants everyone to be saved and come to the knowledge of the truth.

For there is one God and one mediator between God and man, a man Jesus Christ, who gave Himself—a ransom for all" (1 Tim. 2:3–5).

Paul returns again to the same idea in the first epistle of Timothy. "This saying is trustworthy and deserves full acceptance. In fact, we labor and strive for this, because we have put our hope in the living God, who is the Savior of everyone, especially of those who believe" (1 Tim. 4:9, 10).

Paul's point is not that everyone will be saved, but that the Gospel is for everyone who will receive God's only solution to mankind's sin. God wants everyone saved. Jesus died for all. He is the only Savior. In the words of Jesus from His farewell discourse, "no one comes to the Father except through Me" (John 14:6). So the fundamental question is not, "Can everyone be saved?" It is, "Will you believe?" It is not a matter of divine capacity. It is a matter of human willingness to believe God's good news!

Conclusion

So, let me leave you with three concluding thoughts.

1. **Do not think that God's salvation is not for you. It is!**
2. **Do not think that Jesus did not die for you. He did!**
3. **Do not think that this message of salvation is not for you. It is!**

In a Theology of Christmas, the Gospel's capacity is for whosoever! Will you believe in Him?

ADDITIONAL SERMONS AND LESSON IDEAS

Taking the Next Step

2 Peter 1:3–9
By Rev. Brian Bill

Charlie Brown is at bat and strikes out again. As he trudges back to the bench, he laments: "Rats! I'll never be a big-league player. I just don't have it! All my life I've dreamed of playing in the big leagues, but I know I'll never make it." Lucy turns to console him: "Charlie Brown, you're thinking too far ahead. What you need to do is set some more immediate goals. . . . See if you can walk out to the mound without falling down!"

Do you ever feel like that spiritually? Many of us wonder if we'll ever be in the "big leagues" with our Christian faith.

Have you ever looked at a mature believer and wished you could be like him or her? Most of us want instant growth, forgetting that what is behind a godly life is a person who has gone through struggles and trials. Spiritual development only comes through practicing spiritual disciplines, such as time in the Word, prayer, fellowship, fasting, giving, witnessing, and serving. Let's remember that spiritual growth is intentional, not automatic. There are two truths to balance in this regard:

1. **God is committed to our growth** (1 Cor. 3:6, 7; Isa. 60:21).
2. **We must take responsibility for our growth** (2 Peter 3:18; 1 Peter 2:2; 2 Cor. 10:15).

It's not all up to God, and it's not all up to us. God has designed it so that we work in partnership with Him (see Phil. 2:12, 13).

In the book of 2 Peter, Peter is concerned that Christians have become complacent and spiritually stalled. False teachers have been spreading dangerous doctrine, and persecution has become prevalent. On top of all this, a second generation of believers has lost their spiritual passion. Peter's purpose is to remind these Christ-followers that the gospel transforms lives, that discipleship involves discipline, and that spiritual growth is intentional, not automatic.

Let's hold on to these three life-changing proclamations:

1. **We have all that we need** (1:3, 4). We can unleash God's power when we utilize God's promises.
2. **We must use all that we have** (1:5–7). The phrase "make every effort" is quite strong. It refers to eagerness, earnestness, and zeal, and has the idea of moving quickly and trying as hard as possible (see Ex. 12:11).
3. **When we grow, it will show** (1:8–9). No believer should be barren. We don't have to grow colder as we grow older. You can become whomever you want at any time. It is never too late to serve God.

We have all we need and, when we use all that we have, we will grow and it will show—no matter how many times we fall down.

Five Minutes After Death

Luke 16:19–31
By Dr. Adrian Rogers

1. Contrast in life (Luke 16:19–21)
   A. The rich man and the beggar described in Luke 16 were very different.
   B. Life is full of inequities:
      i. Congenital inequities
      ii. Material inequities (Ps. 62:10)
      iii. Social inequities
2. Contrast in death (Luke 16:22)
   A. The Bible states that the rich man died and was buried.
   B. The Bible doesn't say that the beggar was buried. The beggars of that day were often discarded when they died without a proper burial.
3. Contrast in eternity (Luke 16:22, 23)
   A. The beggar died and was carried by the angels to heaven, where he experienced the glories of heaven (Luke 16:22)
      i. Heaven is all that the all-beneficent loving heart of God would desire for you.
      ii. Heaven is all that the omniscient mind of God could design for you.
      iii. Heaven is all that the omnipotent hand of God could prepare for you.
   B. The Bible says that the rich man was in hell, where he experienced the agonies of hell. I believe in hell because Jesus teaches it (Matt. 5:29, 30), the death of Jesus demonstrates it, and the justice of God demands it.
      i. Hell will be sensual misery (Luke 16:23–25; Matt. 25:41).
      ii. Hell will be emotional misery (Luke 16:25)
      iii. Hell will be eternal misery (Luke 16:26; Heb. 9:27)
      iv. Hell will be spiritual misery (Luke 16:27–29)

This sermon was aired on Love Worth Finding *October 24, 2010.*

WEEK 52

SERIES: A THEOLOGY OF CHRISTMAS

A Theology of Engagement

Luke 1:35
By Dr. Jerry Sutton

Introduction

Luke 1:26 relates that, "In the sixth month (of Elizabeth's pregnancy with John the Baptist), the angel Gabriel was sent by God to a town in Galilee called Nazareth." The angel here relates to Mary what God is doing. In his explanation, the angel Gabriel says, "The Holy Spirit will come upon you, and the power of the Most High will overshadow you. Therefore the Holy One to be born will be called the Son of God" (Luke 1:35).

In this description of the events related to Christmas, I want you to be keenly aware of the full engagement of the Trinitarian God. He is one God in three persons fully engaged in the unfolding drama of redemption. It is not one God taking different forms at different times—which is called *modalism*, a concept that has been repeatedly rejected throughout the history of Christianity.

The One God, who is forever and constantly in three Persons, is completely engaged in the quest to prepare and secure humanity's salvation.

Consider the work of the Father.

Angels identify Him as the "Most High One." Gabriel was sent from Him (1:26). Gabriel tells Mary that "the Lord is with you" (1:28). She also hears that she has "found favor with God" (1:30). He is Father to the Son (1:32). He is the one who will give Jesus the throne of His father (from the human perspective) David (1:32).

When the angel says, "Nothing will be impossible for God," he is referring to the Father. In this Christmas miracle, the Father is fully engaged!

Notice, too, the work of the Son.

In short, Christmas focuses on his arrival. The angel tells Mary, "you will conceive and give birth to a son, and you will call His name Jesus. He will be great and will be called the Son of the Most High. . . he will reign over the house of Jacob forever, and His kingdom will have no end" (1:31–33). And again the angel says, "Therefore the holy One to be born will be called the Son of God" (1:35). Luke 2:7 describes the event: "then she gave birth to her first-born Son, and she wrapped Him snugly in cloth and laid him in a manger. "

Now the point of all this is to note Jesus Christ's incarnation. He has forever been the Son of God. For eternity past, He always has been. Yet, at this super-natural point in time, He lays aside His glory, wraps Himself in human flesh, and enters the world in the form of an infant. Jesus is the Father's gift to the world (John 3:16).

Luke 2:52 summarizes His human development: "and He kept on increas-ing in wisdom and stature and in favor with God and man." From His self-emptying (see Phil. 2:5–11), and from His humanity, He had to mature. Here we are told that He matured intellectually, physically, spiritually, and socially.

He came, full of grace and truth (John 1:14, 17), to point a lost world to salvation. Yet, in His atonement, He not only pointed humanity to salvation, He provided salvation to the lost world.

In His death, burial, and resurrection, Jesus provided victory over mankind's two great enemies: sin and death. On the cross, He conquered sin. The prophet declared, "The Father laid upon Him in the iniquity of us all" (Isa. 53:6). And with His resurrection, Jesus conquered the enemy of death. Jesus conquered both (1 Cor. 15:57), and when we enter into a relationship with Him, we know that our sins are forgiven and that we need not fear death.

At Christmas, Jesus the Son of God was fully engaged. He was sent by the Father with the Mission of providing salvation for this fallen world.

Notice, finally, the work of God's Holy Spirit.

Gabriel relates to Mary, "The Holy Spirit will come upon you" (1:35). He was the agent delivering the Son into Mary's body. He was also fully engaged in the communication of the Savior's arrival. He revealed to Simeon, "that he would not see death before he saw the Lord's Messiah." Luke tells us further: "Guided by the Spirit, he (Simeon) entered the temple complex" where he saw, held, and blessed the baby Jesus (Luke 2:25–27).

What the Holy Spirit did for Simeon, He does for us, as well. Jesus tells us several truths concerning the Spirit's work. John 14:16 tells us that the Father would send another Counselor or Comforter who is the Spirit of Truth. John 14:26 points out that He will "teach you [disciples] all things and remind you of everything I have told you." John 15:26 tells us that He will "testify of Me [Jesus]." John 16:8 declares, "when He comes, He will convict [convince] the world about sin, righteousness, and judgment." In John 16:13, 14, Jesus promises, "when the Spirit of truth comes, He will guide you into all truth. . . . He will glorify Me."

Jesus teaches us that the Spirit will comfort us, teach us, guide us, convict us, and point us to Jesus! And this same Holy Spirit who is active in the world today was fully engaged at the Incarnation of Christ, the very first Christmas!

Conclusion

So what are we saying? The Trinitarian God—Father, Son, and Holy Spirit—was fully engaged in the preparation of your salvation! The Father planned and executed it. The Son, through His incarnation and atonement, provided it. And the Holy Spirit points us to God's provision and draws us to Jesus.

If God is so fully engaged in the preparation of our salvation, does it not seem right to you to respond to God's invitation to believe in Christ and be saved?

ADDITIONAL SERMONS AND LESSON IDEAS

Serving without Thanks

Luke 17:7–10

By Rev. Brian Bill

Do you know the difference between a servant and a volunteer? A volunteer picks and chooses when and even whether to serve. A servant serves no matter what. A volunteer serves when convenient; a servant serves out of commitment. Someone said it well: "The servant does what he is told when he is told to do it. The volunteer does what he wants to do when he feels like doing it."

First Peter 2:16 challenges us to "live as servants of God." The issue is not *whether* we will serve, but *where* we will serve.

In Luke 17:7–10, Jesus reveals the superiority of serving over volunteering. There are four standards of servanthood found in this parable.

1. **A servant's work is not always sensational (7*a*).** Sometimes we recruit people to a ministry by telling them how fun and exciting it is to serve. The truth is that serving is strenuous and not always thrilling.
2. **Serving must be sustained (7*b*, 8).** The job description for a servant is very simple and straightforward: "Do everything your Master commands."
3. **Serving is a sacrifice (9).** We are not entitled to a word of thanks or appreciation. Our focus is often on our feelings, whereas this servant was determined just to do his job.
4. **Serving is satisfying (10).** Think of it this way: the Lord of glory has you in His service. In that sense, serving is very satisfying because it's an honor and privilege!

One of the best biblical images of this single-minded resolve to deflect devotion from self to the Savior is found in Ps. 123:2. When the master moves his finger, the servant falls in line. When he says "jump," the servant says, "How high?"

Lorne Sanny, the founder of the Navigators, once said, "You know you're a servant by how you act when you're treated like one."[1] When you're treated like a servant, do you get offended? When someone forgets to say "thanks," do you go in the tank?

Let's work at saying, "I was just treated better than I should have been because I am an 'unworthy' servant."

Remember that, in God's sight, the real superstars are simple servants.

Endnotes

[1] Lorne Sanny, "Five Ideals of the Navigators," *http://www.discipleshiplibrary.com/pdfs/J260. pdf* (accessed January 29, 2011).

The Final Judgment

Revelation 20:11–15
By Dr. Adrian Rogers

1. The setting described (Rev. 20:11)
    A. The throne
    B. The judge is Jesus Christ (John 5:22; Rev. 1:13–16)
2. The summons delivered (Rev. 20:12–13)
3. Who will be called to the judgment?
    A. The out-and-out sinner
    B. The self-righteous
    C. The procrastinator
    D. Lost church members
    E. Those who have never heard the gospel (Luke 12:47, 48)
4. The secrets displayed (Rev. 20:12, 13)
    A. Ecclesiastes 12:14
    B. Romans 2:16
    C. Matthew 12:36
    D. Luke 12:2-3
5. The sentence determined (Rev. 20:13–15)
    A. The sureness of it (Rom. 14:11, 12)
    B. The severity of it (Heb. 10:28–31)
        There are three parts to every trial. First, the evidence is presented. Second, the accused makes his defense. Finally, the verdict is handed down.

This sermon was aired on Love Worth Finding *on October 3 and 10, 2010.*

FUNERAL SERMONS

FUNERAL SERMON

The Life More Than Meat!

Matthew 6:25–31

By Dr. Calvin Miller

"Is not the life more than meat and the body than raiment?" The Master paused at this point in His discourse and surveyed His hillside congregation. If the life was only food and the body was only clothes, then those whom Jesus talks to in Matthew would likely never know life, for never had He seen more evidence of malnutrition and shabby apparel than that which the Palestinian peasantry likely exhibited. He resumed His sermon by calling attention to the birds and the numberless, wild flowers which mosaicked the hillsides, yet He had asked a fundamental question, "Isn't life more than food?" To this question, the rabble could only reply, "Life must be more than food!"

Still, Christ did not speak this question to exalt poverty or condemn wealth. He was attempting to illustrate one simple truth, that, lord or serf, prince or peon, rich or poor, the materialistic approach to life is inadequate. He was teaching them the wisdom in preferring the Bread of Life to the physical loaves, the Water of Life to Evian, and treasures in heaven to treasures on earth.

Just as this materialistic approach was inadequate in the day of Christ, so it is inadequate today. Yet, for all its inadequacy, it is all too common. The desire for gain and the thirst for possessions, these never abate. And though one might expect to find them primarily in the upper class, this is not the case. The materialistic demon has grasped the middle- and lower-class people as well as the upper class. This emphasis exists through every medium of our culture; it gives a commonality to the statesman and the traitor, the vulgar and the pious, and even the clergy and the barfly.

Every purchase we make increases our love of materialism. How pathetic it is to realize how common this approach to life really is and how inadequate it is! We spend all those energies that might be given to God in pursuit of perishable possessions.

This is not only a common approach to this life, it is an insufficient approach. No amount of possessions can satisfy; they only incite greed for more, like drinking sea water!

We can see how this materialistic approach to our existence is so terribly insufficient in light of the time when we must meet God, the Father of our Lord Jesus Christ. We can see all the clearer how important it is to place our affections on our Redeemer and not on the wood, stone, and stubble gods of our materialistic pantheon. We need to see both God and His will as our sole reason for existence. When we have placed God in His proper position in our lives, we see not only the inadequacy of materialism, but the true adequacy of the real life, the spiritual life. Its lack of popularity is due in the main to its stringent demands of courage and self-denial. Yet the foundation stones of courage are only held together by the mortar of self-denial. This discipline of the spiritual life is difficult to practice and virtually impossible to perfect, for ultimate self-denial is the absolute end of materialism. This means that one pours out one's self and pours in God.

At the risk of seeming redundant, I must repeat that, although the "Christ-life" is not common, it is the only adequate life. It is sufficient for this life. Christ graphically demonstrates this truth in the wilderness experience where, for nearly six weeks, He had fasted. As human as He was divine, Jesus at times felt weak with hunger. In His lonely wilderness abode, His hunger seemed to gnaw upon His conscience. In the mind one can perceive Him, as He looks upon a tiny crack in a huge rock; with but one word from God and this tiny crevasse could gush crystal waters to soothe the parched throat of the Master, who daily was subject to the hot sirocco winds of the desert. In this lonely place, who would know if He should have used the power of God to hang the luscious grapes of Galilee on some twisted desert shrub? And there was one particular stone which looked every bit as round and brown as the loaves He had seen so often on the hearth at Nazareth; one seemingly insignificant quantum of God's power, and this bit of bitumen or sandstone or feldspar or granite or whatever it was could become parched meal for the lips of the hungry Christ. But to use God's power to His own selfish ends was a direct antithesis to all He would say later about self-denial. After all, "Isn't the life more than meat and the body than raiment?" Here the Christ of the desert proved conclusively that the spiritual approach is all sufficient in this life.

This is actually the lesson that YHWH tried to teach His children in the wilderness of Sinai. Man can live without all of the material goods he believes necessary, but he can have no real existence without God. For forty years of no seedtime or harvest, they existed in the trackless wastes of Sinai; they could not have lived forty days without the help of God Almighty. Thus, as Christ said in the desert, "Man shall not live by bread alone, but by every word that proceedeth out of the mouth of God."

There is a real sense in which Christ asks everyone the question, "Is not the life more than meat?" He asks the question and waits for our response. Yet the life which is more than the material is a paradoxical life. Life begins when one dies to self or, as Galatians 2:20 puts it, when one is "crucified with Christ." It is a dialectic of eternal proportions. It is a paradox which one must meet and answer correctly.

> Strange paradox, this Christian Life!
> It does not seek for self to say,
> "I own the world!" Still pressed by strife,
> It treads on felt its quiet way.
> It rolls through cluttered history,
> Unchecked by age or timeless woe.
> It is the truth which sets men free;
> It is the only worth I know.
> Enduring and eternal life!
> None other paradox could say,
> That what one gains in owning Christ,
> He gains by giving self away.
> Nor could another truth express
> When man gives God control,
> He has not lost a destiny,
> He has but gained his soul.
>
> —Original

The question Jesus asked was not, "Which is more important, the spiritual life or the material life?" The question is between the transient and eternal: "Which is more important, God or goods?" "What indicates success, salary or salvation?" "What is the goal of life: that a man possess much, or that he be much possessed of God?"

Let us meet the issue squarely! Let us decide what life in Christ is, and let us determine to own it, though it cost us all to purchase it!

FUNERAL SERMON

A Precious Departure

Psalm 116:15

By Dr. Dean Register

Some verses of Scripture puzzle us. At first pause, we wonder how the death of a loved one could be delightful to God. Isn't death our enemy? Isn't death the rotten fruit of our sin, the product of the curse hanging over the head of every one of us? So how could the death of our friend be precious to God? What do we need to understand about the impact of Psalm 116:15? How do we view the death of a godly person as precious to God? By allowing Scripture to interpret Scripture, I believe we can grasp the truth of this statement when we realize three factors.

1. **The death of a Christ-follower is precious to God because suffering has ceased.** The Hebrew word translated "precious" (*yaqar*) denotes something valuable and splendid. In death, suffering ends for a child of God. It is a splendid matter to God. Revelation 21:4 states that, in heaven, pain and suffering cannot exist. We watched while our friend suffered and battled illness; we marveled at our friend's endurance and faithfulness. God notices suffering, too! God smiled and saw a splendid transformation, when our dear friend's heart beat its last beat here on earth, and he drew his first breath in heaven. Frances Havergal wrote many hymns of faith, including "Take My Life and Let It Be." On the last day of her life, she asked a friend to read Isaiah 42 to her. When the friend read the sixth verse—"I, the Lord, have called you in righteousness. I will take hold of your hand. I will keep you"— Miss Havergal stopped her friend and whispered, "Called... Held... Kept! I can go home on that."[1] By faith, our friend was called home, and now he is "held and kept" in the bliss of Heaven where suffering cannot intrude.

2. **The death of a Christ-follower is precious to God because sorrow gives way to celebration.** Sorrow is a constant companion on our earthly journey. Sometimes sorrow lingers far behind, beguiling us into thinking it no longer stalks us, but suddenly its melancholy face will appear beside us, threatening

to steal our joy. Jesus was well-versed in sorrow. He was called a "man of sorrows acquainted with grief" (Isa 53:3). In His humanity, He felt the sting of death's sorrow. When his friend Lazarus died, "He wept" (Jn 11:35).

We, too, weep for a friend and a loved one, but our sorrow yields to God's purpose. Yes we grieve, but our sorrow contains the seed of hope, and our hope is a robust anticipation of eternal life with Christ. With Christ, there is no more sorrow, because He wipes away all the tears of our grief (Rev. 21:4).

3. **The death of a Christ-follower is precious to God because separation gives way to glorification.** The Bible states that, when believers are absent from the body, they are present with the Lord (2 Cor. 5:6, 7). Jesus told the disciples, "I will receive you to Myself, so that where I am you may be also" (John 14:3). When John wrote about the new heaven and earth in Revelation, he noted that there was "no more sea" (21:1). Interpreters have wrestled with the significance of "no more sea," but many agree that the *sea* was a metaphor of separation. The sea surrounded John in his prison at Patmos. It was a barrier that isolated him from fellowship with other believers on the mainland. Consequently, John emphasized the unhindered unity regarding eternal life with Christ.

In heaven with Christ, there is no separation or isolation. There are no depressing farewells that sting the soul, no anxious goodbyes to wound those who love Him. There is indescribable purity, uncontainable satisfaction, irresistible love, and undeniable completion. Theologians call it glorification—the ultimate exclamation of our salvation and the perfecting of our resurrection body.

C. S. Lewis wrote about glorification like this: "To be on the inside of some door which we have always seen from the outside, is no mere neurotic fancy, but the truest index of our real situation. And to be at last summoned inside would be both glory and honor beyond all our merits and also the healing of that old ache."[2]

I'm glad Lewis mentioned "that old ache." We all sense it. We all feel the longing for completion, and only when the old ache gives way to glorification will our imagination merge into reality at the feet of Jesus.

Conclusion

The physical death of a Christ-follower is precious to God. He treasures the arrival of His own like a loving Father who waits expectantly for a reunion with his child. As deeply as we loved our friend, His Savior loved him most. While "here," our friend lived faithfully. Now "there," our friend lives perfectly.

Endnotes

[1] John Maxwell, "Deuteronomy" in *The Communicator's Commentary* (Waco, TX: Word, 1987), 348.

[2] C. S. Lewis, *The Weight of Glory* (San Francisco: Harper Collins 1949), 42.

FUNERAL SERMON

When Life Falls Apart

(The Death Of A Child)

Mark 5:21–43
By Dr. Dean Register

The pain of our grief is bearable only because we have a Savior who identifies with our sorrow (Heb. 4:15). He not only understands our heartache, He feels it with us. During His earthly ministry, Jesus demonstrated His deep love for children. In response, they darted past the disciples' blockade to huddle around Him. Jesus never turned children away. To the contrary, He told adults that, unless they became like children, they would not enter the Kingdom of Heaven (Luke 18:15–17). Jesus loved their eagerness and sincerity. He applauded their simple trust. Today we have gathered with our brokenness and anguish. Life has fallen apart and the torn pieces are still raw as we cry out for His touch. The heaviness in my own heart pushes me to the edge. I want so much today to dry your tears and fix your pain, but I have no ability. So I bid you to join with me as we all turn our eyes upon Jesus and learn what He taught a daddy named Jairus when his daughter was dying. Jairus discovered three vital truths that sustained him when life fell apart.

First, Jairus took his burden to Jesus unashamedly. Jairus was a religious leader. He was a synagogue ruler. He directed worship for synagogue meetings and scheduled rabbis to speak and teach. He knew the Scripture. His rich spiritual heritage and his familiarity with the Law and the Prophets, however, could not eradicate a broken heart. His little girl was dying, and he was a desperate parent. Consequently, Jairus ran to Jesus and begged for help. Casting aside his public image and professional etiquette, he fell down at the feet of Jesus. Only Jesus can handle a burden that drives us to our knees. Precious family, your Savior sees your sorrow, and He hears your anguished cry. Do not hold back. Instead, pour out your soul's trauma to the One who knows you better than anyone.

Second, Jairus travelled with Jesus despite delays and interruptions. Notice what Jesus did when Jairus pled for His intervention. Jesus went with him! Jesus meets us at the point of our grief. He goes where our tears flow. As Jairus and Jesus made their way through the crowd toward Jairus' home, a woman interrupted the process. She, too, needed Jesus. She was slowly dying, and doctors were helpless to heal her condition. If I had been Jairus I would have been frustrated by the delay. My personal grief would have blinded me to the grief of another. Everyone in this room today is grieving, and what seems to us as the pointless loss of a precious child may in fact be a life-changing moment of faith for another person.

Dear family, keep traveling with Jesus! I know it may seem insensitive of me to ask you to trust His heart when you cannot trace His hand. On this journey through the valley of "why?" others have watched your faith and have been prompted to reach out for Jesus because they have seen Him travelling with you. When Walter Winchell, the famous World War 2 radio commentator, heard that the Port of Singapore had fallen under enemy control, he closed his broadcast by saying, "Singapore has fallen, but the Rock of Ages stands".[1] Such is your hope and confidence. Your world has fallen, but your Savior, the Rock of Ages, still stands, and He intercedes for you.

Third, Jairus believed Jesus would do what He said. When a messenger told Jairus that his daughter had just died, Jesus commanded Jairus not to fear. He also commanded him to have faith. A parent of less devotion would have caved in and given up. Instead, Jairus believed deep down in the canyon of his soul that he could depend on Jesus no matter what the outcome. Jesus tenderly spoke life back into Jairus' daughter and, to the jaw-dropping astonishment of everyone, she got out of bed and walked around. Obviously, Jesus didn't grant physical healing to everyone. He didn't breathe life back into every child who died. But He always did what He said He would do! Our comfort and joy today is the realization that the greatest healing Jesus offers is not one that is temporary, but one that is eternal. He did not forget your little one. He did not bypass your child. Jesus ushered your beloved child into everlasting life. Furthermore, upon the authority of His Word, I assure you that your Savior has made arrangements for a reunion that exceeds your fondest dreams! He always does what He says He will do. He conquered sin at the cross, and He vanquished death by His resurrection. Today is not the final chapter. It is the preface to a new edition of life where death cannot invade, suffering cannot intrude, and sin cannot infect.

Endnotes

[1] Talmadge C. Johnson, *Look For the Dawn* (Nashville: Broadman, 1943), 58.

SUGGESTED WORSHIP SERVICES

WEEK 1 SERVICE

Prelude: *Great is the Lord*—Instrumentalist

Call to Prayer for the New Year: Pastor with all men at front of church

Call to Praise: Congregation

I Have Decided to Follow Jesus (v1, v2, v1, v3, v1 in C) (NBH 434)

Worship in Prayer: Pastoral Staff

Welcome: Pastoral Staff

Welcome Song (meet and greet during song): Pastoral Staff

Bind Us Together (2x in F) (NBH 390)

Scripture Reading: Worship Leader with the Congregation

Romans 12:1–2; Philippians 3:7–14 (See below)

Praise and Worship: Congregation

It is Well With My Soul (c in Bb, mod v 4, c in C) (NBH 447)

Prayer of Intercession, Dedication, and Praise: Pastor

Sanctuary (1x in D; 1x in Eb with Tag (NBH 588)

Worship with Our Gifts: Pastoral Staff

Praise and Worship During Offering

I Will Serve Thee (2x in Eb) (NBH 377)

Message: *The Biblical Model for Family*

Hymn of Response/Invitation: Worship Leader and Congregation

I Surrender All (v 1c, v 3c in C) (NBH 433)

Hymn of Benediction: Congregation

Great Is the Lord (1x in C) (NBH 61)

Postlude: *Great is the Lord*—Instrumentalists

Scripture Reading

Romans 12:1–2; Philippians 3:7–14 (New International Version, ©2011)

Worship Leader: Therefore, I urge you, brothers and sisters, in view of God's mercy, to offer your bodies as a living sacrifice, holy and pleasing to God—this is your true and proper worship.

Congregation: Do not conform to the pattern of this world, but be transformed by the renewing of your mind. Then you will be able to test and approve what God's will is—his good, pleasing and perfect will.

Worship Leader: But whatever were gains to me I now consider loss for the sake of Christ.

Congregation: What is more, I consider everything a loss because of the surpassing worth of knowing Christ Jesus my Lord, for whose sake I have lost all things.

Worship Leader: I consider them garbage, that I may gain Christ and be found in him, not having a righteousness of my own that comes from the law, but that which is through faith in Christ—the righteousness that comes from God on the basis of faith.

Congregation: I want to know Christ—yes, to know the power of his resurrection and participation in his sufferings, becoming like him in his death, and so, somehow, attaining to the resurrection from the dead.

Worship Leader: Not that I have already obtained all this, or have already arrived at my goal, but I press on to take hold of that for which Christ Jesus took hold of me.

Congregation: Brothers and sisters, I do not consider myself yet to have taken hold of it. But one thing I do: Forgetting what is behind and straining toward what is ahead,

Worship Leader: I press on toward the goal to win the prize for which God has called me heavenward in Christ Jesus.

WEEK 2 SERVICE

Prelude (CH 213/214): *We Bring the Sacrifice/He Made Me Glad*—Instrumentalist

Prayer of Worship: Worship Pastor

Call to Praise: Congregation

Come, Now is the Time to Worship (2x in D) (NBH 30)

Welcome: Pastoral Staff

Welcome Song (meet and greet during song): Pastoral Staff

What a Mighty God We Serve (2x in D) (NBH 64)

There is a Redeemer (v1c, v2c, v3c in D) (NBH 279)

Scripture Reading: Worship Leader with the Congregation (See Scripture Reading Below)

Praise and Worship: Congregation

Redeemed, How I Love to Proclaim It (v1c, c in G) (NBH 280)

Prayer of Dedication and Praise: Pastor

I Exalt Thee (2x in F) (NBH 36)

Worship with Our Gifts: Pastoral Staff

Praise and Worship During Offering

Blessed Be the Lord God (1x in Bb, 1x in C) (NBH 37)

He is Lord (2x in F) (NBH 277)

Message: *What Every Marriage Needs*

Hymn of Response/Invitation: Worship Leader and Congregation

Sanctuary (1 x in D; 1 x in Eb) (NBH 588)

Hymn of Benediction: Congregation

He Has Made Me Glad (NBH 579

Postlude: (CH 213/214): *We Bring the Sacrifice/He Made Me Glad*—Instrumentalist

Scripture Reading

Worship Leader: The LORD lives: may my rock be praised. The God of my salvation be exalted.

Reader 1: Be exalted, Lord, In Your strength; we will sing and praise your might.

Reader 2: Proclaim with me the LORD's greatness; let us exalt his name together.

Reader 3: I will praise You in the great congregation; I will exalt You among many people.

Worship Leader: God, be exalted above the heavens; let Your glory be over the whole earth.

Reader 1: Though the LORD is exalted. He takes note of the humble; but He knows the haughty from afar.

Reader 2: For you, Lord are the most High over all the earth;

Reader 3: You are exalted above all the gods.

Worship Leader: The Lord is great in Zion; He is exalted above all the peoples.

Reader 1: We exalt You, my God the King,

Reader 2: We exalt You, our God and King

Reader 3: We exalt You and praise your name forever and ever.

Worship Leader: We exalt you.

Reader 1: We exalt You.

Readers 1 and 2: We exalt You (louder)

Readers 1, 2, and 3: We exalt You (excited and very loud)

Worship Leader and Readers 1, 2, and 3: We exalt You forever and ever. (Big, full, and louder)

WEEK 3 SERVICE

Prelude: *Lord, I Lift Your Name on High* (2x in D) (NBH 347)—Instrumentalist

Prayer of Worship: Worship Pastor

Call to Praise: Congregation

All Hail King Jesus (1x in F) (NBH 295)

Welcome: Pastoral Staff

Welcome Song (meet and greet during song): Pastoral Staff

All Hail King Jesus (2x in F) (NBH 295)

He is Exalted (2x in F) (NBH 296)

Majesty (2x in Bb) (NBH 297)

Worship with Our Gifts: Pastoral Staff

Praise and Worship During Offering

Lord, I Lift Your Name on High (2x in D) (NBH 347)

I Know Whom I Have Believed (v1c, v2c, v4 c in D) (NBH 353)

Prayer of Dedication, Intercession, and Praise: Pastor

Spirit of the Living God (2x in F) (NBH 330)

Scripture Reading: Matthew 24:36, 42; 25:331, 32, 39; I John 3;2, 3 NIV (See Scripture Reading Below)

Praise and Worship: Congregation

Days of Elijah (2x in Ab) (NBH 289)

The King is Coming (2x in Ab) (NBH 291)

Message: *How Not to Start a Marriage*

Hymn of Response/Invitation: Worship Leader and Congregation

Spirit of the Living God (2x in F) (NBH 330)

Hymn of Benediction: Congregation

Lord, I Lift Your Name on High (2x in D) (NBH 347)

Postlude: *Lord, I Lift Your Name on High* (2x in D)—Instrumentalist

Scripture Reading

Worship Leader: When the Son of Man comes in His glory, and all the angels with Him, then He will sit on the throne of His glory.

Congregation: All the nations will be gathered before Him, and He will separate them one from another, just as a shepherd separates the sheep from the goats.

Worship Leader: But we know that when he appears, we shall be like Him, for we shall see Him as He is. Everyone who has this hope in Him purifies himself, just as He is pure.

Congregation: Now concerning that day and hour no one knows: neither the angels in heaven, nor the Son: except the Father only.

Worship Leader: So this is the way the coming of the Son of man will be: Then two men will be in the field; one will be taken and the other left.

Congregation: Therefore be alert, since you don't know what da your lord is coming.

WEEK 4 SERVICE

Prelude: *Praise the Name of Jesus* (NBH 322)—Instrumentalist

Call to Praise: Congregation

  All Hail the Power of Jesus' Name (v1c, v2c, v4c in F) (NBH 314)

Prayer of Worship: Worship Pastor

Welcome: Pastoral Staff

Welcome Song (meet and greet during song): Pastoral Staff

  Bless the Name of Jesus (2x in C) (SPW 100)

  His Name is Wonderful (2x in F) (NBH 315)

  At the Name of Jesus (2x in Bb) (NBH 316)

  There's Something About That Name (1x in Eb) (NBH 317)

Prayer of Dedication, Intercession, and Praise: Pastor

  Jesus, Your Name (v1, v2, v3 x C) (NBH 312)

Worship with Our Gifts: Pastoral Staff

Praise and Worship During Offering

  His Name is Life (2x in D) (NBH 318)

Scripture Reading: Reader's Team (See Scripture Reading Below)

Praise and Worship: Congregation

  Your Name (v1c, v2c in Ab) (NBH 326)

Message: *Drink Water from Your Own Cistern*

Hymn of Response/Invitation: Worship Leader and Congregation

  He is Lord: (1 x F, 1x G) (NBH 277)

Hymn of Benediction: Congregation

  Lord, I Lift Your Name on High (2x in D) (NBH 347)

Postlude: *Lord, I Lift Your Name on High* (2x in D)—Instrumentalist

Scripture Reading

Reader 1: In your relationships with one another, have the same mindset as Christ Jesus:

Reader 2: Who, being in very nature God, did not consider equality with God something to be used to his own advantage;

Reader 3: Rather, he made himself nothing by taking the very nature of a servant, being made in human likeness.

Reader 1: And being found in appearance as a man,

Reader 2: He humbled himself

Reader 3: By becoming obedient to death

All: — even death on a cross!

Reader 1: Therefore

Reader 2: Therefore

Reader 3: Therefore

Reader 1: God exalted him to the highest place and gave him the name that is above every name,

Reader 2: That at the name of Jesus

Reader 3: That at the name of Jesus (stronger)

Reader 1: At the name of Jesus (stronger) every knee should bow,

Reader 2: in heaven and

Reader 3: on earth

Reader 1: and under the earth,

Reader 2: and every tongue acknowledge that Jesus Christ is Lord,

All: to the glory of God the Father.

WEEK 5 SERVICE

Prelude: *We Bring the Sacrifice*—Instrumentalist

Prayer of Worship: Worship Pastor

Worship and Praise

   Holy Spirit Rain Down (2x in F) (NBH 335): Congregation

Baptismal Celebration: Pastoral Staff

Prayer: Pastoral Prayer

Welcome Pastoral Staff

Hymn of Welcome: (meet and greet):

   We Bring the Sacrifice (2x in D) NBH 581): Congregation

Worship and Praise: Congregation

   He Is Exalted (2x in F) (NBH 296)

   Jesus, Lord to Me (1x in F, 1 x in G) (NBH 300)

   He is Lord (1 x F, 1 x G) (NBH 277)

Scripture Reading (Responsive: See Below) Proverbs 3:1–9 (NKJV)

Hymn of Surrender

   Take My Life and Let it Be (v1, v2, v3 in F) (NBH 534): Congregation

Sermon: *How to Parent While Keeping Your Sanity*—Pastor

Hymn of Response/Invitation: *In My Life, Be Glorified* (3 x in D) (NBH 542)

Hymn of Benediction: *He Is Exalted* (1x in F) (NBH 296)—Congregation

Postlude: *We Bring the Sacrifice*—Instrumentalist

Scripture Reading

Worship Leader: 1 My son, do not forget my law, But let your heart keep my commands;

Congregation: 2 For length of days and long life And peace they will add to you.

Worship Leader: 3 Let not mercy and truth forsake you; Bind them around your neck, Write them on the tablet of your heart,

Congregation: 4 And so find favor and high esteem In the sight of God and man.

Worship Leader: 5 Trust in the LORD with all your heart, And lean not on your own understanding;

Congregation: 6 In all your ways acknowledge Him, And He shall direct your paths.

Worship Leader: 7 Do not be wise in your own eyes; Fear the LORD and depart from evil.

Congregation: 8 It will be health to your flesh, And strength to your bones.

Worship Leader: 9 Honor the LORD with your possessions, And with the firstfruits of all your increase; 10 So your barns will be filled with plenty! May the Lord add His blessings to the reading of His Word. Amen.

WEEK 6 SERVICE

Prelude: Joyful, Joyful, We Adore Thee (NBH 13)—Instrumental

Call to Worship: Pastoral Staff

Call to Praise: *I Will Bless the Lord* (2x in F) (NBH 14)

Welcome: Pastoral Staff

Hymn of Welcome: *Great and Mighty* (2x in Eb) (NBH 20): Congregation

Praise and Worship: Congregation

   He is Lord (c in F, c in G) (NBH 277)

   I Live (2 times in G) (NBH 278)

   There Is A Redeemer (v1,c, v2,c, v3,c in D) (NBH 279)

Prayer of Praise: Pastoral Staff

   I Sing Praises (v1, v2 in G) (NBH 17)

   Glorify Thy Name (v1, v2, v3 in Bb) (NBH 18)

Offertory Prayer: Pastor

Offertory Praise: *Knowing You* (v1c, v2c, v3c) (NBH 487): Praise Team

Sermon: *What Every Child Needs*—Pastor

Hymn of Invitation: *Jesus, Lord to Me* (2x in F, 1x in G) (NBH 300): Congregation

   Benediction Hymn: *I Sing Praises* (1x in G) (NBH 17): Congregation

   Postlude: *I Sing Praises* (1 x in G, 1x in Ab) (NBH 17)

WEEK 7 SERVICE

Prelude: *Forever* (2x in G) (NBH 99)—Instrumentalist

Prayer of Worship: Worship Pastor

Call to Praise: Congregation

Shine, Jesus Shine (v1c, v2c in Ab) (NBH 491)

Welcome: Pastoral Staff

Welcome Song (meet and greet during song): Pastoral Staff

Shine, Jesus Shine (v3c, c in Ab) (NBH 491)

Shout to the Lord (v1c, c in Bb) (NBH 133)

Scripture Reading: Worship Leader with the Congregation

(See Scripture Reading Below)

Praise and Worship: Congregation

My Jesus, I Love Thee (v1, v4 in F) (NBH 552)

You Are My All in All (v1c, v2c in F)

Worship with Our Gifts: Pastoral Staff

Praise and Worship During Offering

The Potter's Hand (NBH 441): Praise Team

Message: *Dysfunctional Families Can Change*

Hymn of Response/Invitation: Worship Leader and Congregation

Here I Am to Worship (c, v1c, v2c in F) (NBH 130)

Hymn of Benediction: Congregation

Shine, Jesus Shine (v1c in Ab) (NBH 491)

Postlude: *Shine, Jesus Shine* (2x Ab) (NBH 491)—Instrumentalist

Scripture Reading

Worship Leader: I am the light of the world. Anyone who follows Me will never walk in the darkness but will have the light of life.

Congregation: For God, who said, "Light shall shine out of darkness": He has shone in our hearts to give the light of the knowledge of God's glory in the face of Jesus Christ.

Worship Leader: He is the radiance of his glory, the exact expression of his nature, and He sustains all things by His powerful word.

Congregation: In the same way, let your light shine before men, so that they may see your good works and give glory to your Father in heaven.

Worship Leader: The LORD will shine over you, and his glory will appear over you. Nations will come to your light, and kings to the brightness of your radiance.

WEEK 8 SERVICE MOTHER'S DAY

Prelude: *This is the Day* (2x in Eb) (NBH 571)—Instrumentalist

Prayer of Worship: Worship Pastor

Call to Praise: Congregation

Come, Thou Almighty King (v1, v3 in F, v4 in G) (NBH 336)

We Declare Your Majesty (2x in G) (NBH 65)

Welcome: Pastoral Staff

Welcome Song (meet and greet during song): Pastoral Staff

This is the Day (2x in Eb) (NBH 571)

Worship with Our Gifts: Pastoral Staff

(Praise and Worship During Offering)

Bless His Holy Name (2x in Eb) (NBH 151)

Worthy, You Are Worthy (1x in Eb, 1x in F) (NBH 142)

Scripture Reading: Worship Leader and Congregation

(See Scripture Reading Below)

Praise and Worship: Congregation

You Are My All in All (v1c, v2c in F) (NBH 143)

Message: *A Godly Mother Models Godly Living*

Hymn of Response/Invitation: Worship Leader and Congregation

The Heart of Worship (c, 2c in Eb) (NBH 127)

Hymn of Benediction: Congregation

Give Thanks (1x in F) (NBH 576)

Postlude: This is the Day (2x in Eb) (NBH 571)—Instrumentalist

Scripture Reading

Selections from Proverbs 31

Worship Leader: It is hard to find a good wife, because she is worth more than rubies.

Congregation: Her husband trusts her completely. With her, he has everything he needs.

Worship Leader: She does him good and not harm for as long as she lives.

Congregation: She gets up while it is still dark and prepares food for her family.

Worship Leader: She does her work with energy, and her arms are strong.

Congregation: She knows that what she makes is good. Her lamp burns late into the night.

Worship Leader: She welcomes the poor and helps the needy.

Congregation: She makes coverings for herself; her clothes are made of linen and other

expensive material.

Worship Leader: She is strong and is respected by the people.

Congregation: She looks forward to the future with joy.

Worship Leader: She speaks wise words and teaches others to be kind.

Congregation: She watches over her family and never wastes her time.

Worship Leader: Her children speak well of her.

Congregation: Her husband also praises her,

Worship Leader: Charm can fool you, and beauty can trick you,

but a woman who respects the Lord should be praised.

Congregation: Give her the reward she has earned;

she should be praised in public for what she has done.

WEEK 9 SERVICE FATHER'S DAY

Prelude: *Brethren, We Have Met to Worship* (2x in G) (NBH 386)—Instrumentalist

Welcome: Pastoral Staff

Welcome Song (meet and greet during song): Pastoral Staff

Soon and Very Soon (v1, v2, v3 in G) (NBH 599)

He Has Made Me Glad (2x in D) (NBH 579)

We Bring a Sacrifice of Praise (2x in D) (NBH 581)

Prayer of Dedication, Intercession, and Praise: Pastor

(See Scripture Reading Below)

Sanctuary (1x in D, 2x in Eb) (NBH 588)

Scripture Reading: Men's Reading Group

Brethren, We Have Met to Worship (v1, v4 in G) (NBH 386)

Faith of Our Fathers (v1, v3 in G) (NBH 594

Worship with Our Gifts: Pastoral Staff

(Praise and Worship During Offering)

Find Us Faithful (2x in Eb) (NBH 598)

Let It Be Said of Us (v1c, v2c in D) (NBH 597): Men's Ensemble

Message: *A Godly Father Will Lay His Children on the Altar*

Hymn of Response/Invitation: Worship Leader and Congregation

We Will Glorify (1x in D, 1x in Eb) (NBH 22)

Hymn of Benediction: *Forever* (chorus only) (NBH 99): Congregation

Postlude: *Forever* (2x in G) (NBH 99)—Instrumentalist

Scripture Reading

ALL: To the elders among you!

Reader 1: I appeal as a fellow elder,

Reader 2: A witness of Christ's sufferings

Reader 1: And, one who also will share in the glory to be revealed:

ALL: Be shepherds of God's flock!

Reader 3: Serve as overseers—not because you must, but because you are willing

Reader 4: As God wants you to be

Reader 1: not greedy for money, but eager to serve;

ALL: Eager to Serve.

Reader 2: Not lording it over those entrusted to you,

Reader 3: But being examples to the flock.

All: And, when the Chief Shepherd appears

Reader 4: The Chief Shepherd

Reader 1: You will receive the crown of glory that will never fade away.

ALL: Young Men!

Reader 1: In the same way, be submissive to those who are older.

ALL: All of you!

Reader 2: Clothe yourselves with humility toward one another.

Reader 1: "God opposes the proud"

Reader 4: He gives grace to the humble."

ALL: Humble yourselves!

Reader 3: Humble Yourselves under God's mighty hand

Reader 2: That He may lift you up!

Reader 1: That He may lift you up at the right time time.

ALL: Cast your care on Him.

Reader 1: Because he cares for you.

ALL: Be self-controlled

Reader 2: And alert.

Reader 4: Your enemy the devil prowls around like a roaring lion **Reader 3:** Looking for someone to devour.

ALL: Resist him!

Reader 2: Stand firm in the faith

Reader 1: Your brothers throughout the world are undergoing suffering

Reader 3: The God of all grace,

Reader 4: Who called you to his eternal glory in Christ

Reader 2: After you have suffered a little while

Reader 1: Will himself restore you and make you strong

Reader 2: firm

Reader 3: And, steadfast.

Reader 4: To him be the power for ever and ever.

Reader 1: Amen.

Reader 4: Amen.

Reader 2: Amen.

Reader 3: Amen.

ALL: Amen

WEEK 10 SERVICE

Prelude: *I Could Sing of His Love Forever* (NBH 116)—Instrumental

Call to Worship: Pastoral Staff

Call to Praise: *Come Thou Fount* (v1c, v2c, v3c in C) (NBH 95)

Welcome: Pastoral Staff

Hymn of Welcome

　Surely Goodness and Mercy (v1c, v2c in Eb) (NBH 91)

　Think About His Love (2x in Eb) (NBH 102)

　The Heart of Worship (c, v2c in Eb) (NBH 127)

Prayer of Praise: Pastoral Staff

　Great Is Thy Faithfulness (v3c in D, c in Eb) (NBH 96)

Offertory Prayer: Pastor

Offertory Praise: *Grace Alone* (NBH 112): Praise Team

Sermon: *Accept No Imitations, Part 1*—Pastor

Hymn of Invitation: *Just As I Am* (redtiemusic.com): Congregation

Benediction Hymn: *Rock of Ages* (1 x in G) (NBH 126): Congregation

Postlude: *Rock of Ages* (v1c, c in G) (NBH 126)—Instrumentalist

WEEK 11 SERVICE

Prelude: *Jehovah Jireh* (2x in Em) (NBH 124)—Instrumentalist

Prayer of Worship: Worship Pastor

Call to Praise: Congregation

Sing to the King (v1c, v2c in F) (NBH 129)

Hosanna (Praise is Rising) (v1c, v2c in G) (NBH 132)

Welcome: Pastoral Staff

Welcome Song (meet and greet during song): Pastoral Staff

Jehovah Jireh (2x in em) (NBH 124)

He Is Jehovah (v1c, v3c in em) (NBH 118)

Scripture Reading—Worship Leader with the Congregation

(See Scripture Reading Below)

Praise and Worship: Congregation

Open Our Eyes, Lord (v1, v2 w/tag in D) (NBH 426)

I Must Tell Jesus (v1c, v2c in D) (NBH 424)

Tell it to Jesus (chorus only tag last 2 measures) (NBH 425)

Praise and Worship During Offering

Be Exalted, O Lord (NBH 19 in Bb): Praise Team

Message: *Accept No Imitations, Part 2*

Hymn of Response/Invitation: Worship Leader and Congregation

Into My Heart (2x in F) (NBH 418)

Hymn of Benediction: Congregation

Soon and Very Soon (1x in G) (NBH 599)

Postlude: *Soon and Very Soon* (2x in G) (NBH 599)—Instrumentalist

Scripture Reading

Selections from Psalm 16

Worship Leader: Keep me safe, my God, for in you I take refuge.

Congregation: I say to the LORD, "You are my Lord; apart from you I have no good thing."

Worship Leader: LORD, you alone are my portion and my cup;   you make my lot secure.

Congregation: I will praise the LORD, who counsels me; even at night my heart instructs me.

Worship Leader: I keep my eyes always on the LORD. With him at my right hand, I will not be shaken.

Congregation: You make known to me the path of life; you will fill me with joy in your presence, with eternal pleasures at your right hand.

WEEK 12 SERVICE

Prelude: *Sing to the King* (2x in F) (NBH 129)—Instrumentalist

Prayer of Worship: Worship Pastor

Call to Praise: Congregation

Sing to the King (2x in F) (NBH 129)

Welcome: Pastoral Staff

Welcome Song (meet and greet during song): Pastoral Staff

I Will Sing of the Mercies (2x in C) (NBH 625)

Worship with Our Gifts: Pastoral Staff

(Praise and Worship During Offering)

Holy, Holy, Holy (v1, v2 in D, v4 in Eb) (NBH 68)

This is Holy Ground (v1 in Eb) (NBH 71)

We Are Standing on Holy Ground (2x in Eb) (NBH 72)

Scripture Reading: Psalm 95:3; 96:4, 99:2, 145:8, 147:5: Reader's Group

(See Scripture Reading Below)

Praise and Worship: Congregation

Be Thou My Vision (v1c, v4c in D) (NBH 83)

He is Here (2x in D) (NBH 94)

Message: *It's the Gospel Truth*

Hymn of Response/Invitation: Worship Leader and Congregation

Change My Heart, O God (2x in C) (NBH 529)

Hymn of Benediction: Congregation

His Strength is Perfect (2x in F) (NBH 460)

Postlude: Sing to the King (2x in F) (NBH 129)—Instrumentalist

Scripture Reading

Psalm 95:3; 96:4, 99:2, 145:8, 147:5

ALL: The LORD is a GREAT God.

Reader 1: A GREAT King above all gods.

Reader 2: The LORD is great and is highly praised.

Reader 3: He is feared above all gods.

All: The LORD is GREAT in Zion;

Reader 2: HE is exalted above all the peoples.

Reader 3: The LORD is gracious and compassionate,

Reader 1: Slow to anger and great in faithful love.

ALL: Our LORD is great

Reader 1: Vast in power;

Reader 2: His understanding is infinite.

ALL: GREAT IS THE LORD.

Reader 1: GREAT IS THE LORD!

Reader 2: GREAT IS THE LORD!

Reader 3: GREAT IS THE LORD!

Reader 1: The Lord is GREAT

ALL : And, GREATLY to be praised.

WEEK 13 SERVICE

Prelude: *Great Is The Lord* (2x in C) (NBH 61)—Instrumentalist

Call to Praise: Congregation

Great Is The Lord (2x in C) (NBH 61)

Welcome: Pastoral Staff

Welcome Song (meet and greet during song): Pastoral Staff

Come, Now is the Time to Worship (2x in D) (NBH 30)

There Is None Like You (2x in G) (NBH 109)

Hallelujah (Your Love is Amazing) (c, v1c, v2c, c in G) (NBH 100)

Worship with Our Gifts: Pastoral Staff

(Praise and Worship During Offering)

This is My Father's World (v1, v3 in D) (NBH 46)

Come Thou Fount (vs 1 in D vs 3 in Eb) (NBH 98)

Scripture Reading: Worship Leader and Congregation

(See Scripture Reading Below)

Prayer of Dedication, Intercession, and Praise: Pastor

We Will Glorify (v1, v2 in D v4 in Eb) (NBH 22)

He Knows My Name (v1, c, c in Eb) (NBH 44)

Message: *The Mask*

Hymn of Response/Invitation: Worship Leader and Congregation

Open our Eyes Lord (2x in D) (NBH 426)

Hymn of Benediction: *Ancient of Days* (1x in Bb) (NBH 62)—Congregation

Postlude: *Ancient of Days* (2x in Bb) (NBH 62)—Instrumentalist

Scripture Reading

Worship Leader: In you, LORD my God, I put my trust.

Congregation: No one who hopes in you will ever be put to shame, but shame will come on those who are treacherous without cause.

Worship Leader: Show me your ways, LORD, teach me your paths.

Congregation: Guide me in your truth and teach me, for you are God my Savior, and my hope is in you all day long.

Worship Leader: Remember, LORD, your great mercy and love, for they are from of old.

Congregation: Good and upright is the LORD; therefore he instructs sinners in his ways.

Worship Leader: He guides the humble in what is right and teaches them his way.

Congregation: All the ways of the LORD are loving and faithful toward those who keep the demands of his covenant.

WEEK 14 SERVICE

Prelude: *O Magnify the Lord* (2x in D) (NBH 134) Instrumental

Call to Worship: Pastoral Staff

Call to Praise: *Awesome God* (2x in em 1x in fm) (NBH 63)

Welcome: Pastoral Staff

Hymn of Welcome

Victory Chant (v1, v2, v3 in G) (NBH 299)

God of Wonders (v1c, v2c in G) (NBH 51)

Offertory Prayer: Pastor

Offertory Praise

Redeemed, How I Love to Proclaim It (c, v1c, v2c, v3c, v4c in G) (NBH 280)

Down At the Cross (c, v1c, v3c in G) (NBH 252)

Lamb of Glory (v1c, v2c in G) (NBH 260)

Sermon: *The Most Important Question*—Pastor

Hymn of Invitation: *Just As I Am* (redtiemusic.com): Congregation

Benediction Hymn: *Rock of Ages* (1 x in G) (NBH 126): Congregation

Postlude: *Rock of Ages* (v1c, c in G) (NBH 126)—Instrumentalist

WEEK 15 SERVICE

Prelude: *Shine, Jesus, Shine* (1x in Ab) (NBH 491) Instrumentalist

Scripture Reading—Reader's Group

(See Scripture Reading Below)

Because We Believe (v1c, v2c, v3c in C) (NBH 519)

Prayer of Worship: Pastor

Welcome: Pastoral Staff

Welcome Song (meet and greet during song): Pastoral Staff

Victory in Jesus (v1c, v2c, v3c in F) (NBH 499)

Trust and Obey (c, v1c, v3c, v4c in F) (NBH 500)

Worship with Our Gifts: Pastoral Staff

(Praise and Worship During Offering)

Tis So Sweet to Trust in Jesus (v1c, v4c in G) (NBH 502)

Now I Belong to Jesus (c, v1c, v3c in G) (NBH 503)

Prayer of Dedication, Intercession, and Praise: Pastor

Still (v1c, v2c in C) (NBH 459)

His Strength is Perfect (2x in F) (NBH 460)

Message: *The Two Don't Mix*

Hymn of Response/Invitation: Worship Leader and Congregation

In His Time (v1, v2 in Eb) (NBH 522)

Hymn of Benediction: Congregation

Shine, Jesus, Shine (chorus only in Ab) (NBH 491)

Postlude: Victory in Jesus—Instrumentalist

Scripture Reading

(Selections from Romans 10)

ALL: This is . . . the message concerning faith that we proclaim:

Reader 1: If you declare with your mouth, "Jesus is Lord," and believe in your heart that God raised him from the dead, you will be saved.

Reader 2: For it is with your heart that you believe and are justified, and it is with your mouth that you profess your faith and are saved.

ALL: As Scripture says,

Reader 2: "Anyone who believes in him will never be put to shame."

Reader 3: For there is no difference between Jew and Gentile—the same Lord is Lord of all and richly blesses all who call on him,

Reader 4: "Everyone who calls on the name of the Lord will be saved."

Reader 1: How, then, can they call on the one they have not believed in?

Reader 2: And how can they believe in the one of whom they have not heard?

Reader 3: And how can they hear without someone preaching to them?

Reader 4: And how can anyone preach unless they are sent?

Reader 1: As it is written:

ALL: "How beautiful are the feet of those who bring good news!"

WEEK 16 SERVICE

Prelude: *Shine on Us* (2x in D) (NBH 89)—Instrumentalist

Prayer of Worship: Worship Pastor

Call to Praise: Congregation

Joyful, Joyful, We Adore Thee (v1 in F, v2 in G) (NBH 13)

Welcome: Pastoral Staff

Welcome Song (meet and greet during song): Pastoral Staff

I Will Celebrate (2x in F) (NBH 572)

I Will Bless the Lord (2x in F) (NBH 14)

Worship with Our Gifts: Pastoral Staff

(Praise and Worship During Offering)

Nothing But the Blood (v1c, v2c, v4c in F) (NBH 223)

At Calvary (v1c, v4c in Bb) (NBH 245)

The Old Rugged Cross (c, v1c, v4c in Bb) (NBH 230)

Scripture Reading: Worship Leader and Congregation

(See Scripture Reading Below)

Praise and Worship: Congregation

The Power of the Cross (v1c, v4c in C) (NBH 232)

Message: *Living By Grace*

Hymn of Response/Invitation: Worship Leader and Congregation

I Surrender All (v1c, v3c in C) (NBH 433)

Hymn of Benediction: Congregation

The Trees of the Field (2x in em) (NBH 570)

Postlude: *The Trees of the Field* (2x in em) (NBH 570)—Instrumentalist

Scripture Reading

Hebrews 1:1–4; 2:9; 2 Cor. 2:4

Worship Leader: In the past God spoke to our ancestors through the prophets at many times and in various ways,

Congregation: but in these last days he has spoken to us by his Son, whom he appointed heir of all things, and through whom also he made the universe.

Worship Leader: The Son is the radiance of God's glory and the exact representation of his being, sustaining all things by his powerful word.

Congregation: After he had provided purification for sins, he sat down at the right hand of the Majesty in heaven.

Worship Leader: So he became as much superior to the angels as the name he has inherited is superior to theirs.

Congregation: But we see Jesus, crowned with glory and honor because he suffered death, so that by the grace of God he might taste death for everyone.

Worship Leader: For to be sure, he was crucified in weakness, yet he lives by God's power.

Congregation: Likewise, we are weak in him, yet by God's power we will live with him.

WEEK 17 SERVICE

Prelude: *I Will Bless the Lord* (2x in F) (NBH 14)—Instrumentalist

Welcome: Pastoral Staff

Welcome Song (meet and greet during song): Pastoral Staff

Days of Elijah (c 2x in Ab) (NBH 289)

Blessed Be the Name (c, v1c, v4c in Ab) (NBH 310

Crown Him King of Kings (2x in Ab) (NBH 301)

Scripture Reading: Reader's Group

(See Scripture Reading Below)

Prayer of Dedication, Intercession, and Praise: Pastor

Take the Name of Jesus With You (c, v1c, v2c, v4c in G) (NBH 313)

Jesus, Your Name (v1, v2, v3 in C) (NBH 312)

His Name is Wonderful (1x w Tag in F) (NBH 315)

Worship with Our Gifts: Pastoral Staff

(Praise and Worship During Offering)

At the Name of Jesus: Praise Team or Solo

Message: *The Case for Faith*

Hymn of Response/Invitation: Worship Leader and Congregation

He Knows My Name (v1c, v2c in Eb) (NBH 44)

Hymn of Benediction: *I Sing Praises* (1x in G) (NBH 17): Congregation

Postlude: *I Sing Praises* (1x in G, 1x in Ab) (NBH 17)—Instrumentalist

Scripture Reading

ALL: Hallelujah.

Reader 1: Hallelujah, What a Savior

ALL: Hallelujah, what a Savior.

Reader 1: For you know that you were redeemed from your empty way of life inherited from the fathers,

Reader 2: Not with perishable things, like silver or gold,

Reader 3: But with precious blood of Christ,

Reader 4: Like that of a lamb without defect or blemish.

Reader 1: The Son of Man did not come to be served,

Reader 2: But to serve,

Reader 3: And to give his life

Reader 4: A ransom for many.

Reader 2: For to those who are perishing the message of the cross is foolishness,

Reader 3: But to us

Reader 4: But to us who are being saved

ALL: It is God's power.

Reader 1: For it is written:

Reader 4: I will destroy the wisdom of the wise,

Reader 3: And I will set aside the understanding of the experts.

Reader 2: But as for me,

Reader 3: But as for me,

Reader 1: But as for me,

Reader 4: I will never boast about anything except the cross of our Lord Jesus Christ, though whom the world has been crucified to me and I to the world.

Reader 1: Hallelujah.

Reader 2: Hallelujah, What a Savior

ALL: Hallelujah, what a Savior.

WEEK 18 SERVICE

Prelude: *Lord, I Lift Your Name on High* (Chorus 2x in G) (NBH 347)—Instrumentalist

Call to Praise: Congregation

Praise the Name of Jesus (2x in D) (NBH 322)

His Name is Life (2x in D) (NBH 318)

I Will Serve Thee (2x in Eb) (377)

Welcome: Pastoral Staff

Welcome Song (meet and greet during song): Pastoral Staff

Lord, I Lift Your Name on High (Chorus 2x in G) (NBH 347)

Jesus, Name Above All Names (2x in Eb) (NBH 320)

There's Something About That Name (1x in Eb) (NBH 317)

Prayer of Dedication, Intercession, and Praise: Pastor

There's Something About That Name (1x in Eb) (NBH 317)

Scripture Reading: Worship Leader and Congregation

(See Scripture Reading Below)

In Christ Alone (v1, v2, v3 in D, v4 in Eb) (NBH 506)

Worship with Our Gifts: Pastoral Staff

(Praise and Worship During Offering)

If My People Will Pray (NBH 430): Praise Team

Message: *Law and Promise*

Hymn of Response/Invitation: Worship Leader and Congregation

'Tis So Sweet to Trust in Jesus (v1c, c in G) (NBH 502)

Hymn of Benediction: *Who Can Satisfy?* (chorus only in C) (NBH 507) Congregation

Postlude: *Who Can Satisfy?* (v1c, c C) (NBH 507)—Instrumentalist

Scripture Reading

Hebrews 1:1–4; 2:9; 2 Cor. 2:4

Worship Leader: In the past God spoke to our ancestors through the prophets at many times and in various ways,

Congregation: but in these last days he has spoken to us by his Son, whom he appointed heir of all things, and through whom also he made the universe.

Worship Leader: The Son is the radiance of God's glory and the exact representation of his being, sustaining all things by his powerful word.

Congregation: After he had provided purification for sins, he sat down at the right hand of the Majesty in heaven.

Worship Leader: So he became as much superior to the angels as the name he has inherited is superior to theirs.

Congregation: But we see Jesus, crowned with glory and honor because he suffered death, so that by the grace of God he might taste death for everyone.

Worship Leader: For to be sure, he was crucified in weakness, yet he lives by God's power.

Congregation: Likewise, we are weak in him, yet by God's power we will live with him.

WEEK 19 SERVICE

Prelude: *We Bring the Sacrifice* (2x in D) (NBH 581)—Instrumentalist

Call to Praise: Congregation

Majesty (2x in Bb) (NBH 297)

How Great Thou Art (c, v1c, v4c in Bb) (NBH 6)

Prayer of Worship: Worship Pastor

Welcome: Pastoral Staff

Welcome Song (meet and greet during song): Pastoral Staff

We Bring the Sacrifice (2x in D) (NBH 581)

Holy, Holy, Holy (v1, v2, v3 in D, v4 in Eb) (NBH 68)

Offertory Prayer: Pastoral Staff

Praise and Worship During Offering

All Hail King Jesus (2x in F) (NBH 295)

He Is Exalted (11x in F) (NBH 296) (Change "He" to "You," singing TO God)

More Precious than Silver (2x in F) (NBH 557)

Into My Heart (2x in F) (NBH 418)

Scripture Reading: Worship Leader with the Congregation

(See Scripture Reading Below)

Praise and Worship: Congregation

You Are My King (Amazing Love) (NBH 308): Praise Team or Solo

Message: *Sons of God*

Hymn of Response/Invitation: Worship Leader and Congregation

Spirit of the Living God (2x in F) (NBH 330)

Hymn of Benediction: Congregation

He is Exalted (1x in F) (NBH 296)

Postlude: *He is Exalted* (2x in F) (NBH 296)—Instrumentalist

Scripture Reading

Romans 11:36–12:15

Worship Leader: For from Him and through Him and to Him are all things.

Congregation: To Him be the glory forever. Amen.

Worship Leader: Therefore, brothers, by the mercies of God, I urge you to present your bodies as a living sacrifice, holy and pleasing to God; this is your spiritual worship.

Congregation: Do not be conformed to this age, but be transformed by the renewing of your mind, so that you may discern what is the good, pleasing, and perfect will of God.

Worship Leader: For by the grace given to me, I tell everyone among you not to think of himself more highly than he should think.

Congregation: Instead, think sensibly, as God has distributed a measure of faith to each one.

Worship Leader: Now as we have many parts in one body, and all the parts do not have the same function,

Congregation: In the same way we who are many are one body in Christ and individually members of one another.

Worship Leader: According to the grace given to us, we have different gifts: **If prophecy, use it according to the standard of faith; if service, in service; if teaching, in teaching; if exhorting, in exhortation; giving, with generosity; leading, with diligence; showing mercy, with cheerfulness.**

Congregation: Love must be without hypocrisy. Detest evil; cling to what is good.

Worship Leader: Show family affection to one another with brotherly love. Outdo one another in showing honor.

Congregation: Do not lack diligence; be fervent in spirit; serve the Lord.

Worship Leader: Rejoice in hope; be patient in affliction; be persistent in prayer.

Congregation: Share with the saints in their needs; pursue hospitality.

Worship Leader: Bless those who persecute you; bless and do not curse.

Congregation: Rejoice with those who rejoice; Weep with those who weep.

WEEK 20 SERVICE

Prelude: Instrumentalist

Prayer of Worship: Worship Pastor

Call to Praise: Congregation

Friend of God: (v1c, bridge 2x, c in C) (NBH 484)

Welcome: Pastoral Staff

Welcome Song (meet and greet during song): Pastoral Staff

Everlasting God (2x in Bb) (NBH 121)

I Stand Amazed in the Presence (v1c, v2c in G) (NBH 237)

Hallelujah, What a Savior (v1, v2, v3, v4 in Bb, v5 in C) (NBH 242)

Worship with Our Gifts: Pastoral Staff

(Praise and Worship During Offering)

Lead Me to Calvary (v1c, v4c in D) (NBH 251)

Jesus Paid it All (c 2x in D) (NBH 249)

I Believe in a Hill Called Mt Calvary (c, v3c in Bb) (NBH 246)

Scripture Reading: Worship Leader and Congregation

(See Scripture Reading Below)

Praise and Worship: Congregation

God of the Ages (from *Red Tie Music.com*): Praise Team

Message: *A Personal Plea*

Hymn of Response/Invitation: Worship Leader and Congregation

My Jesus, I love Thee (v1, v4 in F) (NBH 552)

Hymn of Benediction: Congregation

Blessed Be Your Name (c in A) (NBH 26)

Postlude: Blessed Be Your Name (c in A) (NBH 26)—Instrumentalist

Scripture Reading

Worship Leader: The Son is the image of the invisible God, the firstborn over all creation.

Congregation: For in him all things were created: things in heaven and on earth, visible and invisible, whether thrones or powers or rulers or authorities; all things have been created through him and for him.

Worship Leader: He is before all things, and in him all things hold together. And he is the head of the body, the church; he is the beginning and the first-born from among the dead, so that in everything he might have the supremacy.

Congregation: For God was pleased to have all his fullness dwell in him, and through him to reconcile to himself all things, whether things on earth or things in heaven, by making peace through his blood, shed on the cross.

WEEK 21 SERVICE

Prelude: *I'm So Glad* (2x in G) (NBH 568)—Instrumentalist

Welcome: Pastoral Staff

Welcome Song (meet and greet during song): Pastoral Staff

I'm So Glad (v1, v2, v3, v4 in G) (NBH 568)

Soon and Very Soon (v1c, v2c, v3c in G) (NBH 599)

I'll Fly Away (v1c, v2c in G) (NBH 601)

Scripture Reading: Reader's Group

(See Scripture Reading Below)

When the Roll Is Called Up Yonder (c, v1c, v2c, v3c in G) (NBH 600)

My Savior First of All (v1c, v2c in G)(NBH 602)

Prayer of Dedication, Intercession, and Praise: Pastor

The Way of the Cross Leads Home (c, v1c, v2c in F) (NBH 606)

In the Sweet By and By (c, v1, c in F) (NBH 605)

Thank You, Lord (2x in F) (NBH 582)

Worship with Our Gifts: Pastoral Staff

(Praise and Worship During Offering)

He the Pearly Gates will Open (v1c, v3c, v4c in G) (NBH 609): Praise Team or Solo

Message: *Roots*

Hymn of Response/Invitation: Worship Leader and Congregation

Take My Life (Holiness) (c, v1c, v2c in F) (NBH 589)

Hymn of Benediction: *Thank You, Lord* (2x in F) (NBH 582): Congregation

Postlude: *Soon and Very Soon* (v1c, v2c, v3c in G) (NBH 599)—Instrumentalist

Scripture Reading

Revelation 21:1–4, 9–11, 21–24

Worship Leader: Then I saw a new heaven and a new earth, for the first heaven and the first earth had passed away, and there was no longer any sea.

Congregation: I saw the Holy City, the new Jerusalem, coming down out of heaven from God, prepared as a bride beautifully dressed for her husband.

Worship Leader: And I heard a loud voice from the throne saying, "Now the dwelling of God is with men, and he will live with them.

Congregation: They will be his people, and God himself will be with them and be their God.

Worship Leader: He will wipe every tear from their eyes. There will be no more death or mourning or crying or pain, for the old order of things has passed away."

Congregation: One of the seven angels who had the seven bowls full of the seven last plagues came and said to me, "Come, I will show you the bride, the wife of the Lamb."

Worship Leader: And he carried me away in the Spirit to a mountain great and high, and showed me the Holy City, Jerusalem, coming down out of heaven from God.

Congregation: It shone with the glory of God, and its brilliance was like that of a very precious jewel, like a jasper, clear as crystal.

Worship Leader: The twelve gates were twelve pearls, each gate made of a single pearl. The great street of the city was of pure gold, like transparent glass.

Congregation: I did not see a temple in the city, because the Lord God Almighty and the Lamb are the city's temple.

Worship Leader: The city does not need the sun or the moon to shine on it, because the glory of God is its light, and the Lamb is the city's lamp.

Congregation: By its light the people of the world will walk, and the kings of the earth will bring their glory into it!

WEEK 22 SERVICE

Prelude: *Leaning on the Everlasting Arms* (ck redtiemusic.com) Instrumentalist

Welcome: Pastoral Staff

Welcome Song (meet and greet during song): Pastoral Staff

Leaning on the Everlasting Arms (ck redtiemusic.com for arr)

I Stand Amazed in the Presence (v1c, v4c in G) (NBH 237)

O the Blood of Jesus (v1, 2, 3, in D, v4 in Eb) (NBH 226)

The Blood Will Never Lose Its Power (v1c, v2c in Ab)

Worship with Our Gifts: Pastoral Staff

(Praise and Worship During Offering)

Holy Spirit Rain Down (2x in F) (NBH 335)

Shout to the Lord (2x in Bb) (NBH 133)

Scripture Reading: Isaiah 53:1–6 NCV: Worship Leader and Congregation

(See Scripture Reading Below)

Prayer of Dedication, Intercession, and Praise: Pastor

Jesus, Lord to Me (1x in F, 1x in G) (NBH 300)

Message: *Free at Last!*

Hymn of Response/Invitation: Worship Leader and Congregation

Father, I Adore You (v1, v2, v3 in F) (NBH 566)

Hymn of Benediction: *My Tribute* (Chorus only in Bb) (NBH 577) Congregation

Postlude: *My Tribute* (c, v1c, c in Bb) (NBH 577)—Instrumentalist

Scripture Reading

Isaiah 53:1–6 NCV

Worship Leader: Who would have believed what we heard? Who saw the Lord's power in this?

Congregation: He grew up like a small plant before the Lord, like a root growing in a dry land.

Worship Leader: He had no special beauty or form to make us notice him; there was nothing in his appearance to make us desire him.

Congregation: He was hated and rejected by people. He had much pain and suffering.

Worship Leader: People would not even look at him. He was hated, and we didn't even notice him.

Congregation: But he took our suffering on him and felt our pain for us.

Worship Leader: We saw his suffering and thought God was punishing him.

Congregation: But he was wounded for the wrong we did; he was crushed for the evil we did.

Worship Leader: The punishment, which made us well, was given to him, and we are healed because of his wounds.

Congregation: We all have wandered away like sheep; each of us has gone his own way.

Worship Leader: But the Lord has put on him the punishment for all the evil we have done.

WEEK 23 SERVICE

Prelude: *I Will Enter His Gates* (v1c, c in D) (NBH 579)—Instrumentalist

Scripture Reading: Reader's Group
(See Scripture Reading Below)

Call to Praise: Congregation
Sing to the King (v1c, v2c in F) (NBH 129)
Here I Am to Worship (c, v1c, v2c in F) (NBH 130)

Prayer of Worship: Worship Pastor

Welcome: Pastoral Staff

Welcome Song (meet and greet during song): Pastoral Staff
I've Got Peace Like a River (v1,2,3,1 in G) (NBH 618)
O How I Love Jesus (v1c, v4c with last line (because) 2x as tag in G) (NBH 626)
Oh How He loves you and me (2x in Ab) (NBH 170)

Offertory Prayer: Pastoral Staff

Praise and Worship During Offering
I Will Sing the Wondrous Story (c, v1c, v5c, c in D) (NBH 633)
A Child of the King (v1c, v3c in D) (NBH 632)

Prayer of Intercession, Praise, and Worship: Congregation
Something Beautiful (2x in Eb) (NBH 623)

Message: *Now What Do We Do?*

Hymn of Response/Invitation: Worship Leader and Congregation
The Longer I Serve Him, The Sweeter It Grows (c, v1c in G) (NBH 374)

Hymn of Benediction: *I Will Enter His Gates* (Chorus only) (NBH 579)
Congregation

Postlude: *I Will Enter His Gates* (v1c, c in D) (NBH 579)—Instrumentalist

Scripture Reading

Reader 1: My heart is confident, Oh God.
Reader 4: My heart is steadfast, Oh Lord.
Reader 3: My heart is trusting, Oh Sovereign.
Reader 2: My heart is fixed on You, Oh Great Redeemer.
ALL: I Will Sing Praise.

Reader 2: I will sing praise in the morning.

Reader 3: I WILL sing praise at noon.

Reader 4: I will SING praise in the evening.

Reader 1: I will praise you for your faithfulness, Oh God.

Reader 2: I will sing to You with a harp. Holy One of Israel

Reader 3: I will sing of faithful love and justice, Most Sovereign and Just God.

Reader 4: I will sing praise to you, MY Lord.

ALL: We Will Sing. (confident)

ALL: We Will Sing Praise. (Louder)

ALL: We Will Sing PRAISE to our Most High God. (Much Louder)

WEEK 24 SERVICE

Prelude: *Hallelujah* (c, v1c, v2c, c in G) (NBH 100)—Instrumentalist

Call to Praise: Congregation

  Forever (v1, v2, c, v3, c, c in G) (NBH 99)

  I Could Sing of Your Love Forever (2x in G) (NBH 116)

Prayer of Worship: Worship Pastor

Welcome: Pastoral Staff

Welcome Song (meet and greet during song): Pastoral Staff

  This is the Day (2x in Eb) (NBH 571)

Worship with Our Gifts: Pastoral Staff

  (Praise and Worship During Offering)

  Amazing Grace (v1, v2, v5 in G) (NBH 104)

  Grace, Greater than All Our Sins (c, v1c in G) (NBH 105)

  Hallelujah (c, v1c, v2c, c in G) (NBH 100)

Scripture Reading: Worship Leader and Congregation

  (See Scripture Reading Below)

Praise and Worship: Congregation

  Think About His Love (2x in Eb)(NBH 102)

Message: *The Great Conflict*

Hymn of Response/Invitation: Worship Leader and Congregation

  My Jesus, I Love Thee (v1, v3, v4 in F) (NBH 552)

Hymn of Benediction: Congregation

  Hallelujah (chorus only 2x in G) (NBH 100)

Postlude: *Hallelujah* (c, v1c, v2c, c in G) (NBH 100)—Instrumentalist

Scripture Reading

Worship Leader: Sing to the Lord, you who do what is right; honest people should praise Him.

Congregation: Praise the Lord on the harp; make music for him on a ten-stringed lyre.

Worship Leader: Sing a new song to him; play well and joyfully.

Congregation: God's word is true, and everything he does is right.

Worship Leader: He loves what is right and fair; the Lord's love fills the earth.

Congregation: The sky was made at the Lord's command.

Worship Leader: By the breath from his mouth, he made all the stars.

Congregation: He gathered the water of the sea into a heap.

Worship Leader: He made the great ocean stay in its place.

Congregation: All the earth should worship the Lord; the whole world should fear him.

Worship Leader: He spoke, and it happened. He commanded, and it appeared.

Congregation: Happy is the nation whose God is the Lord, the people he chose for his very own.

Worship Leader: The Lord looks down from heaven and sees every person.

Congregation: From his throne he watches all who live on earth.

Worship Leader: He made their hearts and understands everything they do.

Congregation: Our hope is in the Lord. He is our help, our shield to protect us.

Worship Leader: We rejoice in him, because we trust his holy name.

Congregation: Lord, show your love to us as we put our hope in you.

WEEK 25 SERVICE

Prelude: *I Will Call Upon the Lord* (2x in C) (NBH 498)—Instrumentalist

Call to Praise: Congregation

Who Can Satisfy My Soul Like You (v1c, v2c in C) (NBH 507)

Welcome: Pastoral Staff

Welcome Song (meet and greet during song): Pastoral Staff

I Will Call Upon the Lord (part 1, 2x; part 2, 2x in C) (NBH 498)

Revive Us Again (v1c, v3c, c in F) (NBH 493)

Just a Closer Walk with Thee (v1c, v3c in Bb) (NBH 473)

Prayer of Dedication, Intercession, and Praise: Pastor

Draw Me Close (v1c, v2c in Bb) (NBH 482)

Worship with Our Gifts: Pastoral Staff

(Praise and Worship During Offering)

Like A River Glorious (v1c, v2c, in F v3c in G) (NBH 516)

Scripture Reading: Psalm 73:23–26, 28: Reader's Team (See Scripture Reading Below)

Praise and Worship: *Still* (NBH 459): Praise Team

Message: *The Litmus Test*

Hymn of Response/Invitation: Worship Leader and Congregation

His Strength is Perfect (2x in F) (NBH 460)

Hymn of Benediction: Congregation

Yes, Lord, yes (1 x in Eb) (NBH 445)

Postlude: *Yes, Lord, yes* (2 x in Eb) (NBH 445)—Instrumentalist

Scripture Reading

Psalm 73:23–26, 28; 75:1

Reader 1: You hold me by my right hand.

Reader 2: You guide me with your counsel, and afterward you will take me into glory.

Reader 3: Whom have I in heaven but you?

Reader 2: And earth has nothing I desire besides you.

Reader 1: My flesh and my heart may fail, but God is the strength of my heart and my portion forever.

Reader 2: As for me, it is good to be near God.

Reader 3: I have made the Sovereign LORD my refuge;

Reader 1: I will tell of all your deeds.

Reader 2: We praise you, God.

Reader 3: We praise you, for you name is near.

All: We praise you for your wonderful goodness.

WEEK 26 SERVICE

Prelude: Mighty is our God (2x in Bb) (NBH 59)—Instrumentalist

Prayer of Worship: Pastor

Welcome: Pastoral Staff

Welcome Song (meet and greet during song): Pastoral Staff

Great is the Lord (2x in C) (NBH 61)

Worship with Our Gifts: Pastoral Staff

(Praise and Worship During Offering)

All the Way My Savior Leads Me (v1, v3 in F) (NBH 474)

Jesus is All the World to Me (v1, v2, v3 in G) (NBH 475)

In the Garden (c, v1c, v2c in G) (NBH 476)

Scripture Reading: Worship Leader and Congregation

(See Scripture Reading Below)

Prayer of Dedication, Intercession, and Praise: Pastor

Step by Step (2x in F) (NBH 480)

Turn Your Eyes Upon Jesus (c, v1c, v3c in F) (NBH 413)

Message: *Good Saint Care*

Hymn of Response/Invitation: Worship Leader and Congregation

Bind Us Together (2x in F) (NBH 390)

Hymn of Benediction: Congregation

There is None Like You (2x in G) (NBH 109)

Postlude: Mighty is our God (2x in Bb) (NBH 59)—Instrumentalist

Scripture Reading

Psalm 145:1–3, 8–13, 17–21

Worship Leader: I praise your greatness, my God the King; I will praise you forever and ever.

Congregation: I will praise you every day; I will praise you forever and ever.

Worship Leader: The Lord is great and worthy of our praise;

Congregation: No one can understand how great he is.

Worship Leader: The Lord is kind and shows mercy. He does not become angry quickly but is full of love.

Congregation: The Lord is good to everyone; he is merciful to all he has made.

Worship Leader: Lord, everything you have made will praise you; those who belong to you will bless you.

Congregation: They will tell about the glory of your kingdom and will speak about your power.

Worship Leader: Then everyone will know the mighty things you do and the glory and majesty of your kingdom.

Congregation: Your kingdom will go on and on, and you will rule forever.

Worship Leader: The Lord will keep all his promises;

Congregation: He is loyal to all he has made.

Worship Leader: Everything the Lord does is right.

Congregation: He is loyal to all he has made.

Worship Leader: The Lord is close to everyone who prays to him, to all who truly pray to him.

Congregation: He is loyal to all he has made.

Worship Leader: He gives those who respect him what they want.

Congregation: He is loyal to all he has made.

Worship Leader: He listens when they cry, and he saves them.

Congregation: He is loyal to all he has made.

Worship Leader: The Lord protects everyone who loves him,

Congregation: He is loyal to all he has made.

Worship Leader: I will praise the Lord. Let everyone praise his holy name forever.

WEEK 27 SERVICE

Prelude: *Great and Mighty* (2x in Eb) (NBH 20)– Instrumentalist

Call to Praise: Congregation

I Sing Praises (2x in G) (NBH 17)

Glorify Thy Name (v1, v2, v3 in Bb with interlude) (NBH 18)

Prayer of Worship: Worship Pastor

Welcome: Pastoral Staff

Welcome Song (meet and greet during song): Pastoral Staff

Days of Elijah (c 2x in Ab) (NBH 289)

Blessed Be the Name (c, v1c, v4c in Ab) (NBH 310)

Crown Him King of Kings (2x in Ab) (NBH 301)

Scripture Reading: Reader's Group

(See Scripture Reading Below)

Crown Him King of Kings (1x in A) (NBH 301)

Offertory Prayer: Pastoral Staff

Praise and Worship During Offering

Battle Hymn of the Republic (v1, c, c in Bb)

America the Beautiful (v1, v3 in Bb; v4 in C) (NBH 641)

My Country 'Tis of Thee (v1, v4 in F) (NBH 646)

Prayer of Intercession, Praise, and Worship: Congregation

God of Our Fathers (v1, v2, v4 with choral tag in Eb) (NBH 642)

Message: *The Inviolable Law*

Hymn of Response/Invitation: Worship Leader and Congregation

Freely, Freely (v1c, v2c in Eb) (NBH 627)

Hymn of Benediction: *Great and Mighty* (1x in Eb) (NBH 20): Congregation

Postlude: *Great and Mighty* (2x in Eb) (NBH 20)—Instrumentalist

Scripture Reading

Worship Leader: You, your children, and your grandchildren must respect the Lord your God as long as you live. Obey all his rules and commands

Congregation: The Lord our God is the only Lord.

Worship Leader: Love the Lord your God with all your heart, all your soul, and all your strength.

Congregation: Always remember these commands I give you today.

Worship Leader: Teach them to your children, and talk about them when you sit at home and walk along the road, when you lie down and when you get up.

Congregation: Write them down and tie them to your hands as a sign. Tie them on your forehead to remind you, and write them on your doors and gates.

Worship Leader: Respect the Lord your God. You must worship him and make your promises only in his name.

Congregation: Do not worship other gods as the people around you do, because the Lord your God is a jealous God.

Worship Leader: Remember how the Lord your God has led you.

Congregation: Obey the commands of the Lord your God, living as he has commanded you and respecting him.

Worship Leader: Praise the Lord your God for giving you a good land.

WEEK 28 SERVICE

Prelude: *This is the Day* (1x in Eb) (NBH 571)—Instrumentalist

Call to Worship: Pastor

  Because We Believe: (v1c, v2c, v3c in C) (NBH 519)

Prayer of Worship: Worship Pastor

Welcome: Pastoral Staff

Welcome Song (meet and greet during song): Pastoral Staff

  Everlasting God (2x in Bb) (NBH 121)

  Made Me Glad (v1c, v2c in Bb) (NBH 120)

Worship with Our Gifts: Pastoral Staff

  (Praise and Worship During Offering)

  Like A River Glorious (v1c, v2c in F, v3c in G)

  Lord, I Give You My Heart (2x in G) (NBH 528)

Scripture Reading: Worship Leader and Congregation

  (See Scripture Reading Below)

  As the Deer (v1c, v2c in D) (NBH 554)

  Jesus, Draw Me Close (2x in G) (NBH 553)

Prayer of Dedication, Intercession, Praise, and Worship: Congregation

  The Greatest Thing (v1, v2, v3 in F) (NBH 527)

Message: *The Centrality of the Cross*

Hymn of Response/Invitation: Worship Leader and Congregation

  Only Believe (2x in C) (NBH 512)

Hymn of Benediction: Congregation

  My Life is In You, Lord (2x in G) (NBH 518)

Postlude: *This is the Day* (1x in Eb) (NBH 571)—Instrumentalist

Scripture Reading

Psalm 30

Worship Leader: I will praise you, Lord, because you rescued me. You did not let my enemies laugh at me.

Congregation: Lord, my God, I prayed to you, and you healed me.

Worship Leader: You lifted me out of the grave; you spared me from going down to the place of the dead.

Congregation: Sing praises to the Lord, you who belong to him; praise his holy name.

Worship Leader: His anger lasts only a moment, but his kindness lasts for a lifetime.

Congregation: Crying may last for a night, but joy comes in the morning.

Worship Leader: You changed my sorrow into dancing. You took away my clothes of sadness, and clothed me in happiness.

Congregation: I will sing to you and not be silent. Lord, my God, I will praise you forever.

WEEK 29 SERVICE

Prelude: *Everlasting God* (2x in Bb) (NBH 121)—Instrumentalist

Welcome: Pastoral Staff

Welcome Song (meet and greet during song): Pastoral Staff
My Life is In You, Lord (2x in G) (NBH 518)
Rock of Ages (2x in G) (NBH 126)

Prayer of Dedication, Intercession, and Praise: Pastor
(See Scripture Reading Below)
You Are My Hiding Place (2x in bm) (NBH 125)

Scripture Reading: Reader's Group
Grace Alone (v1c, v2c in C) (NBH 112)

Worship with Our Gifts: Pastoral Staff
(Praise and Worship During Offering)
Take the Name of Jesus With You (v1c, v2c, v4c) (NBH 313)
Jesus, Your Name (v1, v2, v3 in C) (NBH 312)
His Name is Wonderful (1x w Tag in F) (NBH 315)

Message: *How to Be a Worshiper*

Hymn of Response/Invitation: Worship Leader and Congregation
Lord, Be Glorified (v1, v2, v3 in D) (NBH 542)

Hymn of Benediction: *Great is the Lord* (Chorus only in C) (NBH 61):
Congregation

Postlude: *Ancient of Days* (1x in Bb) (NBH 62)—Instrumentalist

Scripture Reading

Reader 1: Happy is the person whose sins are forgiven, whose wrongs are pardoned.

Reader 2: Happy is the person whom the Lord does not consider guilty and in whom there is nothing false.

Reader 3: I said, "I will confess my sins to the Lord," and you forgave my guilt.

Reader 4: For this reason, all who obey you should pray to you while they still can.

ALL: You are my hiding place.

Reader 1: You protect me from my troubles and fill me with songs of salvation.

Reader 2: The Lord says, "I will make you wise and show you where to go.

Reader 3: I will guide you and watch over you.

Reader 4: The Lord's love surrounds those who trust him.

ALL: Good people, rejoice and be happy in the Lord.

WEEK 30 SERVICE

Prelude: *Forever* (v1, v2, c, v3c, c in G) (NBH 99)—Instrumentalist

Scripture Reading: II Chron. 5:1—Reader's Group

(See Scripture Reading Below)

Call to Worship

Forever (v1, v2, c, v3c, c in G) (NBH 99)

Prayer of Worship: Pastor

Welcome: Pastoral Staff

Welcome Song (meet and greet during song): Pastoral Staff

Victory Chant (v1, v2, v3 in G) (NBH 299)

Blessed Be Your Name (v1, v2, c, v3, v4, c, bridge, c in A) (NBH 26)

Prayer of Dedication, Intercession, and Praise: Pastor

Isn't He (2x in G) (NBH 214)

Worship with Our Gifts: Pastoral Staff

(Praise and Worship During Offering)

I Give You My Heart (2x in G) (NBH 528)

Change My Heart, O God (2x in C) (NBH 529)

I'd Rather Have Jesus (v3c in C) (NBH 530) (v3 solo using "You're" for "He's")

Here I Am to Worship (c in F) (NBH 130)

Message: *The Day the Preachers Stopped Preaching*

Hymn of Response/Invitation: Worship Leader and Congregation

Hymn of Benediction: Congregation

Postlude: *Victory Chant* (v1, v2, v3 in G) (NBH 299)—Instrumentalist

Scripture Reading

Reader 1: Finally all the work Solomon did for the Temple of the Lord was finished.

Reader 2: He brought in everything his father David had set apart for the Temple—

Reader 3: all the silver

Reader 4: and gold

Reader 2: and other articles.

Reader 1: And he put everything in the treasuries of God's Temple.

Reader 4: So all the Israelites came together with the king during the festival in the seventh month.

Reader 1: King Solomon and all the Israelites gathered before the Ark of the Agreement and sacrificed so many sheep and bulls no one could count them.

Reader 2: Then all the priests left the Holy Place.

Reader 3: All the priests from each group had made themselves ready to serve the Lord.

Reader 1: All the Levite musicians—

Reader 4: Asaph,

Reader 3: Heman,

Reader 2: Jeduthun,

Reader 1: And all their sons and relatives—stood on the east side of the altar.

ALL: They were dressed in white linen

Reader 1: And played cymbals,

Reader 2: harps,

Reader 3: and lyres.

Reader 4: With them were one hundred twenty priests who blew trumpets.

Reader 1: Those who blew the trumpets and those who sang together sounded like one

person as they praised and thanked the Lord.

Reader 2: They sounded like one.

Reader 3: They Praised

Reader 4: and thanked the Lord . . .

Reader 1: As One

ALL: As One

Reader 2: They sang as others played their trumpets,

Reader 3: cymbals,

Reader 4: and other instruments.

Reader 1: They praised the Lord with this song:

ALL: "Blessed be the name of the Lord, His love endures forever.

Reader 1: He is good;

ALL: His love endures forever."

Reader 2: He is Righteous;

ALL: His love endures forever.

Reader 3: He is Holy;

ALL: His love endures forever.

Reader 4: He is Awesome;

ALL: His love endures forever.

Reader 2: He is Everlasting;

ALL: His love endures forever.

Reader 3: Then . . .

Reader 1: The Temple of the Lord was filled with a cloud.

Reader 2: The priests could not continue their work because of the cloud,

Reader 3: Because . . .

Reader 2: Because of the cloud.

Reader 4: Because . . .

ALL: The glory of the Lord filled the Temple.

WEEK 31 SERVICE

Prelude: *You Are God Alone* (2x in Bb) (SPW 3)—Instrumentalist

Call to Praise: Congregation

Almighty (c, v1c, v2c in F) (NBH 4)

How Great Is Our God (c, v1c, bridge, c in Bb)

How Great Thou Art (c,v1,c in Bb) (NBH 6)

How Great Is Our God (c, v2c in Bb) (NBH 5)

You Are God Alone (2x in Bb) (SPW 3)

Welcome: Pastoral Staff

Welcome Song (meet and greet during song): Pastoral Staff

You're Worthy to Be Praised (2x in F) (NBH 29)

Prayer of Dedication, Intercession, and Praise: Pastor

I Worship You, Almighty God **(2x in F)**

Scripture Reading: Worship Leader and Congregation

(See Scripture Reading Below)

I Will Bless the Lord **(2x in F) (NBH 14)**

Worship with Our Gifts: Pastoral Staff

(Praise and Worship During Offering)

I Give You My Heart (1x Solo, 1x PT, 2x w/congregation in G) (NBH 528)

Message: *Enough to Transfer Us to the Heavenlies*

Hymn of Response/Invitation: Worship Leader and Congregation

Change My Heart, O God (2x in C)

Hymn of Benediction: *Almighty* (2x in F) (NBH 4): Congregation

Postlude: *Almighty* (2x in F) (NBH 4)—Instrumentalist

Scripture Reading

Worship Leader: God, be merciful to me because you are loving.

Congregation: Because you are always ready to be merciful, wipe out all my wrongs.

Worship Leader: Wash away all my guilt and make me clean again.

Congregation: I know about my wrongs, and I can't forget my sin.

Worship Leader: You are the only one I have sinned against; I have done what you say is wrong.

Congregation: You are right when you speak and fair when you judge.

Worship Leader: I was brought into this world in sin. In sin my mother gave birth to me.

Congregation: You want me to be completely truthful, so teach me wisdom.

Worship Leader: Take away my sin, and I will be clean.

Congregation: Wash me, and I will be whiter than snow.

Worship Leader: Make me hear sounds of joy and gladness; let the bones you crushed be happy again.

Congregation: Turn your face from my sins and wipe out all my guilt.

Worship leader: Create in me a pure heart, God, and make my spirit right again.

Congregation: Do not send me away from you or take your Holy Spirit away from me.

Worship Leader: Give me back the joy of your salvation. Keep me strong by giving me a willing spirit.

Congregation: Then I will teach your ways to those who do wrong, and sinners will turn back to you.

Worship Leader: God, save me from the guilt of murder, God of my salvation, and I will sing about your goodness.

Congregation: Lord, let me speak so I may praise you.

Worship Leader: You are not pleased by sacrifices, or I would give them. You don't want burnt offerings.

Congregation: The sacrifice God wants is a broken spirit. God, you will not reject a heart that is broken and sorry for sin.

WEEK 32 SERVICE

Prelude: *Awesome God* (1 x in Em, 1x in Fm) (NBH 63)—Instrumentalist

Call to Praise: Congregation

Jesus, What a Friend For Sinners (v1c, v2c, v3c in F v5 in G) (NBH 156)

Prayer of Worship: Worship Pastor

Welcome: Pastoral Staff

Welcome Song (meet and greet during song): Pastoral Staff

He is Exalted (2x in F) (NBH 296)

Majesty (2x in Bb) (NBH 297)

Scripture Reading: Reader's Group

(See Scripture Reading Below)

There Is A Redeemer (v1c, v2c, v3c in D) (NBH 279)

I Will Sing of My Redeemer (v1c, v3c, c in G) (NBH 285)

Offertory Prayer: Pastoral Staff

Praise and Worship During Offering

Come, Thou Fount of Every Blessing (v1, v2 in D, v3 in Eb) (NBH 98)

Think About His Love (2x in Eb) (NBH 102)

Prayer of Intercession, Praise, and Worship: Congregation

Jesus, What a Wonder You Are (2 in F) (NBH 147)

Message: *Enough to Build a Heavenly Life!*

Hymn of Response/Invitation: Worship Leader and Congregation

Surely the Presence of the Lord (2x in D) (NBH 158)

Hymn of Benediction: *What A Mighty God We Serve* (1x in C)(NBH 64):
Congregation

Postlude: *Mighty Is our God* (1x in Bb) (NBH 59) Instrumentalist

Scripture Reading

I Corinthians 1:30; I Peter 1:18–24; Isaiah 40:6–8

Worship Leader: Because of God you are in Christ Jesus, who has become for us wisdom from God.

Congregation: In Christ we are put right with God, and have been made holy, and have been set free from sin.

Worship Leader: You know that in the past you were living in a worthless way, a way passed down from the people who lived before you. But you were saved from that useless life.

Congregation: You were bought, not with something that ruins like gold or silver, but with the precious blood of Christ, who was like a pure and perfect lamb.

Worship Leader: Christ was chosen before the world was made, but he was shown to the world in these last times for your sake.

Congregation: Through Christ you believe in God, who raised Christ from the dead and gave him glory. So your faith and your hope are in God.

Worship Leader: Now that your obedience to the truth has purified your souls, you can have true love for your Christian brothers and sisters. So love each other deeply with all your heart.

Congregation: You have been born again, and this new life did not come from something that dies, but from something that cannot die. You were born again through God's living message that continues forever.

Worship Leader: The Scripture says, "All people are like the grass, and all their glory is like the flowers of the field. The grass dies and the flowers fall, but the word of the Lord will live forever." And this is the word that was preached to you.

WEEK 33 SERVICE

Prelude: *I Could Sing of Your Love Forever* (2x in F) (NBH 116)—Instrumentalist

Prayer of Worship: Worship Pastor

Welcome: Pastoral Staff

Welcome Song (meet and greet during song): Pastoral Staff

 He is Jehovah (v1, c, v2, c, v3, c in Em) (NBH 118)

 Blessed Be Your Name (v1, v2, c, v3, v4, c, c in A) (NBH 26)

Worship with Our Gifts: Pastoral Staff

(Praise and Worship During Offering)

 We Will Glorify (v1, v2, v4 in D) (NBH 22)

Scripture Reading: Worship Leader and Congregation

 (See Scripture Reading Below)

 I Sing Praises (2x in G) (NBH 17)

 Glorify Thy Name (v1, v2, v3 in Bb with interlude) (NBH 18)

 Be Exalted, O God (2x in Bb) (NBH 19)

Prayer of Dedication, Intercession, Praise, and Worship: Congregation

 He Giveth More Grace (v1c, v2c in D) (NBH 113): Praise Team

Message: *Enough to Build a Heavenly Church!*

Hymn of Response/Invitation: Worship Leader and Congregation

 You Are my hiding Place (2x in D) (NBH 125)

Hymn of Benediction: Congregation

 Jehovah Jireh (1x in Em) (NBH 124)

 Postlude: *Jehovah Jireh* (1x in Em) (NBH 124—Instrumentalist

Scripture Reading

Psalm 18

Worship Leader: I love you, Lord. You are my strength.

Congregation: The Lord is my rock, my protection, my Savior. My God is my rock.

Worship Leader: I can run to him for safety.

Congregation: He is my shield and my saving strength, my defender.

Worship Leader: I will call to the Lord, who is worthy of praise, and I will be saved from my enemies.

Congregation: In my trouble I called to the Lord. I cried out to my God for help.

Worship Leader: From his temple he heard my voice; my call for help reached his ears.

Congregation: He took me to a safe place. Because he delights in me, he saved me.

Worship Leader: The Lord spared me because I did what was right. Because I have not done evil, he has rewarded me.

Congregation: I have followed the ways of the Lord; I remember all his laws and have not broken his rules.

Worship Leader: The Lord rewarded me because I did what was right, because I did what the Lord said was right.

Congregation: Lord, you are loyal to those who are loyal, and you are good to those who are good.

Worship Leader: You are pure to those who are pure, but you are against those who are bad.

Congregation: You save the humble, but you bring down those who are proud.

Worship Leader: The ways of God are without fault. The Lord's words are pure.

He is a shield to those who trust him.

Congregation: Who is God?

Worship Leader: Only the Lord.

Congregation: Who is the Rock?

Worship Leader: Only our God.

Congregation: God is my protection. He makes my way free from fault.

Worship Leader: You protect me with your saving shield.

Congregation: You support me with your right hand.

Worship Leader: You have stooped to make me great.

Congregation: You give me a better way to live, so I live as you want me to.

Worship Leader: The Lord lives! May my Rock be praised.

Congregation: Praise the God who saves me!

Worship Leader: God gives me victory over my enemies and brings people under my rule.

Congregation: So I will praise you, Lord, among the nations. I will sing praises to your name.

WEEK 34 SERVICE

Prelude: *Sing to the King* (2x in F) (NBH 129)—Instrumentalist

Prayer of Dedication, Intercession, and Praise: Pastor

Sing to the King (v1c, v2c in F) (NBH 129)

Welcome: Pastoral Staff

Welcome Song (meet and greet during song): Pastoral Staff

Rock of Ages (2x in G)(NBH 126)

Hosanna (Praise Is Rising) (v1c, v2c, in G)

Scripture Reading: Reader's Group

(See Scripture Reading Below)

O God, Our Help in Ages Past (v1, v2, v3, v4, in Bb v6 in C) (NBH 122)

Children of the Heavenly Father (v1, v2, v3, v4 in C) (NBH 123)

Worship with Our Gifts: Pastoral Staff

(Praise and Worship During Offering)

Here I Am to Worship (v1c, v2c in F) (NBH 130)

Message: *Enough to Build a Heavenly Home!*

Hymn of Response/Invitation: Worship Leader and Congregation

Shout to the Lord (2x in Bb)(NBH 133)

Hymn of Benediction: *Hosanna* (v1c, c in G) (NBH 135)—Congregation

Postlude: *Let There Be Glory, Honor, and Praise* (1x G/Ab) (NBH 139)—
Instrumentalist

Scripture Reading

Reader 1: God is our protection and our strength.

Reader 2: He always helps in times of trouble.

Reader 3: So we will not be afraid even if the earth shakes,

Reader 4: Or the mountains fall into the sea,

Reader 1: Even if the oceans roar and foam,

Reader 2: Or the mountains shake at the raging sea.

ALL: AMEN!

Reader 1: Nations tremble and kingdoms shake.

Reader 2: God shouts and the earth crumbles.

Reader 3: The Lord All-Powerful is with us;

Reader 4: The God of Jacob is our defender.

ALL: AMEN!

Reader 1: Come and see what the Lord has done,

Reader 2: Come and see

Reader 3: Come and see

Reader 4: Come and see

Reader 2: The amazing things he has done on the earth.

Reader 3: He stops wars everywhere on the earth.

Reader 4: He breaks all bows and spears

Reader 1: and burns up the chariots with fire.

ALL: AMEN!

Reader 1: God says,

Reader 4: "Be still and know that I am God.

Reader 1: I will be praised in all the nations;

Reader 3: I will be praised throughout the earth."

Reader 2: The Lord All-Powerful is with us;

Reader 4: The God of Jacob is our defender.

ALL: AMEN! AMEN! AMEN!

WEEK 35 SERVICE

Prelude: *O Magnify the Lord* (2x in D) (NBH 134)—Instrumentalist

Scripture Reading: Reader's Group
(See Scripture Reading Below)

Call to Worship
Let There Be Glory and Honor and Praise (2x G, 1x Ab) (NBH 139)

Prayer of Worship: Pastor

Welcome: Pastoral Staff

Welcome Song (meet and greet during song): Pastoral Staff
O Magnify the Lord (v1c, v2c in D) (NBH 134)
Thine Is the Glory (v1c, v3c in D) (NBH 138)

Worship with Our Gifts: Pastoral Staff
(Praise and Worship During Offering)
Bless his Holy Name (c, v1c, v2c, v3c in Eb) (NBH 151)
Worthy, You Are Worhy (v1, v2 in Eb, v3 in F) (NBH 142)
You Are My All in All (v1c, v2c in F) (NBH 143)

Prayer of Dedication, Intercession, and Praise: Pastor
Praise You (2x in Bb) (NBH 146)

Message: *Entering the Kingdom*

Hymn of Response/Invitation: Worship Leader and Congregation
I Surrender All (v1c, v2c in C) (NBH 433)

Hymn of Benediction: Congregation
I Have Decided to Follow Jesus (v1, v2, v1 in C) (NBH 434)

Postlude: *Jesus, What a Wonder You Are* (1x in F) (NBH 147)—Instrumentalist

Scripture Reading

Selections from Psalm 29 (NCV)
ALL: Praise the Lord,
Reader 1: Praise the Lord, you angels;
ALL: Praise the Lord.
Reader 2: Praise the Lord's glory and power.
ALL: Praise the Lord.

Reader 3: Praise the Lord for the glory of his name;

ALL: Worship the Lord!

Reader 4: Worship the Lord because he is holy.

ALL: The Lord's voice is heard over the sea.

Reader 1: The glorious God thunders;

ALL: The Lord thunders over the ocean.

Reader 2: The Lord's voice is powerful;

Reader 3: The Lord's voice is majestic.

Reader 4: The Lord's voice breaks the trees;

Reader 1: The Lord's voice makes the lightning flash.

Reader 2: The Lord's voice shakes the desert;

Reader 3: The Lord's voice shakes the oaks and strips the leaves off the trees.

Reader 4: In his Temple everyone says, "Glory to God!"

ALL: "Glory to God!"

Reader 3: The Lord will be King forever.

Reader 4: The Lord blesses his people with peace.

Reader 1: And, ALL the people said: Amen

ALL: "AMEN!"

Reader 2: Praise the Lord"

ALL: PRAISE THE LORD!

Reader 1: Glory to God!

ALL: GLORY TO GOD!

WEEK 36 SERVICE

Prelude: *Bless the Lord, O My Soul* (1x in G, 1x in Ab) (NBH 8)—Instrumentalist

Call to Praise: Congregation

Joyful, Joyful We Adore Thee (v1, v2 in F interlude v3 in G) (NBH 13)

Prayer of Worship: Worship Pastor

Welcome: Pastoral Staff

Welcome Song (meet and greet during song): Pastoral Staff

You Are Holy (2x in F) (NBH 70)

Amazing Grace (v1, v2, v3 in F, v5 in G)(NBH 104)

Scripture Reading: Reader's Group

(See Scripture Reading Below)

There is None Like You (c, c, v, c in G) (NBH 109)

Grace Greater than Our Sin (c, v1c, v3c in G) (NBH 105)

Offertory Prayer: Pastoral Staff

Praise and Worship During Offering

Come, Let Us Worship and Bow Down (2x in D) (NBH 7)

Bless the Lord, O My Soul (1x in G, 1x in Ab)

Prayer of Intercession, Praise, and Worship: Congregation

Enough (v1c, v2c, bridge, c in G0 (NBH 114)

Message: *Passion for the Kingdom*

Hymn of Response/Invitation: Worship Leader and Congregation

I Need Thee Every Hour (v1, v2, v3, v5 in G) (NBH 423)

Hymn of Benediction: *Bless the Lord, O My Soul* (1x in G) (NBH 8): Congregation

Postlude: *I Sing Praises* (2x in G) (NBH 17)—Instrumentalist

Scripture Reading

Psalm 86 (NCV)

Worship Leader: Lord, there is no god like you and no works like yours.

Congregation: Lord, all the nations you have made will come and worship you. They will honor you.

Worship Leader: You are great and you do miracles.

Congregation: Only you are God.

Worship Leader: Lord, teach me what you want me to do, and I will live by your truth.

Congregation: Teach me to respect you completely.

Worship Leader: Lord, my God, I will praise you with all my heart, and I will honor your name forever.

Congregation: You have great love for me.

Worship Leader: You have saved me from death.

Congregation: But, Lord, you are a God who shows mercy and is kind.

Worship Leader: You don't become angry quickly.

Congregation: You have great love and faithfulness.

WEEK 37 SERVICE

Prelude: *I Will Bless the Lord* (2x in F) (NBH 14)—Instrumentalist

Scripture Reading: Senior Pastor and Worship Pastor

(See Scripture Reading Below: By the Senior Pastor and Worship Pastor)

Prayer of Worship: Worship Pastor

How Great Is Our God: (v1c, v2c in Bb) (NBH 5)

How Great Thou Art: (c, v1c, v2c in Bb) (NBH 6)

How Great Is Our God: (c, bridge, c in Bb) (NBH 5)

Welcome: Pastor

Welcome Song (meet and greet during song): Pastoral Staff

Almighty (c, v1c, v2c in F) (NBH 4)

Worship with Our Gifts: Pastoral Staff

(Praise and Worship During Offering)

I Will Bless the Lord (2x in F) (NBH 14)

I Worship You, Almighty God (2x in F) (NBH 16)

Prayer of Dedication, Intercession, Praise, and Worship: Congregation

Worthy of Worship (v1c, v2c, v3c in F) (NBH 3)

Message: *Proclaiming the Kingdom*

Hymn of Response/Invitation: Worship Leader and Congregation

I Exalt Thee (v 2x, c 2x in F) (NBH 36)

Hymn of Benediction: Congregation

I Will Bless the Lord (2x in F) (NBH 14)

Postlude: *Bless the Lord, O My Soul* (1x D, 1x Eb) (NBH 8)—Instrumentalist

Scripture Reading

I Chronicles 16:8–15, 23–34, 36 (NASB)

Senior Pastor: Oh give thanks to the LORD, call upon His name; Make known His deeds among the peoples.

Worship Pastor: Sing to Him, sing praises to Him; Speak of all His wonders.

Senior Pastor: Glory in His holy name; Let the heart of those who seek the LORD be glad.

Worship Pastor: Seek the LORD and His strength; Seek His face continually.

Senior Pastor: Remember His wonderful deeds which He has done, His marvels and the judgments from His mouth,

Worship Pastor: He is the LORD our God; His judgments are in all the earth.

Senior Pastor: Remember His covenant forever, The word which He commanded to a thousand generations,

Worship Pastor: Sing to the LORD, all the earth; Proclaim good tidings of His salvation from day to day.

Senior Pastor: Tell of His glory among the nations,His wonderful deeds among all the peoples.

Worship Pastor: For great is the LORD, and greatly to be praised; He also is to be feared above all gods.

Senior Pastor: For all the gods of the peoples are idols, But the LORD made the heavens.

Worship Pastor: Splendor and majesty are before Him, Strength and joy are in His place.

Senior Pastor: Ascribe to the LORD, O families of the peoples, Ascribe to the LORD glory and strength.

Worship Pastor: Ascribe to the LORD the glory due His name; Bring an offering, and come before Him; Worship the LORD in holy array.

Senior Pastor: Tremble before Him, all the earth; Indeed, the world is firmly established, it will not be moved.

Worship Pastor: Let the heavens be glad, and let the earth rejoice; And let them say among the nations, "The LORD reigns."

Senior Pastor: Let the sea roar, and all it contains; Let the field exult, and all that is in it.

Worship Pastor: Then the trees of the forest will sing for joy before the LORD; For He is coming to judge the earth.

Senior Pastor: O give thanks to the LORD, for He is good; For His lovingkindness is everlasting.

Worship Pastor: To give thanks to Your holy name, And glory in Your praise."

Senior Pastor: Blessed be the LORD, the God of Israel, From everlasting even to everlasting

WEEK 38 SERVICE

Prelude: *Let There Be Praise* (2x in F) (NBH 39)—Instrumentalist

Welcome: Pastoral Staff

Welcome Song (meet and greet during song): Pastoral Staff
Sing Hallelujah (to the Lord) (2x in D) (NBH 35)

Scripture Reading: Reader's Group
(See Scripture Reading Below)
I Exalt Thee (2x in F) (NBH 36)
Blessed Be the Lord God Almighty (v, c in Bb, c in C) (NBH 37)
Awesome in this Place (2x in C) (NBH 38)

Worship with Our Gifts: Pastoral Staff
(Praise and Worship During Offering)
O Lord, You're Beautiful (v1, v2 in D) (NBH 34)

Prayer of Dedication, Intercession, and Praise: Pastor
Fairest Lord Jesus (v1, v2, v3 in D) (NBH 47)
O Lord, You're Beautiful (v3 in D) (NBH 34)
Fairest Lord Jesus (v4 in Eb) (NBH 47)

Message: *Jehovah!*

Hymn of Response/Invitation: Worship Leader and Congregation
Here I Am to Worship (2x in F) (NBH 130)

Hymn of Benediction: *What A Mighty God We Serve* (2x in D) (NBH 64)—Congregation

Postlude: *Mighty Is Our God* (2x in Bb) (NBH 59)—Instrumentalist

Scripture Reading

ALL: Lord our Lord,

Reader 1: your name is the most wonderful name in all the earth!

Reader 2: It brings you praise in heaven above.

Reader 3: You have taught children and babies to sing praises to you

Reader 4: I look at your heavens, which you made with your fingers.

Reader 1: I see the moon and stars, which you created.

ALL: Which YOU created.

Reader 1: But why are people even important to you?

Reader 2: Why do you take care of human beings?

Reader 4: You made them a little lower than the angels and crowned them with glory and honor.

Reader 3: You put them in charge of everything you made.

Reader 2: You put all things under their control:

Reader 1: all the sheep, the cattle,

Reader 2: and the wild animals,

Reader 3: the birds in the sky,

Reader 4: the fish in the sea,

Reader 1: and everything that lives under water.

ALL: Everything?

Reader 1: You created Everything, O Lord.

ALL: Everything!

Reader 1: Everything was made by you. And everything belongs to you.

ALL: Lord our Lord,

Reader 1: Your name is the most wonderful name in all the earth!

All: Amen.

WEEK 39 SERVICE

Prelude: *Great Is the Lord Almighty* (c, v1c in Gm) (NBH 349)—Instrumentalist

Welcome: Pastoral Staff

Welcome Song (meet and greet during song): Pastoral Staff

Yes, Lord, yes (2x in Eb) (NBH 445)

Prayer of Worship: Pastor

Call to Worship

Lift Up Your Heads (2 x in G) (NBH 53)

God of Wonders (v1c, v2c, bridge, c in G) (NBH 51)

Prayer of Dedication, Intercession, and Praise: Pastor

Agnus Dei (2x in A) (NBH 54)

Worship with Our Gifts: Pastoral Staff

(Praise and Worship During Offering)

Holy, Holy, Holy (v1, v2, v3 in D, v4 in Eb) (NBH 68)

Holy Ground (2x in Eb)(NBH 72)

Scripture Reading: Reader's Group

(See Scripture Reading Below)

Holy, Holy (v1, v2, v3, v4, v5 n C) (NBH 74)

Message: *Jehovah Jireh*

Hymn of Response/Invitation: Worship Leader and Congregation

Open our Eyes, Lord (2x in D) (NBH 426)

Hymn of Benediction: Congregation

Great is the Lord Almighty (chorus only in Gm) (NBH 349)

Postlude: *My Life is In Yours, Lord* (2x in D) (NBH 518)—Instrumentalist

Scripture Reading

Isaiah 6

Worship Leader: In the year that King Uzziah died, I saw the Lord sitting on a very high throne. His long robe filled the Temple.

Congregation: Heavenly creatures of fire stood above him. Each creature had six wings: It used two wings to cover its face, two wings to cover its feet, and two wings for flying.

Worship Leader: Each creature was calling to the others: "Holy, holy, holy is the Lord All-Powerful. His glory fills the whole earth."

Congregation: Their calling caused the frame around the door to shake, as the Temple filled with smoke.

Worship Leader: I said, "Oh, no! I will be destroyed. I am not pure, and I live among people who are not pure, but I have seen the King, the Lord All-Powerful."

Congregation: One of the heavenly creatures used a pair of tongs to take a hot coal from the altar. Then he flew to me with the hot coal in his hand.

Worship Leader: The creature touched my mouth with the hot coal and said, "Look, your guilt is taken away, because this hot coal has touched your lips. Your sin is taken away."

Congregation: Then I heard the Lord's voice, saying, "Whom can I send? Who will go for us?"

Worship Leader: So I said, "Here I am. Send me!

WEEK 40 SERVICE

Prelude: *Rock of Ages* (2x in G) (NBH 126)—Instrumentalist

Call to Praise: Congregation

Hosanna (Praise is Rising) (v1c, v2c in G) (NBH 132)

Beautiful One (v1c, v2c in C) (NBH 128)

Welcome: Pastoral Staff

Welcome Song (meet and greet during song): Pastoral Staff

Great is the Lord Almighty (c, v1c, v2c, v3c in Gm) (NBH 349)

Prayer of Dedication, Intercession, and Praise: Pastor

Holy Spirit Rain Down (2x in F) (NBH 335)

Scripture Reading: Entire Praise Team

(See Scripture Reading Below)

Wonderful, Merciful Savior (v1c, v2c, v3c in Bb) (NBH 162)

Worship with Our Gifts: Pastoral Staff

(Praise and Worship During Offering)

Shout to the Lord (2x in Bb) (NBH 133)

Message: *Jehovah Nissi*

Hymn of Response/Invitation: Worship Leader and Praise Team

Just As I Am (McIntyre Setting see redtiemusic.com):

Hymn of Benediction: *My Tribute* (chorus only 1x in Bb) (NBH 577):
Congregation

Postlude: *My Redeemer Lives* (2x in D) (NBH 271)—Instrumentalist

Scripture Reading

Selections from Titus 3:4–7; Psalm 115:1–2; Ephesians 5:4–10

Worship Leader: God's mercy is great, and he loves us very much. Though we were spiritually dead because of the things we did against God, he gave us new life with Christ. You have been saved by God's grace.

Praise Team Reader 1: It was not because of good deeds we did to be right with him. He saved us through the washing that made us new people through the Holy Spirit. God poured out richly upon us that Holy Spirit through Jesus Christ our Savior.

Praise Team Reader 2: Being made right with God by his grace, we could have the hope of receiving the life that never ends. And he raised us up with Christ and gave us a seat with him in the heavens.

Praise Team Reader 3: He did this for those in Christ Jesus so that for all future time he could show the very great riches of his grace by being kind to us in Christ Jesus. I mean that you have been saved by grace through believing.

Praise Team Reader 4: You did not save yourselves; it was a gift from God. It was not the result of your own efforts, so you cannot brag about it. God has made us what we are.

Worship Leader: This is why we say together,

Entire Praise Team: "Not to us, LORD, not to us but to your name be the glory . . . because your love and faithfulness are true."

WEEK 41 SERVICE

Prelude: *Holiness (Take My Life)* (2x in F) (NBH 589)—Instrumentalist

Call to Praise: Congregation

My Life Is In You, Lord (2x in G) (NBH 518)

I Give You My Heart (2x in G) (NBH 528)

Prayer of Worship: Worship Pastor

Welcome: Pastoral Staff

Welcome Song (meet and greet during song): Pastoral Staff

I Have Decided to Follow Jesus (v1, v2, v1, v3, v1, v4, v1 in C) (NBH 434)

I'll Tell the World That I'm a Christian (v1 in D) (NBH 368)

I Know Whom I Have Believed (v1c, v2c, v3, v4 in D) (NBH 353)

Scripture Reading: Reader's Group

(See Scripture Reading Below)

Song for the Nations (v1, v2, v3, v4, v5 in Ab) (NBH 365)

Offertory Prayer: Pastoral Staff

Praise and Worship During Offering

Freely, Freely (v1c, v2c in Eb) (NBH 627)

People Need the Lord (2x in C) (NBH 359)

Prayer of Intercession, Praise, and Worship: Congregation

Open Our Eyes, Lord (v1, v2 in D) (NBH 426)

Message: *Jehovah Rophe*

Hymn of Response/Invitation: Worship Leader and Congregation

I Give All to You (v1, v2, v3 in C, v4 in D) (NBH 442)

Hymn of Benediction: *Soon and Very Soon* (1x in G) (NBH 599): Congregation

Postlude: *Freely, Freely* (v1c, c in Eb) (NBH 627)—Instrumentalist

Scripture Reading

John 20:19–23; Matt 28:18–20; Acts 1:6–11

Worship Leader: This is the strategy Jesus gave his disciples for taking worship to the nations:

Reader 1: When it was evening on the first day of the week, Jesus' followers were together. The doors were locked, because they were afraid of the elders.

Reader 2: Then Jesus came and stood right in the middle of them and said, "Peace be with you."

Reader 3: After he said this, he showed them his hands and his side. His followers were thrilled when they saw the Lord.

Worship Leader: Then Jesus said again, "Peace be with you. As the Father sent me, I now send you."

Reader 1: After he said this, he breathed on them and said,

Worship Leader: "Receive the Holy Spirit."

Reader 2: Then Jesus came to them and said,

Worship Leader: "All power in heaven and on earth is given to me. So go and make followers of all people in the world.

Reader 3: Baptize them in the name of the Father and the Son and the Holy Spirit.

Reader 1: Teach them to obey everything that I have taught you, and I will be with you always, even until the end of this age."

Reader 2: When the apostles were all together, they asked Jesus,

Reader 1: "Lord, are you now going to give the kingdom back to Israel?"

Reader 3: Jesus said to them,

Worship Leader: "The Father is the only One who has the authority to decide dates and times. These things are not for you to know.

Reader 1: But when the Holy Spirit comes to you, you will receive power. You will be my witnesses—in Jerusalem,

Reader 2: In all of Judea,

Reader 3: In Samaria,

Reader 1: And in every part of the world."

Worship Leader: After he said this, as they were watching, he was lifted up, and a cloud hid him from their sight.

Reader 1: As he was going, they were looking into the sky. Suddenly, two men wearing white clothes stood beside them.

Reader 2: They said,

Reader 3: "Men of Galilee, why are you standing here looking into the sky?

Worship Leader: Jesus, whom you saw taken up from you into heaven, will come back in the same way you saw him go."

WEEK 42 SERVICE

Prelude: *Firm Foundation* (2x in F) (NBH 510)—Instrumentalist

Prayer of Worship: Worship Pastor

Welcome: Pastoral Staff

Welcome Song (meet and greet during song): Pastoral Staff

Friend of God (2x in C) (NBH 483)

Who Can Satisfy? (c, v1c in C) (NBH 507)

Worship with Our Gifts: Pastoral Staff

(Praise and Worship During Offering)

Knowing You (v1c, v2c, v3c in C) (NBH 487)

Blessed Assurance, Jesus Is Mine (c, v1c, v2c, c in C) (NBH 446)

Scripture Reading: Worship Leader and Congregation

(See Scripture Reading Below)

My Faith has Found a Resting Place (v1c, v2c, v3, v4c, v5c,c in G) (NBH 454)

Prayer of Dedication, Intercession, Praise, and Worship: Congregation

It Is Well with My Soul (v1c, v3c in Bb, v4c in C) (NBH 447)

Message: *Jehovah Shalom*

Hymn of Response/Invitation: Worship Leader and Congregation

Precious Lord, Take My Hand (v1, v2 in G) (NBH 450)

Hymn of Benediction: Congregation

In Moments like These (1x in D) (NBH 451)

Postlude: *I Will Call Upon the Lord* (v 2x, c 2x in C) (NBH 498)—Instrumentalist

Scripture Reading

Psalm 91

Worship Leader: Those who go to God Most High for safety will be protected by the Almighty.

Congregation: I will say to the Lord, "You are my place of safety and protection. You are my God and I trust you."

Worship Leader: God will save you from hidden traps and from deadly diseases.

Congregation: He will cover you with his feathers, and under his wings you can hide. His truth will be your shield and protection.

Worship Leader: You will not fear any danger by night or an arrow during the day.

Congregation: You will not be afraid of diseases that come in the dark or sickness that strikes at noon.

Worship Leader: At your side one thousand people may die,

or even ten thousand right beside you, but you will not be hurt.

Congregation: You will only watch and see the wicked punished.

Worship Leader: The Lord is your protection; you have made God Most High your place of safety.

Congregation: He has put his angels in charge of you to watch over you wherever you go.

Worship Leader: The Lord says, "Whoever loves me, I will save. I will protect those who know me.

Congregation: They will call to me, and I will answer them. I will be with them in trouble; I will rescue them and honor them.

Worship Leader: I will give them a long, full life, and they will see how I can save."

WEEK 43 SERVICE

Prelude: *New Name in Glory* (2x in Ab) (NBH 616) Instrumentalist

Welcome: Pastoral Staff

Welcome Song (meet and greet during song): Pastoral Staff

I'll Fly Away (v1c, v2c, v3c in G) (NBH 601)

Soon and Very Soon (v1, v2, v3 in G) (NBH 599)

When We All Get to Heaven (v1c, v2c, v4c in C) (NBH 603)

Scripture Reading: Reader's Group

(See Scripture Reading Below)

Sanctuary (1x in D, 1x in Eb) (NBH 588)

Find Us Faithful (2x in Eb) (NBH 598)

Prayer of Dedication, Intercession, and Praise: Pastor

On Jordan's Stormy Banks (v1c, v2c, v4c in Eb) (NBH 611)

Worship with Our Gifts: Pastoral Staff

(Praise and Worship During Offering)

When the Morning Comes (c, v1c, v3c in Eb) (NBH 615)

Face to Face with Christ, My Savior (c, v1c, v3c in Ab) (NBH 612)

Message: *Jehovah Tisidkenu*

Hymn of Response/Invitation: Worship Leader and Congregation

Something Beautiful (2x in Eb) (NBH 623)

Hymn of Benediction: *On Jordan's Stormy Banks* (Chorus) (NBH 611)
Congregation

Postlude: *Peace Like a River* (2x in G) (NBH 618)—Instrumentalist

Scripture Reading

I Corinthians 15: 51–58; Isaiah 25:8; Hosea 13:14

Worship Leader: But look! I tell you this secret: We will not all sleep in death, but we will all be changed.

Congregation: It will take only a second—as quickly as an eye blinks—when the last trumpet sounds. The trumpet will sound, and those who have died will be raised to live forever, and we will all be changed.

Worship Leader: This body that can be destroyed must clothe itself with something that can never be destroyed. And this body that dies must clothe itself with something that can never die.

Congregation: So this body that can be destroyed will clothe itself with that which can never be destroyed, and this body that dies will clothe itself with that which can never die.

Worship Leader: When this happens, this Scripture will be made true: "Death is destroyed forever in victory." "Death, where is your victory? Death, where is your pain?"

Congregation: Death's power to hurt is sin, and the power of sin is the law.

Worship Leader: But we thank God! He gives us the victory through our Lord Jesus Christ.

Congregation: So my dear brothers and sisters, stand strong. Do not let anything move you. Always give yourselves fully to the work of the Lord, because you know that your work in the Lord is never wasted.

WEEK 44 SERVICE

Prelude: *Celebrate Jesus* (2x in F) (NBH 275)—Instrumentalist

Prayer of Worship: Worship Pastor

Call to Praise: Congregation

  My Redeemer Lives (2x in D) (NBH 271)

  I Live (2x in G) (NBH 278)

Welcome: Pastoral Staff

Welcome Song (meet and greet during song): Pastoral Staff

  He Lives (v1c, v2c, v3c in Ab) (NBH 269)

  Worthy is the Lamb (v, c,c, in A) (NBH 264)

Scripture Reading: Worship Leader with the Congregation

  (See Scripture Reading Below)

Praise and Worship: Congregation

  The Wonderful Cross (v1c, v3, c in C) (NBH 239)

  O the Blood of Jesus (v1, 2, 3 in D, v4 in Eb) (NBH 226)

  Because He Lives (c, v1c, v3c in Ab, c in Bb) (NBH 449)

Offertory Prayer: Pastoral Staff

Praise and Worship During Offering

  Hallelujah, What a Savior (v1, 2, 3, 4 in Bb) (NBH 242)

  I Believe in a Hill Called Mount Calv'ry (c, v2, c in Bb) (NBH 246)

  Hallelujah, What a Savior (v5 in C) (NBH 242)

Message: *Alive and Six Who Said So*

Hymn of Response/Invitation: Worship Leader and Congregation

  Into My Heart (2x in F) (NBH 418)

Hymn of Benediction: Congregation

  Because He Lives (Chorus only) (NBH 449)

Postlude: *Because He Lives* (c, v1c in Ab, c in Bb) (NBH 449)—Instrumentalist

Scripture Reading

Matthew 28:1–8

Worship Leader: After the Sabbath, at dawn on the first day of the week, Mary Magdalene and the other Mary went to look at the tomb.

Congregation: There was a violent earthquake, for an angel of the Lord came down from heaven and, going to the tomb, rolled back the stone and sat on it.

Worship Leader: His appearance was like lightning, and his clothes were white as snow.

Congregation: The guards were so afraid of him that they shook and became like dead men.

Worship Leader: The angel said to the women, "Do not be afraid, for I know that you are looking for Jesus, who was crucified.

Congregation: He is not here; he has risen, just as he said. Come and see the place where he lay.

Worship Leader: Then go quickly and tell his disciples: 'He has risen from the dead and is going ahead of you into Galilee. There you will see him.' Now I have told you."

Congregation: So the women hurried away from the tomb, afraid yet filled with joy, and ran to tell his disciples.

Worship Leader: Suddenly Jesus met them. "Greetings," he said. They came to him, clasped his feet and worshiped him.

Congregation: Then Jesus said to them, "Do not be afraid. Go and tell my brothers to go to Galilee; there they will see me."

WEEK 45 SERVICE

Prelude: *Come into His Presence* (2x in Bb) (NBH 584)—Instrumentalist

Call to Praise: Congregation

Firm Foundation (c, v1c, v2c in F) (NBH 510)

Trust and Obey (chorus only in F) (NBH 500)

Firm Foundation (chorus only in F) (NBH 510)

Prayer of Worship: Worship Pastor

Welcome: Pastoral Staff

Welcome Song (meet and greet during song): Pastoral Staff

I'm So Glad, Jesus Lifted Me (v2, v2, v3, v4 in G) (NBH 568)

Jesus, Draw Me Close (2x in G) (NBH 553)

I Am Thine, O Lord (c, v1c, v3c, v4c in G) (NBH 535)

Scripture Reading: Reader's Group

(See Scripture Reading Below)

In Christ Alone (v1, v2, v3 in D v4 in Eb) (NBH 506)

Offertory Prayer: Pastoral Staff

Praise and Worship During Offering

More Precious than Silver (chorus only 2x in F) (NBH 557)

Take My Life, and let It Be (v1, v2, v3, v4 in F) (NBH 534)

I Give You My Heart (1x in F, 1x in G) (NBH 528)

Prayer of Intercession, Praise, and Worship: Congregation

The Greatest Thing (v1, v2, v3 in F) (NBH 527)

Message: *To Contemplate the Cross*

Hymn of Response/Invitation: Worship Leader and Congregation

Change My Heart, O God (2x in C) (NBH 529)

Hymn of Benediction: *Father, I Adore You* (v1, v2, v3 in F) (NBH 566): Congregation

Postlude: *The Trees of the Field* (2x in Em) (NBH 570)—Instrumentalist

Scripture Reading

Phil 3:7–14

Worship Leader: I press on toward the goal to win the prize

ALL: I press on toward the goal to win the prize

Reader 1: But whatever were gains to me I now consider loss for the sake of Christ.

ALL: I press on toward the goal to win the prize

Reader 2: What is more, I consider everything a loss because of the surpassing worth of knowing Christ Jesus my Lord, for whose sake I have lost all things.

Reader 3: I consider them garbage, that I may gain Christ and be found in him.

ALL: I press on toward the goal to win the prize

Reader 4: Not having a righteousness of my own that comes from the law but that which is through faith in Christ

Reader 1: This is the righteousness that comes from God on the basis of faith.

ALL: I want to know Christ (soft)

ALL: I want to know Christ (med loud)

ALL: I want to know Christ (loud)

Reader 2: Yes, to know the power of his resurrection and participation in his sufferings, becoming like him in his death,

Reader 3: And so, somehow, attaining to the resurrection from the dead.

ALL: I press on toward the goal to win the prize

ALL: I press on toward the goal to win the prize

Reader 4: Not that I have already obtained all this,

Reader 3: Or have already arrived at my goal,

Reader 2: But I press on to take hold of that for which Christ Jesus took hold of me.

ALL: Brothers!

ALL: Sisters!

ALL: Brothers and sisters!

Reader 1: This one thing.

Reader 2: This one thing I do.

Reader 3: This ONE thing I do.

Reader 4: Forgetting what is behind and straining toward what is ahead,

ALL: I press on toward the goal to win the prize.

Reader 3: This is the goal!

Reader 4: This is the goal for which God has called me.

ALL: I press on toward the goal to win the prize in Christ Jesus.

WEEK 46 SERVICE

Prelude: *We Bow Down* (2x in D) (NBH 31)—Instrumentalist

Prayer of Worship: Worship Pastor

Come, Now Is the Time to Worship (2x in D) (NBH 300)

Welcome: Pastoral Staff

Welcome Song (meet and greet during song): Pastoral Staff

Great and Mighty (2x in Eb)

Thou Art Worthy (2x in Ab) (NBH 23)

Worship with Our Gifts: Pastoral Staff

(Praise and Worship During Offering)

O Worship the King (v1, v2, v3 in G, v4 in Ab) (NBH 24)

Scripture Reading: Worship Leader and Congregation

(See Scripture Reading Below)

Joyful, Joyful, We Adore Thee (v1 in F, v3 in G) (NBH 13)

Prayer of Dedication, Intercession, Praise, and Worship: Congregation

Let it Rise (2x in G) (NBH 25)

Message: *Raising the Children We Cherish*

Hymn of Response/Invitation: Worship Leader and Congregation

He Knows my Name (v1c, v2c in Eb) (NBH 44)

Hymn of Benediction: Congregation

I Will Bless the Lord (1x in F) (NBH 14)

Postlude: *Bless the Lord, O My Soul* (1x in G, 1x in Ab) (NBH 8)—Instrumentalist

Scripture Reading

Psalm 95:1–7

Worship Leader: Come, let us sing for joy to the LORD;

Congregation: Let us shout aloud to the Rock of our salvation.

Worship Leader: Let us come before him with thanksgiving and extol him with music and song.

Congregation: For the LORD is the great God, the great King above all gods.

Worship Leader: In his hand are the depths of the earth, and the mountain peaks belong to him.

Congregation: The sea is his, for he made it, and his hands formed the dry land.

Worship Leader: Come, let us bow down in worship,

Congregation: let us kneel before the LORD our Maker;

Worship Leader: For he is our God and we are the people of his pasture, the flock under his care.

WEEK 47 SERVICE

Prelude: *He Has Made Me Glad* (2x in D) (NBH 579)—Instrumentalist

Welcome: Pastoral Staff

Welcome Song (meet and greet during song): Pastoral Staff

We Bring a Sacrifice of Praise (2x in D) (NBH 581)

He Has Made Me Glad (2x in D) (NBH 579)

My Heart Is Filled with Thankfulness (v1, v2, v3 in C) (NBH 575)

Scripture Reading: Worship Pastor and Congregation

(See Scripture Reading Below)

We Will Remember (Tommy Walker . . . See Praisecharts.com)

Prayer of Dedication, Intercession, and Praise: Pastor

Great is Thy Faithfulness (v1c, v2c, v3c in D, chorus in Eb) (NBH 96)

Worship with Our Gifts: Pastoral Staff

(Praise and Worship During Offering)

Give Thanks: (2x in F) (NBH 576)

My Tribute: (2x in Bb) (NBH 577)

Message: *God and Nations*

Hymn of Response/Invitation: Worship Leader and Congregation

My Jesus, I Love Thee (v1, v2, v4 in F) (NBH 552)

Hymn of Benediction: *Thank You Lord* (2x in F) (NBH 582): Congregation

Postlude: *He Has Made Me Glad* (2x in D) (NBH 579)—Instrumentalist

Scripture Reading

Deut 6:4–9

Worship Leader: The LORD our God, the LORD is one

Congregation: Love the LORD your God with all your heart and with all your soul and with all your strength.

Worship Leader: These commandments that I give you today are to be on your hearts.

Congregation: Impress them on your children.

Worship Leader: Talk about them when you sit at home and when you walk along the road, when you lie down and when you get up.

Worship Leader: Tie them as symbols on your hands and bind them on your foreheads.

Congregation: Write them on the doorframes of your houses and on your gates.

WEEK 48 SERVICE

Prelude: *Mighty Is Our God* (2x in Bb) (NBH 59)—Instrumentalist

Scripture Reading: Reader's Group

(See Scripture Reading Below)

God of Wonders (2x in G) (NBH 51)

Prayer of Worship: Pastor

Welcome: Pastoral Staff

Welcome Song (meet and greet during song): Pastoral Staff

I'm So Glad, Jesus Lifted me (v1, v2, v3, v4 in G) (NBH 568)

This is Our Father's World (v1, v2, v3 in D) (NBH 46)

Fairest Lord Jesus (v1, v2, v3 in D, v4 in Eb) (NBH 47)

Worship with Our Gifts: Pastoral Staff

(Praise and Worship During Offering)

We Gather Together (v1, v2, v3 in Bb) (NBH 637)

Prayer of Dedication, Intercession, and Praise: Pastor

Breathe (2x in A) (NBH 481)

Message: *Ninety Percent of All Lepers*

Hymn of Response/Invitation: Worship Leader and Congregation

Just As I Am (v1, v2, v3, v5, v6 in C) (NBH 435)

Hymn of Benediction: Congregation

I Have Decided to Follow Jesus (v1, v4, v1 in C) (NBH 434)

Postlude: *Majesty* (2x in Bb) (NBH 297)—Instrumentalist

Scripture Reading

All: May the peoples praise you, Oh God.

All: May All the peoples praise you,

Reader 1: May God be gracious to us and bless us and make his face shine on us—

Reader 2: So that your ways may be known on earth, your salvation among all nations.

All: May the peoples praise you, Oh God!

All: May All the peoples praise you!

Reader 3: May the nations be glad and sing for joy,

Reader 4: For you rule the peoples with equity and guide the nations of the earth.

All: May the peoples praise you, Oh God!

All: May All the peoples praise you!

Reader 1: The land yields its harvest;

Reader 2: God, our God, blesses us.

Reader 3: May God bless us still,

Reader 4: so that all the ends of the earth will fear him.

All: May the peoples praise you, Oh God.

All: May All the peoples praise you!

WEEK 49 SERVICE

Prelude: *How Great Our Joy* (2x in Gm) (NBH 202)—Instrumentalist

Call to Praise: Congregation

O Come, All Ye Faithful (v1c, v2 in G, v3 in Ab) (NBH 199)

Prayer of Worship: Worship Pastor

Welcome: Pastoral Staff

Welcome Song (meet and greet during song): Pastoral Staff

Jehovah Jireh (v1c, v2c in Em) (NBH 124)

You Are My Hiding Place (2x in Bm) (NBH 125)

Scripture Reading: Reader's Group

(See Scripture Reading Below)

What Child Is This? (v1c, v2c, v3c in Em) (NBH 198)

Offertory Prayer: Pastoral Staff

Praise and Worship During Offering

One Small Child (v1, v2, v3, v4 in Dm) (NBH 200)

Emmanuel (2x in C) (NBH 201)

Isn't He? (2x in G) (NBH 214)

Prayer of Intercession, Praise, and Worship: Congregation

All Is Well (v1, v2, v3 in Eb)

Message: *A Theology of Time*

Hymn of Response/Invitation: Worship Leader and Congregation

Into My Heart (2x in F) (NBH 418)

Hymn of Benediction: *Father, I Adore You* (v1, v2, v3 in F) (NBH 566):
Congregation

Postlude: *How Great our Joy* (2x in Gm) (NBH 202)—Instrumentalist

Scripture Reading

ALL: Long ago, God spoke!

Reader 1: God spoke to the fathers by the prophets at different times and in different ways.

Reader 2: In these last days, He has spoken to us by [His] Son, whom He has appointed heir of all things and through whom He made the universe.

Reader 3: He is the radiance of His glory, the exact expression of His nature.

Reader 4: And, He sustains all things by His powerful word.

ALL: In the beginning was the Word,

Reader 1: And the Word was with God,

Reader 2: And the Word was God.

ALL: He was with God in the beginning.

Reader 3: All things were created through Him,

Reader 4: And apart from Him not one thing was created that has been created.

ALL: Life was in Him!

Reader 1: And that life was the light of men.

Reader 2: That light shines in the darkness,

Reader 3: Yet, the darkness did not overcome it.

Reader 4: The true light, who gives light to everyone, **was coming into the world.**

ALL: He was in the world!

Reader 1: And the world was created through Him,

Reader 2: Yet the world did not recognize Him.

Reader 3: He came to His own,

Reader 4: And His own people did not receive Him.

ALL: But to all who did receive Him!

Reader 1: He gave them the right to be children of God,

Reader 2: To those who believe in His name!

Reader 3: Who were born not of blood!

Reader 4: Or of the will of the flesh,

Reader 1: Or of the will of man, but of God.

ALL: The Word became flesh

Reader 1: And took up residence among us.

Reader 3: We observed His glory,

Reader 2: The glory as the One and Only Son from the Father, full of grace and truth.

ALL: The Word became flesh!

Reader 1: And took up residence among us.

ALL: And, (pause) we worship Him.

WEEK 50 SERVICE

Prelude: *Come Christians, Join to Sing* (1x in G, 1x in Ab) (NBH 32)—Instrumentalist

Prayer of Worship: Worship Pastor

Welcome: Pastoral Staff

Welcome Song (meet and greet during song): Pastoral Staff

Go Tell it On the Mountain (c, v1c, v2c in F) (NBH 182)

Good Christian Men, Rejoice (v1, v2, v3 in F) (NBH 183)

Angels We Have Heard on High (v1c, v3c in F, v4c in G) (NBH 184)

Worship with Our Gifts: Pastoral Staff

(Praise and Worship During Offering)

The Birthday of the King (v1c, v2c in G) (NBH 191)

Scripture Reading: Worship Leader and Congregation

(See Scripture Reading Below)

I Heard the Bells on Christmas Day (v1, v2, v3, v4, v5 in D) (NBH 187)

Prayer of Dedication, Intercession, Praise, and Worship: Congregation

Wonderful, Merciful Savior (v1c, v2c, v3c in A) (NBH 162)

Message: *A Theology of Intention*

Hymn of Response/Invitation: Worship Leader and Congregation

The Greatest Thing (v1, v3 in F) (NBH 527)

Hymn of Benediction: Congregation

I Give You My Heart (Chorus only in G) (NBH 528)

Postlude: *O Come, All Ye Faithful* (1x in G, 1x in Ab) (NBH 199)—Instrumentalist

Scripture Reading

Matthew 1:18–25 (NKJV)

Worship Leader: Now the birth of Jesus Christ was as follows:

Congregation: After His mother Mary was betrothed to Joseph, before they came together, she was found with child of the Holy Spirit.

Worship Leader: Then Joseph her husband, being a just man, and not wanting to make her a public example, was minded to put her away secretly.

Congregation: But while he thought about these things, behold, an angel of the Lord appeared to him in a dream, saying, "Joseph, son of David, do not be afraid to take to you Mary your wife, for that which is conceived in her is of the Holy Spirit.

Worship Leader: And she will bring forth a Son, and you shall call His name JESUS,

Congregation: For He will save His people from their sins."

Worship Leader: So all this was done that it might be fulfilled which was spoken by the Lord through the prophet, saying:

Congregation: "Behold, the virgin shall be with child, and bear a Son, and they shall call His name Immanuel," which is translated, "God with us."

Worship Leader: Then Joseph, being aroused from sleep, did as the angel of the Lord commanded him and took to him his wife, and did not know her till she had brought forth her firstborn Son.

Congregation: And he called His name JESUS.

WEEK 51 SERVICE

Prelude: *Sing We Now of Christmas* (2x in G) (NBH 197)—Instrumentalist

Welcome: Pastoral Staff

Welcome Song (meet and greet during song): Pastoral Staff

Amen (c, v1c, v2c in ?) (CH)

Emmanuel (2x in C) (NBH 201)

Away in a Manger (v1 in F) (NBH 205)

Away in a Manger (v2 in F) (NBH 208)

Away in a Manger (v3 in F) (NBH 205)

Scripture Reading: Worship Pastor and Congregation

(See Scripture Reading Below)

Mary, Did You Know? (v1, v2 bridge v3 in Bm) (NBH 209)

Prayer of Dedication, Intercession, and Praise: Pastor

Infant holy, Infant Lowly (v1, v2 in G) (NBH 213)

Worship with Our Gifts: Pastoral Staff

(Praise and Worship During Offering)

I Have Seen the Light (2x in G) (NBH 211)

That's Why We Praise Him (c, v1c, v2c in C) (NBH 218)

Message: *A Theology of Capacity*

Hymn of Response/Invitation: Worship Leader and Congregation

My Jesus, I Love Thee (v1, v4 in F) (NBH 552)

Hymn of Benediction: *Joy to the World* (v1 in D) (NBH 181): Congregation

Postlude: *Joy to the World* (2x in D) (NBH 181)—Instrumentalist

Scripture Reading

December 16, 2012, from Luke 2:8–20

Worship Leader: Now there were in the same country shepherds living out in the fields, keeping watch over their flock by night.

Congregation: And behold, an angel of the Lord stood before them, and the glory of the Lord shone around them, and they were greatly afraid.

Worship Leader: Then the angel said to them, "Do not be afraid, for behold, I bring you good tidings of great joy which will be to all people. For there is born to you this day in the city of David a Savior, who is Christ the Lord.

Congregation: And this will be the sign to you: You will find a Babe wrapped in swaddling cloths, lying in a manger."

Worship Leader: And suddenly there was with the angel a multitude of the heavenly host praising God and saying:

Congregation: " Glory to God in the highest, And on earth peace, goodwill toward men!

Worship Leader: So it was, when the angels had gone away from them into heaven, that the shepherds said to one another, "Let us now go to Bethlehem and see this thing that has come to pass, which the Lord has made known to us."

Congregation: And they came with haste and found Mary and Joseph, and the Babe lying in a manger.

Worship Leader: Now when they had seen Him, they made widely known the saying which was told them concerning this Child.

Congregation: And all those who heard it marveled at those things which were told them by the shepherds.

Worship Leader: But Mary kept all these things and pondered them in her heart.

Congregation: Then the shepherds returned, glorifying and praising God for all the things that they had heard and seen.

Worship Leader: Hallelujah!

Congregation: Hallelujah, Amen!

Worship Leader: Glory to God!

Congregation: Glory to God in the Highest!

WEEK 52 SERVICE

Prelude: *O Come, All Ye Faithful* (v1c in G, v3 in Ab) (NBH 199) Instrumentalist

Scripture Reading: Reader's Group

(See Scripture Reading Below)

Angels, From the Realms of Glory (v1 in A, v4 in Bb) (NBH 179) Praise Team ONLY

The First Noel (Transition from NBH 179, v1c, v4c in D)

Joy to the World (v1, v3 in D, v4 in Eb) (NBH 181)

Prayer of Worship: Pastor

Welcome: Pastoral Staff

Welcome Song (meet and greet during song): Pastoral Staff

Go Tell It On the Mountain (c, v1c, v2c, v3c in F with tag) (NBH 182)

Angels We Have heard on High (v1c, v2c, v3c in F, v4 in G) (NBH 184)

Worship with Our Gifts: Pastoral Staff

(Praise and Worship During Offering)

What Can I Give Him? (2x in Bb) (NBH 207)

Silent Night, Holy Night (v1, v2, v3, v4 in Bb) (NBH 206)

What Can I Give Him? (pick up to m 5 to the end in Bb) (NBH 207)

Prayer of Dedication, Intercession, and Praise: Pastor

Isn't He? (v1, v2 in G) (NBH 214) (Transition into chorus of 199 at same tempo)

O Come, All Ye Faithful (c, v1c, v2c in G, v3 in Ab) (NBH 199) (Gradually get bigger)

Message: *A Theology of Engagement*

Hymn of Response/Invitation: Worship Leader and Congregation

What Child is This? (c, v1c, v3c in Em) (NBH 198)

Hymn of Benediction: Congregation

O Holy Night (Last two phrases of last verse: "Christ is the Lord" in C) (NBH 194)

Postlude: *Joy to the World* (v1 in D, v4 in Eb) (NBH 181)—Instrumentalist

Scripture Reading

Selections from Luke 2:1–14

ALL: And it came to pass!

Reader 1: That in those days that a decree went out from Caesar Augustus all the world should be registered for tax purposes.

ALL: And it came to pass!

Reader 2: That this census first took place while Quirinius was governing Syria.

Reader 3: That So all went to be registered, everyone to his own city.

ALL: And it came to pass!

Reader 4: That Joseph also went up from Galilee, out of the city of Nazareth, into Judea, to the city of David, which is called Bethlehem

Reader 1: That is Because he was of the house and lineage of David,

Reader 2: He journeyed to Bethlehem To be registered with Mary, his betrothed wife,who was with child.

ALL: And it came to pass!

Reader 3: That while they were there, the days were completed for her to be delivered.

Reader 4: And she brought forth her firstborn Son, and wrapped Him in swaddling cloths, and laid Him in a manger!

Reader 1: Because there was no room for them in the inn.

ALL: And it came to pass!

Reader 2: That there were in the same country shepherds living out in the fields, keeping watch over their flock by night.

Reader 3: That And behold, an angel of the Lord stood before them, and the glory of the Reader 4:That the Lord shone around them, and they were greatly afraid.

ALL: And it came to pass!

Reader 1: That the angel said to them,

Reader 2: "Do not be afraid, for behold, I bring you good tidings of great joy which will be to all people.

Reader 3: For there is born to you this day in the city of David a Savior, who is Christ the Lord.

Reader 4: And this will be the sign to you: You will find a Babe wrapped in swaddling cloths, lying in a manger."

ALL: And, it came to pass!

Reader 1: It came to pass! (louder)

Reader 2: It came to pass! (louder and more deliberate)

Reader 3: It came to pass! (more intense and louder)

Reader 4: It came to pass! (Loud)

Reader 1: (Interrupting) That suddenly there was with the angel a multitude of the heavenly host praising God and saying:

Reader 2: " Glory to God!

Reader 2 and 3: " Glory to God in the highest!

Readers 4: " Glory to God in the highest, And on earth

Reader 1: And on the earth

Readers 1 and 4: peace,

Readers 2 and 3: goodwill

Readers 2, 3, and 4: toward men!"

Reader 1: Peace and goodwill toward ALL men!

ALL: And it came to pass that Jesus Christ was born.

EXTRA SERVICE

Prelude: *O Magnify the Lord* (v1c, v2c in D)—Instrumentalist

Call to Worship: Congregation

Hosanna (v1c, v2c in G) (NBH 135)

O For a Thousand Tongues to Sing (v1, v2, v3 in G, v4 in Ab)

Scripture Reading: Reader's Group

(See Scripture Reading Below)

Be Thou My Vision (v1, v2, v3 in D, v4 in Eb) (NBH 83)

Prayer of Worship: Pastor

Welcome: Pastoral Staff

Welcome Song (meet and greet during song): Pastoral Staff

This is the Day (2x in Eb) (NBH 571)

Bless His Holy Name (c, v1c, v2c, v3c in Eb) (NBH 151)

Worthy, You Are Worthy (v1 in Eb, v3 in F)

You are My All in All (v1c, v2c in F) (NBH 143)

Worship with Our Gifts: Pastoral Staff

(Praise and Worship During Offering)

Jesus, What a Wonder You Are (2x in F)

Prayer of Dedication, Intercession, and Praise: Pastor

All Heaven Declares (1x Praise Team, 2x All in A) (NBH 140)

Great Is Thy Faithfulness (v1c, v2c, v3c in D c in Eb) (NBH 96)

Message: Pastor

Hymn of Response/Invitation: Worship Leader and Congregation

Just As I Am (v1, v2, v3, v5, v6 in C) (NBH 435)

Hymn of Benediction: Congregation

I Have Decided to Follow Jesus (v1, v4, v1 in C) (NBH 434)

Postlude: *Sing to the King* (2x in F) (NBH 129)—Instrumentalist

Scripture Reading

Selections from Isaiah 43 and 58

Reader 1: But now, this is what the LORD says—

ALL: "Do not fear!

Reader 2: For I have redeemed you;

ALL: "Do not fear!

Reader 3: For I know you and have a plan for you.

ALL: "Do not fear!

Reader 4: I have summoned you by name; you are mine.

ALL: "Trust in Me!

Reader 1: When you pass through the waters,

ALL: I will be with you;

Reader 2: And when you pass through the rivers,

ALL: They will not sweep over you.

Reader 3: When you walk through the fire,

ALL: You will not be burned;

Reader 4: The flames will not set you ablaze.

ALL: For I am the LORD your God,

Reader 3: The Holy One of Israel, your Savior;

ALL: For I am with you;

Reader 2: The LORD will guide you always;

Reader 1: He will satisfy your needs in a sun-scorched land and will strengthen your frame.

Reader 3: You will be like a well-watered garden,

Reader 4: You will be called Repairer of Broken Walls

Reader 2: And, a Restorer of Streets with Dwellings!

ALL: Blessed be the Name of the Lord!

(Isaiah 43:1–3, 5a, 10–13, 15, 19, 20b–21; 58:11–12)

CHRISTMAS EVE COMMUNION SERVICE

Prelude: *He Is Born* (2x in F) (NBH 190)—Instrumentalists

Prayer of Praise: Pastoral Staff asking Blessing for the Evening

Welcome: Pastoral Staff

Song of Welcome (meet and greet): Congregation

    Joy to the World (v1, v2 in D, v4 in Eb) (NBH 181)

Prayer of Worship and Praise: Pastoral Staff

    The First Noel (v1c, v4c, c in D) (NBH 180)

Communion

Scripture Reading: Matthew 26:26–30: Pastor

Sharing of the Bread

    Tell Me the Story of Jesus (v1, v3 in D) (NBH 220)

    Who Is He in Yonder Stall? (v1c, v2c, v3c, v4c) (Baptist Hymnal [1976] 124)

    Prayer of Thanksgiving for the Bread

Sharing of the Cup

    A Communion Hymn for Christmas (v1, v3, v4, v5 in D) (NBH 402)

    Mary Did You Know? (v1c, v3c in bm) (NBH 209)

    Prayer of Thanksgiving for the Cup

Worship and Praise: Congregation

    O Come, O Come, Emmanuel (v1c, v3c, v4c in em) (NBH 175)

    What Child is This? (v3c in em) (NBH 198)

MISSIONS VIDEO

Offertory Prayer for the Nations: Pastoral Staff

Offertory Praise: Solo and PT Ensemble

    The Birthday of the King (v1c, v2c in G) (NBH 191)

Message: Pastor

Hymn of Invitation: *My Jesus, I Love Thee* (as needed in F) (NBH 552)

Lighting the Candles by Congregation

    Silent Night, Holy Night (v1, v3, v4 in Bb) (NBH 206)

Hymn of Benediction: *Angels We Have Heard on High* (NBH 184): Congregation

Postlude: *God Rest Ye Merry Gentlemen*—Instrumentalists

CHRISTMAS EVE SERVICE

Prelude: *Joy to the World* Instrumental

Christmas Greeting: Pastor and Pastor's Wife Together: (Video Greeting)

Joy to the World . . .

Mary Had a Baby: Solo: Traditional Spiritual

Reading of Scripture: Psalm 46:1–11: Chairman of Deacons and Wife

Christmas Testimony (Video) (3 minute Video)

I Wonder as I Wander: Ensemble

Prayer of Thanksgiving: Chairman of Trustees

Beautiful Baby: Ladies Ensemble

Reading of Scripture: Pastor and Congregation (See Below)

Joy to the World (vs 1,2,4 in D)—Congregation

Prayer of Praise: SS Superintendent

The Lord Has Come . . .

Angels We Have Heard on High (vs 1, 3,4) (CH 278): Congregation

Reading of Scripture: Luke 2:8–14 (NKJV): President of Women's Ministry

Hark, the Herald Angels Sing (v1, 2, 3) (CH 277): Congregation

Reading of Scripture: Luke 2:15–20 (NIV): Associate Pastor

. . . Let Heaven and Nature Sing!

The First Noel (v 1, 6) (CH 265): Congregation

Reading of Scripture: Matthew 1:18–23 (NASB):

O Holy Night: Solo on verses, congregation on chorus

Offering of Praise and Worship: Pastor

Infant Holy, Infant Lowly: Soloist

Away in a Manger: Instrumental Solo

Christmas Message: Pastor

Hymn of Invitation (CH 253) *Silent Night, Holy Night* (v, 1,2,3): Congregation

Prayer of Blessing and Thanksgiving: Pastor

O Come All Ye Faithful (vs1c, v2c, v3c) (CH 249)—Congregation

Postlude: *God Rest, Ye Merry Gentlemen*: Instrumental

Scripture for Christmas Eve Service [KJV]

Pastor: Comfort ye, comfort ye my people, saith your God.

Congregation: The voice of him that crieth in the wilderness, Prepare ye the way of the Lord,

Pastor: Make straight in the desert a highway for our God And the glory of the Lord shall be revealed,

Congregation: And All flesh shall see it together: For the mouth of the Lord hath spoken it.

Pastor: He shall feed his flock like a shepherd: He shall gather the lambs with his arm,

Congregation: And carry them in his bosom, And shall gently lead those that are with young.

BABY DEDICATION SERVICE

Prelude: *This is the Day* (NBH 150): Instrumental

Prayer of Worship: Associate Pastor

Praise and Worship: Congregation

The Family Prayer Song (2x in G) (NBH 655)

Responsive Reading (see below)

Song of Dedication: Congregation

A Christian Home (v1, v2, v3, v4 in F) (NBH 654)

Presentation of Children: Pastor

Songs of Commitment: Congregation

Praise Him, All Ye Little Children (v1, v2, v3 in D) (NBH 650)

Jesus Loves the Little Children (2x in G) (NBH 651)

Dedication of Children: Pastor

Commitment from Parents to Help Nurture this child

Commitment from Grandparents to Help Nurture this child

Commitment from Congregation to Help Nurture this child

Prayer of Dedication: Pastor

Song of Dedication: Congregation

Jesus Loves Me (v1c, v2c in C) (NBH 652)

Song of Thanksgiving: Congregation

Praise Him, Praise Him (v1c, v3c in G) (NBH 149)

Postlude: *Family Prayer Song* (chorus in G) (NBH 655): Instrumental

Scripture for Baby Dedication

Worship Pastor: As for me and my house, we will serve the Lord.

Congregation: Train up a child in the way he should go and when he is old he will not depart.

Worship Pastor: Whoever welcomes this little child in My name welcomes Me.

Grandparents: Let the little children come to me . . . for the kingdom of heaven belongs to such as these.

Worship Pastor: You have prepared praise from the mouths of children and nursing infants.

Parents: Neither height nor depth, nor anything else . . . . will be able to separate us from the love of God.

SHARPENING YOUR PREACHING SKILLS

Preaching on the Family
By Dr. David Wheeler

In the book *Family to Family*, Jerry Pipes and Victor Lee deal with some key issues related to the destruction of the American family. In chapter one, entitled "Healthy Families," they equate the modern family to the instructions related to operating a pressure cooker:

- Check pressure regulator vent and pressure indicator stem and safety tube openings before opening.
- For best results, fill one-half to two-thirds full. Do Not Overfill.
- Indicator stem rises when cooker is under pressure.
- When fully pressurized, the regulator will "hiss and rock." This is normal and allows excessive steam to escape.[1]

Unfortunately, while such a comparison may seem extreme, it is nonetheless reasonable considering the shape of the modern family. In fact, Pipes and Lee continue this line of thought by giving "The Seven Marks of a 'Hurried' Family." They are:

- Can't relax.
- Can't enjoy quiet.
- Never feel satisfied.
- Absence of absolutes.
- They are suffering servants—great people who do wonderful things for others, but are unhappy because they do good things for wrong reasons.
- There is a storm rumbling beneath the calm.
- They are "world class" overachievers.[2]

If all of this is accurate, then it becomes imperative that the contemporary pastor should understand how to best communicate with families. This is especially true in the pulpit. May I also say, this is especially challenging.

Always Keep in Mind

God created the family before He created the church. Therefore, it has always been His design that faith should be passed through the lineage of family members.

Think about it: back in biblical days, it was normal to have several generations of family members living under the same roof. It was also normal to share several meals together every day. It was during these times and others that one's faith was passed to children and grandchildren. It reminds me of God's instructions to the Israelites in Deuteronomy 6:1–9 (Amplified Bible):

> Now this is the instruction, the laws, and the precepts which the Lord your God commanded me to teach you, that you might do them in the land to which you go to possess it, That you may [reverently] fear the Lord your God, you and your son and your son's son, and keep all His statutes and His commandments which I command you all the days of your life, and that your days may be prolonged. Hear therefore, O Israel, and be watchful to do them, that it may be well with you and that you may increase exceedingly, as the Lord, the God of your fathers, has promised you, in a land flowing with milk and honey. Hear, O Israel: the Lord our God is one Lord [the only Lord]. And you shall love the Lord your God with all your [mind and] heart and with your entire being and with all your might. And these words which I am commanding you this day shall be [first] in your [own] minds and hearts; [then] You shall whet and sharpen them so as to make them penetrate, and teach and impress them diligently upon the [minds and] hearts of your children, and shall talk of them when you sit in your house and when you walk by the way, and when you lie down and when you rise up. And you shall bind them as a sign upon your hand, and they shall be as frontlets (forehead bands) between your eyes. And you shall write them upon the doorposts of your house and on your gates.

From these words, it is obvious that God desires to be honored through the actions of families operating in a proper manner.

The question is, how can the church encourage this to happen? Since this is a book on preaching, the pulpit is obviously one of the many ways to create dialogue and to bring about positive changes.

Suggestions for Preaching on the Family

Preach the Bible

I know this suggestion sounds rather obvious, but don't jump to any premature conclusions. After all, there are way too many preachers who have chosen to abandon biblical exposition in fear that the Bible is somehow boring. These preachers often feel that their people will not listen unless they subscribe to clever sermons addressing practical questions.

While this approach is not inherently wrong if the answers are firmly grounded in Scripture, if not monitored closely, the practice can easily result in the misuse of Scripture where both context and meaning are sacrificed on the altar of shallow entertainment. Strong families are held together by accurate biblical truth.

Preach Through Books of the Bible

While I will freely admit that expository preaching can be packaged in many forms, including preaching on topics from time to time, I still feel that we lose much in the translation when we jump from passage to passage during a sermon. If it is true that families desperately need the glue of biblical teachings to strengthen their bond, then it only makes sense that we should teach the whole council of God through the continuity of preaching through books of the Bible. Again, often in our pursuit to be cute in the pulpit, we do not consider the ramifications on the listeners, especially families, who I fear never quite grasp the importance of biblical truth.

Do Not Avoid Hard Biblical Truths

If there was ever a time in history where families needed a huge dose of biblical truth, it is today. However, for fear of being too straightforward, many pastors unintentionally compromise biblical truth. For instance, it is popular among many "hip" parents to want to be their child's friend. I often address this issue when leading family conferences for local churches. I am shocked how often the pastor feels a bit uncomfortable when I talk about this and other issues related to the parents' responsibility to discipline their children and be the leaders of their families. There seems to be an aversion to addressing issues for fear of upsetting the church body. Let me make this clear: if that is your approach to the pulpit, either repent or quit the ministry. Families need the truth preached as the truth, not as a watered-down suggestion. As it says in John 8:32, "And you shall know the truth, and the truth shall make you free."

Preach to All Types of Families

I will never forget preaching a message one morning on the subject of the family. When the invitation came, I extended the opportunity for several types of decisions related to restoring families spiritually. As several families responded, a young lady approached me and began in a soft but stern voice to chastise me for not addressing single-parent homes. At that point, all I could do was assure her that we did care for her and other single-parents. In the end, I learned that families come in different forms. In addition to two parent homes, there are single-parents, divorced, widows, widowers, and blended families. There are also a growing number of grandparents who are raising their grandchildren, not to mention the singles in your congregation who need guidance in how to find a mate. As mentioned above, preach the Bible; in one way or another, it will address each of these issues.

Know Your People

In the end, the greatest thing that a pastor can do is get to know his people. When this occurs, you will understand the issues that need to be addressed in order to strengthen families.

Be Transparent

When I taught preaching, I often told my students that, in order "to preach an expository message, one has to be willing to live an expository life." This simply means to be real. While you do not want to embarrass your family in the pulpit, it certainly helps other families when we are willing to admit personal struggles. I have found that. when people see us as approachable, both in the pulpit and among the congregation, they are much more likely to receive the teaching as truth that can be applied to any situation.

Endnotes

[1] American Family Association website at *www.afa.net*, as seen in Pipes and Lee, *Family to Family*, NAMB, 1999, p. 7.

[2] Ibid, 8.

Preaching through a Book of the Bible
By Dr. Kent Spann

The most daunting task for the preacher is coming up with one or more sermons every week. The preacher barely gets through his Sunday message for the day before it is time to think about the next Sunday.

Preaching a series helps the preacher, because he is not trying to determine what to preach from week to week. One of the best kinds of series is a series through a book of the Bible.

Blessings of Preaching Through Books of the Bible

I have found many blessings from preaching through books of the Bible.

—It puts the highest emphasis on God's Word. Stephen Rummage, in his book *Planning Your Preaching*, writes:

> Although other methods for planning allow for biblical preaching, preaching through books is an approach that draws maximum attention to the Bible itself as the source of your message. When you preach through a book of the Bible, your congregation becomes aware that Scripture is guiding not only each individual sermon you preach but also the entire direction of your preaching ministry.[1]

—It makes the preacher's weekly preparation easier. Once you have done the background work on your chosen book, you don't have to do it again for the rest of the series. You don't have to determine the context, because you are preaching verses in their context.

Also, you can make better use of your study time, since you know exactly what you are going to study. In addition, you can gather the books and materials you need in advance. You will use those books and materials for the whole series. This saves time and money, both of which are valuable to the preacher.

⚬ It guards against taking passages out of context, since you are preaching from the entire book.

⚬ It helps your audience understand the theme and focus of the book which you are preaching your way through.

⚬ It keeps you from preaching only your favorite texts, and stops you from avoiding difficult texts.

⚬ It honors the book as it was written by the author under the inspiration of the Holy Spirit.

Getting Started

If you have never preached through an entire book of the Bible, it can seem like a daunting task. The rule of thumb is to break a large project into bite-sized pieces.

1. **Select the book of the Bible for your sermon series.** If you have never preached through a book of the Bible, begin with a short book. Don't start with the book of Isaiah or the Gospel of Matthew; start with 1 John or Philippians.

Here are some questions that help me determine the book I should preach:

⚬ Which book speaks to me? If I am interested in my subject, then my preaching will be interesting. I have found that God speaks out of my own personal walk.

⚬ Which book speaks to the current needs of my audience?

⚬ Is your congregation experiencing trials and tribulations? Preach through 1 Peter or James. Does your congregation need doctrine? Preach through Romans. Does your congregation need to better understand the nature of the church? Preach through Ephesians. Does your congregation need to learn about leadership? Preach through Nehemiah.

⚬ Which book speaks to the present times and conditions?

⚬ During the period of economic uncertainty in 2010–11, I preached through the book of Habakkuk. The title of my series was "Tough Questions for Tough Times." I highlighted the tough questions Habakkuk was asking God—questions God's people were asking during uncertain times.

⌒—Which book will fit in my time frame? If you can only allot six weeks for a series, you probably don't want to preach through the book of Genesis.

⌒—What is the Lord saying to me?

2. **Gather your resources.** The advantage of doing a book study is that you know the materials you need for your study. Here are a few of the resources you should gather:

⌒—Commentaries on your book

⌒—A good Bible handbook that gives you an overview of all the books of the Bible.

⌒—A Bible Dictionary

⌒—Sermonic material from other preachers. Preaching is always enriched by reading great preaching. A great free resource is *http://preceptaustin.org/commentaries_by_verse.htm*. Use the drop down option under collections. There you will find all the books of the Bible. Click on your book and unlock a wealth of commentaries and sermonic material by some of the best.

3. **Read and reread the book.** Before you look at any material, take time to read through the book yourself. I like to print out the book I am preaching through so I can mark it up. As I read, I mark it with different color highlighters. Here are the things I will highlight:

⌒—Things I need to study, such as words or phrases

⌒—Themes I discover

⌒—Cross references that come to mind

⌒—Questions I have about a word, verse, or chapter

⌒—How God spoke to me

⌒—Applications for the text

4. **Do a background study of the book.** If you have never done a background study, get a copy of Rick Warren's book *Personal Bible Study Methods.* There is a chapter on doing background studies that is excellent. You will also find his other chapters helpful in your study of your Bible book.

5. **Create an outline of the book.** I recommend the chapter in Warren's book, "The Book Survey Method of Bible Study."

6. **Determine your preaching portions.** The size of your preaching portions will be determined by the timeframe you have and the size of the book. When I preached through the book of Acts, I did one chapter per sermon. When I preached through Galatians, I created several sermons under each chapter.

   You can use the subheadings in the version of your Bible as a guide. You can also look at how others have broken up their sermons.

7. **Develop a series title for your book study.** Here are some examples of titles I have used:

—Galatians: "The Gospel Truth"
—Acts: "The Church on Fire"
—Habakkuk: "Tough Questions for Tough Times"
—Nehemiah: "Lessons on Leadership"

8. **Study your preaching portion for the week using good Bible study techniques and the tools you have gathered.**

9. **Prepare your sermon.**

10. **Pray, pray, pray!**

Keys to a Good Series on Books of the Bible

I want to close with some keys to preaching through books of the Bible.

—Start your preparation early. A good book study requires some advance preparation. It is not something you probably want to start the Monday before the Sunday. Take time to look ahead.

⟶ Avoid a long, drawn-out series, especially for Sunday mornings. How long is too long is best determined by you. It is probably longer than you think if the sermons are well prepared and interesting. You might have to divide a large book like Genesis or Isaiah into sections. You could cover one section a year. You can also do a thematic study of a book that doesn't require you to cover every section of verses.

⟶ Make each message stand alone. The reality is that no one is going to be there for every sermon in the series.

⟶ Bring each message home to your audience. Don't just deliver content from the book. Make it applicable by showing them how it speaks to their lives. Make it alive by illustrating it.

⟶ Make progress in your series. If your audience sees progress, they will stay with you and not lose interest. Otherwise, the series will become laborious for your audience and you.

⟶ Tie it together. Keep pulling the material together. Most books of the Bible can be easily read in a few hours; you are going to preach it over weeks. One suggestion is to preach a final message where you summarize all they have learned from the book. You can highlight key themes from the book.

Conclusion

Preaching through books of the Bible can be both rewarding and satisfying. Your life and your congregation's life will be enriched as you unlock the rich treasures of God's Word. It is also hard work, but work that is well worth it.

In this volume, you will find two book studies. One is a study through Galatians, entitled "The Gospel Truth." The other is a study through the book of Jonah. Blessings on you as you preach God's Word book by book.

Endnotes

[1] Stephen Nelson Rummage, *Planning Your Preaching*, (Grand Rapids: Kregel, 2002), 81.

Ministering To People In Special-Needs Situations

Dr. David Wheeler[1]

> Then the king said, "Is there not still someone of the house of Saul, to whom I may show the kindness of God?" And Ziba said to the king, "There is still a son of Jonathan who is lame in his feet."
>
> —2 Samuel 9:3

Overview

Individuals with special needs and their families represent one of the largest unchurched people groups in the United States. With this in mind, it is imperative that local congregations catch the vision and learn to minister to this group through the love and compassion of Christ. According to special education teachers and those fluent in this kind of ministry, the most effective approach is family-to-family (relational) contact through genuine concern and servant-oriented ministries.

A Dose of Reality

I recall walking through a Mexican restaurant one day in Fort Worth, Texas, when I passed a young girl sitting in a wheelchair. I proceeded to engage the girl and her family by asking if I could speak to the "most beautiful young lady in the restaurant." The girl smiled as I introduced myself to her and the parents by letting them know that I had a special needs child, Kara, who has mild cerebral palsy.

I then proceeded to ask the family about their involvement in a local church. Knowing the horrible track record of many congregations over the years in relating and adapting to special needs families, I was not surprised at the immediate and awkward silence. It was only after I gently pushed for a response that the parents finally replied with the statement, "We used to attend." Eventually, they shared with a note of confusion how their eight year-old daughter could be lovingly mainstreamed into a public school (secular) classroom, but was ignored and forced to remain in the nursery at church.

As the parent of a special needs child, you can imagine the horror and embarrassment I felt for Christ's body, the church, when I heard the above story. Unfortunately, based on statistics and personal experience, this is an all too common testimony of many families. Along the same lines, I recently met a beautiful sixteen year-old girl with mild Down syndrome at a local church. Her parents were brokenhearted about the apparent indifference of the youth group. We watched with great disappointment as the young woman stood alone after lunch without the slightest attempt from the youth group (or anyone else for that matter) to engage her in conversation or to invite her to join their activities. To them, she might as well have been invisible.

Initiating a Special Needs Ministry

There are several steps to take to begin an effective special-needs ministry. To begin with, one must clear up any misconceptions relating to special-needs individuals. First, most people tend to lump all impairments into the same category, with the assumption that physical needs are always related to mental deficiency. Nothing could be farther from the truth. Like everyone else, special-needs children and adults must be dealt with individually. The truth is, those with physical or mental challenges need the saving grace of the Gospel message. In many cases, these individuals will excel beyond their supposed difficulties and often become bold evangelists and compassionate ministers of the Gospel.

This leads to the second misconception that somehow special-needs individuals must always have limitations placed upon their activities and behavior. This is a wrong assumption. If you are the Christian parent of a special-needs child, or a layman in a local church with the privilege of mobilizing people into ministry, please know that, like all other Christians, those with physical or mental impairments must also be obedient to the call of God upon their lives. This means that the church must not limit their community involvement in ministry for the sake of protecting a person who has a special need. In most cases, these individuals can be very effective in ministry, and often become an asset to the outreach and caring ministry of the church.

For instance, suppose there is a family dealing with a special-needs situation in your community. Who could be better prepared to minister to this family evangelistically? They already understand many of the difficulties and challenges. It only takes a sacrifice of time, a strong trust in God, genuine concern, and a willingness to listen and get involved in kingdom business. In the end, this will rebuild the family atmosphere of your church, create lasting memories, and develop a greater confidence among both the physically and mentally challenged, as well as the family members involved.

Consider the testimony of one family of a child with cerebral palsy who participated in door-to-door servant evangelism projects by allowing their excited young girl to be the first person met at the door bearing gifts. In one case, it was fudge at Christmas; in another instance, it was batteries for smoke detectors, or bags of microwave popcorn with a card attached stating "pop in and visit our church some time." Those visited were introduced to each participant, given a special gift by a "special" child, and then told that "Christ loved them." In some of those cases, they prayed with individuals; in others, they were able to share the Gospel. In every instance, the participants learned the same important lessons about fulfilling the great commission, regardless of physical or mental limitations. Both the young girl and those visited received an extraordinary blessing. Imagine what would happen if the lay leaders of your church adopted these individuals and volunteered to go with the families as they ministered in the community.

A third misconception, and probably the most disheartening, is the idea that, since you do not know what to say to a person with a special need, the best thing to do is to not say anything at all. Unfortunately, this approach often comes across as rude or indifferent. Worst of all, it usually results in staring, which magnifies the situation and makes the person with the special need feel even more self-conscious and out of place.

I recall one evening shortly after our four year-old special-needs daughter learned to walk. We celebrated by going to her favorite restaurant. As she walked out of the restaurant, she insisted, as always, on doing it herself. So we held the front doors open wide as she stumbled out, nearly falling several times. A young couple stood over to the side and rudely glared at Kara as we celebrated her independence. To say the least, I was irritated by the couple who stared and never smiled or offered a word of encouragement. It was then that I walked over to them and made the statement, "I am very sorry for the way Kara is walking. I told her to get away from the bar or this [stumbling] would be the result." The look on their faces was priceless.

In most cases, a proper response is to simply ask the person about his malady, or better yet, offer assistance if needed. Let the person tell his story while you be a good listener. Whatever you do, speak plainly (not slowly) and be yourself. People with special needs are like everyone else: they want to be loved, and they need a relationship with Christ.

As far as ministering within special-needs situations, consider several options, like providing "parents' night out" opportunities, especially where the needs are chronic and demand round-the-clock care. I recently heard of a family like this where the parents had not been alone in more than three years because of required round-the-clock care. No wonder the divorce rate is so high.

In some cases, the situation may demand securing a nurse who is trained to administer proper care. In many other situations, you may only require a mild dose of patience, a listening ear, and a special ability to administer the love of Christ. Ask the Lord to show you how to proceed.

You might also consider preparing meals, mowing yards, offering to do small repair jobs, or providing some new clothes. If they are good quality, consider offering some of the slightly used clothes that your children have outgrown. In addition, one person expressed the need for volunteers to do grocery shopping. By the way, always be careful to respect handicap parking at the mall, church, or at the grocery store.

In addition, go through your church and ask for an honest assessment related to the accessibility needs of the disabled. Be open about negative attitudes and fears. Lead the way in educating your church. Contact Joni and Friends on the Internet (*www.joniandfriends.org*), or secure a local special-education teacher to lead the training. You can also provide free community education for parents of special-needs children about federal laws, public programs, and how to best represent their children.

Most important, do not give up, even if the special-needs family does not respond immediately. Remember that, above all people, they know the difference between loving concern and pity. These individuals do not need our pity. On the contrary, they need Jesus and the affirmation of dignity, love, compassion, and self-worth that is inherent to the gospel.

Conclusion

Ministering to the disabled is not complicated. Always remember that there is no one-size-fits-all solution. You must plan to minister to the whole family, not just the person with the disability. Begin by researching community-based opportunities for ministries. Start by asking questions. Care. Be honest about your attitudes and prejudices. As a goal, include and engage the disabled and their families into the ministries of the church. In doing so, you will help them find their ultimate fulfillment in Christ. Be proactive.

Endnotes

[1] This article is adapted from David Wheeler, "Special Needs," *Nelson's Church Leader's Manual for Congregational Care* (Nashville: Thomas Nelson, 2010), 229–35.

SHEPHERDING GOD'S PEOPLE

Ministering in Times of Grief

Dr. Kent Spann[1]

Grief is a universal human experience. Not a day passes that someone does not experience some type of grief. The Bible is full of accounts of people, both righteous and unrighteous, who experienced deep grief. David, the man after God's own heart, experienced the full gamut of grief. He lost children (2 Sam. 12:15–18; 13:37; 18:33), a best friend, and also a king (2 Sam. 1:17–27). He even suffered the grief of betrayal by a best friend (Ps. 55:12–14). Certainly you cannot talk about grief in the Bible without mentioning Job.

Even Jesus, the perfect man, was not immune to the pain of grief. He grieved over the hardness of men's hearts (Mark 3:5). He was also filled with sorrow and grief in the face of the cross (Matt. 26:36–44; Mark 14:32–42).

Grief Defined

Grief is the natural human response to loss. It is a deep and sometimes very intense emotional suffering. Other things may accompany it, such as physical issues like fatigue or sickness, and mental issues such as a preoccupation with thoughts of the individual, or extreme thoughts such as committing suicide. At grief's core, however, is emotional suffering. It is a sad and lonely state.

The Process of Grief

Some materials refer to stages of grief, while others refer to cycles of grief. Really, it is more of a process than a stage. The terminology of stages indicates an orderly step by step process which is not always the case. Granger E. Westberg identifies ten stages of grief in his book *Good Grief*. Here is the list:

1. We are in a state of shock.
2. We express emotion.
3. We feel depressed and lonely.
4. We may experience physical symptoms of distress.
5. We may become panicky.

6. We feel a sense of guilt about the loss.

7. We are filled with anger and resentment.

8. We resist returning.

9. Gradually, hope comes through.

10. We struggle to affirm reality.[2]

The grieving process normally lasts from one to three years.

Ministering in a Time of Death

Every minister knows the feeling of receiving the phone call and hearing the sound of a distressed congregant. Somehow, they manage to tell you that their spouse or parent has died. Those first few moments on the phone are so important. Listen and pray for God's guidance. Be sure to express your condolences. Ask if you may come and visit with them. The reason you need to ask is that they may not want company presently. If they want a visit, find out the best time and place to visit with them. Finally, pray with them on the phone if they are okay with that, especially if you are not going to be able to visit them for a while.

Based on the cultural and church protocol as well your personal practice, you will need to decide whether to make a personal visit. Some ministers only make visits in the case of immediate family, while others will visit in any death situation.

Here are a few guidelines when making your ministry visit.

1. **Be aware of what is happening when you walk in the door.** Is there a crowd of people, or is the person alone? Is the bereaved lying down or moving around?

2. **Be sensitive to the person when you arrive.** The bereaved person might want to hug you, but he might not. The bereaved may want to talk, but then again he may not.

3. **Keep your words brief.** Let those grieving talk if they want to. Many times, they will want to recall memories or what happened when the person died.

4. **Offer practical support such as making phone calls, picking up people at the airport, or making hotel arrangements.**

5. Ask if you can read Scripture and pray with them.

Ministering to the grieving doesn't end with the funeral. Aftercare is very important to those grieving. Determine how and when you will follow up. Contact the bereaved on special anniversaries such as a birthday, wedding anniversary, and most importantly the year anniversary of the person's death. Encourage the person to get into a grief support group. Pray for the person.

Living Losses

While grief is certainly the normal response to death, it is also the response to life. Living losses occur in the course of living life. There is the husband grieving as his wife of twenty years walks out the door for good. Parents experience grief as their child makes poor life choices, resulting in pain for both the parent and child. There can be the loss of a dream. For some, it is the loss of one's health to an injury or a debilitating disease. It may be the loss of a job. It can involve the loss of a friend.

The difference in grieving losses to death and living losses is closure. For example, when a spouse dies, there can be closure; that is not the case where a marriage ends in divorce.

The truth is that people don't know how to grieve living losses. Most don't understand that living losses lead to grief. Most sweep it under the rug. The problem is that it comes up later in bad ways.

How can we help those experiencing living losses?

1. **Encourage the person to grieve.** Show the person why it is important. Help the individual to understand that grieving is God's way of getting the person through loss.
2. **Help the individual develop a recovery plan.** What is the person going to do now that he or she can't work due to a disability? What is the person going to do in the face of a job loss? How can the individual dream again?
3. **Remind the person that God still has a plan for his or her life** (Jer. 29:11; Rom. 8:28).

4. **Recommend journaling.** Journaling is a lost art in today's culture, but it is extremely therapeutic. Much of the Old Testament is a journal. It is God's people processing life.

5. **Suggest that the person write a letter of closure.** It may be a letter saying goodbye to a dream or vision. It may be a letter of closure after a divorce. This will help the individual to let it go.

6. **Be his or her friend.**

7. **Pray with the person about his or her real concerns.**

Whether it is a living loss or a loss to death, the best thing you can offer is the presence of Christ (Ps. 23:4) and the promise of your presence (1 Thess. 2:8).

Endnotes

[1] This article is adapted from the article "Grief," previously published by Thomas Nelson. Kent Spann, "Grief," *Nelson's Church Leader's Manual for Congregational Care*, (Nashville: Thomas Nelson, 2010), 149–64.

[2] Granger E. Westbrook, *Good Grief: A Constructive Approach to the Problem of Loss* (Minneapolis: Ausburg Fortress, 1997).

Working with Volunteers

By Duane Floro

Working with volunteers can be one of the most rewarding opportunities in ministry. It can also be one of the most challenging. When I first went into the ministry, I assumed that everyone had the same goals and dreams. I soon realized that, not only were they different, but they were held with deep passion. I, like you, sought to bring about change through various methods: in preaching, in strategies, in convincing others that God was on "my side." When all else failed, I simply locked horns until only one of us was left standing. I am sure some of these efforts did not end as I had hoped, but I did come away wiser because of the experience.

1 Chronicles 12 describes a couple of keys to help our understanding of working with volunteers. For King David, this understanding was the difference between life and death. This defined clarity is important in times of war and in times of peace. The definition of the tribe of Zebulun in verse 33 is one clear example of working with volunteers: "men of Zebulun, experienced soldiers prepared for battle with every type of weapon to help David with undivided loyalty."

We learn three principles from this brief passage to help us as we serve with volunteers. First, the followers of King David brought experiences to draw from for future endeavors. In a similar fashion, the volunteers in our settings bring much to the ministry from their life experiences.

Second, the followers of King David are equipped to draw from various resources to carry out the task before them. They knew how to use various weapons (tools) to carry out the tasks before them; so too are the volunteers who come along with us. There is a misconception where some think the secret is in the training. Some say, "the more I can learn, the better I must be." The truth is, it is application, not simply information. Therefore, working with volunteers requires leaders who are equipped to equip.

Finally, the men demonstrated endurance. As King David considered his army, he wanted to know he did not have a group of quitters. Their loyalty in battle and in their everyday lives was paramount. In today's world, we want to know if that person we are counting on is the one who has the stuff to endure to the end. The attention span for many has grown short, as various things pull them in numerous directions. We live in a day of information and activity overload. It is necessary for volunteers to see the goal, to be prepared to endure, and to understand clearly their role in the journey. A similar idea can be found in sports. It is conditioning. To the occasional observer, it seems unnecessary, but the coach understands that training now is how one builds future champions.

As you build upon volunteers' experiences, equip them and support them so that they may endure. It aids volunteers to have them set boundaries to achieve personal goals. It is the old adage: "we want people to finish, and finish well."

Here are six keys to leading volunteers:

— Relationships: A leader values relationships, serving side by side in the trenches of the work. The leader must be an engineer that is a "builder of bridges" into the lives of volunteers.

— Time: A leader invests personal and ministerial time in volunteers. A good leader remembers the details, and this takes time.

— Vision: A leader personalizes the vision by drawing the images on the canvas of the volunteer. Once the vision is cast, the volunteers color in the final work of art. Make the vision not simply "my vision," but "our vision."

— Goals: A leader seeks volunteers to reach the goal. The leader must have personal wins in order for volunteers to feel safe following the leader by devoting their time, talents, and treasures. A good leader helps volunteers to experience wins, too. Achieving meaningful and significant goals helps people stay on board.

— Partnership: A leader sees the partnership in ministry. One day, we will hand off all we do to another. Volunteers should understand the movement of ministry. This is first modeled in the leader. It is the ability to transition from ministry leader to recruiter, to trainer, to supporter, to encourager. This allows volunteers to sense personal responsibility, acknowledge clear accountability, and to be empowered to achieve the goals of the ministry.

Training: Leaders equip volunteers to carry out the ministry by providing multiple venues for volunteer training. The leader must see the big picture to develop a training strategy that aids the overall goals of the ministry, and must hear the needs of the volunteers as they serve. The point is guiding, not driving.

The development of volunteers is a priority. I am reminded of the story of the professor who stood before the class with an empty jar. First placing large rocks in the jar until they reached the top, the professor asked, "Is this jar now full?" After some discussion the professor poured in gravel. As the class watched, the professor added sand and finally water, until the water stood level with the top of the jar. The professor finally asked, "What have we learned today?" One said, "There is always room for something else." Another, piped in, "just keep pouring until it overflows."After a moment, the professor said, "These are interesting responses, but what we really learned today is: 'if you don't put the big rocks in first, they will never fit.'" May we first "put in" the priorities of working with volunteers, so that we have a long and wonderful ministry together.

SHEPHERDING THE SHEPHERD

Leading by Faith

By Dr. Bill Elliff

How do you lead three million grumbling people across the desert? This was the task given to Moses, and he discovered early that he would never succeed in this leadership task if he didn't operate by one key principle: faith.

Whether it's leading three million, three hundred, or thirty, faith is the non-negotiable element of authentic biblical leadership. You can scan a thousand secular books, get the latest tips and tricks on leadership, but they will all fail if you do not operate God's way. And in God's economy, everything is always about believing in Him. In fact, He goes so far as to say that "whatever is not of faith is sin," and "without faith it is impossible to please God" (Romans 14:23, Hebrews 11:6).

The reason for God's stubbornness on this is simple: He wants to lead. He knows that even the best leaders are blind without His vision, timid without His courage, ignorant without His knowledge, and foolish without His wisdom. We were never designed to lead anything without Him. And the key in the ignition that connects us to the leadership of God is the key of faith.

Beginning in Faith

The first step of faith is the admission of our need. It took Moses many years to get this. Forty years after he escaped Egypt after killing an Egyptian, God confronted a humbled Moses at a burning bush that was not consumed. When called to lead, Moses said the exact words God needed to hear: "I can't." God had molded His leader into a humble man who was aware of his own deficiencies and desperately in need of Someone beyond himself. He was ready.

Any man who thinks he can lead by himself is illustrating the worst kind of foolishness. Such humanistic pride will always lead to faulty plans, and those who serve under that type of leadership will pay a huge price.

Great leaders are broken and humble, which leads to dependence. There is a simple way to evaluate yourself as a leader on this point. How much do you pray and pursue God through His Word? If you can go a day or a week without fervent communication with God, it is a clear indication that you think you can handle your leadership responsibilities on your own. You are not leading by faith.

Hearing by Faith

The wise leader looks to God. He knows that God has plans and thoughts that are higher and better than his own, which can only be discerned by the illumination of God's Word through His Spirit. So he goes to God in dependency. He listens. This leader burns up His Bible. He understands that he cannot bluff his way through leadership, making up fancy strategic plans without the Lord's guidance. The seasoned Moses retreated often. When faced with problems, he prayed prayers that are recorded as an evidence of His faith.

Jesus, as a man, operated in precisely the same manner. "I do nothing on my own initiative," He said on numerous occasions (John 5:30; 8:28; 12:49; 14:10). He was always listening to the Father, and Jesus always said what He heard the Father say. Jesus always did what He saw the Father do. In this way, God the Father was actually leading through Jesus the man. And we must do the same.

Are you hearing? Are you listening on a daily basis to find God's direction for your life and your people? When faced with a leadership challenge, do you figure it out or cry out? Are you operating out of God-initiation? Do the plans that you propose to your people come hot from the kitchen of heaven?

Standing by Faith

What leader has not offered what he believes to be God's plan, only to be opposed? What is a leader to do? He must stand by faith. Moses led his congregation to the threshold of the promised land, but the people shrank back in doubt when faced with incredible prosperity, peppered with a few giants in their way. Moses and his faith-filled assistants gave a faithful answer to their objections. They reminded the people that their enemies would be like bread—nourishing and easily consumed with the Lord's help (Numbers 14:9). Moses led by faith and stayed in faith for the forty years that God's people wandered, until God delivered them into His promise.

Any faith venture will be opposed. Count on it. The only salvation for a leader is the promise of God, given in the presence of God to the servant of God. That promise cements a faith that is immovable. You must stand by faith.

Rejoicing by Faith

When a leader is used by God to accomplish God's work, who does he thank? By faith, he turns to the One who gave Him the direction, confirmed it to him along the way, gave him the ability to stand, and brought faith to its fulfillment. The hardest part of faith is finishing well, while giving God the credit for what He alone has accomplished. Many a leader has forgotten faith at this critical juncture and failed to rejoice in God alone.

And God rejoices in a leader's faith. It is no wonder that God's final reward acknowledges this one characteristic. It is what God is looking for. It is what honors Him as the ultimate leader and puts the servant leader in the proper posture for true, God-glorifying success.

It will be the leader's greatest joy to hear God say, "Well done, thou good and *faith*ful servant!"

Bob Russell

From Pennsylvania Farm Boy to Mega-Church Preacher
By Ruth Schenk

When Bob Russell retired after forty years at Southeast Christian Church in Louisville, Kentucky, he led one of the largest churches in the nation, preaching to more than 20,000 on weekends; wrote fourteen books; and was in demand as a speaker at churches and conferences around the country. But he was never impressed with himself, and he always gave God the glory.

Early years in ministry weren't glamorous. That first Sunday at Southeast Christian Church on June 12, 1966, Bob Russell preached a twenty-minute sermon to 177 people in the basement of a red brick house. Furnace pipes lined the ceiling above his head, and the choir sang *God Bless America* from their perch near the furnace. No one in that first Sunday gathering dreamed that Southeast would be a mega-church someday—perhaps Bob least of all.

He grew up in Conneautville, PA., a small, one-stoplight town with an ice cream stand, ballpark, and market. His parents were strict with their six children: no playing ball on Sundays, no excuses for not attending church, and no skipping family devotions. Bob called it a good training ground.

No one heard Bob talk about being a preacher in those days. His life revolved around sports. As the quarterback for the football team, point guard on the basketball team, and shortstop on the baseball team, he chose chores that made room for practice after school. He had no love for the family cow, but milked her at dawn, scrubbing his hands like a surgeon to shed the smell of the barn. Dreams of a college basketball scholarship seemed certain during Bob's senior year in high school. The Conneautville Indians won every game until the last quarter of the state championship, when they lost a heartbreaker in the final seconds. Bob was so devastated by the defeat that his parents sent him to visit his older sister Roseanne at Cincinnati Bible College.

A few weeks later, after a disappointing official visit to a college where he'd been offered a basketball scholarship, Bob told this dad that he wanted to be a preacher. No one was more surprised than those who knew him best.

Bob studied preaching at Cincinnati Bible College, played basketball, and fell in love with Judy Thomas. They were quite different. His passion was sports; she loved music. He wanted to preach. Judy told friends that she'd never marry a preacher. They dated through college, got engaged on Christmas Eve 1964, and married in 1965.

Believing that God blesses the preparation as well as the presentation, Bob reserved at least twenty hours a week to prepare his sermon and practiced it out loud at least four times before stepping into the pulpit. His goal was to make the gospel understandable and personal. He wove stories with biblical truth. People laughed at stories about Bandit, the family dog who never loved Bob. The feeling was mutual. People identified with homespun stories about the boys bickering in the car, about cramming gifts in the trunk one Christmas Eve, about Bob's die-hard support of the University of Louisville, and about getting lost on a trip because he refused to ask for directions. Bob ended every service with a simple invitation to accept Christ and be baptized. Hundreds walked forward to commit their lives to Christ and be baptized.

Realizing that ministry takes a toll of families, he determined to be home most evenings, and began reserving family time on the calendar. When tee-ball, soccer, and basketball games began, Bob and Judy were in the bleachers.

By the end of Bob's first decade at Southeast, more than eight hundred people were making their way to the church early to snatch a parking space, then waiting in line to get into the church for a seat in one of the stiff wooden pews. Before long, the Pennsylvania farm boy who planned to spend his life preaching in a small country church was preaching to thousands. In the next forty years, Bob preached more than two thousand weekend sermons, and the church grew from sixty to more than twenty thousand members. There were four "one-time-only" building campaigns to make room for more. Elders stretched finances and resources as far as they thought possible every time, but outgrowing buildings became a way of life at Southeast.

Bob's forty-year-record is rare in a culture where the average preacher changes churches every five years. In the end, it was never about the buildings or the programs. It was always about introducing people to Christ. In looking at Bob's ministry, the number that means the most is 37,000. That's the number of people who made their way to the front of the church to make Christ the Lord of their lives. That legacy will last.

Bob retired as the senior minister at Southeast in June 2006. He founded Bob Russell Ministries to mentor young preachers. He continues to write, speak, and preach the same Gospel message in a way that changes lives.

Billy Sunday (1862–1935)

By Ruth Schenk

Over thirty-nine years, Billy Sunday preached to more than one hundred million people under big white revival tents. Crowds were intrigued by the professional baseball player turned evangelist. No one knows how many "walked the sawdust trail" to accept Christ, but some say it was more than one million people.

Billy Sunday was an unlikely preacher. He was born in Ames, Iowa in 1862, a month before his father died of disease while serving in the Union Army. His mother, Mary Jane Sunday, and the children moved in with her parents for a few years. She later remarried, but her second husband deserted the family. Sunday was ten years old when his mother took him to the Soldiers' Orphans Home in Glenwood, Iowa. He was fending for himself by the time he turned fourteen.

Sunday began playing organized baseball for a fire brigade team in Marshall-town, Iowa when he was eighteen. His natural talent impressed scouts with the Chicago White Stockings. They signed him to a professional contract in 1883. Sunday struck out four times in his first game and seven more times in the next three games before getting a hit. His seven-year professional baseball career had its ups and downs, but he was always popular with fans and teammates.

On a Sunday afternoon in Chicago during the 1886 baseball season, Sunday and several of his teammates stopped to hear a gospel team from the Pacific Garden Rescue Mission. Originally drawn by hymns that his mother used to sing, Sunday began attending services at the mission and decided to become a Christian.

Teammates and fans saw him change as Sunday stopped drinking, swearing, and gambling. He began speaking in churches and YMCAs. In March 1891, Sunday traded his $3,000 a year salary in professional baseball for $75 a month as the assistant secretary for the Young Men's Christian Association. He began preaching in small towns in Iowa and Illinois. He called it the "kerosene circuit" because they had no electricity.

In a nation that worshipped winners, Sunday used his reputation as a baseball player to attract crowds. In 1907, in Fairfield, Iowa, Sunday organized local businesses into two baseball teams and scheduled a game between them. Sunday came dressed in his professional uniform and played on both sides.

When Sunday began to attract crowds larger than rural churches or town halls could accommodate, he pitched rented canvas tents. Sunday would put the tents up and keep them up during good and bad weather. He even slept in them at night. After Sunday's tent was destroyed in a snowstorm, he required towns to build temporary wooden tabernacles before he arrived.

As the crowds got larger and the administrative demands harder, Billy and his wife Helen hired a full-time nanny for their four children so that Helen could manage the revivals. She hired musicians, custodians, advance men, and Bible teachers of both sexes who reached out in schools and hospitals during the day to encourage people to attend services at night. Well ahead of their time, they had nurseries for the children so their parents could concentrate on the message.

The tabernacle floors were covered with sawdust to dampen the noise of shuffling feet and people going forward during the invitation. People coming forward to accept Christ on those sawdust floors became known as "hitting the sawdust trail."

Sunday was an animated preacher who often ran from one end of the platform to the other, sometimes diving across the stage as if he were sliding into home plate. He smashed chairs to emphasize his points, and charmed crowds with baseball stories and impersonations.

By 1910, Sunday was front-page news in cities like Philadelphia, Detroit, Boston, and New York City. Newspapers often printed his sermons in full, and during World War 1, stories of his campaigns often surpassed news of the war.

Over the course of his career, Sunday probably preached to more than one hundred million people, face-to-face, without microphones. Before his death, Sunday estimated that he preached nearly twenty thousand sermons, which averages forty-two per month from 1896 to 1935. During his heyday, he often preached more than twenty times a week to huge crowds.

The Sundays supported themselves through freewill offerings, which could be small or large depending on the crowd. The Sundays never owned a car and gave away most of what they received in offerings.

Tragedy marred the Sundays' final years. Their three sons got involved in the very things that he preached against, and the Sundays paid blackmail money to several women to keep the scandals quiet. In 1932, the Sundays' daughter died of what seems to have been multiple sclerosis, and their oldest son committed suicide in 1933.

When Sunday had a heart attack in 1935, doctors told him to stay out of the pulpit, but he ignored the doctor's advice. He died on November 6, 1935, a week after preaching his last sermon on the text, "What must I do to be saved?"

BABY DEDICATION

Infant's Name: _____

Significance of Given Names: _____

Date of Birth: _____

Date of Dedication: _____

Siblings: _____

_____

Paternal Grandparents: _____

Maternal Grandparents: _____

Life Verse: _____

Notes: _____

_____

_____

_____

_____

BAPTISMS AND CONFIRMATIONS

Date   Name   Notes

_____

_____

_____

_____

_____

_____

_____

_____

_____

_____

_____

_____

_____

FUNERAL REGISTRATION

Name of Deceased: _____

Age: _____

Religious Affiliation: _____

Survivors:

    Spouse: _____

    Parents: _____

    Children: _____

    Siblings: _____

    Grandchildren: _____

Date of Death: _____

Time and Place of Visitation: _____

Date of Funeral or Memorial Service: _____

Funeral Home Responsible: _____

Location of Funeral or Memorial Service: _____

Scripture Used: _____ Hymns Used: _____

Eulogy By: _____

Others Assisting: _____

Pallbearers: _____

_____

Date of Interment: _____ Place of Interment: _____

Graveside Service: Yes_____ No _____

FUNERALS LOG

Date	Name of Deceased	Scripture Used

MARRIAGE REGISTRATION

Bride: _____

    Religious Affiliation: _____

    Parents: _____

Groom: _____

    Religious Affiliation: _____

    Parents: _____

Date of Wedding: _____

Location: _____

Ceremony Planning By: _____ Minister _____ Couple

Others Assisting: _____

_____

Maid / Matron of Honor: _____

Best Man: _____

Wedding Planner: _____

Date, Time, Location of Rehearsal: _____

Reception: _____ All Wedding Guests _____ Invitation Only

Reception Location: _____

Photography: _____ During Ceremony _____ After Ceremony

Date of Counseling: _____ Date of Registration: _____

Miscellaneous: _____

MARRIAGES LOG

Date	Names of Couple	Scripture Used

SERMONS PREACHED

Date	Text	Title / Subject

SCRIPTURE INDEX BY WEEK